The M   Britain
Current Debates and Developments

edited by

Jane Stokes and Anna Reading

First published 1999 by
PALGRAVE MACMILLAN
Houndmills, Basingstoke, Hampshire RG21 6XS and
175 Fifth Avenue, New York, N.Y. 10010
Companies and representatives throughout the world

PALGRAVE MACMILLAN is the global academic imprint of the Palgrave
Macmillan division of St. Martin's Press, LLC and of Palgrave Macmillan Ltd.
Macmillan® is a registered trademark in the United States, United Kingdom
and other countries. Palgrave is a registered trademark in the European
Union and other countries.

ISBN 0–333–73062–3 hardcover
ISBN 0–333–73063–1 paperback

This book is printed on paper suitable for recycling and made from fully
managed and sustained forest sources.

A catalogue record for this book is available from the British Library.

Editing and origination by Aardvark Editorial, Mendham, Suffolk

Printed and bound in Great Britain by
Antony Rowe Ltd, Chippenham and Eastbourne

*This book is dedicated
to our students*

Contents

List of Figures

List of Tables

Acknowledgements

The authors and publisher wish to thank the following for permission to use copyright material:

The Advertising Association for Figures 2.1, 2.2 and 2.3 from *The Advertising Statistics Yearbook 1998*.
AC Nielsen-MEAL and Haymarket Campaign Publications Ltd for the data in Tables 2.1 and 2.2 from *Campaign Report* (1998).

Every effort has been made to trace all the copyright holders but if any have been inadvertently overlooked the publishers will be pleased to make the necessary arrangements at the first opportunity.

Notes on Contributors

Richard Collins is Head of Education at the British Film Institute. He has published widely on the media; his latest book is *From Satellite to Single Market: New Communication Technology and European Public Service* (Routledge, 1998).

James Cornford is based at the University of Newcastle's Centre for Urban and Regional Development Studies. He has been researching the role of communications and media industries for the development of cities and regions for ten years.

Simon Cottle is Professor of Media Communication at Bath Spa University College. He is the author of *TV News, Urban Conflict and the Inner City* (Leicester University Press, 1993), *Television and Ethnic Minorities: Producers and Perspectives* (Avebury, 1997) and, with A. Hansen, R. Negrine and C. Newbold, *Mass Communication Research Methods* (Macmillan, 1998). He is currently editing *Ethnic Minorities and the Media: Changing Cultural Boundaries* to be published later this year (Open University Press) and preparing a new book called *Communicating Conflict*.

Andrew Crisell lectures in Media and Communication at the University of Sunderland. He is the author of *Understanding Radio* (1994) and *An Introductory History of British Broadcasting* (1997) both of which are published by Routledge.

Richard Crownshaw is currently finishing his doctoral thesis on representations of the Holocaust in American Culture at the University of Sussex. He also teaches English and American literature at Goldsmiths College.

Jacqui Gabb is currently studying for a DPhil at the University of York, Centre for Women's Studies, having previously worked as a Senior Lecturer in Media. Her media research is primarily concerned with lesbian and/or queer media.

Peter Goodwin is a Senior Lecturer in the Department of Journalism and Mass Communication, University of Westminster. He is a member of the Centre for Communication and Information Research Group and Course Director of Westminster's BA Media Studies. He is author of *Television Under the Tories: Broadcasting Policy 1979–1997* (BFI, 1998).

John Hill is Professor of Media Studies at the University of Ulster. His publications include: *Sex, Class and Realism: British Cinema 1956–63* (1986);

Cinema and Ireland (co-author) (1987); *Border Crossing: Film in Ireland, Britain and Europe* (co-editor) (1994); *The Oxford Guide to Film Studies* (co-editor) (1998) and *British Cinema in the 1980s: Issues and Themes* (1999).

Paul McDonald is Senior Lecturer in Media at South Bank University. His recent research publications include the two volumes of *Screen International's World Film Distribution Report* (EMAP Media/Market Trading International).

Peter Meech is a Senior Lecturer in the Department of Film and Media Studies, University of Stirling, and a member of the Stirling Media Research Institute.

Bart Moore-Gilbert is Senior Lecturer in English at Goldsmiths College, University of London. He is the author of *Postcolonial Theory: Contexts, Practices, Politics* (London, 1978) and *Kipling and 'Orientalism'* (London, 1988). He is currently writing a monograph on Hanif Kureishi for Manchester University Press.

Jenny Owen is Senior Lecturer in Media at South Bank University. She is currently writing a book about crime and the media.

Julian Petley lectures in Media and Communications in the Department of Human Sciences at Brunel University. His most recent publication is *Ill Effects: Media Violence Debates* co-edited with Martin Barker (Routledge, 1997). He is one of the founders of the *British Journalism Review* and sits on its editorial board. He is Vice-Chair of the Campaign for Press and Broadcast Freedom.

Anna Reading is a Senior Lecturer in Media at South Bank University. She is the author of *Polish Women, Solidarity and Feminism* (1992) and researched with Colin Sparks *Communism, Capitalism and the Mass Media* (1997). She is on the editorial board of *Media, Culture and Society*. She is also the author of six stage plays performed around Britain and abroad.

Hillegonda Rietveld is Senior Lecturer in Media and Society at South Bank University. She actively takes part in contemporary dance culture and has published various articles on this topic and is the author of *This is Our House: House Music, Cultural Spaces and Technologies* (Ashgate, 1998).

Kevin Robins is Professor of Communications, Goldsmiths College, University of London. He is the author of *Into the Image* (Routledge, 1996) and (with Frank Webster) *Times of the Technoculture* (Routledge, 1999).

Jay Russell is a writer whose novels include *Celestial Dogs*, *Blood* and *Burning Bright.* His short stories and reviews have been widely published in Britain and the US. His website can be found at: http://www.sff.net/people/jrussell.

Professor Scannell is Director of Research for the School of Communication, Design and Media, University of Westminster. He is a founding editor of *Media, Culture and Society* and has written widely on broadcasting. His publications include *A Social History of British Broadcasting* (Blackwell, 1991) with D. Cardiff and *Radio, Television and Modern Life* (Blackwell, 1996).

Aleks Sierz is a freelance journalist and theatre critic of *Tribune*. He also teaches journalism at Goldsmiths College, University of London, and has published many articles about contemporary theatre. He is currently writing a book about 'in-yer-face' drama for Faber & Faber.

Jane Sillars is a Lecturer at Stirling University and a researcher in the Stirling Media Research Institute. Her main interest lies with questions of nationality and representation.

Ben Slater was co-editor of *Entropy*, a magazine of experimental culture. Based in Bristol, he teaches Print Media at the University of West of England and is a freelance journalist, film producer and cinema programmer.

Murray Smith is Senior Lecturer in Film Studies at the University of Kent. He is the author of *Engaging Characters: Fiction, Emotion and the Cinema* (Oxford) and the co-editor of *Film Theory and Philosophy* (Oxford) and *Contemporary Hollywood Cinema* (Routledge).

Colin Sparks is Professor of Media Studies at the Centre for Communication and Information Studies in the University of Westminster.

Jane Stokes is Senior Lecturer in Media and Society at South Bank University. She is the co-editor of this volume and author of *On Screen Rivals: The Cinema and Television in Britain and America* (Macmillan, 1999).

Introduction

JANE STOKES

Today is a very exciting time to be studying *The Media in Britain*, and this book aims to convey some of the thrill the editors and contributors experience working as media scholars. We explore some vitally important questions such as: 'Who controls the media in Britain?'; 'How are media companies adjusting to the digital era?' and 'What is *British* about the media and the texts they generate?' *The Media in Britain* addresses subjects of importance to everyone interested in contemporary British culture and society. Especially useful to people who are studying the media at undergraduate level, this book will offer something to think about to the uninitiated and the media specialist alike.

One reason why studying the British media is so important is because of the central role the media will play in helping to determine what kind of a country we live in as we enter the new millennium. The last century has seen changes in the media more profound than at any time in our history: the expansion of photography and cinema; the popularizing of the press; the introduction of radio and television; the development of the computer – all have made their impact on life in Britain during the past one hundred years. But the rate of change has been accelerating and in the last decade the adoption of digital technology in all areas of economic and cultural life has been profound. Broadcasting technology was developed at the beginning of the twentieth century, but as analogue broadcasting is replaced by digital, the medium enters a new phase of unpredictable revolution. And it is not just broadcasting that will be affected: printing, telephony, cinema – all media must adjust to radical shifts in the ways their messages are produced, distributed and received. The future holds enormous potential to transform the media terrain.

Sometimes it is difficult for the student of the media to keep up with the pace of change. In *The Media in Britain* we take stock of the state of the media in our country. In Part I, we examine *The Structure of British Media Industries* and look at the key industries of publishing, advertising, the press, broadcasting, cinema, music and new media. The seven chapters in Part I survey the main players in each industry and indicate the current areas of interest and debate. There are recurring themes across many areas of the media, for example, the introduction of new technologies, the changing role of the state or the expanding influence of multinational companies. Some of these themes will be discussed in more detail in the introduction to Part I which also offers an overview of the media industry in Britain today.

One of the most important influences on the shape of the media in Britain is, of course, the government. Part II investigates *Regulation and Media Policy*, demonstrating how inextricably entwined the realms of British politics and media have become. The Conservative governments of 1979–96 had a profound influence on all areas of British life, not least on the structure and identity of the media and culture industries. The current parliament seems prepared to engage actively in developing media policies that promote the industry and embrace the new media. One of the Labour government's first moves was to rename the Department of National Heritage the Department of Culture, Media and Sport, thereby broadening and updating its remit. As Secretary for this new Department, Chris Smith has raised the profile of the British media industries and the level of debate about their importance to our cultural life. The media produce artefacts (films, television programmes, magazines) that not only reflect the culture in which they are made, but also contribute to the development of that culture. The chapters in Part II show the relationship between policy decisions and the shape of the media in Britain.

In Part III, *Media Material: Content and Representation*, a wide range of chapters explore the diverse content of contemporary British media. Here you will find a broad span of approaches to media analysis. Some of the chapters examine the kinds of material that are usually studied in media text books: such as newspapers, magazines, television and the Internet. Some invite the reader to question the traditional boundaries of the field of media studies by investigating areas of practice that are not usually included in surveys of the field. Here you will find essays on the theatre, novels, and museums. The range of texts discussed is enormously varied and includes *Trainspotting*, *Gardeners' World*, *Blind Date*, *The Stephen Lawrence Story*, *The Buddha of Suburbia* and The Imperial War Museum. The chapters in this section collectively build up a kaleidoscope of the kinds of media being produced in Britain today. Each chapter presents a different approach to the study of the media, showing the wealth of methodologies currently available to the scholar of the media in Britain.

This book aims to interest and excite the reader in the stimulating area of media studies. We hope you will enjoy reading it and that it will encourage you to enter into the lively and continuing debate about the future of the media in Britain.

PART I

THE STRUCTURE OF BRITISH MEDIA INDUSTRIES

JANE STOKES

The types of media industries in Britain are the same as in most other countries: books, newspapers, television programmes, films and music are among the media produced and sold here. But the exact nature of the texts that the British media industries produce is unique. The exact historical and cultural location of each medium gives the industries in Britain a different identity from those of media in other countries. Thus television programming in Britain is different from that you would find in Germany, Trinidad or America because of the different histories of these countries and the specific relationship of television to other media there. Exactly what kinds of newspaper we read or television programmes we watch are dependent in large part on the history of publishing or broadcasting and the structure of the media environment in which they exist. The structure of the media industry contributes to the character of our country, and is also a product of our history. This section offers an overview of the media, and in this introduction I will provide a brief summary of the media industries in Britain.

British people are used to thinking of our economy as 'mixed' – with the public sector and private industry both having a role to play. It is useful to think of the media in these terms, too: the public and private sectors have interests in the media and both contribute to the shape and character of the British scene. The role of the state in supporting, censoring or regulating the media differs from one country to another and, indeed, from one industry to another. For example, television is an area that is very highly regulated by most European governments, and the British are no exception. In Britain, the British Broadcasting Corporation (BBC) – one of the most important broadcasters – is funded by a licence fee determined by the government and is closely regulated by the state. The impact of the state on the media economy is discussed in Part II of this volume. Part I of *The Media in Britain* explores the structure of the principal media industries, delving into the history where that is necessary to understand the contemporary composition.

The seven chapters that follow are presented in approximate historical order, beginning with 'Publishing' which examines the book and periodical trade. This chapter begins by offering a brief history of publishing in Britain.

The origins of all media can be traced to the introduction of the printing press to Britain by William Caxton. The focus of this chapter is on books and magazines (newspapers are examined in detail in Chapter 3). 'Publishing' discusses the development of the publishing house and the relationship between publishers and booksellers. Special attention is paid to the expansion of American retailers, such as Borders, into the British market. The impact of new digital technologies on the book business is also discussed. The parallel history of the magazine is also chronicled in this chapter and I pay special attention to the dominance of the leading magazine publishers, IPC and EMAP, over the British periodical business. This chapter shows how the most traditional of media have responded to the challenges of new technology and demonstrates that publishing is a vital and dynamic medium.

The relationship between publishing and advertising has a long history: Peter Meech shows how the first newspapers included advertisements – many of them for books – in his introduction to the analysis of the advertising industry in Britain. Meech provides an overview of the history of advertising in Britain and focuses his discussion on the industry since the 1980s. The Thatcher period is identified as central to the development of the relationship between advertising and the broader media industries. (This period is also considered as key to changes in broader media policy discussed in Part II.) The mechanisms for regulating advertising, including the role of the Advertising Standards Authority, are discussed. Meech presents current data that show the close dependence on the financial support advertising provides to television, the press and the cinema. Finally, Meech argues that the centrality of advertising to media is assured: even the 'new' medium of the Internet relies heavily on advertising and corporate sponsorship.

The relationship between advertising and the press is further discussed and problematized by Colin Sparks. In his chapter, Sparks discusses the London-based newspapers that comprise the national press in Britain: the *Sun*; the *Mirror*; the *Star*; the *Mail*; the *Express*; the *Telegraph*; the *Financial Times*; the *Guardian*; the *Independent* and *The Times*. For Sparks, the most important role of the press is to provide a public forum for debate about political life: a healthy democracy is dependent on a free and open press. In this regard he finds the British press lacking. Sparks compares the press in Britain with that of other countries and finds that the oligopolistic competition under which the British press operates is not conducive to the full participation of readers in the democratic process. Sparks argues that the concentration of ownership, the reliance on advertising and the tendency towards an increasingly tabloid press present powerful dangers to contemporary democracy. Sparks concludes that the free market in Britain is incompatible with a free press.

In contrast to the press, broadcasting in Britain has never operated as a free market. Television and radio are probably the most heavily regulated of the media in Britain. Andrew Crisell begins his discussion of 'Broadcasting: Television and Radio' by considering the relationship between public service broadcasting and democratic principles. He examines the introduction of

Independent Television and the development of the duopoly of ITV and BBC which has dominated the history of broadcasting in Britain. Crisell shows how the tensions between public service and commercial imperatives have shaped the development of broadcasting. In discussing more recent trends in the industry, Crisell considers the impact of new technologies and deregulation. The expansion of radio and television services in recent years is discussed, as is the question of the future of the BBC in a more competitive, multichannel, multidelivery-system broadcasting world.

Television and radio in Britain have always been dominated by indigenous operators, largely because governments have carefully controlled the industry to limit the input of non-British players. The British cinema, by contrast, has often sought government intervention, but has been dominated by non-British players: the overwhelming influence of Hollywood is a feature of most European film industries. John Hill puts recent claims for a 'revival' in British cinema in context in his chapter and shows how the power of Hollywood dominates British efforts. Hill also explores how new initiatives such as Channel 4's *Film on Four* have made an impact on the relationship between the film and television industries in Britain.

The recorded music market is the subject of Chapter 6, where Paul McDonald assesses the importance of music among the media in Britain. Here the place of the British music industry within the global music industry is explored. The relationship between the British and American industries is considered and the importance of EMI, the only British 'major' is considered. The impact of new technologies, especially the World Wide Web, on music is discussed. Of special concern to McDonald is the question of rights and copyrights in the face of increasingly easy circulation of music properties.

The last chapter in this section, by James Cornford and Kevin Robins, explores the impact of new media, including CD-ROM, Internet and the World Wide Web, on the media environment. Cornford and Robins ask what is new about the 'new media'? New media, they argue, characteristically enable innovation in the areas of *convergence*, *compression* and *interactivity*. In terms of ownership and control, however, Cornford and Robins demonstrate that many traditional media operators exercise a powerful influence. Picking up on the discussion by Meech in his chapter on advertising, the authors of this chapter examine the importance of commercial sponsorship of websites. Despite claims that the Internet can allow publishing for all, Cornford and Robins argue that it is dominated by big business. The use of new digital technologies in traditional media like television and newer media such as computer games is discussed here. Finally, though, Cornford and Robins conclude that: 'what the new technologies permit is the refinement, extension and embellishment of traditional media.' Which brings us full circle to the beginning of our chronological survey and the observation that even publishing, the first mass medium, is flourishing and expanding in the new media age.

Some Key Themes

Throughout all of the chapters in Part I, *The Structure of British Media Industries*, three interrelated themes emerge which I would like to briefly tease out:

1. concentration of ownership
2. globalization, and
3. the impact of new technologies.

Concentration of Ownership

Media scholars and political commentators become very exercised by the worry that the ownership of the media in Britain might be concentrated in the hands of too few people. The idea of a single person controlling a number of media outlets threatens the principles of a free and open press. The spectre of the media baron intervening directly in the politics of the nation has been feared by many (Curran and Seaton, 1991). It is an issue raised by Colin Sparks in his chapter. Contemporary commentators of the British media frequently identify a non-British citizen, Rupert Murdoch, as a latter-day media mogul. Through his American-based company, News International Corporation, Murdoch owns several British media companies, including *The Times* and the *Sun* newspapers and BSkyB satellite television.

The main fear arising out of concentration of ownership is that a company may exert a monopoly over a medium. Governments are able to use anti-monopoly legislation to ensure that no one company or interest exercises an unfair market position. There are controls on cross-media ownership, too: that is, the percentage of interests in one medium which a company may own in another medium. For example, no single company can control more than 15 per cent of the total television market (measured by audience share). Radio is also restricted: no company may own more than one national radio licence, while at a local level, companies are restricted to 35 local licences or 15 per cent of the radio market as defined by the Radio Authority. But such limits on media ownership can prove counter productive. Legislation prescribing growth in one medium has prompted some media companies to expand into neighbouring industries, creating ever more diverse portfolios. British media companies are becoming ever more complex as a result, expanding into related media and leisure interests. They are also collaborating with domestic and international partners to form new companies and conglomerates, which serves to complicate the British media scene further.

Owning diverse media interests can leave a company open to accusations of unfair practices by using power in one market to exercise leverage in another. The sheer scale of the company also means it can use pricing as a marketing method to gain what is perceived by some to be an unfair advantage. Thus, *The Times* was offered at considerably below production cost to boost its circulation, something the company could only afford to do because of the deep pockets of the parent company. The price war, aimed at gaining control of the quality newspaper market in Britain, is estimated to cost News International between £20 and £50 million pounds *per annum* (Peak and Fisher, 1998). The fact that one proprietor can use his financial muscle to manipulate the market in such a way has a potentially deleterious effect on the industry as a whole, as argued by Colin Sparks in Chapter 3.

In Britain a few large companies dominate the media industries, and the main ones are shown in Table 1. We can see from this table that Granada is the largest media company in Britain in terms of revenues and number of employees. Starting in the film business, Granada diversified into live entertainment, was an early player in commercial television and now incorporates hotel and restaurant chains. It is a highly diversified company with wide experience of British media and entertainment. From Table 1 we can see that the leading media companies in Britain tend to have interests in a range of industries – not always media-related. The tendency in the British media, and globally, is towards greater concentration of ownership and bigger, more consolidated, companies.

Most of the industries discussed in this section of *The Media in Britain* are vulnerable to concentration of ownership. In the area of publishing, recent history is littered with buy-outs and mergers which are leaving the hundreds of publishing houses in Britain in the control of a handful of international conglomerates. In the newly deregulated broadcasting industry a newer trend is evident. In the television industry the BBC held a state monopoly for many years, but today production is being opened up and new independent companies are beginning to flourish. However, there are relatively few companies with sufficient expertise and capital to exploit the potential offered by new television delivery systems. Granada, Pearson and BSkyB are leading the way in providing new television services. The concentration of ownership in the hands of relatively few large companies continues to characterize the British media.

Globalization

Globalization is the tendency for organizations to operate on an increasingly global scale. The media industries, in keeping with other industries, are becoming increasingly global in reach. Some media developed along international lines early in their history: the news agency Reuters is the second largest media company in Britain and relies for its success on its global chain of offices. The advertising industry, too, has always had international agencies; cinema grew up along the trade routes of the great empires at the beginning of the twentieth century. Many of the media industries have pioneered global marketing of their products to audiences around the world.

These media industries have been at the vanguard of globalization, operating in an international arena.

Many of the main players on the British scene are not British in origin. The film industry in Britain, as in the rest of Europe, is dominated by that of Hollywood, as John Hill explains in Chapter 5. British publishing, as we shall see in Chapter 1, is dominated by the German company Bertelsmann AG, while Dutch companies VNU and Elsevier have long held interests here. The top circulation tabloid newspaper, the *Sun*, and the 'newspaper of record', *The Times*, are owned by the US company, News International Corporation.

News International operates on a global scale and this may sometimes lead the organization to act in one market to gain an advantage in another market. For example, when Rupert Murdoch halted the publication of a book by Chris Patten, former British Governor of Hong Kong, the most plausible explanation seemed to be that this was to protect his company's interests in China. Rupert Murdoch is keen to develop his interests in China, which include a share in the main Communist newspaper, *The Peoples' Daily,* and the Asian satellite company, Star. The importance of the burgeoning Asian market to News International seems to have influenced a decision about publishing in the British market. As they operate in an increasingly global economy, media corporations make decisions based on strategic advantages in a bigger arena than the nation state. Decisions made in the interests of market dominance in another part of the world may not be to the advantage of users of the media in Britain. The business ethic that is driving globalization undermines the authority of the national state.

An often ignored fact in debates about the globalization of the media market is the fact that British companies are often successful in overseas markets. Table 1 shows the diverse countries where the main British operators have interests and it is clear that these companies are every bit as international in focus as their overseas competitors. Globalization goes two ways and more and more British companies are making expansion overseas a priority. Much of the current imperative towards globalization is being driven by new technologies which allow media material to be produced, disseminated and received on an increasingly transnational scale. British media companies are well equipped to play a significant role in the globalization of media industries.

New Technology

The phenomenal growth in new technologies, especially digital technologies, has redrawn the map of media ownership and control in Britain and the rest of the world. All of the industries discussed in this section of the book have been influenced by technological innovations, especially the introduction of digital technologies. Traditional media industries earn their money by creating, distributing and exhibiting the mediated artefacts. New technology enables simpler generation of these artefacts; more rapid distribution through the interconnected infrastructure of the Internet and greater access to the means of originating work and of reproducing the work of others. The unique skills of the typesetter, the audio engineer, the camera operator, the cinema projectionist are all threatened by digital technologies which herald a multimedia revolution in which the differences between print, sound and image are no longer germane.

Multimedia technologies not only generate new media, such as the Internet (discussed in Chapter 7), but also engender new relations among pre-existing media. Perhaps the most important of the traditional media to be reinvented by digital technology is the telephone. Recent years have witnessed a phenomenal growth in telephone use prompted by the increased use of computers and the development of fibre optic cables. The growth of new phone lines is now outstripping that of cable. The telephone companies are now more powerful than ever, but the computer companies are those that are riding the boom: IBM and Microsoft are now among the largest and most profitable companies in the world. The pattern of the media industry in Britain, and across the world, is being redrawn by the expansion in digital technology. New media industries are being spawned and traditional media industries reformed by new technologies, as we see in all of the chapters to follow.

The Major British Media Companies

Throughout this book the question of what is British about the media in Britain is raised repeatedly. But, with concentration of ownership and an increasing tendency towards globalization reinforced by new technologies, the idea of a British media company is difficult to define.

So, what constitutes a 'media company'? Traditional categories of the press and broadcasting are insufficient to account for the range of media operators in Britain today. Given the integration of telephony with new media, we should perhaps include them in our list of leading media companies. British Telecom employ nearly 130,000 people and their revenues stood at £14,935 million in 1997 (Dun and Bradstreet, 1998) which exceeds the traditional media companies in Table 1. Since they currently make most of their money from telephone services it would be misleading to include them among media companies, but for how much longer can we neglect telephony from the media industries? Another company that has been excluded from our rostra of British media companies is EMI, a British company that is also the leading music publisher in the world. Their annual revenues of £3988 million make them slightly larger than Granada, but they are not generally considered a media company because their interests extend beyond the parameters of 'media' as it is usually defined.

When it comes to defining a company we find even this is problematic in the British media arena. One interest which is not, technically speaking, a

Table 1 Holdings of major British registered media companies by revenue

Company	Revenue (£000,000)	Employees	Media interests	Non-media interests	Countries where company has holdings or subsidiaries
Granada	3,816.90	66,850	Granada Film; Granada UK Rental and Retail; Granada Television; Granada Video; Harman Radio; Granada Computer Services	Little Chef; Travelodge; Granada Nightclubs	Angola, Belgium, Canada, Congo, Eire, France, Germany, Hong Kong, Netherlands, Singapore
Reed International	3,381.00	25,800	Reed Elsevier plc; Elsevier Science Publications; Heinemann Publishers; Hamlyn Publishing; Octopus Books; Essex County Newspapers	Reed Travel Group; Reed Holiday	Australia, Belgium, Canada, Eire, France, Italy, Japan, Netherlands, Malaysia, Singapore, Spain, Thailand
Reuters Holdings plc	2,914.00	14,917	Reuters Ltd; Reuters Television Satellite Service; Uplink Ltd International		Australia, Brazil, Canada, Cyprus, Denmark, Eire, France, Germany, Hungary, Hong Kong, Japan, Luxembourg, Netherlands, New Zealand, Spain, Sweden, Turkey, United Arab Emirates, USA
Pearson plc	2,186.00	17,383	The *Financial Times*; Channel 5; Pearson Television; Thames Television; Penguin Books; Future Publishing; Addison Wesley; Longman	The Tussauds Group: Madame Tussauds, Alton Towers, Chessington World of Adventures	Australia, Canada, France, Germany, Greece, Italy, India, Indonesia, Japan, Malaysia, Mexico, Netherlands, New Zealand, Singapore, Spain, USA, Venezuela,
United News and Media plc	1,990.70	18,318	MAI; Anglia Television Group; Meridian Broadcasting; the *Daily Express*; the *Sunday Express*; United Publications Ltd; Visual Communications Group	Blenheim Group plc; Ludgate Inc.; MAI Holdings; Miller Freeman Ltd	Australia, Belgium, Denmark, France, Germany, Hong Kong, Italy, Japan, Netherlands, Sweden, Switzerland, USA
Carlton Communications plc	1,677.50	10,607	Carlton Books; Carlton Television; Central Television; Carlton Films; Carlton Screen Advertising; Technicolor; The Moving Picture Company Ltd; Atlantic Satellite Communications; Direct Television		Australia, Belgium, Canada, Denmark, Eire, France, Germany, Hong Kong, Italy, Japan, Mauritius, Netherlands, Spain, USA
British Sky Broadcasting Group plc*	1,270.01	4580	BSkyB; Sky Channel; Sky Radio		
Daily Mail and General Trust	1,006.60	10,383	Associated Newspaper Holdings; Northcliffe Newspapers Group; *Daily Mail*; *Mail on Sunday*; *Evening Standard*; Channel 8 Ltd; Channel 9 Ltd		Australia, France, Hong Kong, Netherlands, Singapore, USA

*BSkyB is 40% owned by News International, but is a British registered company.
Source: Dun and Bradstreet (1998) *Who Owns Whom*.

company, but which is a major player in the British media scene, is the BBC. The BBC is a public corporation, funded out of licence fees paid by every television owner in the country. In 1994 the BBC launched BBC Worldwide to market its programmes and spin-off magazines around the world. The BBC is attempting to reach global commercial markets: it is part-owner of European Channel Management with Pearson Television and Cox Communications; it also is a 20 per cent shareholder in the Australian subscription television station UKTV with partners Pearson and Foxtel. The BBC is not included in our list of media companies because it is not, strictly speaking, a company, but a public corporation.

Table 1 includes the companies which have media as their primary or sole concern and which accrue revenues over £1000 million a year. They are listed in rank order of income, revealing Granada Group plc to be the largest media company in Britain, although a large amount of this revenue is from non-media interests such as their hotel and leisure chain. Much of the wealth of British media companies comes from overseas: Table 1 also lists those countries in which the listed companies own subsidiaries or interests according to Dun and Bradstreet (1998).

The British media industry is thus very complicated and the British media company is equally complex. It is important that we understand just how complex they are if we are to keep abreast of the many changes that are occurring in the media today.

Many of the largest media companies in Britain are not British: the most infamous is News International Corporation, owned by the notorious Rupert Murdoch. There are several international companies that are larger: Bertelsmann AG is the largest media company in the world; Time-Warner and Microsoft can give Murdoch a run for his money and are both powerful players in the British media.

This book focuses on the media in Britain and we will see that much of the media used in Britain are not British in origin. At the same time, British media companies are active players overseas and are often very successful in marketing British products in the international arena. The world of media studies has to recognize the international perspective of today's media industry if it is to keep up with current debates and development in the industry. The chapters in this section of *The Media in Britain* provide a thorough and stimulating overview of the main media industries in Britain and the main challenges confronting them in the future.

References

Curran, J. and Seaton, J. *Power Without Responsibility. The Press and Broadcasting in Britain*, 4th edn. London: Routledge, 1991.

Dun and Bradstreet *Who Owns Whom 1998/99* Volume 1: *United Kingdom and Ireland*. High Wycombe, Bucks: Dun and Bradstreet, 1998.

Peak, S. and Fisher, P. (eds) *The Media Guide 1988 (Guardian)*. London: Fourth Estate, 1998.

CHAPTER 1

Publishing

JANE STOKES

Publishing is the longest lived of the media in Britain, and one of the most influential. The publishing industry can trace its antecedents to the Middle Ages when the first hand-produced manuscripts were made and read by the religious elite. The medium of books first became industrialized following the development of a printing press with movable type in Germany during the middle of the fifteenth century by Johann Gensfleisch zum Gutenberg. A mechanical printing press was first introduced to England in 1476 by William Caxton, who ran a printer's shop near Westminster Abbey (Feather, 1991). The printing press helped advance the 'technologizing of the word' (Ong, 1982) and revolutionized the way ideas and information were disseminated. Gutenberg's invention mechanized literacy and led to the expansion of reading; printing gradually evolved into a mass medium such that books were no longer the preserve of the elite. The success of the printing press was dependent on various social factors including a critical mass of readers. In modern Britain, universal education ensures a literate public which is a prerequisite to publishing's centrality in our intellectual and cultural life.

Ever since the printing press was introduced to London, publishing has been a site of struggle between those who are driven by the profit motive and those who see books as fulfilling a more elevating, high culture, role. Printing helped create a mass public for the first time in European history, but also mobilized dissent against the elites of church and aristocracy: it democratized literacy and challenged the hegemony of elites. Today, the often divisive distinction between the 'mass' and the 'literary' markets is testament to a long history of ideological argument about the role of books. Underlying such distinctions is the controversial notion that some kinds of books are more worthy than others. What is beyond dispute is that books and periodicals have been produced on an increasingly large scale since the introduction of the printing press (Steinberg, 1996).

In its half a millennium history publishing has seen off many putative rivals. With the introduction of each new mass medium the demise of the book has been forecast. The cinema; broadcasting; sound recording; the computer – all have presented challenges to Britain's longest established media industry, threatening to bring about the end of literacy. Indeed, a key book in the history of British cultural studies claims that the twentieth-century mass media are responsible for a decline, not in literacy itself, but in the uses of literacy (Hoggart, 1958). Richard Hoggart argues that, although more people than ever before were reading in Britain in the 1950s, the commercial nature of their reading material debased the activity. The mass media, according to Hoggart, are responsible for the devaluation of reading in our society. A similar argument has been rehearsed with respect to television's deleterious effect on society. Writers have been eager to denounce the impact of broadcasting on literacy and reading, the most influential of these is perhaps Neil Postman's *Amusing Ourselves to Death* (1986). Despite many fearful prognostications, the book has survived and continues to flourish (Dennis *et al.*, 1997).

Publishing is a highly influential, dynamic player in the British media field. It is a flexible industry which has survived the many social changes that have occurred in the modern age; books are a malleable medium, able to deal with almost any subject matter and capable of transforming potential threats from rivals into publishing opportunities – witness the number of books and magazines currently in press about computing, for example. But, most importantly, publishing has survived because of the centrality of literacy to contemporary Western society. This chapter looks at two different products of the publishing industry: books and periodical publishing. It also looks at the increasingly important role of the bookshop and the book superstore in the book and periodical trade.

The impact of printing on the culture of European countries has been so vast as to be almost impossible to assess. Lucien Febvre and Henri-Jean Martin (1990 [1958]) study the very earliest books produced and consider how they have impacted scholarship and learning since the fifteenth century. They show how mechanized printing gradually changed the kinds of books being produced, bringing reading and book ownership beyond the confines of the clergy. Elizabeth Eisenstein (1979) sees the printing press as instrumental in bringing about the Protestant revolution which has been so important to the history of Europe. For Eisenstein, the printing press enabled the publication of literature that challenged the hegemony of the Papacy in the western world. John Thompson goes so far as to argue that publishing was crucial to the development of 'modernity' and argues that modern society itself is, in large part, the product of the press (Thompson, 1995). For S.H. Steinberg, a historian of printing, 'the history of printing is an integral part of the general history of civilization' (Steinberg, 1996, p. 1). There can be no doubt that publishing has had an enormous influence on the culture and society of Europe, including Britain.

The first books to be published in England were religious *incunabula* which bore a very close relationship to the handmade manuscripts that preceded them (Smith, 1994). Not only did early books imitate the style of the manuscripts, they also used the same themes: books of Gospels, prayer books and hagiographies were typical. Like the hand-produced manuscripts, *incunabula* were usually written in Latin – the language of the medieval clerisy. Gradually, more secular themes began to develop and books were produced in the vernacular languages (Febvre and Martin, 1990). The development of mechanical book production necessarily created a tension between the traditional book producers – mostly religious men – and the rising mercantile classes who made up the new printers and booksellers. A wider reading public poses a challenge to groups who fear that the expansion of access to ideas and information will threaten their hegemony. Until the current time, the history of publishing in Britain has been dogged by the ideological conflict between those who would maintain the elitism of reading and those who want to expand literacy. In recent times, for example, the introduction of the paperback was decried by some because it was feared that the elite control over the content of books would be lost.

The tension between 'popular' and 'elite' is also evident in regularly published journals, newspapers and magazines, often referred to as 'periodical publishing'. Periodical publishing in Britain dates back to the seventeenth century and has spawned both magazines and newspapers (Curran and Seaton, 1991). The newspaper industry is discussed in Chapter 3 of this volume by Colin Sparks; it falls within the purview of this essay to consider the weekly and monthly publications. In most discussions of the press in Britain, it is newspapers that are typically highlighted, while magazines are generally ignored. They are both manifestations of the same medium, however, and both trace their origins to the *corantos* of the seventeenth century, prototype periodicals that carried news of overseas events and shipping. Publications such as *The Moderate Messenger* or *The Faithful Post* (both first published in 1653) are early examples. While the newspaper is now generally a daily publication focused on current affairs, the magazine is more infrequently published (usually monthly or weekly) and more specific in focus.

All sectors of the publishing industry have seen growth in the 1990s, with profits increasing every year (ICC, 1998). In addition, there have been several vigorous takeover campaigns for successful titles and companies which are testament to the liveliness of the industry. Despite being the oldest of the mass media, publishing is one of the most dynamic and exciting.

The British Publishing Houses

Many of the most famous British publishing houses have very long and illustrious histories. Companies like Longman, founded in 1724; Macmillan, over 150 years old; and Hodder and Stoughton, established in 1868, continue to trade. Today there are hundreds of publishers in Britain, between them publishing approximately 100,000 books each year. The top selling publishers in Britain are shown in Table 1.1.

Table 1.1   The top selling publishers in Britain in 1997

Publisher (Parent Co.) {Origin}	Total Gross £ 1997	Total Copies 1997
Transworld (Bertelsmann AG) {Germany}	36,654,804	6,061,376
HarperCollins (News International) {USA}	30,070,170	4,379,487
Macmillan (Holtzbrinck) {Germany}	22,583,672	3,527,559
Random House (Bertelsmann AG) {Germany}	19,811,544	3,198,963
HodderHeadline {United Kingdom}	19,264,073	2,828,157

Sources: *The Bookseller*, 16 January 1998; Dun and Bradstreet, 1998.

Transworld is the publisher that dominates the popular end of the market, with imprints such as Corgi and Bantam on its rostra. Britain's most successful publisher is owned by the giant German conglomerate, Bertelsmann AG – the biggest media company in the world. The second largest grossing company, HarperCollins, is owned by News International, the American-based international conglomerate with multiple interests in the British media scene. Publishing in Britain, and elsewhere in the world, is an increasingly global phenomenon and many familiar British publishing houses are owned by non-British companies: conglomerates from Europe or the US now dominate British publishing. These patterns of globalization and conglomeration are evident in other areas of the media in Britain, as subsequent chapters in this section of the book will show.

American companies are among those currently leading the twin dynamics of globalization and convergence in the media around the world. Certainly, the most active acquisitors in the British publishing industry in recent years have been American companies: Random House has been one of the most aggressive newcomers entering the British market with the purchase of both Chatto & Windus and Cape (Chatto & Cape) in 1987, followed by Century Hutchinson in 1989 and Reed Consumer in 1997. Today, Random House owns a whole stable of publishing companies, including many of Britain's most venerable houses. The volatility of the publishing market is such that no company is immune from takeover: Random House were purchased in 1998 by Bertelsmann for an estimated £840 million (Moss and Barrie, 1998). Each of the major publishers in Britain owns several publishing houses and imprints, as we see in Table 1.2. This is evidence of the increasing conglomeration of publishing in Britain; it shows that formerly independent publishing houses are now increasingly owned by larger concerns.

Table 1.2 The main imprints of the leading British publishers

Trans-world	HarperCollins	Macmillan	Random House	Hodder Headline
Anchor	Collins	Macmillan Press	Arrow	Edward Arnold
Bantam	Flamingo	Pan	Century	Delta
Black Swan	Fontana	Papermac	Heinemann	Headline Review
Corgi	HarperCollins	Picador	Hutchinson	Hodder & Stoughton
Doubleday	Marshall Pickering	Sidgwick & Jackson	Methuen	Hodder Christian
Partridge Press	Thorsons		Pimlico	Liaison
	Times Books		Secker & Warburg	New English Library
	Voyager			

Sources: Dun and Bradstreet, 1998; Seaton, 1997.

What kinds of books are sold in Britain today, and by whom? Table 1.3 lists the ten top selling paperbacks in 1997, and we can see that four of these were published by Corgi, an imprint of Transworld. The globalization of the popular book market is further evident from this table when we observe that overseas publications compete well with British imprints in the British market. Only half of the books in the top ten are published by British companies. This shows how international the market for books is in Britain.

By cross-referencing Tables 1.2. and 1.3 above, we can see that the most popular books in Britain are sold by major corporations with global media interests. Bertelsmann and News International, the two biggest players in the British publishing scene, have interests in a number of different media. This 'cross-media ownership' can be used to advantage to promote products made in one medium in another, for example, using newspapers to push books or films made by another company within the same stable. Even greater advantages can accrue in the age of digital media because convergence can also be of benefit (see Chapter 7 of this volume for further discussion of this point). Cross-media ownership legislation in Britain has been relaxed in order to encourage British companies to become larger and better able to compete in a global market. However, the most integrated media companies in the British media scene continue to be non-British owned.

Table 1.3 The ten top selling paperbacks in Britain in 1997

Title	Author	Imprint	Nationality	Total Sales
The Runaway Jury	John Grisham	Arrow	US	1,015,256
The Evening Class	Maeve Binchy	Orion	Ireland	1,002,676
Angela's Ashes	Frank McCourt	Flamingo	Ireland	723,559
Bridget Jones's Diary	Helen Fielding	Picador	British	679,342
The Fourth Estate	Jeffrey Archer	HarperCollins	British	669,363
Icon	Frederick Forsyth	Corgi	British	618,867
Cause of Death	Patricia Cornwell	Warner	US	590,300
Appassionata	Jilly Cooper	Corgi	British	575,862
The Upstart	Catherine Cookson	Corgi	British	568,979
Malice	Danielle Steel	Corgi	US	558,038

Source: *The Bookseller*, 16 January 1998.

The book market, like the film industry, can be volatile at times and publishing is subject to being skewed by the occasional blockbuster, with titles by Delia Smith or about the royal family being especially saleable in recent years. Sales of a title are likely to increase if a film or television programme of the book is shown or if publication coincides with, or accompanies, a television series. For example, Michael Ondaatje's *The English Patient* was first issued in 1993, but in 1997, the year that the film of the book was released, it sold a further 487,367 copies (Hamilton, 1998). When *Captain Corelli's Mandolin* was featured on the BBC radio programme, *Book at Bedtime*, in July 1997, sales doubled the following month (*The Bookseller*, 6 February 1998). Film and television broadcasts have a significant effect on library borrowing too, increasing the number of issues of classic and modern novels (Book Marketing Update, 1996). Broadcasters and film production companies are keen to exploit their product by publishing spin-off publications. The BBC now vigorously supports books of series, as do other television companies, and these now constitute a rapidly growing area of publishing. Prizes, most notably the Booker, have a huge impact on book sales with the nominated titles guaranteed lucrative publicity. Arundhati Roy's first novel, *The God of Small Things*, winner of the 1997 Booker Prize, went on to become an international best seller. The great media coverage awarded to the winners of prizes helps to differentiate their work from the thousands of new titles issued each year and guarantees increased sales. However, Bookers are awarded to 'literary' books, which rarely outsell the 'mass market' popular paperbacks. In Britain, in 1997, the top selling paperback was by John Grisham, one of the world's most popular authors: *The Runaway Jury* sold over a million copies for Arrow, an imprint of Random House. This one book made up almost one-third of the paperback sales for Random House (see Table 1.1). Table 1.3

shows the top selling authors are mostly tried and tested names: Frederick Forsyth; Catherine Cookson; Danielle Steel; Jeffrey Archer – these writers produce mass market novels which are the mainstay of the publishing industry. The mass market may be eschewed by cultural elitists, but it provides the bread and butter of the publishing industry. Although books may have an image of being 'high culture', in fact today most are popular titles aimed at the mass market and produced by giant transnational corporations.

The British Bookshop

The relationship between the publisher and bookseller is a very complex one; the two trades only becoming separate relatively late in the history of books. The success or failure of a book often depends on its availability and promotion at the retail end: publishers rely on bookshops to stock and push their titles. The Net Book Agreement 'the cornerstone of the whole structure of British publishing in the twentieth century' (Feather, 1991, p. 148), was a crucial contract between publishers and booksellers in Britain, which came into being at the beginning of the century, on 1 January 1900. It was initiated by the publishing industry to prevent booksellers discounting their products, and enabled publishers to fix the prices at which retailers could sell their books. When the Net Book Agreement was finally abandoned in 1995, because it was considered to be a restraint of trade, publishers feared a return to rampant discounting and were worried they would lose control over the prices at which their products could be sold on the retail market. Despite anguished warnings about the deleterious effects on publishing, the end of the Net Book Agreement has not had much impact, and the trade has remained relatively unchanged. During the first few years there was considerably less discounting of books than many expected; despite doleful predictions of a reduction of the number of titles, publishers continue to produce more books. According to Matt Seaton, 'publishers are putting out more and more books, with shorter print runs and at lower and lower margins – all chasing what is, in net terms, less and less consumer spending' (Seaton, 1997, p. 2). But recent evidence shows the contrary: spending on books and profits for the publishing sector as a whole have continued to grow in the 1990s.

One reason for continued growth in the publishing industry is that there have been changes in book retailing which have resulted in consumers having more outlets where they can purchase books. The high-street book trade in Britain has long been dominated by the 200-year-old company WH Smith, Britain's leading stationery supplier and newsagent, with about 500 bookshops in the UK. The more upmarket Waterstone's was founded by a former WH Smith employee, Tim Waterstone, in 1982, to cater to a more literary end of the book trade. Waterstone's quickly grew to challenge the established literary bookstore, Dillons. Dillons was founded in 1936 by Uma Dillon, who later joined forces with the University of London to form Dillons

University Bookshop in 1956. It was acquired by Thorn-EMI in 1995 and has some 85 shops with annual sales of £170 million (McCabe, 1998). The Waterstone's chain of 115 retailers, with annual sales of £200m, is now also owned by EMI. Thus Britain's two leading bookshop names are now part of the EMI retail chain, HMV Media Group, making this one of the strongest retailers of books in Britain. The amalgamation of Dillons and Waterstone's into HMV looks set to create the biggest bookseller in Britain's history, with some 20 per cent of the market. WH Smith, which now incorporates John Menzies, has to take second place for the first time in its history although it still controls a significant 18 per cent of the market. The bookshop in Britain is part of the growing multi-interest media chains.

British bookshops need to be in a strong economic position if they are to withstand the challenge confronting the trade from across the Atlantic. The single most important influence on book retailing in Britain is posed by the new, giant American bookstores Barnes and Noble (currently the biggest bookstore chain in the world) and Borders (the second biggest chain globally). These giant superstore bookshops have considerably more floor space than the average Dillons or Waterstone's, stock many more titles and have a much more user-friendly approach to book buying. The American superstores stock in excess of 150,000 titles, which is far above anything the average high-street British bookshop could carry.

Barnes and Noble and Borders bookstores typically have comfortable chairs and tables where one can sit and read in comfort; children are well catered for; there are story telling events, children's tables and chairs and play areas. These bookstores encourage one to browse by having coffee and snacks for sale in a hospitable environment and providing good public lavatories, which are arguably a must if one is to encourage shoppers to linger! Their revolutionary attitude towards book selling has brought them huge profits in the US. Borders has begun its foray into the British scene by buying the chain Books etc., and opened their first European Books and Music superstore in London's Oxford Street in August, 1998. Waterstone's have risen to the challenge and plan their own, seven-storey store in Piccadilly, London, which they claim will stock 300,000 titles, over a million books and will be the third largest bookshop in the world (Hall, 1998). The expansion of the American superstores into the British market is certainly shaking up the high-street book trade.

In the US, the rapid growth of the giant superstores has caused much speculation about the potentially harmful impacts on the trade. The spectre of independent bookstores closing down in the face of aggressive competition is already a reality in the US. In Britain, the first victims of the large stores are already being identified: Austicks in Leeds and Alison's Books of Bolton were both established independent bookstores that have ceased trading in the face of strong competition. Publishers fear that the range of books will not be published as quantity becomes more important than quality. However, the range of books stocked and the number of books sold has increased and the publishing market overall has been given a fillip by these new entrants.

In Britain, it is possible that we might find a situation where retailing determines more of what is published. Certainly, current trends in the book trade are tipping the balance of power away from publishers and towards retailers. For the book buyer, the prospect of well-stocked, comfortable stores is welcomed: book sales are growing as a result of bigger bookshops. Nicholas Clee maintains:

> After the expansion of bookshop chains such as Waterstone's and Dillons in the late 1980s and early 1990s, bookselling in the UK is entering a new phase, in which the principal retail companies compete to present their outlets as not just shops, but leisure environments. (Clee, 1998, p. 9)

The 'leisure environment' of multimedia shopping has been a growing phenomenon in recent years. In order to reach younger readers, books are now frequently sold in the same retail outlets where people can also buy CDs, electronic games, videos and other media. Stores like Virgin, HMV and Tower offer their customers the opportunity to make purchases in a range of media where books are just part of the mix. The differences between the media forms are being increasingly elided in the high street. WH Smith is a leading outlet for music; Virgin HMV and Tower are primarily music retailers who do a busy trade in books, periodicals, posters, videos, electronic games and so on.

Traditional bookshops face a further threat from advances in new technology, especially given that selling over the Internet can bypass traditional retailers. Amazon.com is a leading retailer of books on the Internet making book buying easy for the computer literate. Often computer users are the natural constituency for booksellers: bookworms and techies are both information hungry animals. While Amazon.com shift record numbers of books, at the time of writing they have yet to make a profit. Conventional operators are now developing their own web presence and offer Internet sales. For example, WH Smith owns the Internet Bookshop (www.bookshop.co.uk), the largest Internet book retailer in Europe. Other providers of books on-line include Bookpages (www.bookpages.co.uk) and The Book Pl@ce (www.thebookplace.com). Meanwhile new forms of sales are growing on the Internet: some books have even been given away, for example Bruce Sterling's *The Hacker Crackdown*, published by Penguin (Ollier, 1998). This has enormous implications for the control of publishing properties. The problems of maintaining copyright in the age of electronic data and *http* are legion. Alex Hamilton speculates on the impact of the expansion of the Internet and fears, 'copyright will leak like a sieve all over the universe' (Hamilton, 1998, p. 21).

Electronic publishing is a challenge that traditional publishers have found it difficult to adjust to: early attempts at CD-ROM publishing, for example, have now been abandoned by many. New entrants to publishing are better able to use digital technology to target niche markets more precisely than the traditional companies. One of the disadvantages of traditional publishing is the huge amount of waste generated by the publication of books that will not sell and that must be pulped: more books are wasted than are sold. The company Original On-Line utilizes electronic publishing to get round this problem by only producing a physical copy of a book after it has been ordered. Another outlet, the Download Bookstore (www/.psi.net/download-bookstore) provides a discount service for clients to download books (Ollier, 1998). Digital technology allows for the industry to produce to order and enables a more targeted production line. Ironically, then, the new technology permits the reintroduction of bespoke publishing which has been lost since the introduction of mass production.

British Periodical Publishing

Contemporary periodical publishing is one of the most flexible and dynamic of the media in Britain, due in no small measure to the speed with which the industry is able to generate new products. A new magazine can be launched in a matter of weeks by well-capitalized companies with experienced management. Magazines are able to respond rapidly to changes in new technology as well as to changes in gender and social relations by targeting publications at relevant groups. It is worth noting that, well before the launch of the modern 'lads' magazines, such as *Loaded*, periodical publishing was one of the most highly gendered of the British media. The earliest general interest magazines were directed at a male audience, for example *The Gentlemen's Journal* (1692) and *The Gentleman's Magazine* (1731–1831). These periodicals were aimed at gentlemen who lived in the country and could not reach clubs and social engagements in the metropolis.

Magazines specifically for women are among the most successful titles ever published, and these, too, have their origins in the seventeenth and eighteenth centuries. Titles such as *The Ladies' Mercury* (1693), *The Ladies' Magazine* (1749) and *The Lady's Monthly Museum* (1798) were among the first women's magazines. These were largely aimed at the gentry, or upper middle-class women, and had the goal of improving the minds of their readers through a 'tone of mental and moral uplift well suited to literate, leisured ladies' (Ferguson, 1985, p. 15). Samuel Beeton's *The Englishwoman's Domestic Magazine* was launched in 1852 and cost just two old pennies. One sixth of the price of competitors, it was aimed at more middle-class women who were the wives and daughters of the professional and business classes.

After the 1853 repeal of advertisement duty made it more economic to advertise in newspapers and magazines, there was a huge expansion in both the advertising industry and the publication of popular papers and periodicals. The cover price of many newspapers and magazines fell and more popular titles were created, subsidized by advertising revenues. The complex pattern of interrelationships between advertising and magazines was evident in the earliest days of advertising (see Meech, this volume). Today's 'consumer market' of the periodical trade sometimes elides the difference between copy and advertising, and sponsorship of stories is not uncommon.

There are approximately 10,000 magazines published in Britain today, the precise number is difficult to gauge as the majority are trade publications, distributed through subscription or membership to professional bodies. The most visible elements of the market are the consumer titles that one finds on sale at the local newsagent, although subscription and trade magazines make up a large part of the market (see Table 1.4). The magazine market is dominated by two major concerns: IPC and EMAP. IPC magazines are leaders in the magazine publishing field, with 71 titles in all (Zenith Media, 1997). Formerly owned by the multi-interest publishing conglomerate, Reed, IPC was recently sold to Cinven, an investment company, for £860 million in January 1998 (Barnett, 1998). Cinven began as an offshoot of British Coal Pension Fund in 1977 when the Coal Board had the largest pension fund in the UK (Barnett, 1998). Its interest in IPC is not so much to own a magazine company as to own a leading brand name. IPC publishes several of the top selling consumer magazines in Britain, including *What's on TV*, *Woman's Own* and *Marie Claire*.

The second leader in the field is EMAP (formerly East Midlands Allied Press) which publishes some 90 consumer magazines (Zenith Media, 1997). EMAP is a Peterborough-based publisher recently valued at £1.8 billion with an annual turnover of £850 million and profits growing at 40 per cent per annum. EMAP's top selling magazine is *FHM*, and the company also publishes *More!*, *Empire* and *Smash Hits*. The latest entrant to the magazine business is BBC Worldwide. Launched by the BBC in 1994, BBC Worldwide is the means by which the public Corporation can market its products both globally and in the UK. BBC Worldwide publishes 19 magazines (10 of them in the top 100), with combined sales of over 100 million in 1996 (Peak and Fisher, 1997).

Table 1.4   The leading UK consumer periodical publishers

Company	No. of titles	Main titles in top 100
IPC	23 Marie Claire, NME, TV Times	Loaded, Country Life, Woman's Own,
EMAP	20	FHM, Elle, New Woman, Smash Hits, Bliss
BBC	10	Radio Times, Top of the Pops, Gardeners' World, Good Food
National Magazines	6	Cosmopolitan, Good Housekeeping, Home Beautiful
Condé Nast	3	GQ, Vogue, Home and Garden

Source: Zenith Media Worldwide (1997).

While newspaper sales have decreased in recent years (see Sparks, this volume), there has been a gradual increase in the overall sales of consumer magazines, from 1155 million copies in 1991 to 1454 million copies in 1996, while magazine advertising revenue has nearly doubled since 1986.

The current leading circulation magazine is not a consumer title, but a subscription title, *AA Magazine*, which is distributed to nearly 4 million members of the Automobile Association (see Table 1.5). Television guides take second and third place, *Sky TV Guide* had a circulation of almost three and a half million in 1997, followed by *What's on TV* at close to two million the same year. Half of the top ten circulation magazines are television guides of one kind or another, including the BBC's *Radio Times* and IPC's *TV Times*. It is clear that television viewing has not displaced magazine purchase, but has given magazine publishers a new area in which to publish. This proves the ability of the medium to ameliorate threats from new media by producing titles of interest to users of new media.

Table 1.5   The ten top circulation consumer/customer magazines in the UK

Rank	Publication	Publisher	Circulation*
1	AA Magazine	Redwood Publishing Ltd	3,981,939
2	Sky TV Guide	Redwood Publishing Ltd	3,491,173
3	What's on TV	IPC Weeklies Group	1,702,184
4	Reader's Digest	Reader's Digest Ass'n Ltd	1,492,549
5	A Taste of Safeway Magazine	Redwood Publishing Ltd	1,471,338
6	Radio Times	BBC Worldwide Ltd	1,400,270
7	Somerfield Magazine	Brass Tacks Publishing Co	1,241,493
8	Cable Guide	Cable Guide	1,101,251
9	You and Yours	Mediamark Publishing International Ltd	959,850
10	TV Times	IPC Weeklies Group	892,760

* All circulation figures are based on Audit Bureau of Circulation figures for the period January–June 1997.

Source: Willings Press Guide 1998.

The main characteristic of successful magazine publishing is niche marketing which requires a good sense of the market, high levels of investment capital and flexibility. Finding a community of interest prepared to buy a magazine and matching their demographic profile with an advertising group is a basic skill all periodical publishers must acquire. The real key to launching new magazines has been the ever more effective targeting of increasingly tight consumer niches, not just those for shared interests, such as fashion or fishing, but often for demographic groups with a shared attitude (Garrett, 1998, p. 5).

The huge magazine market is strongly entwined with consumerism. Supported by advertising and linked in with manufacturing and service industries, magazines are able to reinforce marketing strategies of every other industry in Britain. Mike Matthew, chief executive of IPC, summed up the view for Alexander Garrett:

> The UK is one of the most competitive, dynamic and innovative magazine markets in the world, which is constantly creating new sectors and sub-sectors, and I see no reason why it cannot continue to do that indefinitely. (Garrett, 1998, p. 5)

Magazines in Britain have certainly proved themselves able to sustain market positions in the face of competition from abroad and from other media. One of the most successful magazine publishers, EMAP, ascribes its success to its willingness to 'back people who take risks' (Farrelly, 1997, p. 2). In practice, this often means allowing people to float titles and see if they sail. If a magazine does not do well it can be scrapped with no great loss to a company which can afford to back the risk. Kevin Hand, chief executive of EMAP, recognized the importance of imaginative concepts in magazine publishing, even though this might mean backing an occasional failure. Hand told Paul Farrelly about his least favourite title, *Woman on Wheels*:

> It was in the eighties when we thought scooters would be the in-thing for shopping in crowded city centres. It had a free nail file on one side of the cover and a spark-plug cleaner on the other. It was dreadful. It never got past the first edition. (Farrelly, 1997, p. 2)

The fact that *Woman on Wheels* was even contemplated is evidence of the flexibility of the industry. Successful magazine publishing in Britain must be able to identify and cater to every lifestyle and consumer subset.

In conclusion, Britain's oldest medium is having to adopt to a rapidly changing media environment. Like many other media in this country, publishing is increasingly owned and operated by huge multinational companies. Bertelsmann and News International now effectively dominate the British book trade, and most of Britain's most venerable old publishing houses have been absorbed into these giant companies. But British readers may benefit from the fact that the increased investment in books means that there are now more titles published each year than ever before. The retail book trade faces some exciting challenges as bookstores grow into new retail leisure environments. Traditional booksellers may find themselves elbowed out of the business as larger, better stocked and more user-friendly stores threaten their trade. Periodical publishing continues to be dominated by the two leaders IPC and EMAP, both British companies which exploit the precise niche marketing which contemporary magazine publishing allows. The chal-

lenges of the digital age have been patchily responded to: while some periodical publishers have leapt into the fray, some sectors of the publishing
industry still balk at entering the age of the computer.

The arguments that dog publishing still reflect those of the early days of the
industrialization of books: the industry is still divided into trade (mass) and
literary (elite) publishing.

References

Barnett, A. 'Venture capitalists out of a new mould', *Observer* Business Section, (11
January 1998) p. 6.

Book Marketing Update *Tie-ins and Prizes: The Effects on Borrowing through Public
Libraries*. London: Book Marketing Limited, 1996.

Clee, N. 'War of the words', *Guardian* (25 July 1998) p. 9.

Curran, J. and Seaton, J. *Power Without Responsibility. The Press and Broadcasting in
Britain*, 4th edn. London: Routledge, 1991.

Dennis, E.E., LaMay, C.L. and Pease, E.C. (eds) *Publishing Books*. New
Brunswick/London: Transaction Press, 1997.

Dun and Bradstreet *Who Owns Whom 1998/9* Vol. 1: *United Kingdom and Ireland*.
High Wycombe, Bucks: Dun and Bradstreet, 1998.

Eisenstein, E. *The Printing Press as an Agent of Change*. Cambridge: Cambridge
University Press, 1979.

Farrelly, P. 'Publisher with a knock-out punch', *Observer* Business Section (30
November 1997) p. 2.

Feather, J. *A History of British Publishing*. London/New York: Routledge, 1991.

Febvre, L. and Martin, H.-J. *The Coming of the Book: The Impact of Printing,
1450–1800*. Translated by David Gerard. London: Verso, 1990 [1958].

Ferguson, M. *Forever Feminine: Women's Magazines and the Cult of Femininity*. London:
Gower, 1985.

Garrett, A. 'Loaded magazines fire on both barrels', *Observer* Media Section (11
January 1998) p. 5.

Hall, S. 'Shop will have 1m books on six miles of shelves', *Guardian* (28 October
1998) p. 13.

Hamilton, A. 'Alex Hamilton's paperback fastsellers of 1997', *The Bookseller* (16
January 1998) pp. 20–1.

Hoggart, R. *The Uses of Literacy*. Harmondsworth: Pelican, 1958.

ICC *UK Industrial Performance Analysis 1997/8*. Middlesex: ICC Business Publications.
1998.

McCabe, D. 'Arch-rivals to be best pals?', *The Bookseller* (16 January 1998) p. 10.

Moss, S. and Barrie, C. 'Meet some German literary types', *Guardian* (25 March
1998) p. 17.

Ollier, A. 'Selling books in cyberspace', *The Bookseller* (23 January 1998) p. 34.

Ong, W. *Orality and Literacy. The Technologizing of the Word*. London: Methuen, 1982.

Peak, S. and Fisher, P. *The Media Guide*. London: The Guardian/Fourth Estate, 1997.

Peak, S. and Fisher, P. (eds) *The Media Guide 1998 (Guardian)*. London: Fourth
Estate, 1998.

Postman, N. *Amusing Ourselves to Death*. London: Methuen, 1986.

Seaton, M. 'Books in a bind', *Guardian* Media Section (29 December 1997) pp. 2–4.

Smith, M.M. 'The Design Relationship Between the Manuscript and the Incunable', in R. Myers and M. Harris (eds) *A Millennium of the Book: Production, Design and Illustration in Manuscript and Print 900–1900*. Winchester: St. Paul's Bibliographies/Delaware: Oak Knoll Press, 1994.

Steinberg, S.H. *Five Hundred Years of Printing*. New edition, revised by John Trevitt. London: The British Library and Oak Knoll Press, 1996.

Thompson, J.B. *The Media and Modernity. A Social Theory of the Media*. London: Polity Press, 1995.

Willings Press Guide 1998. Teddington, Middlesex: Hollis Directories Ltd, 1998.

Zenith Media Worldwide *UK Media Yearbook*. United Kingdom: Zenith Media, 1997.

CHAPTER 2

Advertising

PETER MEECH

People often look to biology for metaphors to characterize the relationship between advertising and the media. For some, advertising is a parasite, living on the backs of the media and feeding greedily on its hosts. For others, the relationship is better described as symbiotic: just as certain animals or plants have developed ways of surviving that are of mutual benefit, so too have advertising and the media. This chapter examines their close and evolving relationship.

To begin with, the characteristic features of the UK advertising industry are discussed, including its heightened salience in the 1980s, structural changes in the industry since then, and advertising's continuing attempts to demonstrate its value and professionalism to clients and the general public. The second half deals with the economic contribution that advertising makes to the UK media and some of the editorial implications arising from this. Alternatives to traditional ads are also considered, as are changing public attitudes to what has become an integral part of popular culture.

Advertising's Recent Past

Modern advertising developed in the second half of the nineteenth century, although its antecedents can be traced back at least as far as the early eighteenth century. The first newspapers carried small classified ads for patent medicines, books or concerts, but it was not until the branding of consumer goods by means of display ads in the Victorian era that advertising acquired many of the features we would recognize today (Nevett, 1982). The twentieth century subsequently saw the increasing professionalization of the practice, the introduction of market research, the expansion of media vehicles, especially television (Henry, 1986), and the growth of the consumer society.

For much of the early post-war period, advertising, particularly of the hard-selling television variety, had been thought of as something of a US import by many people in Britain. A number of American agencies had set up bases in London in the 1920s, of which J. Walter Thompson was the biggest and best known. Later, in the 1950s and 60s, the tendency was for British agencies to be acquired by US predators. In the 1980s, however, British advertising companies began making headlines by taking over established American agencies. Saatchi & Saatchi acquired Compton in 1982, the American-based worldwide network more than twice its size, and, in 1986, the Ted Bates agency. Although this process had in fact begun with other British companies in the late 1970s, the perception that the Saatchi brothers were responsible for exporting so-called creative British advertising to the US was another of the latter's achievements. Also in 1986 WPP, with headquarters in London, took over J. Walter Thompson, the parent company, and subsequently the Ogilvy & Mather agency to become the world's largest advertising organization. Although the UK advertising industry is predominantly London-centred, there are many independently owned agencies or subsidiaries of larger companies to be found elsewhere in the country: Faulds in Edinburgh, for example, or McCann-Erickson in Manchester. But, as with most leading UK media organizations, a strong centripetal force accounts for a concentration in the capital of the main offices of companies such as Lowe Howard-Spink or The Media Centre.

During the 1980s, advertising unquestionably gained a new, high public profile in the UK. Conservative governments played a central role by extending the concept of the market to areas that had previously run on a non-commercial basis. Advertising was heavily used, for example, to assist the privatization of public utilities and publicly owned companies. Charities, churches, trade unions and universities came to feel obliged to buy commercial airtime on television to gain a competitive edge. The first Thatcher administration had itself been helped to gain office in 1979 by the advertising campaign that Saatchi & Saatchi created for it, which included the famous 'Labour isn't working' poster. The inevitable involvement in politics of an industry previously associated in the main with promoting consumer goods was finally recognized by the Labour Party. Since 1987 it too has made increasing use of professional advertising expertise in its general election campaigns.

Advertising in the UK became the epitome of 1980s yuppie culture: febrile, lavish and glamorous. The number of companies and personnel working in the industry and the size of their salaries all grew as advertising budgets increased in line with an expanding economy. But it was not to last. The recession of the early 1990s saw a reduction in promotional budgets with inevitable consequences for the industry. Advertising is by tradition particularly sensitive to the broader economy, reflecting in heightened form both upward and downward trends in the latter, as advertisers concentrate resources on what they perceive as more core activities. The resulting combination of reduced budgets and staff cuts produced a new mood of caution, which has not entirely disappeared despite a general improvement in the national economy in the mid-1990s. Now more than ever cost-effectiveness-conscious advertisers are considering other marketing communications tools to traditional 'above-the-line' advertising. As a result, 'below-the-line' alternatives such as public relations, sales promotion and sponsorship have grown in importance.

It was also during the 1980s that British media studies developed a strong interest in advertising, stimulated by a body of new critical writing. Drawing on the work of Barthes, Althusser and Lacan, Judith Williamson had a lasting influence on the structuralist analysis of magazine ads (Williamson, 1978), while Raymond Williams argued against the irrational appeals of advertising (Williams, 1980). *Media, Culture and Society* devoted a special issue to the subject in 1981, which contains James Curran's classic political economy study of advertising and the UK media (Curran, 1981). Gillian Dyer's broadly based textbook (Dyer, 1982) became a fixture on many undergraduate courses, as did the US-orientated monograph by William Leiss, Stephen Kline and Sut Jhally, first published in 1986 (Leiss *et al.*, 1991). Meanwhile, Kathy Myers (Myers, 1986) persuasively cautioned against demonizing advertising as the handmaiden of capitalism.

The Business of Advertising

A standard way of distinguishing between agencies is according to what they can provide for their clients. The larger companies have traditionally had the resources and expertise to be able to offer a so-called full service. Account planners research the likely customers and their media consuming habits, using survey data such as the government's Social Trends, the Target Group Index and the National Readership Survey. Media planners determine where and when the campaign will appear, and media buyers negotiate the required media space or airtime (Brierley, 1995). One or more creative teams, each comprising a copywriter and art director, design how the campaign will look, sound and read (Douglas, 1984). An agency will also pre-test its advertising for acceptability by a sample group, check that it is carried as agreed with the media and possibly evaluate a campaign's success in achieving the objectives set by the client.

In the past it was customary for advertisers to assign responsibility for such work to a single agency, with whom they built up an enduring relationship of mutual trust and confidence. Nowadays it is common for accounts to be split among different agencies and for these to change with greater frequency. Competitive pitches are arranged by advertisers at which rival agencies present their ideas for a new campaign. Details of accounts 'on the move' are published regularly in the trade press such as the weekly magazine *Campaign*. Traditionally agencies were paid by withholding 15 per cent of the airtime and space costs which they collected from clients and remitted to the medium concerned. But over the years suspicions grew that some agencies were motivated to buy the most expensive media primarily to boost their own earnings. While payment by commission is no longer the norm – fixed fees and payment by results having become more common (Lace, 1998), the issue of remuneration remains a contentious one for advertisers seeking greater accountability from advertising agencies.

An indication of the size of the major full-service agencies is provided by their billings and staff size. The former are an annual estimate by the market research organization AC Nielsen-MEAL of the costs of the airtime and space bought by agencies on behalf of clients. They are generally held to be more accurate than figures supplied by the agencies themselves. In 1997, for example, the top agency, Abbott Mead Vickers BBDO, had estimated billings of £355.9 million and a staff of 345; Ogilvy & Mather, with a staff of 298, was in second place, with £271.1 million (*Campaign Report*, 1998, p. 3). In total, 17 agencies exceeded the figure of £100 million for the year (see Table 2.1).

Table 2.1   Top ten agencies in 1997

Rank		Agency	Billings*	Billings*
1997	*1996*	*Agency*	*1997 £m*	*1996 £m*
1	1	Abbott Mead Vickers BBDO	355.9	306.8
2	3	Ogilvy & Mather	271.1	254.6
3	5	Saatchi & Saatchi	260.3	224.3
4	2	J. Walter Thompson	252.6	278.2
5	6	BMP DDB	246.6	237.0
6	11	Grey	214.9	159.4
7	10	Bates Dorland	203.9	168.4
8	8	M&C Saatchi	194.7	175.0
9	7	Publicis	192.2	186.5
10	14	McCann-Erickson	182.8	140.8

* AC Nielsen-MEAL figures: all media and other activities.

Source: Campaign Report, 6 March 1998, p. 3.

Maintaining the staff to be able to offer the full range of coordinated activities is a costly business. As a result, several agencies commission the design and production of ads from specialist companies as and when required rather than keeping such creative staff on the payroll. But the biggest development since the 1970s, and particularly since the mid-1980s, has been the dramatic growth of media independents which specialize in the buying of airtime and space in an increasingly complex media system. In a decade a number of these companies, known also as media shops, have outstripped the billings of the main full-service agencies. Zenith Media topped the 1997 list with £615.09 million, followed by TMD Carat with £451.81 million. A further 17 media independents are estimated to have had billings in excess of £100 million (see Table 2.2). By way of consolidating its status as a major player, Zenith maintains an excellent website (www.zenithmedia.com), an indispensable aid for anyone seeking up-to-date information on advertising and marketing.

Table 2.2   Top ten media independents in 1997

Rank 1997	1996	Agency	Billings* 1997 £m	Billings* 1996 £m
1	1	Zenith Media	615.1	554.3
2	2	TMD Carat	451.8	400.7
3	3	MediaVest (The Media Centre)	381.1	357.7
4	4	BMP Optimum (BMP DDB)	351.4	311.1
5	5	Mediapolis	276.1	232.1
6	9	Universal McCann	271.8	220.8
7	8	Initiative Media	259.5	226.9
8	7	New PHD	258.3	227.7
9	11	MediaCom	252.9	210.9
10	6	CIA Medianetwork UK	245.8	230.4

* AC Nielsen-MEAL figures: all media and other activities.

Source: Campaign Report, 6 March 1998, p. 39.

As advertising grew during the twentieth century, its practitioners organized to publicize advertising's benefits and to protect their collective interests. The process of seeking professional status for an activity that was – and
still is – often regarded by some as dishonest and manipulative took an important step forward in 1924 with the founding of the Advertising Association
(AA). Now a federation of 29 different trade associations and professional
bodies, it represents all branches of the industry (advertisers, agencies, media
organizations and support services). The AA's wide-ranging activities include
promoting the value of advertising to opinion leaders, monitoring all UK and
European legislation that relates to advertising, and lobbying policy-makers
on behalf of the industry. The Association is also a useful source of information for members of the public on all aspects of advertising. Other professional bodies with more sectional interests include the Incorporated Society
of British Advertisers (ISBA) representing clients, the Institute of Practitioners in Advertising (IPA) and the Association of Media and Communications Specialists (AMCO), which mainly speak for advertising agencies and
independents respectively, and the Direct Marketing Association (DMA).

Regulating Advertising

A prized aspect of any profession in the UK is the right to regulate its own
activities, rather than being subject to control by the state. This right has been
successfully defended by the UK advertising industry in respect of work
appearing in the press, on posters, in the cinema, on video cassettes and on

teletext as well as direct marketing and sales promotion activities. The Advertising Standards Authority (ASA), established as a limited company in 1962, administers the British Codes of Advertising and Sales Promotion. Complaints from the public against advertisements held to be illegal, misleading, fraudulent or tasteless are considered by the ASA secretariat, which makes recommendations to the ASA's Council, comprising mostly lay members. Those from rival firms are handled by a separate industry-based committee under the supervision of the Authority; however, political advertising, at present, remains exempt from these controls.

With some exceptions, the ASA's adjudications are not widely publicized – indeed the existence of the body itself still has a low profile, despite efforts to raise public awareness through posters and press ads. In ruling against an ad, the Authority can only advise an advertiser on the one hand to withdraw it or not to repeat it and media owners on the other to desist from carrying it. It has no powers to fine those it finds in breach of the code. Such public accountability is an important part of the industry's claim to professional status, but there is a strong element of self-interest involved too. Without (a minimum of) public confidence the industry risks losing its credibility and, as a consequence, its livelihood. There is also the lurking threat of control by statute as is the case in many other countries. For these reasons, advertisers and agencies generally abide by the constraints of the code, while testing the boundaries of the acceptable, in many instances to creative effect. Together with comparable organizations on the Continent, the ASA helped to set up the European Advertising Standards Alliance in 1992 to promote self-regulation in the Single Market within the framework of EU directives on advertising.

In the 1990s, a more calculated attitude began to manifest itself, starting with Benetton's 'transgressive' print and poster ads (Falk, 1997). The strategy of deliberately setting out to breach national advertising codes was later adopted by companies such as Club 18–30 in the UK. Offended members of the public react to the advertising by complaining to the ASA and by writing letters to the press. Momentum grows as editors report and comment on the controversy. The advertisers concerned welcome the editorial coverage, however negative, as a way of stretching free of charge their expensive advertising and of helping to position their brands. By the time the ASA comes to an adjudication, the campaign has often ended, the desired iconoclastic notoriety has been gained for the product and the credibility of the ASA has been compromised. In 1997, for example, the clothing company French Connection UK blatantly ignored pre-publication advice to amend its 'fcuk advertising' slogan in style magazines such as *Marie Claire*, a decision that the ASA subsequently judged to have brought advertising into disrepute (ASA, 1998).

Press ads are free of statutory control as has been the editorial content of the UK press in the modern era. By contrast, radio and television commercials – in parallel with programmes – are subject to regulation by bodies established by Act of Parliament: the Radio Authority (set up in 1991) and the Independent Television Commission (ITC) – the successor, since 1991, of the Independent Broadcasting Authority (see Crisell, Chapter 4 for further discussion of broadcasting in Britain and Goodwin, Chapter 8). A script advisory service and, in the case of television, obligatory pre-viewing attempt to ensure that commercials comply with the respective codes before they are transmitted. Nevertheless, complaints are still made about commercials. If upheld by the relevant authority, these can result in a range of sanctions which include a ban on the offending item, a fine levied on the broadcasting company responsible for its transmission or, in extreme cases, withdrawal of the licence. Like the ASA in other media, the ITC has recently adopted a strategy of promoting on-air its role as a regulator more actively than previously.

Another way of maintaining standards of advertising is the annual peer assessment process leading to awards. This takes place at different levels, from the regional, for example the Scottish Advertising Awards, to the national, for example the Designers' and Art Directors' Awards (D&AD), and the international (Epica), culminating in the International Advertising Film Festival at Cannes with its Gold, Silver and Bronze Lions. Traditionally these have been awarded in recognition of creative excellence in various categories and the trophies themselves subsequently displayed with pride in offices. Reputations, both individual and corporate, are made on the strength of the awards and often lead to a demand for higher fees. But there is a problem for many inside and outside the industry: such awards tend to encourage agency people to focus on artistry to impress their competitor-colleagues at the expense of advertising's primary function of meeting clients' marketing objectives. For this reason, in 1980, annual awards for effectiveness were introduced by the IPA in recognition of the previous lack of balance. By comparison with those for creativity, the judges' selection depends on the more objective process of scrutinizing reasoned accounts of a campaign's success in increasing sales or market share. A set of award-winning papers is published biennially by the IPA as *Advertising Works* and serves to promote the cost-effectiveness of an industry to an often sceptical business world.

The Media and Advertising

Nearly two pounds in every hundred generated in the UK economy is spent on advertising. The actual proportion of advertising expenditure (ad spend) to gross domestic product (GDP) varies from year to year, with periodic upward and downward trends. In the period since the mid-1980s it has consistently been above 1.6 per cent of GDP, with a high of 1.96 per cent in 1989 at the peak of the inflationary boom (Advertising Association, 1998). At the same time ad spend has increased by over half, from £6.74 billion in 1985 to £10.52 billion in 1997, when calculated at constant 1990 prices (see Figure 2.1). This puts the UK in fourth position in a world league table after the

USA, Japan and Germany. However, when ad spend is expressed per head of the population, the UK ranks only eighth out of 16 West European countries, the USA and Japan (Switzerland is by far the biggest per capita spender).

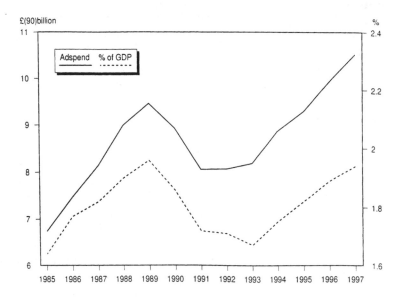

Figure 2.1   Total advertising expenditure at constant (1990) prices and as per cent of GDP (Advertising Association, 1998, p. 3)

The actual sum spent on advertising in the media in 1997 was £13.14 billion, or between £4 and £5 a week for every member of the British public. Contrary to popular understanding, most of this continues to be directed towards the press in its various forms. The print sector, which comprises newspapers (national and regional), magazines (consumer, business and professional) and directories such *Yellow Pages*, still accounts for a little over half of total UK advertising expenditure (53 per cent in 1996). Overall, however, it has been in relative decline for many years, especially as regards display advertising. All the other media by contrast have increased their share since 1985. Proportionally, the biggest growth has come in radio and cinema due to the larger audiences created by the huge expansion of independent local radio (ILR) in the 1980s, the splitting of frequencies and the advent of national commercial radio and by the proliferation of cinema multiplexes. Both sectors' share of the market almost doubled in the period 1985 to 1997, albeit from a low base: from 1.6 per cent to 2.9 per cent in the case of radio, and from an even lower 0.4 per cent to 0.7 per cent for cinema. But translated into cash terms, these are quite significant amounts: £393 million in 1997 for radio, a medium which in the early 1970s had earned only

£1 million (at current prices). The comparable figures for cinema advertising, £88 million and £6 million, indicate a less dramatic trend, but still an upward one (see Figures 2.2 and 2.3).

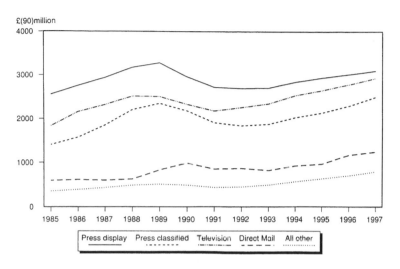

Figure 2.2 Total advertising expenditure by main medium and type at constant (1990) prices (Advertising Association, 1998, p. 4)

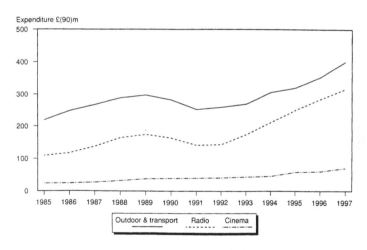

Figure 2.3 Advertising expenditure in the smaller media at constant (1990) prices (Advertising Association, 1998, p. 6)

Of the other mass media, television maintained its strong competitive position, although its share of the market only increased marginally between 1985 and 1997 (from 27.2 per cent to 27.8 per cent). Earning £3.65 billion in 1997, television attracted more than double the advertising revenue of all the national newspapers combined (£1.65 billion) But the bigger picture reveals that television still only accounts for approximately half the ad spend that goes to the press as a whole, which includes regional papers and magazines (£6.97 billion).

Advertising has its own media beyond the press, television, radio and cinema. Poster sites, bus shelters, the sides of buses and taxis, for example, are conventionally brought together under the category of 'outdoor and transport'. This sector also grew during the 1990s, but still only accounts for a little under 4 per cent of total UK advertising expenditure. Larger growth occurred in another area outside the mass media: direct mail registered a share of 11.7 per cent in 1997, compared with 8.8 per cent in 1985. Promotional material delivered by post made striking gains in 1990 at a time when the economic recession led to reduced allocations to conventional advertising. Despite fluctuations caused by improvements in the national economy, direct mail's continuing success (1997 expenditure: £1.54bn at current prices) indicates clearly a desire by many advertisers to target potential customers more accurately than is often possible with the mass media.

Much of the contemporary UK mass media are heavily dependent on advertising revenue for their continuing existence. The degree of economic dependence can be plotted on a spectrum, with 'free' newspapers at one end, representing total reliance, and the BBC, for most of its services, at the other. In between lie commercial radio and television, 'quality' newspapers, 'popular' newspapers, and magazines, roughly speaking in that order. Caution is required here, as some parts of commercial television, notably cable and satellite, are more reliant on subscription revenue than on advertising.

The interdependent relationship between the mass media and advertising extends back to the eighteenth century with the precursors of the modern newspaper. An indication of that relationship remains today in the titles of newspapers such as the Dundee-based *Courier and Advertiser* (established 1810). By contrast, broadcasting in the UK remained for much of its history a public service funded exclusively by the licence fee, a legacy of the BBC's first Director General's abomination of US-style broadcasting. It was to be 30 years before the first commercials were transmitted, in 1955, on the new ITV channel, and more than another decade (in 1972) before radio ads were first heard on local radio stations (ILR). National commercial radio was not launched in Britain until as recently as 1992.

The responsibility for the selling of advertising space and airtime varies from medium to medium. With newspapers and magazines it rests with individual or group advertising departments, whereas three large sales houses operate on behalf of consortia of ITV companies. With the historical addition of each medium funded by advertising, the competition for this revenue stream intensifies. What media executives have to trade is airtime or space and the market obliges them to operate competitively. As a consequence they need regularly to reconsider the rates charged to advertisers and to review their 'product' (for example programming) to make it as attractive as possible to both audiences and advertisers. In the late 1990s, the prospect of an ever-expanding World Wide Web, with globalized advertising, poses a potential challenge to traditional media as well as to space-buying agencies (Kassaye, 1997). The *Guardian* newspaper, having built up a highly profitable media and public service recruitment section, launched RecruitNet, an on-line version of the posts advertised in the paper to add value to its clients.

Broadsheet titles like the *Guardian* have a different economic base from tabloid newspapers, in so far as the greater part of their income derives from display and classified advertising. This long-standing characteristic has led to the suggestion that '[i]n terms of commercial income, upmarket papers are primarily in the advertising business, while down-market papers are primarily in the sales business' (Tunstall, 1996, p. 14). Indeed, James Curran attributes the polarization of the UK press into popular and serious sectors to the historic effect of the distribution of advertising expenditure (Curran and Seaton, 1997). However, both he and Tunstall oversimplify the situation by speaking only of two categories of newspaper, when in fact there is a third: mid-market, middle-brow titles, such as the *Daily Mail*, which have the same format as the so-called 'red top' tabloids (for example the *Sun*), but with a news and features content often more akin to that of the broadsheets. In addition, the latter, in their increased coverage of human interest stories and use of photos and large headlines, have acquired some of the other sector's clothes to broaden their appeal.

Broadsheets, despite smaller circulations, can sell advertising space at higher rates per thousand readers than the tabloids because a larger proportion of their readership are from the higher income groups (socio-economic categories A and B). So long as there is a demand on the part of many advertisers to want to reach such people, broadsheet papers will be happy to supply space at a premium. There is an irony, sometimes overlooked, in the fact that the number of such readers of papers like the *Sun* or the Scottish *Daily Record* exceeds in absolute terms those of more prestigious titles. That advertisers for luxury goods, for example, choose to ignore this can be explained by reference to the concept of editorial environment.

Theorists have long stressed the important role played by context in any communicative act (for example, Jakobsen, 1981). Whether it be the background to a figure in a painting or the social event at which a particular outfit is worn, the immediate context can substantially affect the meaning of the message. From an advertiser's point of view, the medium chosen as the vehicle for the promotional message must not only meet the practical requirement of being accessible to the intended audience; it should also enhance the impact of the advertising, or at least not detract from it. The same press ad appearing in a magazine and a newspaper, targeted at different audiences is affected by the company it keeps. Each editorial environment has its own connotations, of youthful irreverence, for instance, or adult sophistication. Commercial television or radio stations also have their own image, which they work hard to cultivate by their programming and self-promotional activities (more of which later). The right of advertisers to choose the most suitable environment for their advertising is not at issue; what is contentious, however, is the attempt by advertisers to modify that environment to suit their own purposes.

The existence of the ITC and the Radio Authority (and their predecessors) has helped to ensure that the interests of the general viewing public are represented, in terms of programming and advertising. Not only the range of advertisers but the permitted minutage of commercials, their location in the schedule, their promises and executions are all regulated by these bodies (more liberally in the case of radio). Nevertheless, on the principle that 'he who pays the piper calls the tune', it is often alleged that the media follow an agenda set by advertisers rather than one determined by the presumed interests of the general public. In this respect news is an area that offers ample scope for conspiracy theorists. Typically, the threat of the withdrawal of a major account is identified as the reason for an organization's reluctance to investigate a particular story. The problem lies in the fact that documentary proof of cause and effect is difficult to obtain. Meanwhile, most journalists regard advertising as a necessary evil. There is evidence to suggest that fashion magazines are particularly prone to pressure from advertisers. The editor of British *Vogue*, for example, has confirmed that '[t]here is a big relationship between advertising and what goes in the magazine... It's a symbiotic relationship' (Thomas, 1995). But in general advertisers do not wish to be seen as manipulating news agendas, and news organizations have no desire to appear professionally compromised.

A rare instance of advertiser pressure and its consequences entering the public domain occurred in 1987, when the *Star* newspaper set out to lure readers from the *Sun*, its rival, by increasing the daily quota of topless models and by generally spicing itself up. Safeway, Tesco and other supermarket chains reacted by withdrawing their advertising from the paper on the grounds that such editorial changes would not be acceptable to housewives, their main customers, and to their female staff. Faced with these revenue losses and public opprobrium, the paper beat a retreat. A more recent case from the US prompts particular concern. In 1997, the Chrysler Corporation, the car and truck manufacturer, formally requested at least 50 magazines, through its ad agency PentaCom, to 'be alerted in advance of any and all editorial content that encompasses sexual, political, social issues or any editorial that might be construed as provocative or offensive' (cited by Baker, 1997). That this crass attempt at editorial blackmail became public knowledge was highly unusual but indicated the concern felt by groups such as the American Society of Magazine Editors, which rallied against the demand. But the magazine *Esquire* had already changed its mind about publishing a sexually explicit short story for fear of offending the same advertiser.

In the UK there have been attempts by moral pressure groups, such as the National Viewers and Listeners Association, to encourage advertisers to boycott certain films or strands of programming shown on television.

Inspired by the activities of such US lobbying groups as the American Family Association, the NVLA's aim is to force broadcasters to drop material they deem offensive. Channel 4 has been the most frequently targeted station. But its 1986 'red triangle' series of adult films went ahead despite a boycott on the part of some advertisers as did its 1993 Gay Christmas programming. The channel had asserted its editorial independence in facing down its critics.

At the local level, traditional weekly 'paid-for' newspapers have a particularly close relationship with the community they serve. The bulk of the revenue from display and classified advertising comes from local sources. Staff frequently live in the neighbourhood and move in the same social circles as news providers, readers and advertisers. They are in close contact with them and thus directly accountable to an extent unfamiliar to their colleagues on national newspapers and magazines. It is not impossible under these circumstances for an editor boldly to adopt an independent line, perhaps even indulging in investigative or campaigning journalism. However, pragmatic considerations, including tightened budgets, tend to prevent this. The result is that most local titles have become consensual chroniclers of parochial news (Franklin and Murphy, 1991).

This applies in particular to local weekly free newspapers (also known derogatively as freesheets), which mushroomed during the late 1970s and 1980s. Wholly dependent on income from advertising sales, usually with a minimum of editorial content, they provide advertisers with geographically targeted delivery, for example to prosperous suburbs. They thus compete against incumbent local weeklies for advertising revenue but not on news. In the face of this threat, many newspaper groups owning traditional paid-for newspapers launched their own free titles to avert the haemorrhaging of ad revenue to the new kids on the block. The latter soon came to be organized into chains owned by the leading regional publishers, the top five of whom controlled 43 per cent of the total free and paid-for local weekly newspaper circulation by 1995 (Curran and Seaton, 1997). However, the increase in titles should not be confused with editorial diversity or distinction.

A phenomenon commonly found in the local press, although by no means confined to this sector, is the *advertorial*. This hybrid form cloaks a promotional message in the guise of a regular feature article. By doing so advertisers hope to gain the kind of credibility for their product or service – a restaurant, for example – which would accrue from a flattering piece written by a journalist (Goodlad *et al.*, 1997). In the case of an advertorial, however, the journalist is compromised by a business arrangement whereby advertising space has been traded for less-than-objective coverage. As an assignment it is unpopular with many journalists, since it runs counter to notions of professional integrity. The Sales Promotion Code requires these 'advertisement promotions' to be easily distinguished, so readers who prefer editorial and advertising to be separated should look for the label 'advertising feature' or 'special feature' at the top of the relevant page.

This development is closely related to the sponsorship of sections of pages, whole pages or even complete supplements of newspapers or magazines. Many involve crosswords, weather reports, share prices, where the scope for bias is limited and the advertisers concerned are largely interested in creating awareness of their product or service among readers. The sponsored supplement may be indistinguishable from a piece of inserted junk mail. It may, on the other hand, be a valued addition, such as those published periodically by the *Financial Times* on individual countries or specialist topics. Here the reputation of the newspaper for objective reporting acts as a guarantee of resistance to undue pressure from the sponsors. However, no general inference can be derived from the example of the *FT*; it is a special case and not the rule.

In recent years, the range of advertisers on UK television and radio has expanded to include financial institutions, solicitors, and even the police (in Strathclyde at least). As institutions in what has become a 'promotional culture' (Wernick, 1991), each now regards it as essential to publicize its activities via the broadcast media. It is a development that the latter have also begun to embrace, using their own resources in a sustained self-promotional effort. Programme trails have acquired the slick sophistication of their forerunners in the cinema. Advertising for themed evenings, whole seasons' programming, cross-media promotions (for instance radio advertised on television) now rub shoulders with regular commercials. Entire stations are advertised in expensive corporate branding exercises, such as the BBC's 1997 ballooning images and Gill Sans typography. This is less postmodern self-reflexivity, more a strategic attempt to build a degree of audience loyalty in the era of multichannel viewing.

Public attitudes to advertising have become more accepting over the years, especially among the young. The proportion of those questioned, in a four-yearly industry study, who approved of advertising rose from 68 per cent in 1966 to 78 per cent in 1996, with a fall from 25 per cent to 15 per cent of those who disapproved (Advertising Association, 1996). After almost half a century many UK television commercials can claim to be sophisticated, witty, amusing and, above all, well-crafted 'mini-masterpieces' (the term Fedorico Fellini allegedly used in the 1960s to describe the British commercials of that era). Unlike then, today's budgets ensure production values equivalent to many feature films. Distinguished actors and media and sporting celebrities make on-screen appearances or do voice-overs. Styles and formats of popular TV genres, the cinema and pop videos are imitated or parodied in a riot of intertextuality (Fowles, 1996; Goldman and Papson, 1996). In return, television commercials provide material for press columnists to analyse and for presenters of comedy or quiz shows to celebrate or mock. This interrelationship confirms the condition of symbiosis that advertising has achieved with the UK media.

Postscript

The discussion so far has focused almost exclusively on advertising in the conventional media of the press, broadcasting, cinema and outdoors, for two reasons. First, they continue still to attract the overwhelming bulk of ad spend in this country and, second, reasonably reliable statistics on that expenditure are publicly available. Although still in their infancy and comparatively small, the new media, particularly the Internet, have already made an impact (see Cornford and Robins, Chapter 7, for further discussion). Interactivity has given consumers the opportunity to make on-the-spot transactions as well as providing advertisers with valuable personal data. As the practice grows, this kind of information will allow for a more individually tailored approach to the design and targeting of ads. There is also likely to be a growth of reactive advertising, which consumers deliberately seek out for the purposes of information or entertainment. Over the years each of the main media has adapted to meet the competitive challenge of attracting advertisers and audiences created by the advent of newer media. But in the era of the World Wide Web, digital television services and personalized newspapers (the '*Daily Me*'), the advertising environment may change radically in future. Manufacturers of niche brands are expected to continue to find suitable ways of addressing potential customers, but those of products with mass appeal may well encounter difficulties in reaching consumers cost-effectively. If so, Nicholas Negroponte, the Massachusetts Institute of Technology communications guru, is perhaps right in declaring: 'I think if I was Procter & Gamble, I'd be buying billboard space. A lot of it' (www.zenithmedia.com, 1997).

References

Advertising Association *Public Attitudes to Advertising*. London: AA, 1996.

Advertising Association *Advertising Statistics Yearbook 1998*. Henley-on-Thames: NTC, 1998.

Advertising Standards Authority *ASA Monthly Report*, 80 (January 1998).

Baker, R. 'The Squeeze', *Columbia Journalism Review*, September/October 1997.

Brierley, S. *The Advertising Handbook*. London: Routledge, 1995.

British Codes of Advertising and Sales Promotion, 9th edn. London: Committee of Advertising Practice, 1995.

Campaign Report, London: Haymarket Campaign Publications, 6 March 1998.

Curran, J. 'The impact of advertising on the British mass media', *Media, Culture and Society*, **3**, 1 (1981) pp. 43–69.

Curran, J. and Seaton, J. *Power without Responsibility*, 5th edn. London: Routledge, 1997.

Douglas, T. *The Complete Guide to Advertising*. London: Macmillan, 1984.

Dyer, G. *Advertising as Communication*, London: Routledge, 1982.

Falk, P. 'The Benetton-Toscani effect: testing the limits of conventional advertising' in M. Nava, A. Blake, I. MacRury and B. Richards (eds) *Buy This Book: Studies in Advertising and Consumption*. London: Routledge, 1997, pp. 64–83.

The Media in Britain

40

Fowles, J. Advertising and Popular Culture. Sage: CA, London and New Delhi, 1996.
Franklin, B. and Murphy, D. What News? The Market, Politics and the Local Press. London: Routledge, 1991.
Goldman, R. and Papson, S. Sign Wars: The Cluttered Landscape of Advertising. New York: Guilford Press, 1996.
Goodlad, N., Eadie, D., Kinnin, H. and Raymond, M. 'Advertorial: creative solution or last resort?', International Journal of Advertising, 16 (1997) pp. 73–84.
Henry, B. (ed.) British Television Advertising. The First 30 Years. London: Century Benham, 1986.
ITC Code of Advertising Standards and Practice. London: Independent Television Commission, 1995.
Jakobsen, R. 'Linguistics and poetics' in Selected Writings, Volume 3. The Hague: Mouton, 1981, pp.18–51.
Kassaye, W.W. 'The effect of the World Wide Web on agency-advertiser relationships: towards a strategic framework', International Journal of Advertising, 16 (1997) pp. 85–103.
Lace, J. Paying for Advertising. London: ISBA, 1998.
Leiss, W., Kline, S. and Jhally, S. Social Communication in Advertising, 2nd edn. London: Routledge, 1991.
Myers, K. Understains: The Sense and Seduction of Advertising. London: Comedia, 1986.
Nevett, T. Advertising in Britain. A History. London: Heinemann, 1982.
Thomas, L. 'Fashion editors profit from designer gifts', Sunday Times, 22 October 1995.
Tunstall, J. Newspaper Power. Oxford: Oxford University Press, 1996.
Wernick, A. Promotional Culture. London: Sage, 1991.
Williams, R. 'Advertising: The Magic System' in R. Williams (ed.) Problems in Materialism and Culture: Selected Essays. London: Verso, 1980, pp. 170–95.
Williamson, J. Decoding Advertisements. London: Marion Boyarsm, 1978.

Electronic source:
www.Zenithmedia.com, 1997

CHAPTER 3

The Press

COLIN SPARKS

This chapter looks at aspects of the UK press. There are more than 1000 newspapers distributed in this country, and more than 10,000 magazines. It is obviously not possible to say very much about that vast range of material in one short chapter, and I have been forced to be very selective indeed. The main focus here is on the ten London-based titles that constitute the national daily press. I have made some references to other aspects of the press industry, but it is usually as a contrast with the main theme of this article.

Making this choice means a number of important issues in the printed media are not treated at all, most obviously those raised by magazines. These come in a variety so enormous that most people have no conception of the kinds of titles that are available. Even a visit to WH Smith's is misleading, since many trade publications, which form the bulk of titles, never make it to the newsagents' shelves. Jane Stokes, in Chapter 1, looks in detail at periodical publishing.

A focus on the newspaper press does, however, have one very important advantage. It throws into sharp relief the issue of the relationship between the mass media and political democracy. Historically, 'freedom of the press' has been one of the key issues around which the struggle for democracy has been fought (Siebert, 1965; Hollis, 1970; Curran and Seaton, 1988). Today, no theory of democracy could possibly be taken seriously if it did not discuss the mass media in general, and the newspaper press in particular, as key elements in the constitution of political life. Much intellectual debate over this issue in the last ten years has revolved around the issue of 'the public sphere', and its main theorist argued that 'today newspapers and magazines, radio and television, are the media of the public sphere' (Habermas, 1974, p. 49).

With regard to newspapers, which are not obliged, as are broadcasters in the UK, to be impartial in accounts of the political process, a major issue of debate has always been whether the structure and organization of the press permits the expression of the plurality of views necessary to democratic political debate. At the time of writing, for example, there are intense debates among politicians and journalists over whether the granting of a right of privacy to individuals would unduly restrict press freedom, and whether legislation designed to prevent unfair competition should be modified to prevent the kinds of price war that can lead to the closure of titles. One of the main themes of this chapter is to enquire why the press has the structure it has, and what the implications of that structure are for the functioning of newspapers in a democracy.

In the newspaper press itself, a concentration on the national daily press marginalizes some other very important sections of newspaper publishing. The political geography of the British Isles means that there are very important papers, that arguably fulfil 'national' functions in Scotland and Wales, or that have important and unique functions in the six counties of Northern Ireland, which are not classified as 'national papers' in the sense that is used in this article. Even within England, there are important regional papers that have substantial and regular amounts of national and international news, that would require attention in a fuller study. As it is, they are here lumped together with what can only be considered the much more parochial interests of the local press proper. Again, this choice has the virtue of highlighting more clearly the issues at stake with regard to the relationship between newspapers and the state. All of the important questions about democracy, as well as others about standards of reporting and of taste, are particularly sharply about the national daily press.

The Press Market

As Table 3.1 shows, there are more than 1000 newspapers published in the United Kingdom. Of these, more than half, both in terms of number of titles and numbers of copies, are 'freesheets', pushed through people's doors, usually on a weekly basis and dependent entirely on advertising revenue for income. At the other extreme, in 1995, the ten titles that make up the national daily press accounted for 12,933,000 out of an overall total of 18,741,000 daily circulation. In other words, 69 per cent of all daily newspapers distributed in this country were in that year edited in London and circulated throughout the country six mornings a week. The paid-for local press, despite its considerable economic importance to advertisers, is a minority press both in its weekly and its daily forms. At the time of writing, the national press retained more or less the same dominant position. As Table 3.3 shows, the average circulation of the leading ten national daily titles was 13,750,061 in 1997.

Table 3.1   The number of titles and the circulation of newspapers published in the UK by kind of publication

	Number	Circulation
Dailies	101	18,741,000 (a day)
Weeklies	473	6,370,000 (a week)
Sundays	20	16,460,000 (Sunday)
Freesheets	685	33,020,000 (total)
Total	1279	–

Source: Féderation Internationale des Editeurs de Journaux, *World Press Trends*, 1995.

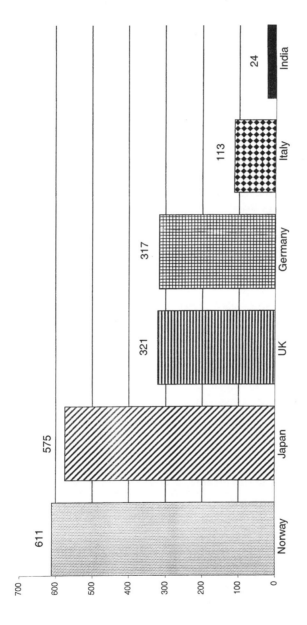

Figure 3.1 Daily newspaper circulation per 1000 of population (1994) in six countries

In most respects, the UK is a fairly middling consumer of newspapers. As Figure 3.1 shows, newspaper circulation per 1000 of the population falls into the middle band of European newspaper circulation. People here are much less likely to buy a newspaper than are Norwegians, Swedes or Finns, but much more likely to do so than the Irish, French, Italians or Spanish. In Europe, their behaviour is closest to the Germans, the Danes and the Dutch. More widely, although the Japanese buy many more newspapers than people here, citizens of the USA buy many fewer. Outside of the developed world, consumption is usually an order of magnitude lower.

These overall averages, however, conceal the extent to which the dominance of the national daily press constitutes a highly unusual feature of the UK press. There are a number of titles that constitute nationally produced and circulated newspapers, like the *Sporting Life* (1997 average circulation 52,634), and a couple of daily political titles whose true circulation is hard to discover but is unlikely to be greater than 10,000, but they have not been included here. The ten top titles are clearly different in scale, accounting for at least 99 per cent of the total circulation, and form a distinct group. The smallest circulation among these is the *Financial Times*, which in the six months to June 1997 recorded a paid circulation of 312,723, of which around 200,000 was in the UK. By contrast, the largest circulation was for the *Sun*, which during the same period recorded a paid circulation of 3,789,168. The figures in Table 3.2 attempt to give some kind of international perspective on this. As can be seen, the top selling newspaper in the UK is far from the biggest internationally in circulation terms, although it would appear relatively larger (as, even more clearly, would the Norwegian case) if the figures were adjusted for population size. More important than this is that only in Norway and Japan of the countries tabulated here are there other newspapers circulating nationally on a similar scale. In the other cases, the press markets are dominated by more local forms. The UK press is distinctive in that there is a large group of big-circulation national newspapers that dominate the press scene.

Table 3.2   Circulation of leading newspapers in different countries

Country	Newspaper	Circulation
UK	*Sun*	3,919,000
USA	Wall Street Journal	1,780,422
Germany	*Bild Zeitung*	4,436,118
France	*Ouest-France*	790,132
Italy	*La Repubblica*	652,601
Japan	*Yomiuri Shimbun*	10,085,025
Norway	*Verdens Gang*	386,137
India	*Malayala Manorama*	748,788

Source: Féderation Internationale des Editeurs de Journaux, *World Press Trends*, 1995.

The reasons for this peculiar structure are not well understood. The best we can do is to list possible factors. These are particularly clearly seen by way of contrasts with other countries, but it is impossible to specify exactly what their individual influence has been on the formation of this national market. The first, and most obvious, is that Britain constitutes a large and relatively prosperous population concentrated within a small geographical area. Using the new technology of the nineteenth century, the steam locomotive, it was technically possible as early as the 1870s to distribute a centrally produced newspaper to much of the population. The technical possibility of national newspapers was more or less coincident with the birth of the modern commercial press in Britain, and, from very early on, the local and regional newspapers faced increasing national competition (Lee, 1976). The obvious contrast here is with the USA, where a railway journey from New York to Los Angeles took several days and thus prohibited the economical production of a national daily newspaper. In fact, it was only in the 1980s, with the development of satellite transmission and remote printing technology that it became feasible to produce a newspaper with national coverage in the USA, by which time the country had already been covered for a century by a dense network of local papers. In fact, both the *Wall Street Journal* and *USA Today*, the two largest-circulation newspapers in the country, and the first truly national newspapers, were ones that built themselves around this new technology of the twentieth century.

A second, related, factor is the relatively concentrated nature of political power in Britain. Political, economic, legal and social power are highly concentrated in London, in sharp contrast with the much more regionalized societies of the USA and Germany. In those countries, state and land are repositories of real power and the doings of the national government can often seem distant and perhaps less important. In Britain, while the provincial press does certainly devote attention to the doings of local and regional authorities, these are relatively powerless bodies. Any active citizen wanting to know about the political and economic life of the country needs also to buy and read newspapers that focus on the doings of parliament and city in London.

In contrast with the even more politically centralized case of France, however, the tradition of politically owned newspapers has been much weaker in Britain. There has not, for the forty years since the death-agonies of the *Daily Herald*, been a formally Labour paper in Britain, and there has never been a significant Communist press here. There have been no subsidies, either directly from political parties or partisan individuals, or indirectly from the state, that have sustained a political press in much of the rest of Europe. Although newspapers in Britain are obviously and stridently partisan, they are not party newspapers in the formal sense, and have not been so since the end of the Second World War, at the very latest (Koss, 1990).

Newspapers in Britain are first and foremost businesses. They do not exist to report the news, to act as watchdogs for the public, to be a check on the doings of government, to defend the ordinary citizen against abuses of power, to unearth scandals or to do any of the other fine and noble things that are sometimes claimed for the press. They exist to make money, just as any other business does. To the extent that they discharge any of their public functions, they do so in order to succeed as businesses. This commercial logic has done its work very thoroughly in Britain. In that, it has been powerfully aided by the fact that there have been no substantial extra-economic interventions in the press. There have been no invasions and occupations, no collaboration and resistance, no revolutions or coups, to overturn press ownership and economics. The nearest there has been was the period from 1939 to 1956 when newsprint was rationed, and in which the normal logic of the commercial press was modified by the limits on advertising space that resulted.

The consequence of all of this is that the British press is a truly capitalist press. Compared with the other main international contenders, the British press is much freer. It is not freer in its ability to report and comment, as later chapters in this book make clear. It is much freer in the sense that it is the product of an almost untrammelled free market economy. If we want to see the strengths and the weaknesses of a media system based on the free market, then it is before our eyes.

A Competitive Market

One of the most important, and unusual, features of the British national daily press is that it exists in a competitive market. Competition, of course, is the lifeblood of capitalism. Without competition, none of the allegedly beneficial effects of the private ownership of the means of production can occur. It is not, however, universally the case that those newspapers that so vigorously defend the virtues of competition and the free market have experienced its benefits at first hand. The most striking example is that of the USA. There are more than 1500 daily newspapers in the USA, but the vast majority (around 99 per cent) of them operate in conditions of local monopoly. Although they might compete with other media for advertising and, on the margin, with the proto-national titles we have discussed above, or with the other 'tiers' of newspaper provision in the same geographical region, hardly any of them face direct, head-on competition from another, hostile, daily newspaper out to steal their readers and their advertisers (Picard, 1988). This is the normal situation of the British national daily press.

Each of the ten national daily titles faces direct competition, but there are some special features of this competition that mean that it is not quite as intense as it might appear at first sight. It is not really the case that the editor of each newspaper has to fight the editors of all of the other nine for readers, or that the advertising manager of each newspaper has to fight the advertising managers of all the others for business. The two factors that modify this apparent war of all against each are ownership structure and market segmentation. The ten titles are in fact the property of seven large media companies, all of which have substantial other media interests. The ownership pattern, and the most recently available circulation figures, are presented in Table 3.3. As can be clearly seen, a very small number of firms dominate the market in circulation terms. Two companies account for more than 50 per cent of circulation and the top four have nearly 90 per of the total. This is a level of concentration that most economists would describe as 'oligopoly': that is, a market in which a small number of companies have an overwhelmingly dominant position.

Table 3.3   Ownership and circulation of the national daily press (1997)

Group	Title	Circulation Jan–June 97	Group market share %
News International	Sun	3,789,168	33
	The Times	747,750	
Mirror Group	Daily Mirror	3,062,766*	24
	Independent	257,010	
DMGT	Daily Mail	2,152,874	16
MAI	Daily Express	1,237,300	14
	Star	657,040	
Hollingsworth	Daily Telegraph	1,124,640	8
GMT	Guardian	408,790	3
Pearson	Financial Times	312,723**	2
Total for top ten titles		13,835,841	>99
Market share of top four firms			87

* Includes The *Daily Record*, the sister-paper published in Scotland.
** Includes the circulation of the international editions (around 120,000).

Source: Audit Bureau of Circulation, *National Newspapers: Six Monthly Averages for the 1990s*, 1997.

In fact, the degree of oligopoly is even greater than the overall figures suggest. As we will show later, the readers of different newspapers are stratified in quite clear ways. The overall market can be subdivided into at least two, and most accurately three, different sub-markets. In the quality market there are the five broadsheet titles (*The Times*, the *Daily Telegraph*, the *Guardian*, the *Independent* and the *Financial Times*); in the mid-market there are two titles (the *Daily Mail* and the *Daily Express*); in the popular market, there are three titles (the *Sun*, the *Daily Mirror*, the *Star*). There is relatively little crossover in readership between these different titles, and there are important differences in the nature of the advertising sold in each sector. Competition is largely within the three different market segments (Sparks,

1995). Consequently, in none of the markets is there the kind of robust competition that is claimed, not least by the editorial writers of most of the newspapers in question, to be so characteristic of capitalism and so beneficial to humanity.

Oligopoly is a problem for capitalism because of the way in which the free market is supposed to work. The function of competition is to make sure that companies constantly innovate and cheapen their goods in order to increase their market share. If any company gains an advantage, others will sooner or later find ways of getting on level terms. Prices are kept down and profits tend to be averaged out across the whole of industry. If there are relatively few companies in a market, then it is likely that, either wittingly or unwittingly, they will tend to raise prices and enjoy profits above the norm, and be reluctant to invest in new plant and machinery. Oligopoly, and still more monopoly (where there is only one firm in the market), is thus a situation in which a few companies benefit at the expense both of other firms and the consumer. In theory, other capitalists from outside the particular market in question should compare their profits with those enjoyed by the oligopolists and decide that they too would like get more than their fair share. They then enter the market and render it more competitive. This removes the conditions that have led to abnormal profits in the first place, and the system has demonstrated the wonderful self-corrective properties that led Adam Smith to talk about the hidden hand.

In practice, there are often barriers to entry that prevent this taking place. Newspapers are a classic example of such a situation. The only successful wholly new entrant into the UK national press market in the last thirty years was Rupert Murdoch, who purchased the *Sun* in 1967. While two sectional newspapers (the *Financial Times* and the then *Manchester Guardian*) did manage to become properly national newspapers, as part of larger media groups, the other attempts have all failed. The case of the *Independent* is exemplary here. The first part of the story is exactly what economic theory says should happen. The paper was founded by a group of journalists who gained very substantial backing from finance houses eager to enjoy the supposed opportunities for profit. But far from restoring market equilibrium, it proved impossible for the paper to survive on its own, and it was taken over by other media companies, most notably the company that already ran the *Daily Mirror*. At the time of writing, it continues to publish, but even with this wealthy patron its future must be very uncertain, since its circulation has been in steady decline for nearly a decade. The characteristic form in which new capitalists enter this market is by taking over an existing firm. Since this involves no new product, it does not increase competition, and thus does not modify the conditions of oligopoly.

The overall picture of the UK national daily press is thus one of markets characterized by oligopolistic competition. Because none of the players has much to gain by driving down prices, the normal form that competition takes in this kind of market is through what is called 'product differentiation'.

Instead of making their products cheaper, the owners of national daily newspapers strive to make their products unique and uniquely valued. It is this kind of competition that explains much that is distinctive about the press. It lies behind the industry myth of the 'scoop', in which one news team manages to produce a product that is so unique that it has an overwhelming competitive advantage. The nature and content of what counts as a 'scoop' varies depending on the market segment. In the quality press, it can be some kind of revelation that the government would like to keep quiet. In the popular press, sexual shenanigans, particularly those involving the royal or the rich, are clearly scoop material.

In the real world, the kinds of unique event that fit perfectly the need to produce a differentiated but attractive product do not occur at twenty-four hour intervals, six days each week. Much of the business of 'journalism' lies in finding, or constructing, and then reporting, or distorting, events so that they becomes stories that satisfy the need for innovative product differentiation. Many of what are often thought of as the excesses of the popular press, such as sensationalizing, invading privacy, making up stories and so on, result directly from the need to produce a differentiated product. Far from being deviations from some pure norm of journalism, they are the inevitable result of the kind of competition in which the different titles are engaged.

On a much more mundane level, the slightly different combinations of news and commentary, not to mention political alignment, that are such obvious features of the press are also examples of product differentiation. In particular, the notorious party political biases of the printed press, which differ so strikingly from the broadcast media, can be seen as part of the process of product differentiation. Only in situations of monopoly, or near monopoly, when a newspaper is trying to attract readers from right across the political spectrum, does it make sense to be impartial and balanced. When there is competition, then political bias is a part, albeit a relatively minor part, of product differentiation.

It is important to note that there is one significant exception to the general rule that oligopolistic competition takes place through product differentiation rather than price cutting. In the situation where there has been a sharp decline in the size of the market, firms will find that they have excess capacity. Using plant and machinery at less than their optimum outputs involves increased costs per unit of output. This undermines the basis for the excess profits that oligopolists enjoy. There is thus a pressure on individual firms to try to expand their market share to reach optimum output, and price competition is one of the ways that they might achieve this. The UK price war of the 1990s was almost a textbook example of this process. All sectors of the market fell quite sharply from the late 1980s. All the firms had excess capacity, and in 1993 News International launched a price war in a successful attempt to increase the market share of its titles.

A Stratified Market

The three markets we have identified within the overall daily national press market are most clearly differentiated by the nature of their readers. Although we do not have anything that can properly be called a sociological analysis of the readership of the press, the 'social grade' of the different readers is exhaustively studied. Social Grade is a classification system developed by the advertising industry to help them understand people's consumption habits. It breaks all adults down into five grades: A (Upper Professional); B (Lower Professional); C1 (Routine Clerical); C2 (Skilled Manual); D (Unskilled Manual); E (Economically Inactive). Newspaper readership is classified by the social grade of the household's chief income earner. Using this classification the five broadsheet titles all have more than 50 per cent of their readers in grades A and B; the two mid-market titles both have between 20 and 30 per cent of their readers in those categories; while the three popular titles all have less than 10 per cent of A and B readers.

The social profile of the readers of *The Times* and the *Sun* is compared with those of the population as a whole in Figure 3.2. As is immediately clear, the readership of these two different kinds of newspapers is centred on different social groups. Although the nature of the definitions of social grade are constructed differently, it would be reasonable to conclude from this material that there is strong evidence that the readership of the quality press is predominantly upper and middle class, while the readership of the popular press is predominantly working class.

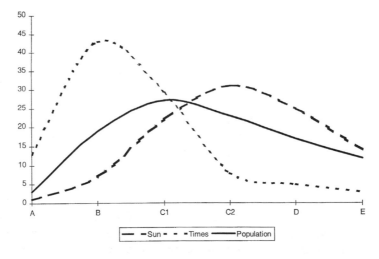

Figure 3.2   Social structure of readership of *The Times* and the *Sun* compared to the total population (National Readership Survey, 1996)

This market stratification has two very important consequences. The first concerns the economic effect of socially differentiated readership patterns (Sparks, 1995). Paid-for newspapers, like most advertising-supported media commodities, exist in what is called a 'dual product market'. There is one market in which the newspaper sells itself to the consumers. From this, it raises circulation revenue. There is, however, a second market in which the newspaper sells its readership to advertisers wishing to gain the attention of large numbers of particular kinds of people. From this it raises advertising revenue. These markets have different characteristics. In the first market, all people are equal. The 25 pence paid out for a copy of a popular newspaper, or the 40 pence paid out for a quality paper, is the same whether it comes out of the pocket of a millionaire, a media studies lecturer, or a student. All that matters to the company running the newspaper is that it gets enough purchases, and the bigger its circulation, the bigger the resulting revenue.

The second market is different. It matters very much to the advertiser whether the person reading the paper is a millionaire, a media studies lecturer, or a student, because they each have different amounts of money to spend, and are likely on average to spend it in different sorts of ways. If you are selling holiday estates in the Bahamas, then you do want to reach as many millionaires as possible, because among them are your customers. On the other hand, you are not very interested in either lecturers or students, since most of them do not have enough money even to think about your products. As a consequence, you will try to buy advertising space in the sorts of news-papers read by rich people.

If you are trying to recruit people to teach media studies in a British university or college, then you are not very interested in millionaires, nor most students. You want to reach those people who are willing, and preferably able, to teach media studies for the sort of rotten money that you are prepared to pay. So you advertise in the sorts of paper read by lecturers and final-year doctoral students. In other words, advertisers are interested in reaching partic-ular target audiences with a known propensity and ability to purchase the particular kinds of commodities they are selling. Knowing how best, and most cheaply, to reach these different audiences is one of the most important skills an advertising agency offers its clients.

These differences are exhaustively researched, by the National Readership Survey (NRS) among others. Rich readers are much more interesting to advertisers than other people. As Hemingway noted, when Scott Fitzgerald said: 'The very rich are different from you and me', someone replied, 'Yes, they have more money'. The rich are more interesting to advertisers in just the same way: because they have more money. They need the same sort of things as everybody else, like toilet rolls and socks and washing powder. But they also buy things, like business-class air tickets, BMWs, large residential properties and expensive clothes, that poor people do not have the money for. Luxury goods, notoriously, have high prices and high margins. The attention of people who buy them is at a premium. As Table 3.4 shows, the published costs of reaching 1000 of the readers of the *Daily Telegraph* is about 4.5 times greater than reaching 1000 of the readers of the *Sun*. In the extreme case of the *Financial Times*, it is around three times greater even than the *Daily Telegraph*. The result of this is that those newspapers that can show they reach large numbers of rich people are able to command high prices for advertising space, even if the prices they end up charging will in practice be discounted from the published figures.

Table 3.4   Cover prices and advertising rates

Title	Cover Price (p)	Column Centimetre (£)	B&W Page (£)	Colour Page (£)	Cost Per 1000 for B&W Page (£)
Sun	25	146	34,700	42,800	3.40
Star	28	39	9433	15,092	4.52
Mirror	30	106	27,500	34,900	4.30
Mail	35	104	26,208	37,800	5.08
Express	35	85	20,285	31,500	7.24
Telegraph	40	88	38,500	47,000	15.15
FT	70	75	33,600	42,200	46.86
Guardian	45	36	15,500	16,000	12.17
Independent	40	32	14,000	18,000	16.15
The Times	35	45	19,000	25,500	9.98

Source: NTC, *Advertising Pocket Book*, 1997.

From the point of view of selling advertising, then, what matters to a newspaper is not the total number of readers its attracts but the social composition of its audience. It can either go for as many readers as possible, accepting that they will necessarily be relatively poor, and thus less attractive to advertisers, or concentrate on reaching a much smaller, but very much richer, audience that is very attractive to advertisers. In the past, it has certainly been the case that for a newspaper aimed at the richer segment of the audience to increase its circulation beyond a certain point meant that the increased costs of production and distribution outweighed the additional revenue, since the new audience consisted of poorer people for whom advertisers would not pay a premium. It was thus in the interests of the owners of elite newspapers to restrict the circulation of their papers in order to maximize their profits.

The consequence is that there are two rather different business models operating in the national daily press. By the standards of most newspapers in the developed world, which would expect to raise between 80 and 100 per cent of their revenue from advertising, the UK national daily press is relatively heavily dependent upon subscription sales. In the case of the popular press, it is conventionally reckoned that only 20 per cent of revenues come from advertising (Henry, 1978). The popular press is under a great deal of pressure to maximize sales, and a big circulation is a condition for survival. The quality press, on the other hand, receives around 60 per cent of its revenue from advertising. It is possible to sustain a competitive product on a much lower circulation than is the case with the popular press.

The mid-market newspaper *Today* was closed as irredeemably loss-making by News International in 1995. Its average circulation was then 566,302, which was larger than that of three quality papers that continue trading to this day. This ability to charge high prices to reach relatively few readers is sometimes called an 'advertising subsidy', and it certainly allows a relatively large number of titles to thrive in the narrow quality market in a way that is not possible for middle-market and popular newspapers. These latter need much larger circulations, and there are therefore fewer of them in each sector of the market.

The second consequence relates very closely to these different business models. The popular press are under market pressure to try to reach the widest possible audiences, and thus must prioritize the kinds of material that will sell vast quantities. Quality newspapers are much less interested in maximizing circulation, and are concerned to prioritize the kinds of material that will sell to particular kinds of people. Indeed, for them, maximizing circulation can be counter-productive (Corden, 1953). This difference in content affects the ways in which the press actually inform their readers about important public issues. Press freedom is such an important issue, and the press is so important to democracy, because it is in and through the press that citizens can learn about the world in which they are living and debate the choices facing them. Only in this way can they be expected to exercise informed choices about how, and by whom, their society shall be governed.

We may term this the 'public enlightenment' function of the press, and it is this aspect of its activity that most press theory concentrates on. The quality press, despite its many limitations, certainly provides this kind of information in abundance. It can be argued that the mid-market press carries at least a modicum of this sort of material. It cannot be argued that the popular press contains more than a tiny amount of public enlightenment. In other words, the newspaper press in which public enlightenment is a prominent feature accounts for around 20 per cent of the total circulation. Those titles that devote at least some attention to the issues account for around 25 per cent of total circulation. The majority of newspapers circulated in Britain today, however, have hardly any role in the provision of public enlightenment.

In a ratio of four to one, the newspaper reading population of the UK chooses titles that provide more detailed information about sport, celebrity scandals and popular entertainment than about politics and economics. Because of the structure of the readership for different newspapers, the social reality behind this is that, while the middle and upper classes are relatively well provided with the kinds of information and opinion necessary to democratic political life, the bulk of the white collar and manual working class are not. The price, language, content and general aura of the quality press act as an effective deterrent to the majority of the population, who are thereby excluded from the chance to be fully informed about the way in which their society is being run.

To say that the majority press concentrates very heavily on issues other than the narrow world of official politics and economics is not to say that the material it carries is unimportant, or that people are fools for preferring what it does talk about. Obviously, the popular press does carry some narrowly political information, particularly at election times. Obviously, sport, scandal and soap have political implications, even within the narrow official definitions of politics. More generally, it is true that, as the slogan has it, the personal is political. One can make out a strong case that the content of the popular press is actually much more important to the lives of the people who read it than is the material in the serious press. The coexistence of political democracy, expressed in various de facto rights and in periodic but infrequent elections, and economic tyranny, expressed in the daily subordination that everyone experiences the moment they start work, has the effect of making the former very remote from the lives of most people. It is quite understandable that most people would prefer to read about things that matter to them and which they might influence, rather than the arcana of power over which they have no real power (Sparks, 1988).

All of these things are true, but they simply act to reinforce the claim that the state of the British press presents a crisis for democracy. Free-to-air broadcasting has provided some amelioration of this crisis. In the public service form universal in the UK up until the 1990s, broadcasting was mandated to reach all of the population – or at least as much of it as was technically possible. This took both a physical form, in the transmitter network, and a social form, in the evolution of accessible public service broadcasting. While it is clearly not the case that any news service is the equivalent in terms of range and depth of coverage to the quality press, it is certainly true that broadcasting reached large sections of the population who without it would have had little or no contact with public affairs. Whether the increasing importance of encoded services will permit this counter-influence to continue is an open question.

A Declining Market?

It is commonly argued that the printed press is in crisis because the habit of reading newspapers is in decline. There is an apparent truth to this. The daily national press market stood at 17,320,000 in 1957. Forty years later, it was 13,835,841, a fall of around 20 per cent. As Figure 3.3 shows, while the decline has not been without interruptions, it is nevertheless well established. A trend such as this, lasting for over forty years, must certainly be considered a significant social phenomenon. Of course, the rate of decline is magnified by the choice of axes in this graphical presentation, and with another range it would appear a much more modest phenomenon. It is also true that if one projects the trend line into the future, it would not be until 2057 that circulation dipped below the 10,000,000 mark. In other words, on present trends, a century would result in only a 40 per cent drop in circulation. On the other hand, the UK population has increased over that timescale, so the proportion of people reading a newspaper has fallen even more rapidly than the absolute number. It seems therefore that talk of the imminent collapse of the press is much exaggerated, but that it is indeed a slowly declining medium.

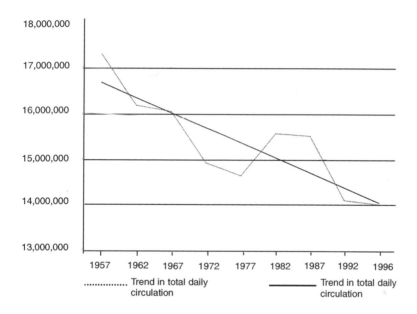

Figure 3.3   National daily press circulation over forty years (Sparkes, 1995; Audit Bureau of Circulation 1997)

Against that observation, we need to set a number of other factors. If we cast our net more widely, it is not at all clear that the whole of print culture is in decline. It is true that the paid-for local and regional newspaper sector is in even sharper decline than the national daily press, but the magazine sector is booming. It was estimated that there were just under 3000 publications of all sorts in 1900, but by 1989 there were nearly 7500 (Sparks, 1991). Since then, as Jane Stokes has shown in Chapter 1, there has been a further very sharp growth. If newspapers are declining, magazines are booming.

Second, even within the national daily newspaper press, the global figures for circulation conceal quite different and contradictory movements. Figures 3.4, 3.5 and 3.6 show the direction of change in the quality, middle and popular sectors. (Again, they have all been drawn with axes that exaggerate the variations from the trend line.) As is clear, the popular sector has had its ups and downs but has grown slightly. The quality sector has seen modest but sustained growth. The bulk of the decline has been in the middle market. If one repeats the projection of the trend line into the future, as Figure 3.7 shows, this middle sector crosses the zero line in around 2025, and a similar exercise for the quality press shows the two sectors crossing about now.

Considered in more detail, then, the claim that readership of print products is a dying habit is one that needs to be qualified. It is certainly true that the market is changing. The magazine sector has shown a consistent trend of growth over almost a century, while the overall readership of newspapers peaked in the 1950s and has been in decline since then. The newspaper market has, over the last forty years, polarized sharply into an elite quality sector and a mass popular sector. Both of these sectors have grown modestly.

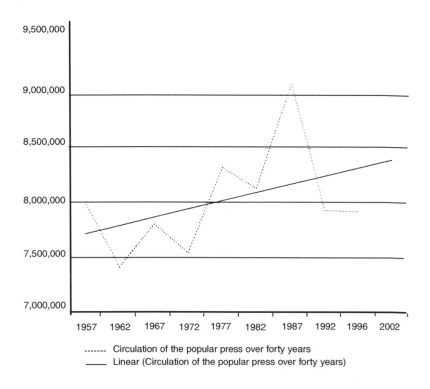

Figure 3.4   Trend in the cirulation of the popular press over forty years (Sparks, 1995; Audit Bureau of Circulation, 1997)

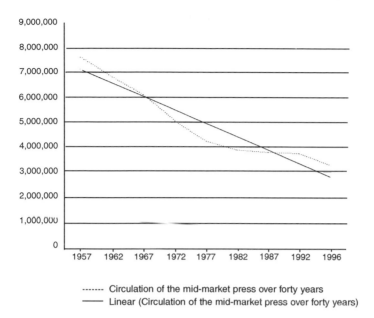

Figure 3.5 Circulation of the mid-market press over forty years (Sparkes, 1995; Audit Bureau of Circulation, 1997)

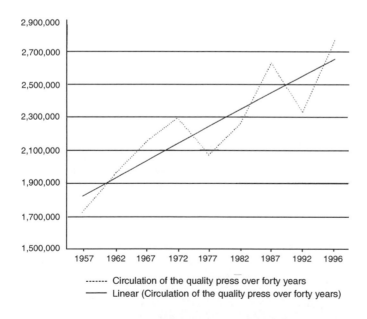

Figure 3.6 Circulation of quality press over forty years (Sparkes, 1995; Audit Bureau of Circulation, 1997)

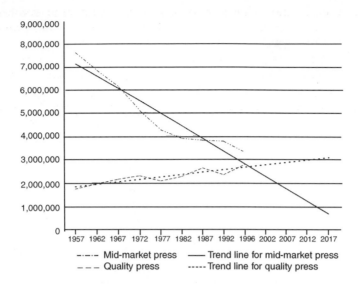

Figure 3.7   Projections for the circulation of the mid-market and quality press
(Sparkes, 1995; Audit Bureau of Circulation, 1997)

The case of the quality press is an interesting one. The core readership of this sector is among the highly educated sector of the population. Growth has been steady over the decades, but it is on average only around 1 per cent per annum. Given that the number of people with higher education is rising rapidly, these titles are, despite an increase in their total circulation, reaching a smaller and smaller sector of a rapidly expanding sector of the market. Over the past few years, there have been marked changes to the editorial material carried by these newspapers, which has often been described as a process of 'tabloidization'. It could be argued that this constitutes an attempt, so far relatively unsuccessful, to reposition these newspapers to win readers among the growing layer of educated people who at present do not have the newspaper reading habit. The recent price wars, which have been particularly acute in this sector, can also be seen as an attempt to extend the market to this layer (Sparks, 1998).

Conclusions

The major features of the UK national daily press are well explained by the workings of the market. The absence of any serious social or political disruption during the epoch of the modern press means that the logic of a commercially based press has been worked through very thoroughly. The fact that geographical concentration allows it to serve a relatively large number of people, together with the fact that it operates in a relatively wealthy country means that a number of titles are able to sustain themselves.

Taken together, these factors mean that the national daily newspaper press is a particularly good example of a competitive press in a stratified society. The dependence upon advertising revenue has meant that the press itself has stratified into three different kinds of products, each of which is aimed at markedly distinct audiences. The richest group is relatively well served, with five titles, while the two less wealthy groups have a narrower range of choices. The products that serve the richest audience are approximations to the newspaper of democratic mythology. The others are quite different commodities.

The oligopolistic nature of the market means that product differentiation is the prime form of competition between titles. Because no titles approximate to monopoly positions, a partisan political stance represents one, relatively minor, form of product differentiation. The intense competition for circulation between the popular press means that there is an in-built tendency to attempt to gain 'scoops' in those areas known to be attractive to readers. The lurid, sensational and sometimes offensive material that dominates the mass market press is the logical and inevitable consequence of its economic position.

None of these elements can be traced to the shortcomings of individuals. Newspaper proprietors may be, in the main, bullying reactionary bigots who force their editors to print politically biased material. But even if they were self-denying liberal paragons, it would still make sense for editors to act in the same way, because that is the best business model available to them. Again, editors and journalists may well be moral defectives with no sense of their responsibility to society and to the people upon whose lives they so pruriently report. But even if they were saintly ascetics, it would still make sense for them to publish the same sorts of material, because that is what best secures the competitive position of their newspapers.

Producing a press that sees as its main task the production of material that informs all of its readers objectively about the dangers and opportunities of their world, that presents them impartially with a range of informed opinions about desirable policy options, and that sees as one of its main functions providing them with a forum in which to articulate their own views and opinions, is an impossibility in a free market.

References

Audit Bureau of Circulation *National Newspapers: Six Monthly Averages for the 1990s*. Berkhamstead: Audit Bureau of Circulation, 1997.

Corden, W. 'The maximization of profit by a newspaper', in *Economic Studies 20*. 1953, pp. 181–90.

Curran, J. and Seaton, J. *Power without Responsibility. The Press and Broadcasting in Britain*, 3rd edn. London: Routledge, 1988.

Féderation Internationale des Editeurs de Journaux *World Press Trends*. Paris: FIEJ, 1995.

Habermas, J. 'The public sphere: an encyclopedia article', *New German Critique*, **3** (Fall 1974) pp. 49–55.

Henry, H. 'The Pattern of Press Revenues', in H. Henry (ed.) *Behind the Headlines – the Business of the British Press. Readings in the Economics of the Press*. London: Associated Business Press, 1978, pp. 9–30.

Hollis, P. *The Pauper Press*. Oxford: Oxford University Press, 1970.

Koss, S. *The Rise and Fall of the Political Press in Britain*. London: Fontana, 1990.

Lee, A. *The Origins of the Popular Press: 1855–1914*. London: Croom Helm, 1976.

National Readership Survey *NRS:* Volume One. London: National Readership Survey, 1996.

NTC *Advertising Pocket Book*. Henley on Thames: NTC, 1997.

Picard, R. 'Measures of concentration in the daily newspaper industry', *Journal of Media Economics*, **1**, 1 (1988) pp. 61–74.

Siebert, F. *Freedom of the Press in England 1476–1776*. Urbana, IL: University of Illinois Press, 1965.

Sparks, C. 'The popular press and political democracy', *Media, Culture and Society*, **X**, 2 (1988) pp. 79–87.

Sparks, C. 'Goodbye, Hildy Johnson: The Vanishing "Serious Press"', in P. Dahlgren and C. Sparks (eds) *Communication and Citizenship: Journalism and the Public Sphere in the New Media Age*. London: Routledge, 1991.

Sparks, C. 'Concentration and market entry in the UK national daily press', *European Journal of Communication*, **10**, 2 (1995) pp. 179–206.

Sparks, C. 'Are newspapers price inelastic? Lessons from the UK price war 1993–97' in Robert Picard (ed.) *Evolving Media Markets: Effects of Economic and Policy Changes*. Turkue, Finland: Economic Research Foundation for Mass Communication, 1998, pp. 212–38.

CHAPTER 4

Broadcasting: Television and Radio

ANDREW CRISELL

This chapter considers the present structure of British broadcasting in the light of both its past and its future. First, its historical development is traced in terms of the distinctive philosophy that has shaped it. Then, as it begins to be transformed by radical new technologies, the problems and issues it faces are outlined and some likely new developments suggested.

'A High Democratic Purpose': The Idea of Public Service Broadcasting

The statutory framework for British broadcasting that was created during its birth and infancy in the 1920s was sturdy enough to last until the middle of the 1980s. For the most part it was determined, or at least inspired, by technology: there was no room on the wavebands for more than a small number of broadcasting organizations. Until 1955 the BBC therefore enjoyed a domestic monopoly of television and, until 1973 (apart from three years in the 1960s, when a flotilla of pirates rode the airwaves), a domestic monopoly of radio. Even when these monopolies were ended, the BBC's commercial rivals were locked into a single composite structure, which provided the Corporation with only one source of competition on a national scale, and as we shall see, even these commercial rivals were required to subscribe to a similar broadcasting philosophy. The regional contractors of the commercial TV network formed a unified system under the control of the government-appointed Independent Television Authority, and the local radio operators made up a similar unified system under its successor, the Independent Broadcasting Authority (IBA), which took responsibility for both media from 1972.

The philosophy that informed British broadcasting was that of 'public service' and was conceived largely by the first Director General of the BBC, John Reith (Briggs, 1961). He held that because of the scarcity of wavelengths broadcasting should be a service of information, education and entertainment for everyone in the community who wanted it, free from the direct influences of both government and commerce. To this end the programme schedules within a single network strove not only to provide 'something for everyone' but 'everything for someone' – to expose the individual listener to the widest possible range of content. Hence each network carried a mixture of programming (Scannell and Cardiff, 1982) in which routine scheduling was mostly avoided. As part of this philosophy the BBC has always been funded by a receivers' licence fee, not by advertising, for the latter would drive output towards the maximization of audiences and the neglect of unprofitable minorities.

Likewise, the 1954 Television Act imposed public service duties on the system of commercial television that it brought into being. Although funded from advertising, 'independent' television (ITV) was obliged to offer a range and balance of programming, a fact that moderated competition between the two broadcasters, especially when after the findings of the Pilkington Report (1962) ITV was more tightly policed. Hence from 1955, monopoly in broadcasting was replaced not so much by full-blooded competition as by *duopoly* – by two broadcasters serving broadly similar objectives. When further networks were launched – BBC 2 in 1964 and a second ITV channel in 1982 – they were simply locked into the same system. Although Channel 4 was quite separate from ITV, in being a national operation under the direct control of the IBA, and in commissioning all its programmes instead of making them, it was not concerned with maximizing its audience. Indeed, it was not even obliged to sell its own advertising. This was done within their respective regions by the ITV companies, who then kept the proceeds and contributed to the upkeep of Channel 4 according to their respective means.

New Technologies and the Beginnings of Deregulation

The history of British broadcasting since the mid-1980s is largely an account of how this public service duopoly has been disturbed by a succession of technological developments, and of government efforts to devise a new statutory framework which would partly curb and partly exploit them. The rest of this chapter will survey the broadcasting landscape that is emerging and consider future problems and likely trends. It will focus on television, as the main medium, but include a word or two on radio.

Although both BBC 2 and Channel 4 were locked into the duopoly, there was a sense in which they modified it, even if they did not actually destabilize it. Together they doubled the number of networks that the viewer could choose to watch and marked the first tentative steps towards 'niche' broadcasting or 'narrowcasting'. Moreover, as a commissioner rather than a maker of programmes, Channel 4 enabled more independent producers to gain access to the viewing public. Instead of being confronted by two TV networks, each committed, in theory at least, to a comprehensive mixture of output, viewers could thus choose more specialized programming, much of it created by individuals who were not directly employed by either the BBC or ITV.

There were one or two other significant developments before the mid-1980s. From 1974 Teletext, and from the end of the 1970s, video cassette recorders (VCRs) enabled viewers to put their television sets to uses other than the reception of conventional broadcasts. These technologies created a further fragmentation and specialization of the mass audience and so weakened the old public service rationale of generalist programming that the Annan Committee (1977) used the new viewing habits to attempt a revised rationale of the concept.

The next major development was satellite broadcasting, which began in Britain in 1983 as a feed to the cable companies, but from 1989 could be beamed directly into people's homes via a 'dish' and a decoder – a technology known as 'direct broadcasting by satellite' (DBS). The first DBS service was operated by Rupert Murdoch's Sky TV, which was based in Luxembourg and consisted of several channels funded mainly by subscription but with some advertising. The short but epic history of satellite television (see Negrine, 1988, 1994; Horsman, 1997) was marked during the 1980s by Sky's pre-emptive strikes in securing such programme sources as Disney and the Hollywood studios and in launching before its rival, British Satellite Broadcasting (BSB) – the latter a culmination of sluggish and misjudged attempts by the broadcasting establishment to create its own DBS service. After lasting only a few months, BSB was absorbed by Sky at the end of 1990 to form BSkyB, an operation that has since prospered by buying the rights to blockbuster movies and major sporting events.

We will focus here on just two related lessons to be learned from the history of DBS. First, the capital costs of setting up and running a satellite service are so huge as to be sustainable only by large consortia rather than individual broadcasting organizations: during its first years BSkyB was funded not just by Murdoch's media empire but by companies such as Granada TV, Reed International, Chargeurs and the Pearson Group. Second, satellite broadcasting is inevitably a transnational, even a global, business: both its operators and its transmissions (known as 'footprints') transcend national frontiers. BSkyB itself is based abroad and its majority shareholder, News Corporation, is a worldwide operation, all of which makes it harder for individual countries like Britain to regulate the access, conduct and content of satellite broadcasting. When BSB merged with Sky, the Independent Television Commission instructed it to demerge or cease broadcasting by the end of 1992. Had BSkyB taken any notice, Britain would now have no DBS service at all.

The development of cable TV was another threat to the old BBC/ITV duopoly. Although wired broadcasting is almost as old as the atmospheric kind, it gathered impetus at the end of the 1970s with the arrival of fibre optic cables with vastly increased capacity – 250,000 times that of ordinary telephone wire (Bowen, 1994). Glimpsing its informatic potential, the government conceived the idea of a national cable infrastructure that could be entertainment led and privately funded (Negrine, 1985); and acting on the recommendations of the Hunt Committee (1982), it offered eleven regional franchises which were to be regulated by the Cable Authority.

Because broadcasting was seen as merely instrumental to cable's main business of linking computers and telephones (activities known respectively as 'informatics' and 'telecoms'), and because its operators saw themselves even more than satellite operators did as carriers rather than content producers, cable television was treated as supplementary to the BBC/ITV duopoly instead of in competition with it. As part of the channel packages that they offered to the viewer in return for a subscription, the cable companies were therefore obliged to carry all of the four conventional services. Most of the other channels would be supplied, for want of an alternative, by the satellite operators – which ultimately meant BSkyB.

The significance of cable technology has already been implied. It has enormous potential to offer telecoms and informatic services in parallel with broadcasting: but it can also make broadcasting itself a potentially interactive process. Viewers will soon be able to send messages back to broadcasters, ordering or modifying live programmes and feature films (the latter facility known as NVOD or 'Near Video-On-Demand') and summoning other associated services. Cable is thus an example *par excellence* of media convergence or integration. But between them, cable and satellite have a further significance: they not only offer many more channels than conventional broadcasting, but include sophisticated subscription and pay-per-view facilities. By the mid-1990s BSkyB had developed a lead in conditional access technology, the means by which channels can be offered or denied to viewers, through its subsidiary News Datacom (Horsman, 1997). In the longer term this could spell the end of, or at any rate a vastly reduced role for, the 'free to air' broadcasting presently provided by the BBC and ITV.

But it is the imminent development of digitization which will give the *coup de grâce* to the old broadcasting dispensation. To view digital transmissions audiences will need to buy either a new TV set or a set-top adaptor. Since as many as ten digital channels can occupy the frequency space presently occupied by a single analogue service (BBC, 1997), audiences will then be able to receive hundreds of channels delivered by cable, satellite and terrestrial means, with widescreen pictures and CD quality sound. Hence digitization will surely hasten and intensify the effects of the earlier technologies we outlined above: the scaling up of broadcasting organizations; globalization; narrowcasting; interactivity and media convergence. As an instance of the latter, the screening of a major new drama might be accompanied by supplementary material – documentaries, archive film, interviews – which the viewer could either watch at the same time or utilize off-line (BBC, 1997).

Riding the Tiger: the Search for a New Political Framework

The government's attempts to provide a framework for these developments were largely enshrined in the Broadcasting Acts of 1990 and 1996. The framework was partly shaped by the government's own belief that communications technology was occupying an ever more central and strategic role in economic affairs, and by its preference for the market rather than the state as the engine of the economy (Garnham, 1998). It aimed to get business to pay for what otherwise would have to come from the public purse, yet also to enhance business efficiency and public choice by stimulating market competition.

The 1990 Act split the IBA into the Independent Television Commission (ITC), which would be given responsibility for cable and satellite as well as ITV, and the Radio Authority, and both bodies were to facilitate broadcasting competition by regulating with a lighter touch. Since the proliferation of channels had weakened the rationale for the original notion of public service broadcasting, the regional ITV franchises would be reallocated not primarily on programming merits – although a 'quality threshold' was mentioned – but by auction. After 1993 Channel 4 would be obliged to sell its own advertising, and although it would still be linked with the main ITV regional network for some years to come through a 'safety net' agreement on advertising revenue, the connection between them would ultimately be severed. Competition and viewer choice would be further enlarged by a new ITV Channel 5, which would be run as a single national franchise, and all broadcasters, including the BBC, were required to commission not less than 25 per cent of their programme material from independent producers.

However, the 1990 Act maintained restrictions on multiple media ownership, which immediately came under strain. As we saw, the ITC was quite powerless to prevent the launch of BSkyB, with which the regional ITV companies could compete only by growing bigger and more efficient. Ownership restrictions were therefore eased in 1993, prompting a rash of takeovers and coalitions. Carlton TV, United News and Media and Granada emerged as the three big players on the ITV regional network, and in 1995 the latter's alliance with BSkyB was cemented with the launch of the Granada Sky Channel.

Even the new Channel 5 – a national, not merely regional, franchise – was not large enough to prove especially tempting, partly because it would cover only 85 per cent of the country and oblige its operator to re-tune 90 per cent of the VCRs therein. In 1992 it attracted only one, unsuitable, bidder and had to be readvertised. However, it was awarded in 1995 to a consortium of Pearson, United News and Media and the Luxembourg-based company CLT, which launched a service of tabloid TV in 1997.

The general tendency of 'scaling up' within the commercial broadcasting sector was further abetted by the 1996 Act, which relaxed ownership restrictions even more. Since then, ITV has been characterized by an increasing concentration of broadcasting ownership, by increasing cross-media ownership, and by increasing globalization, with the regional companies becoming part of multinational media conglomerates (Franklin, 1997). Only BSkyB and the Mirror Group have been too large for the remaining limits on the size of media share (Horsman, 1997).

Lend Me Your Ears: the Situation of Radio

Most of these technological, political and organizational developments have affected radio as well as television. However, back in the 1950s there was less pressure to end the BBC's monopoly of radio than of TV. Why? The Corporation's achievements were greater in the former than in the latter. It had had thirty years' experience of sound broadcasting, which included a distinguished war record. By contrast its TV service was fairly new, starved of funding, and run with scant appreciation of its potential (Goldie, 1977). Yet in what was now a booming post-war economy the medium's value to advertisers was becoming all too clear. Until 1964, then, the less glamorous medium of radio was left entirely in the hands of the BBC, apparently facing total eclipse as its audiences leached away to television. What revitalized it were the arrival of the transistor and the explosion of interest in pop music (as symbolized by the offshore pirate stations) – two factors that extended radio's possibilities as a 'secondary' or background medium and thus made it more attractive to commercial interests (Crisell, 1997). The development of VHF in 1955 also made room on the waveband for a multitude of local stations, which a Labour government authorized in 1967 but only as an extension of the BBC's monopoly. It was in 1972 that the structure of radio at last began to mirror the TV duopoly: a Conservative government inaugurated commercial radio, albeit on a local rather than regional basis, to be regulated along with ITV by the IBA, and with public service obligations (Barnard, 1989; Crisell, 1994).

By the time national commercial radio arrived, an astonishing 70 years after the launch of the first BBC service and as a result of the 1990 Broadcasting Act, the radio and TV landscape was, as we have seen, no longer viewable in terms of the old duopoly but a site of open competition. Classic FM arrived in 1992, to be followed a year later by Virgin 1215, and in 1995 by Talk Radio. A few regional stations were also authorized and many more local ones, 160 of which were broadcasting by 1995 (Seymour-Ure, 1996). Like ITV, independent local radio (ILR) has recently been characterized by consolidation and is now largely divided among three companies: Capital Radio, GWR, and East Midlands Allied Press (Franklin, 1997).

Like television, radio is contemplating a digital future and under the 1996 Broadcasting Act the Radio Authority has been given responsibility for assigning the 'multiplexes' or bundles of digital frequencies (each of which is able to carry at least six stations) to both public and commercial broadcasters, and for regulating the services they provide. All of the present national stations are guaranteed a place within the system. The BBC has already been broadcasting a digital service of its five networks since September 1995, but its geographical coverage is limited and listeners require special receivers. Under the new system it will acquire one of two national multiplexes, the other going to the existing national commercial stations. At least one other multiplex will be assigned to local services (Franklin, 1997).

Television's Beckoning Digits

Digital television has already arrived, and it is rumoured that the government aims to phase out analogue TV by about 2013. For digital satellite, BSkyB has formed a consortium known as British Interactive Broadcasting (BIB) with British Telecom, Midland Bank and Matsushita Electric of Japan, the owners of Panasonic. Its embryo television service, carrying pay-per-view movies and top sporting events, launched as Sky Digital on 1 October 1998, but the full BIB package, offering around 200 channels, some of conventional television and others of an interactive nature such as NVOD and home shopping channels, is expected in 1999.

Satellite operators dismiss the idea that interactivity is impossible by DBS and without a direct cable link. They claim that their present service need only be supplemented by a modem and a separate phone line to provide a 'return path' (Horsman, 1997). Nevertheless this method will not enjoy the capacity of cable and there will be insufficient bandwidth to allow the viewer instant control in the form of immediate films on demand or stop, rewind and fast-forward facilities. From a limited menu, NVOD could be provided simply by carrying the same film at staggered intervals on six satellite transponders: the viewer would then have to wait no more than a few minutes in order to watch it. But the viewer could preschedule programmes across different channels only if their transmission times did not clash (Barden, 1996).

Cable television has got off to a poor start in Britain and has an unclear digital future. For reasons outlined elsewhere (Horsman, 1997), it has been forced into a costly reliance on BSkyB's programming; it differed from American cable TV in following rather than preceding the arrival of the VCR; until 1992 it was not allowed to offer telecoms, a much more profitable business than carrying broadcasting; and thanks to the anachronistic regional basis on which the first franchises were allotted, the industry is fragmented and lacks a unified brand image. But as it struggles to compete with other forms of broadcasting, the predictable economies of scale have occurred and there are now only two main companies, Cable and Wireless Communications and Telewest. It is likely that these will combine to provide a single multichannel digital cable service, although one which will again depend heavily on feeds from BSkyB. But as we have seen, its fibre optic cables can carry a lot of return information, thus offering its customers a greater degree of interactivity and media convergence than other forms of broadcasting can.

The allocation of licences for digital terrestrial television has been assigned to the ITC. Six multiplexes are available. One has been allocated to the BBC, which will offer BBCs 1 and 2 free of charge, together with two themed subscription channels, BBC Choice and BBC News 24, which is at present available only on analogue (BBC, 1997). A second multiplex has gone to ITV and Channels 4 and 5, which will all be free, as at present, but supplemented by two subscription channels, an ITV 2 and Channel 4 Film Club (FilmFour), which specializes in art-house movies. Three other multiplexes have been awarded to ONdigital (formerly British Digital Broadcasting), a consortium of Carlton, Granada, and British Telecom which launched on 15 November 1998. Its pay TV channels include offerings from BSkyB, such as Granada Sky, plus three channels jointly operated by the BBC and the American cable and satellite company, Flextech, with which the Corporation has a deal for the distribution of its programmes in the United States. The joint channels comprise BBC Horizon (documentary and wildlife programmes), BBC Style and Showcase (lifestyles), and BBC One TV, a televised version of Radio 1 FM. The remaining multiplex has been reserved for interactive services: home shopping and banking, Internet access, ticket reservation (McCann, 1997a).

What will Become of Auntie?: the Future of the BBC

When we review these digital developments we can predict that several, largely interrelated, tendencies and dilemmas, which are already present in broadcasting, will continue and even intensify; but it is hard to foresee how some of the dilemmas might be resolved. Let us begin with the future of the BBC. In a television system that will extend to hundreds of channels, many of them themed, the old Reithian concept of public service broadcasting will no longer be necessary or even viable: it will not make sense to attempt comprehensive mixed programming on just one or two of these channels. Moreover, if the BBC controls only a handful of the channels available and regularly commands only a fraction of the audience, how can it continue to lay claim to a licence fee that must be found by all the viewers, even those who are paying subscriptions to other broadcasters? We might therefore seek to redefine public service as a service to otherwise unserved minorities, but to expect every single viewer to pay for it would still be unreasonable.

In anticipation of change – the licence arrangement is due to be reviewed in 2006 – the present Director General, John Birt, is striving to reduce the BBC's dependence on licence revenue by developing its commercial potential and introducing tighter financial disciplines in the form of producer choice and the 'internal market'. But are there other conceivable notions of public service which will enable the BBC to continue to distinguish itself from its rivals?

One 'public service' role might be for the BBC to offer a subscription service to those minorities which would not be catered for by other, more commercially minded broadcasters. But the only minorities that commercial broadcasters would be likely to neglect would be those from whom they could not make money – and this means that if the BBC undertook to serve them, it would still have to find income additional to that which it received from their subscriptions. The cynical wisdom at BSkyB is that in the present broadcasting environment the only kinds of programme that viewers are willing to subscribe to are big movies, top sporting events and pornography (Horsman, 1997). But even if money could be made from certain kinds of minority, they are unlikely to be those who stood to gain most from the old, Reithian kind of public service – the less affluent, less educated and less able-bodied (Garnham, 1994). The minorities who could afford to pay for their interests would probably be 'highbrow', but most of the programmes they require – news and current affairs, serious drama, opera, ballet, classical concerts – are expensive to produce, and it is certain that the subscription revenue they would generate could not hope to match the income which the BBC currently derives from the licence fee.

The BBC might also maintain its claim to be a public service broadcaster on the unique quality and range of its news and current affairs provision. Many other broadcasters now seek to offer little more than entertainment: within ITV, for example, there are undoubtedly pressures to reduce and popularize news output (Franklin, 1997). In this context the BBC's mission to inform, educate and explain, which very much accords with the preferences of its own director general, seems ever more impressive. BBC News 24 was launched on analogue in 1997 and is set to become a digital subscription service in the near future. The BBC's international newsgathering infrastructure is stronger than either BSkyB's or CNN's and – a significant advantage – News 24 is presently being supplied to the cable operators free of charge (McCann, 1997b). But in one way or another the BBC's news operation will have to be paid for in the future – and there is some evidence that the global demand for news is by no means insatiable.

The likeliest way in which the BBC will seek to survive as a public service broadcaster has been sketched out by Franklin (1997). He points out that in 1996, John Birt hived off two BBC divisions, Production and Resources, as part of his plan to make the Corporation leaner and fitter, more of a publisher-broadcaster than a producer-broadcaster. It is possible that these two divisions will acquire separate, commercial status, while the remaining divisions – Broadcast, News, World Wide and Corporate Centre – could collectively be funded as a publisher from a reduced licence fee, and derive extra income from the commercial services of BBC World Wide. Meanwhile, both of the commercial concerns, Production and Resources, could market programmes and services to commercial broadcasters as well as supplying the residuary Corporation.

These activities would be part of a trend whose continuation we can predict with much more confidence: a convergence in broadcasting between the commercial, private sectors and the non-commercial, public sector to a point where they will be virtually indistinguishable. This convergence is already under way. In partnership with the private company Flextech, the BBC has created a four-channel package of repeat programmes called UKTV – which is carried by the highly commercial BSkyB, not to mention the cable operators.

But if the BBC needs the private sector, the private sector also needs the BBC. BSkyB is itself a fertile source of programming, as the ITC recently acknowledged. Although the latter preferred the programmes of a rival bidder, Digital Television Network, it awarded a digital terrestrial franchise to ONdigital because the latter had access to the prime content from BSkyB, which would induce more viewers to switch over to the new technology (McCann, 1997a). Yet even BSkyB will have difficulty in filling all its channels, over 100 of them on its satellite service alone: the BBC, from its great public service treasure house, will be an invaluable supplier of content, and is in any case part of ONdigital's package of channels as well as occupying its own separate multiplex.

Some Other Developments and Dilemmas

These alliances and combinations are all part of the relentless scaling up that is now necessary in broadcasting. Consortia will operate at all digital levels, thus spreading the capital costs of technological development, satellite access, and the purchase or production of programmes and services to fill scores of channels. These consortia are typically alliances between carriers (BT, Flextech), manufacturers of media technology (Matsushita), and makers or commissioners of programme material (Granada, the BBC). But within them there is likely to be some adjustment of functions. With the blurring of boundaries between broadcasting and other media, book publishers and software manufacturers may become programme makers; programme makers may become programme commissioners; broadcasting carriers like the BBC may become no more than programme makers and/or commissioners. Telecoms and TV rental companies may become broadcasting carriers, especially as in the year 2000 the government is expected to lift its ban on the broadcasting of entertainment by BT.

In this brave new digital world BSkyB is perceived to be the clear winner. First, it controls access to *all* digital channels because it has a clear lead in the technology of encryption and decryption – in developing the necessary set-top boxes. Second, the purchasers of all forms of pay-TV will have to be processed through a sophisticated subscriber management system, which BSkyB also has in place. Third, it is the main satellite broadcaster to Britain. Fourth, even though it was obliged to relinquish its shareholding in ONdigital, the latter's licence depends on retaining access to premier sports events and movies – and BSkyB is the sole provider of these. Hence without having to put any money into ONdigital, Sky will get 70 per cent of its revenue. Fifth, while DBS does not incorporate the interactive, high-capacity technology of cable, BSkyB's connections with British Telecom through both BIB and ONdigital will give it direct access to, and a potential share in, the home shopping market.

Mention of interactivity and home shopping reminds us that the key to the digital future will not simply be the superabundance of channels but viewer control (Barden, 1996); and the viewer's experience will if anything confirm that convergence and blurring of corporate identities we have just been describing. As an instrument of viewer control, subscription will become a much more significant part of television revenue than ever before. It will increase relative to advertising – even now, BSkyB gains little more than 10 per cent of its revenue from advertisers (Horsman, 1997) – and may even sound the knell of old-fashioned 'free to air' broadcasting.

In this climate of extreme consumerism, themed channels will be more attractive than mixed programme channels because the subscriber will know exactly what she is going to get. It is significant that the BBC's mixed programme networks, 1 and 2, will remain free in the future, whereas its themed channels, including News 24, will be funded from subscription. Although there are grounds for believing that some mixed programme networks have a future (Barwise and Gordon, 1998), many media analysts foresee a continuing growth in 'niche' channels (Paterson, 1998).

But increased audience control will have a further consequence. Just as a customer in a bookshop does not expect to have to pay for every woman's magazine on the rack when she selects just one of them, so in the longer term the viewer will wish to subscribe to individual *programmes* rather than to channels or packages of channels – to move to an exclusive system of pay-per-view. She will wish to preschedule and reschedule the programmes she has plucked eclectically from a variety of channels and to store her schedule until she is ready to view it. And in the selection she makes she will also resemble the bookshop customer in being mainly attracted to the title and content of what she buys without really noticing who its 'publisher' happens to be.

Yet even if customers continue to subscribe to whole channels or packages of channels, it will as often as not be clear to them that these are the patch-worked products of different broadcasting organizations rather than the creation of one broadcaster alone. Hence the brand image of individual organizations is likely to fade, and as I have already suggested, this will pose a particular problem for the BBC, which seeks to maintain a distinctive public service identity. In the terrestrial digital system, for instance, the BBC will have its own multiplex: but it will also show programmes on the multiplexes owned by ONdigital, sometimes in collaboration with Flextech and sometimes not. It will, moreover, be in the same bundle of channels as Carlton, Granada and BSkyB, and the viewer will also know that even programmes appearing under its own imprint may well have been commissioned from an outside source. Finally, and perhaps most decisively, the viewers' consciousness of the BBC as a separate and different broadcaster will be dulled by the fact that they will have to pay for programmes in exactly the same way as they pay for everybody else's.

It may still, however, be lamented that even if viewers grow less aware of different brand images, BSkyB will continue to dominate the broadcasting landscape. Yet the game is changing so rapidly that no player's ascendancy can be taken for granted. The rights to screen premiership soccer, which BSkyB clinched in 1992 and 1996, were brilliant coups, securing its subscriber base until 2001. But its subscriptions are slowing down in the hiatus before digital conversion, and it now draws 60 per cent of its new subscribers from cable, which is showing better growth than the core satellite business (Horsman, 1997).

BSkyB faces a further problem. Just as digital broadcasting begins to take hold at the turn of the century, its premiership soccer deal will expire. With a glut of channels, it is not inconceivable that a scaling down, as well as a scaling up, might take place; that is to say, a number of leading clubs might well acquire their own exclusive TV channels, rather as they now have their own Internet websites, and televise their matches directly to the public on a pay-per-view basis (Horsman, 1997). With the 'Manchester United Channel', viewers would have a much greater sense of content than carrier, indeed their traditional sense of a 'broadcaster' might vanish altogether. But more to the point, BSkyB could find that a major source of its popularity – and income – could also vanish. This explains its audacious bid in the autumn of 1998 to buy Manchester United Football Club for £624 million. But Rupert Murdoch has been thwarted, for, perceiving a potential conflict of interests, the government referred his bid to its Monopolies and Mergers Commission, where it was turned down.

Let us draw comfort from our ignorance. In the present broadcasting landscape, conglomerates and megalomaniacs seem to be taking a firm stance. Yet the ground underneath is quicksand.

References

Annan Committee *Report of the Committee on the Future of Broadcasting, 1977*. Cmnd 6753, 1977.
Barden, S. 'Let's get digital', *Independent on Sunday Business*, (8 December 1996) p. 3.
Barnard, S. *On the Radio: Music Radio in Britain*. Milton Keynes: Open University Press, 1989.
Barwise, P. and Gordon, D. 'The Economics of the Media', in A. Briggs and P. Cobley (eds) *The Media: An Introduction*. Harlow: Addison Wesley Longman, 1998, pp. 192–209.
BBC *The BBC's Digital Service Proposition: A Consultation Document*. London: British Broadcasting Corporation, 1997.

Bowen, D. 'After the media earthquake', *Independent on Sunday* (6 March 1994) p. 9.

Briggs, A. *The History of Broadcasting in the United Kingdom* – Volume I: *The Birth of Broadcasting*. London: Oxford University Press, 1961.

Crisell, A. *Understanding Radio*, 2nd edn. London: Routledge, 1994.

Crisell, A. *An Introductory History of British Broadcasting*. London: Routledge, 1997.

Franklin, B. *Newszak and News Media*. London: Edward Arnold, 1997.

Garnham, N. 'The broadcasting market', *Political Quarterly*, **65**, 1 (1994) pp. 11–19.

Garnham, N. 'Media Policy', in A. Briggs and P. Cobley (eds) *The Media: An Introduction*. Harlow: Addison Wesley Longman, 1998, pp. 210–23.

Goldie, G. *Facing the Nation: Television and Politics, 1936–1976*. London: The Bodley Head, 1977.

Horsman, M. *Sky High: The Inside Story of BSkyB*. London: Orion Business Books, 1997.

Hunt Committee *Report of the Inquiry into Cable Expansion and Broadcasting Policy*, Cmnd 8679, 1982.

McCann, P. 'Great TV – but no new shows', *Independent* (25 June 1997a) p. 5.

McCann, P. 'There's a lot more on offer, but do we want it?', *Independent* (1 November 1997b) p. 20.

Negrine, R. (ed.) *Cable Television and the Future of Broadcasting*. London and Sydney: Croom Helm, 1985.

Negrine, R. (ed.) *Satellite Broadcasting: The Politics and Implications of the New Media*. London: Routledge, 1988.

Negrine, R. *Politics and the Mass Media in Britain*, 2nd edn. London: Routledge, 1994.

Paterson, R. 'Contemporary Television: A Framework for Analysis', in A. Briggs and P. Cobley (eds) *The Media: An Introduction*, Harlow: Addison Wesley Longman, 1998, pp. 127–39.

Pilkington Committee *Report of the Committee on Broadcasting 1960*, Cmnd 1753, 1962.

Scannell, P. and Cardiff, D. 'Serving the Nation: Public Service Broadcasting before the War', in B. Waites, T. Bennett and G. Martin (eds) *Popular Culture: Past and Present*. London: Croom Helm, 1982, pp. 161–88

Seymour-Ure, C. *The British Press and Broadcasting since 1945*, 2nd edn. Oxford: Basil Blackwell, 1996.

CHAPTER 5

Cinema

JOHN HILL

A British Cinema Revival?

In some ways, British cinema in the 1990s would appear to be in good shape. Following a drop to an all-time low of 54 million in 1984, cinema admissions have been steadily rising, reaching 137 million in 1997. This growth has been accompanied by the opening of new cinemas and a rising number of cinemas and cinema screens. Thus, since 1987 the pattern of cinema closure has been reversed and, between 1987 and 1997, the number of UK cinemas rose from 677 to 747 and actual screens from 1277 to 2383 (*Screen Finance*, 1998a) (see Table 5.1). This may be linked to the rapid growth of multiplexes (purpose-built cinemas with multiple screens commonly located on greenfield sites) following the opening of the first UK multiplex in Milton Keynes in late 1985. By 1997, the number of multiplexes had risen to 142 and accounted for over half of all UK cinema screens and an even higher proportion of all cinema visits.

Table 5.1   UK sites and screens
1984–96

Year	Total Sites	Total Screens
1984	660	1271
1987	677	1277
1990	737	1685
1991	724	1789
1992	735	1845
1993	723	1890
1994	734	1969
1995	743	2019
1996	742	2166
1997	747	2383

Source: Screen Finance/BFI.

At the same time, there seems to have been a certain revival of British film-making. During the 1980s British film production fell to its lowest levels since 1914. However, since 1989 (when only 30 films were made), film numbers have risen, totalling as many as 128 in 1996 (the highest figure since the 1950s, see Table 5.2). The 1990s have also witnessed a number of outstanding commercial successes for British films. In 1994, *Four Weddings and a Funeral* was the most popular film in Britain, taking over £27 million at the UK box office and a further $52 million in the US. In 1996, *Trainspotting* took over £12 million at the UK box office (and a further $16 million in the US) while, in 1997, *The Full Monty* became the biggest grossing film ever in the UK, earning over £40 million at home and $133 million worldwide. However, while these figures are striking, what they nonetheless disguise are the continuing weaknesses of British film production more generally.

Table 5.2 Number of UK films produced 1989–96

1989	30
1990	60
1991	59
1992	47
1993	67
1994	84
1995	78
1996	128
1997	112

Source: Screen Digest/BFI.

Although there has been an upsurge of cinema-going in recent years, to which the popularity of films such as *The Full Monty* has contributed, British audiences are in the main going to see American rather than British films. This is reflected in the high numbers of Hollywood films on British screens and the relatively low levels of market share taken by British films at the UK box office. During the 1990s, US films have generally accounted for over 80 per cent, and often over 90 per cent, of UK revenues while British films have struggled to top 10 per cent. In 1997, the market share of British films did rise as high as 23 per cent but this figure was largely the result of the performance of just two films, the UK co-production *Bean* and *The Full Monty*. Although these films did extraordinarily well, the Top 50 most popular films at the UK box office were still overwhelmingly Hollywood productions (*Men In Black, The Lost World: Jurassic Park, 101 Dalmatians, Batman and Robin, Liar Liar, Jerry Maguire, Scream, Con Air* and so on).

What this also indicates is that, despite the growing number of British films being made, the vast bulk of British films do relatively poorly at the box office. Indeed, many of the films made in Britain in the 1990s have not been seen in cinemas at all. Over 30 per cent of British films made since 1991, and over 50 per cent of films made in 1995 and 1996, have not been released. Moreover, of those films that were released in 1995 and 1996, only about a quarter secured general UK exhibition (*Screen Finance*, 1998b). The perception of the increasing strength of the British film industry in the 1990s, in this respect, has tended to derive from the exceptional popularity of a small number of films rather than from the genuinely widespread success of British productions.

Moreover, while the economic performance of the most successful British films has been outstanding by British standards, they are still relatively modest by the standards of Hollywood. So, while *The Full Monty* may have beaten both *Men In Black* and *The Lost World* at the UK box office, each of these films earned around four times the gross of *The Full Monty* worldwide. Similarly, while *Four Weddings and a Funeral* outperformed *The Lion King* in the UK it still only earned around one-sixth of the Disney film in the US. As for *Trainspotting*, its US earnings (high for a British film) were still insufficient to win it a place in the US Top 100 for 1996. Indeed, the only 'British' film to appear in the US Top 100 for that year was the Hollywood-backed *Sense and Sensibility*.

The purpose of these points is not in any way to belittle the achievements of films such as *Trainspotting* and *The Full Monty* but rather to place them in context. The accomplishments of these films do not, on their own, add up to a revival of British film-making nor do they seriously challenge the global dominance of Hollywood cinema. Indeed, one of the ironies of *The Full Monty*'s success is that the film was actually financed by the subsidiary of a Hollywood major, Fox Searchlight (established in 1994 as part of a strategy to target niche markets), and undoubtedly benefited from the distribution and marketing advantages that association with a Hollywood major brought. In this respect, despite the resurgence of cinema-going in Britain and the successes of a few films, British film production in the 1990s is still overshadowed by Hollywood, an industry whose films have dominated British screens since the end of the First World War. In order to understand why British film-making is in the situation that it is, it is necessary to begin by examining the reasons for Hollywood's success.

The Power of Hollywood

It is, of course, worth remembering that film-making is a particularly high-risk business. Each film is to some extent a 'prototype' and it is difficult to predict accurately which films will do well and which will not. As a result, while the profits from film-making can be great, many films – including some which seem to be reliable 'commercial' prospects – may perform badly (as the notorious example of the Arnold Schwarzenegger vehicle *The Last Action Hero* will testify). Indeed, the Hollywood studios routinely expect to carry losses on some of the films they make and it is still a rough rule of thumb that, purely within theatrical markets (that is, from showings in cinemas), only 2 out of 10 films turn a profit. The continuing success of Hollywood, therefore, has depended upon its ability to spread the financial risks of production in such a way as to make film-making, more or less, consistently profitable. There are a number of ways in which this has been accomplished.

The first factor relates to scale of production. US film production is dominated by the Hollywood studios or 'majors': Warner Bros, Disney/Buena Vista, Paramount, MCA/Universal, Twentieth Century Fox, Columbia/TriStar and MGM/UA (the weakest of the group). These studios are in a position to finance production from their own resources and characteristically invest in a slate of productions of around 10–20 films per annum. In doing so, it is generally expected that the revenues that they generate from the most successful films will outweigh the losses made on the others. In this respect, Hollywood production relies upon a 'critical mass' of production that allows it to ride the failures that inevitably accompany 'commercial' film-making.

The Hollywood studios also make films of a particular type. They attempt to minimize the 'uncertainty' of film production by recombining elements that have proved successful in the past. This involves the use of big-name stars (who can now command extraordinarily high salaries on the basis of their assumed box-office appeal), proven talent (such as writers and directors), the 'remaking' of earlier successes in the form of sequels or generic types and the use of spectacular 'state-of-the-art' special effects. These features also make Hollywood films very costly and certainly far more expensive than those of any other country. Indeed, Hollywood's domination of the international box office in the 1980s and 90s is clearly associated with the rise of the blockbuster, or 'event' movie, and the growing film costs that are associated with it. Thus, in 1980, the average cost of a studio film (including domestic advertising) was an estimated $13.7 million (*Screen Finance*, 1994). By 1996 the corresponding figure had risen to $59.7 million, with many of the studios' highest profile, or 'tentpole', movies costing considerably more. Thus, a substantial proportion of the big studio films released in 1997, such as *Men In Black, The Lost World: Jurassic Park, Batman and Robin, Dante's Peak*, and *Speed 2: Cruise Control*, cost well over $100 million (*Screen Finance*, 1997).

However, if Hollywood relies upon a scale of production (in terms of both the number and cost of films made) that is beyond the means of other film industries (the average cost of 'wholly' British films in 1996, for example, was only £1.6 million), Hollywood's global dominance does not rest on production strategy alone. For while it is common to think of Hollywood in terms of studios (and hence production), the economic might of the Hollywood majors derives, above all, from their integration of production (which the studios may only finance) with distribution (that is, the renting of films to cinemas). The 'studios', in this sense, are as much film distributors as they are film producers and it is their commanding position within distribution, in both the US and elsewhere, that is the primary source of their economic might. As the major distributors of film in the US, for example, they are able to limit the access of independent and non-US distributors to the US market and, thus, command a disproportionately high box-office share in proportion to the number of films released. The size of the US home market (one of the biggest in the world and the most important for the majority of Hollywood films) also ensures that a sizeable proportion (if not all) of production costs are recouped in the US and, therefore, that films can be sold competitively (and with reduced distribution costs) overseas.

The huge sums that the majors spend on promotion is worth noting in this regard. A key part of the studios' strategy in the US in recent years has been to back up their biggest films with a widespread release (often on over 2000 screens) and saturation marketing. A particular premium is placed on 'opening big' on a film's first weekend and this makes the role of advertising (particularly on the television networks) especially important in generating admissions. This is then reflected in the very high sums – nearly half of average negative (that is, production) cost – that are spent by the Hollywood majors on advertising and the production of prints. This scale of release and promotion of studio films in the US not only makes it very difficult for non-studio and foreign films to compete successfully in the US market but also creates a 'buzz' around a film that can then be exploited in international markets. Indeed, the gap between the US opening of a film and release elsewhere has been narrowing in order to facilitate the exploitation of a film's release as something of a global 'event'. Thus, within less than three months of its US opening in 1997, *Men in Black* was in box-office top tens across Europe as well as in Australia, Brazil, and Hong Kong (*Screen International*, 1997b). This is a measure not only of the effectiveness of Hollywood's international distribution network but also its success in promoting films on a global scale.

However, the strength of Hollywood in distribution is not solely dependent upon access to cinema screens. What is also apparent is the commanding position that Hollywood occupies within non-theatrical markets as well. Indeed, the great achievement of the Hollywood studios in recent years has been their ability to overcome the financial difficulties that they faced in the late 1960s and early 1970s by taking advantage of the opportunities provided by video, pay-TV and satellite. This can be seen in the changing patterns of revenue streams. In 1980, the returns from theatrical release (both domestic and foreign) accounted for over 75 per cent of US studio revenues. Ten years later this had fallen to 32 per cent (*Screen Finance*, 1993). In the same period, revenues from pay-TV grew from 4.8 per cent to 9 per cent while revenues from video rose dramatically from just 1 per cent to 45 per cent, and then to over 50 per cent by 1996 (*Screen Finance*, 1997). In this respect, Hollywood's pre-eminence in theatrical markets is now matched by a similar dominance of the (rental and sell-through) video market for film.

The growth in the importance of video and pay-TV markets also reflects another aspect of the changing character of Hollywood. Particularly since the mid-1980s, there has been a growing incorporation of the studios into large transnational media conglomerates. Rupert Murdoch's News Corporation now owns Twentieth Century Fox; Sony owns Columbia Pictures; the cable company Viacom (with interests not only in pay-TV but publishing, video rental stores and theme parks) has bought Paramount; Seagram, the Canadian drinks and entertainment group, are owners of MCA/Universal; while Time and Warner Bros have merged to create Time Warner (the world's biggest media corporation). In all cases, these large conglomerates have interests across a range of media, such as television, cable, computer games, recorded music, publishing and theme parks, and their film activities are only a part (albeit an important one) of general entertainment and information business strategies. The value of film to these companies, in this respect, is not simply the revenues that they provide but the platform to other media and consumer markets that they offer. This involves tie-ins such as books, magazines, computer games, toys and soundtracks as well as the licensing of a whole range of consumer products. The huge merchandising campaign accompanying the release of *Jurassic Park*, for example, not only involved lucrative licensing deals with McDonalds and Choice Hotels but also the licensing of an enormous variety of trademarked products, ranging from popcorn and chocolate eggs to boys' briefs, bed headboards and metal TV trays! Indeed, tie-ins and licensing now provide the majors with an even greater source of income than actual film and video rentals and provides yet another example of the ways in which the studios are able to manage the high risks and uncertainties of big-budget film-making and to make a profit from film production. Moreover, as a result of these ownership changes and diversification of interests, the Hollywood majors have strengthened their dominant position within the international film industry. In doing so, they have also made it more difficult than ever for other companies to compete effectively (as the experience of the aspiring major Orion, which went bankrupt, suggests) or for countries outside of the US to sustain film industries that are commercially viable.

The Weaknesses of British Cinema

This may be seen in the case of the UK where the film industry has had to confront some of its greatest difficulties since the 1920s. Historically, the British cinema has adopted two main industrial strategies, either trying to compete directly with Hollywood in the international market or relying primarily on the domestic market for its commercial viability. While the first of these two strategies has always been fraught with difficulties, the second has also proved problematic in recent years. The first strategy has involved the attempt to secure success in the US market by emulating the model (and costs) of Hollywood film-making. This has been attempted at various junctures in the history of British cinema: by Alexander Korda in the 1930s, by Rank in the 1940s, by EMI in the 1970s and then Goldcrest in the 1980s. However, in the absence of those factors (large-scale production, large domestic market, an international distribution and exhibition network) that have provided Hollywood with its competitive advantage, such strategies have always ended in financial disaster. This is illustrated by the collapse of Goldcrest following the failure of three big-budget projects – *Absolute Beginners*, *The Mission* and *Revolution* – aimed at the international market. In this case, the very high financial risks of film production were spread across too few productions, there was no control over distribution in the US market and the company was insufficiently capitalized to be in a position to sustain a run of losses (Eberts and Ilott, 1990). Other companies, such as Handmade and Palace, also aimed for the US market in the 1980s and early 1990s with a different style of cheaper 'independent' production. However, even this kind of policy proved unsustainable in the long run (Hill, 1999). For while 'cracking the US market' has been the holy grail of successive generations of British film-makers, the US has remained a market dominated by Hollywood films and US distribution interests. As a result, the UK share of the US market during the 1990s has barely risen above one or two per cent.

Given these difficulties of competing with Hollywood in the US market, it has been the second strategy – of competition in the domestic market – that has traditionally characterized British film-making and that underpinned British film-making in its heyday in the 1930s and 40s. The basis of this cinema, however, was a size of audience sufficient to sustain the profitability of domestic film-making. As cinema audiences began to decline, especially from the 1950s onwards, the commercial viability of this kind of cinema began to be threatened. As a result, regular British film production (characteristically popular genre film-making) aimed at the domestic market came to a virtual halt after the 1970s when Hammer horror, the *Carry Ons* and the *Confession* films all ceased production. Audiences have, of course, increased since then but cinema admissions in the 1980s and 90s are still relatively small by the standards of previous decades (see Table 5.3). Thus, the 1997 figure of 137 million is only around one-tenth of the admissions figures that were typical of the 1940s. So although, in comparison to the US, the British home market has always been relatively small, it was still large enough, up until the 1970s, for British films to make money. Since then it has become much more difficult for them to do so.

Table 5.3   UK cinema admissions (millions) 1946–96

1946	1,635.00
1950	1,395.80
1960	500.80
1970	193.00
1980	101.00
1984	54.00
1990	97.37
1991	100.29
1992	103.64
1993	114.36
1994	123.53
1995	114.56
1996	123.80
1997	137.00

Source: Screen Digest/BFI.

So, while hits, such as *The Full Monty*, have demonstrated that it is still possible for British films to recoup their costs in the UK market the vast bulk of recent British movies have failed to do so. For example, *Backbeat* (the most popular 'wholly' British film after *Four Weddings and a Funeral* in 1994) only succeeded in earning £1,870,000 of its £2,900,000 production cost at UK cinemas. Moreover, given that only a small proportion (possibly as low as 10–20 per cent) of box-office revenues actually returns to a film's producer (rather than to the exhibitor and distributor), even those films that did 'cover' their costs at the cinema were not necessarily guaranteed a profit. For example, *Brassed Off* (the second most successful British film of 1996), which cost £2,530,000 to make, would still have failed to turn a profit on the basis of its UK revenues of £2,873,429. Inevitably, this has made British films more dependent upon overseas revenues but, as has been seen, the biggest overseas market – the US – has generally failed to offer a reliable source of income for British films.

The decline in size of the UK market, and corresponding weakness of British production, is also related to another significant difference between Hollywood and the British film industry. As has been argued, a key to Hollywood's success has been its integration of distribution and production. In the case of Britain, however, there has been an almost complete divorce within the industry between the different sectors. During the 1940s and 50s, Britain did have its equivalent of the Hollywood studio system whereby two British companies, Rank and ABPC, produced films in their own studios for distribution to their own cinemas. As cinema audiences began to decline, however, the economic basis of this system was undermined and the two British 'majors' not only ended their production programmes but withdrew from investment in production as well. The net result of this was that, from the mid-1980s onwards, the exhibition and distribution sector (responsible for the screening and supply of films) in Britain had virtually no direct ties with the British production sector and, as a consequence, no particular interest in showing British as opposed to Hollywood films.

This problem for British film-makers was reinforced by the growing strength of US exhibitors (that is, cinema owners) and distributors in the UK. It was US exhibitors who were primarily responsible for the opening of multiplexes in the UK and their share of the UK market grew accordingly (see Table 5.4). As a result, three of the five largest exhibitors in the UK are effectively US subsidiaries: UCI (with 254 screens and around 18 per cent of UK box office in 1996) is owned by Paramount and MCA; National Amusements (143 screens) is owned by Viacom (the owner of Paramount); and Warner Village (143 screens) is owned jointly by Warner Bros and the Australian company Village Roadshow (*Screen International*, 1997a). Moreover, the large cinema chains that are not US subsidiaries have established relations, or alignments, with US distributors and are supplied with films by them on a systematic basis. Thus, the Odeon chain (with 351 screens in 1996) is aligned with Twentieth Century Fox, Columbia and Buena Vista (a subsidiary of Disney) while Virgin Cinemas (with 172 screens) and ABC Cinemas (234 screens) are aligned with United International Pictures (UIP) and Warners. As this would suggest, the all-important distribution sector in the UK is even more dominated by US interests than exhibition. Thus, the five largest distributors in Britain (commanding over 80 per cent of box-office share in 1996 and 1997) are also subsidiaries of the Hollywood majors, that is, UIP (which is jointly owned by MCA/Universal, MGM and Paramount), Warner Distributors, Columbia, Buena Vista and Fox.

Table 5.4   US majors' share of UK distribution

Distributor	Percentage market share		
	1995	*1996*	*1997*
Fox	8.5	12.6	20.5
Buena Vista	21.0	20.0	19.9
UIP	23.5	27.5	15.7
Columbia	6.8	9.0	14.8
Warner	20.5	10.9	9.7
Total US majors' share	80.3	80.0	80.6

Source: Screen International.

Inevitably, this domination of the UK exhibition and distribution sectors by US interests has limited the circulation of British films and may be related to the difficulties many British films during the 1990s have experienced in securing a cinema release. It is not, of course, that the US distributors will not distribute British films but that the system inevitably favours those from Hollywood. This is not only because, as subsidiaries of the Hollywood conglomerates, the activities of US distributors in the UK fit in with the global distribution strategies of the studios, but also that there are economic advantages in doing so. Unlike most new British films that have yet to be shown in cinemas, Hollywood films have generally been 'market-tested' in the US where they have also benefited from extensive advertising and promotion. Indeed, one of the reasons that *Four Weddings and a Funeral* did so well at the UK box office was that it had already 'proved' itself in the US where it had opened two months ahead of the UK. Moreover, as London Economics argue, because certain costs have already been met by their parent companies, US distributors in the UK (and the EU more generally) are typically 'biased towards US product' since they require a higher return on a British (or EU) film to achieve the same profit margin as one of their own studio films of equivalent box-office potential (London Economics, 1993). Thus, of the 48 British films made in 1996 that actually succeeded in securing a cinema release, only 10 were handled by one of the five big US distributors (*Screen Finance*, 1998b).

It is, of course, the case, certainly in relation to Hollywood, that theatrical (or cinema) earnings are no longer as important as those from video. And, in the UK, the video market has grown to such an extent that spending on film on video (both rental and retail) in recent years has been three to four times the spending on cinema-going (Selwood, 1996). However, theatrical release of a film remains of crucial importance in establishing a film's value for other markets and the performance of a film on video (especially in the rental market) is heavily influenced (although not completely determined) by its performance in the cinemas. As a result, the video market for film in the UK is dominated by Hollywood titles in much the same way as British screens.

This is also reflected in the dominance of video distribution by the subsidiaries of the Hollywood majors – Warner/MGM, CIC (owned by Universal and Paramount), Buena Vista, Fox Guild and Columbia TriStar – which, in 1995, accounted for nearly 80 per cent of all UK video rentals. Thus, while the Hollywood studios have been able to compensate for the drop in audiences at cinemas by generating revenues from video (and pay-TV), the returns to the British film industry from video have been much less substantial. For example, the most successful 'wholly' British film of 1992, *Peter's Friends* actually earned less on video than it did at the cinemas and the film's combined revenues from UK theatrical box office and video still barely covered the film's costs (Ilott, 1996).

British Film Production

The other main consequence of this separation between the distribution/exhibition sector and production is the pattern of financing film production which it has encouraged. As was previously indicated, the Hollywood system is an integrated one in which the studios finance a slate of films which they then distribute. In the UK, since the demise of the British studio system, there has been no equivalent source of regular finance from the distribution sector. As a result, British film production is primarily carried out on an irregular or one-off basis by relatively small independent production companies. Thus, during the 1980s, no less than 342 production companies were involved in film production and, of these, 250 were involved in only one film (Lewis, 1990). The absence of vertically integrated companies has also meant that British producers have generally had to put together financing from a variety of sources. Typically, these have included a reliance upon a mix of pre-sales (whereby distribution rights to particular territories are pre-sold, usually through a sales agent), funding by government-backed agencies (such as British Screen, the Arts Councils and Scottish Screen) and by television (especially Channel 4 but also the BBC and ITV companies).

The exception to this model in recent years has been Polygram Filmed Entertainment which owns a number of production companies (such as Working Title) and was the biggest investor in British film in 1997. Polygram, which was itself – until recently – owned by the Dutch electronics giant Philips, moved into film in the late 1980s and early 1990s on the back of its success in the music and video business. Although involved in US and European projects as well, Polygram played a significant role in British film-making of the 1990s through their financing or distribution of high-profile successes such as *Shallow Grave*, *Trainspotting*, *Four Weddings and a Funeral* and *Bean*. A part of the company's success, in this respect, derived from its development of an international distribution network and adoption of a Hollywood-style attitude to promotion. Thus, while *Trainspotting* cost only £1,760,000 to make, Polygram spent a further £850,000 on UK advertising as well as taking advantage of profitable tie-ins such as the accompanying CD soundtrack (Finney, 1996). The company also benefited from the shelter of a large multinational conglomerate which helped it to ride the inevitable losses that the film division initially sustained (Dale, 1997). Nevertheless, the returns from Polygram Filmed Entertainment still proved a disappointment to Philips which announced, in 1998, the sale of its share of the company (75 per cent) to Seagram (the owner of Universal). Thus, what began as an ambitious attempt to become a 'European major' in competition with Hollywood has ended with a Hollywood takeover and an uncertain future for the company's production and distribution operations.

The most sustained contribution to British film-making since the 1980s, however, has undoubtedly been television and Channel 4 in particular.

Channel 4 was launched as the fourth UK television channel on 2 November 1982 and, borrowing from the example of German and Italian television, supported the production of feature films by offering either full funding, equity investment or the pre-purchase of television rights. According to the channel's own calculations, it invested £91 million in 264 different films between 1982 and 1992 and the films that it has supported include many of the key British films of the 1980s and 90s such as *My Beautiful Laundrette*, *Letter to Brezhnev*, *A Room with a View*, *The Passion of Remembrance*, *Riff-Raff*, *The Crying Game*, *Four Weddings and a Funeral*, *Shallow Grave* and *Trainspotting*. The prestige that attached to Channel 4 because of its film-making policy also encouraged other television companies to follow suit and the BBC, as well as a number of ITV companies, have had an up and down involvement with film production since the mid-1980s. However, while Channel 4 has been party to a number of major box-office successes, it is also worth noting that, in strict commercial terms, most of the channel's films have made a loss. Channel 4, in this respect, has been able to carry the 'losses' of film production precisely because its primary source of income is from advertising rather than film revenues (Hill, 1996). In this respect, the alliance between film and television that has developed in the UK has provided a particular kind of (partly culturally driven) 'solution' to the problems that British film-making has encountered in the face of Hollywood's global dominance.

For similar reasons, British film-making has also depended on what forms of state support have been available. During the 1980s, the Conservative government, under Margaret Thatcher, sought to subject the film industry to what it believed would be the bracing winds of the free market. It therefore abolished the quota (whereby British cinemas were required to show a certain proportion of British films), ended the Eady levy (whereby a small percentage of exhibitors' earnings was returned to film producers) and abolished the tax incentives which had helped to fuel the would-be 'renaissance' of British film-making in the early 1980s. Rather than invigorating the industry, however, these measures simply reinforced the market weakness of the British film industry which came to rely even more heavily on what government assistance remained (Hill, 1993). Thus, after Channel 4, one of the most important sources of finance for British film has been the government-funded British Screen which has invested in over 120 films (including *The Crying Game*, *Orlando*, *Naked*, *Land and Freedom* and *Butterfly Kiss*) since 1986 (when it replaced the National Film Finance Corporation).

However, the most significant new source of finance, which has partly been responsible for the increasing number of British productions, has been money from the National Lottery administered by the Arts Councils of England, Wales, Scotland and Northern Ireland. Following the announcement of lottery funding for film in 1995, the four Arts Councils had made awards of around £50 million to over 160 films (including features, shorts and documentaries) by the beginning of 1998. As part of a strategy for encouraging the emergence of 'mini-studios', the Arts Council of England also awarded, in 1997, franchises to three film industry consortia – The Film Consortium, Pathé Pictures and DNA Films. And, following the growing evidence of problems of distribution for British films (including those supported by Lottery money), the English Arts Council has also indicated its intentions to support film distribution. Assistance for the distribution of British films via an All-Industry Fund was also a key recommendation of the Film Policy Review Group, set up by the new Labour government in 1997 (Film Policy Review Group, 1998).

Conclusion

The failure of the bulk of new British films to secure a cinema release does, of course, raise the question whether this is simply a matter of distribution or one of fundamental strategy. Critics of the British film industry have argued that its problems are due to an excessive dependence upon television and government support which has led to the production of too many low-budget films that fail to compete in the market place. The argument of this chapter, however, is that British film-making has developed in this way precisely because of the enormous competitive advantages which Hollywood enjoys by virtue of its dominant position within the international film industry. A big-budget Hollywood-style cinema is simply not feasible for the British film industry (although, as many British directors, actors and writers have demonstrated, successful participation in the making of Hollywood films is).

As a result, the British cinema has had to develop ways of 'living with Hollywood' which avoid direct competition with it. This has involved a strategy of differentiation whereby British film-makers have sought to make films that are different from the Hollywood norm and offer audiences distinctive kinds of film experience. This is clearly the case with both *Trainspotting* and *The Full Monty* which have found an audience despite (and, perhaps, because of) dispensing with many of the normal Hollywood ingredients of action-driven narratives, special effects and stars. Other low-budget British films have, of course, fared much less well and, in many cases, there may be good reasons for this. Nevertheless, the structure of the international film industry is heavily weighted against such films and the challenge for the British film industry must be not only to get films made but also to develop strategies that will foster more diverse forms of distribution and exhibition.

References

Dale, M. *The Movie Game: The Film Business in Britain, Europe and America*. London: Cassell, 1997.
Eberts, J. and Ilott, T. *My Indecision is Final: The Rise and Fall of Goldcrest Films*. London: Faber & Faber, 1990.

Film Policy Review Group *A Bigger Picture: The Report of the Film Policy Review Group*. London: Department for Culture, Media and Sport, 1998.

Finney, A. *The State of European Cinema: A New Dose of Reality*. London: Cassell, 1996.

Hill, J. 'Government policy and the British film industry 1979–90', *European Journal of Communication*, 8, 2 (1993) pp. 203–24, 1993.

Hill, J. 'British Television and Film: The Making of a Relationship' in J. Hill and M. McLoone (eds) *Big Picture, Small Screen: The Relations Between Film and Television*. Luton: John Libbey/University of Luton Press, 1996, pp. 151–76.

Hill, J. *British Cinema in the 1980s: Issues and Themes*. Oxford: Oxford University Press, 1999.

Ilott, T. *Budgets and Markets: A Study of the Budgeting of European Film*. London: Routledge, 1996.

Lewis, R. *Review of the UK Film Industry: Report to BSAC*, mimeo. London: British Screen Advisory Council, 1990.

London Economics *Retailing European Films: The Case of the European Exhibition Industry*, A Report for the Media Business School. London: London Economics, 1993.

Screen Finance 'Studio film revenues set to grow by 6.9 per cent in 1993' (5 May 1993) pp. 8–13.

Screen Finance 'Studio film revenues set to grow by 8.8 per cent in 1994' (4 May 1994) pp. 9–14.

Screen Finance 'Studio revenues set to rise by six per cent' (24 July 1997) pp. 6–10.

Screen Finance 'Multiplex building reaches new peak' (5 February 1998a) pp. 8–12.

Screen Finance 'Nearly 60 per cent of British films stuck in distribution bottleneck' (14 May 1998b) 1, pp. 9–11.

Screen International 'UK Preview 1997' (24 January 1997a) pp. 15–41.

Screen International 'Box Office' (19 September 1997b) pp. 33–5.

Selwood, S. (ed) *Cultural Trends 1995: Cultural Trends in the '90s, Part 1*, Issue 25. London: Policy Studies Institute, 1996.

CHAPTER 6

The Music Industry

PAUL MCDONALD

The music industry plays a significant part in Britain's leisure economy. A 1996 study conducted by the National Music Council estimated that the music sector contributed over £2.5 billion in value added to the UK domestic economy (Dane *et al.*, 1996). Based on this estimate, music equalled the value of other key industries, for example water supply (£2.4 billion in 1994), and was larger than organic and inorganic chemicals (£2.1 billion), electrical motors (£1.9 billion), electronic components (£1.7 billion) and shipbuilding (£1.6 billion). The same study showed UK consumer spending on music estimated at £2.9 billion, with music generating 115,163 full-time jobs, nearly 11,000 of which were in the recording industry.

In its entirety, the music market in Britain is made up from earnings from a range of activities. These can be divided between core and peripheral activities:

CORE

- live performance
- recording and manufacturing
- retailing and distribution of recordings
- composition and exploitation of music works
- manufacture, retailing and distribution of musical instruments
- promotion, management and other agency-related activities
- education and training

PERIPHERAL

- radio, television and film, and advertising
- music press
- merchandising
- dance sector (from ballet to dance clubs)
- the manufacture of audio hardware

This chapter concentrates on those activities related to the manufacture, sale and exploitation of recorded music. Initially the chapter provides an overview of the economic value of recorded music in Britain and the concentration of corporate power which dominates the music market. The chapter then progresses to reflect on two trends which have recently been under debate concerning the impact they are having and are likely to continue to have on the British music industry: electronic commerce and commercial piracy. While the chapter focuses on the domestic market for recorded music, it is impossible to see the British market in isolation. Throughout, the chapter therefore considers how Britain is positioned as part of the wider global music business.

The UK Music Market

The economic value of recorded music results from two sources of earnings. Sales of soundcarriers (that is CDs, tapes and vinyl) are recorded as *units*, representing the *volume* of sales, while earnings from sales are calculated as retail *value*. Information on music sales in the UK is published annually by the British Phonographic Industry (BPI). BPI figures have shown that during the 1990s, at constant values, the music market has seen steady growth (Figure 6.1). A second major source of earnings is the royalty revenues accrued from licensing the rights to use musical works. A glance at the small type printed on any tape or CD will usually identify words to the following effect: 'All rights of the producer and of the owner of the recorded work reserved'; 'Unauthorised copying, hiring, renting, public performance and broadcasting of this record prohibited'. What the tape or disc represents is the licensed authority for the consumer to use the recording for his or her private consumption. Music consumers may purchase a CD but they do not own the music recorded on the disc. Owning the disc does not permit the consumer to legally use the recording for a public performance, for example playing in a club, or to use a tape recorder or other technology to make a copy of the recording. The entire recorded music industry, including sales of soundcarriers, is therefore based on transactions over rights.

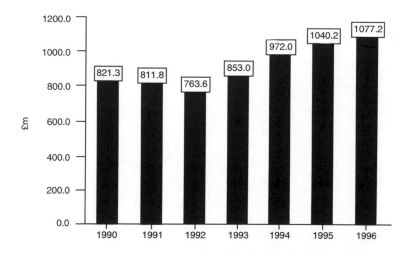

Figure 6.1   UK sales 1990–96 (BPI, 1997a, p. 6)

The right to license the use of the music recorded on the CD remains with the individual or organization who owns the copyright on the musical work. While a CD is a tangible object, the music recorded on the disc is intangible. Copyright law protects the rights of artists and publishers by conceptualizing the intangibility of music creation as 'intellectual property'. Like all property, intellectual property can be traded, purchased and transferred. Copyright law attempts to define the ownership of intellectual property and to control the legitimate uses of such property. After creation, any single musical work may be subject to use in several contexts, including radio and television broadcasts, in-store Muzak, compilation albums, and cover versions by anyone from other signed artists to pub bands. Legislation to protect the value of rights for musical works must be as wide ranging as possible by acknowledging and responding to all the various contexts in which music can be used.

In Britain, there is no intellectual property law specific to music. Instead, musical works are protected under the Copyright, Designs and Patents Act of 1988 (HMSO, 1988). This act specifies that copyright applies immediately an original work is committed to some material form, for example by writing or recording. Economic rights entitle the owner of copyright to fair remuneration resulting from any use of a work he or she owns. With music, the composer is the primary owner of copyright. However, as composers are not primarily business professionals, it is conventional for artists to negotiate the assignment of the rights to their works when signing with a record company to act as the artist's publisher. In turn, collecting societies administer the gathering of royalty revenues from uses of a musical work.

Two main categories of economic rights apply to music: mechanical and performing rights. Mechanical right, or the right to record a piece of music, applies whenever a song is recorded for sale on record, or recorded for the purposes of inclusion in a film, television programme or video. Performing right entitles the holder of a copyright to receive a royalty payment at anytime the music he or she owns is performed in public or broadcast. In Britain, the former are administered by the Mechanical Copyright Protection Society (MCPS), while the latter are managed by the Performing Rights Society (PRS) on behalf of composers and publishers, or the Phonographic Performance Ltd (PPL) representing record companies and their artists.

Mechanical and performing rights represent a significant revenue stream in the music business. In 1996, the MCPS distributed £141,376,438 in royalties to members (MCPS, 1998). The PRS holds over 2.75 million works on file, for a total of 29,366 members, and estimates that each year it processes in excess of 3 million radio performances (PRS, 1997b, 1998b). During 1996, in the UK, the PRS collected a total of £58,078,304 from the uses of music for public performance in a wide variety of contexts (Table 6.1). A further £64,806,986 was collected from radio and television royalties (Table 6.2).

Table 6.1   PRS accounts: public performance royalties 1996

	£	%
Cinemas	2,416,145	4.2
Classical concerts	1,003,008	1.7
Clubs	6,969,121	12.0
Commercials dance halls and discotheques	1,827,611	3.1
Educational establishments	1,036,192	1.8
General purpose	4,441,355	7.6
Hairdressers and waiting rooms	717,815	1.2
Holiday centres	1,167,928	2.0
Hotels, restaurants and cafes	6,917,517	11.9
Industrial premises	2,733,854	4.7
Non-commercial halls	645,740	1.1
Popular concerts	4,940,714	8.5
Public houses	13,151,161	22.7
Shops and stores	5,840,482	10.1
Theatres	375,114	0.7
Transport	1,446,797	2.5
Variety	758,657	1.3
Miscellaneous	1,689,093	2.9
Total public performance royalties	**58,078,304**	**100**
Less expenses	(14,711,201)	
Net distributable revenue	**43,367,103**	

Figures for royalties from United Kingdom, Channel Islands and Isle of Man.
Source: PRS, 1997b, p 44.

Table 6.2   PRS accounts: radio and television
royalties 1996

	£
British Broadcasting Corporation	31,551,529
Independent television and radio	30,846,945
Satellite, Cable, etc.	2,408,512
Total radio and television royalties	**64,806,986**
Less expenses	(10,858,328)
Net distributable income	**53,948,658**

Figures for royalties from United Kingdom, Channel Islands and Isle of Man
Source: PRS, 1997b, p. 44.

As new situations and contexts emerge for the uses of musical works, so the collecting societies must remain responsive to change. For example, with the growth of in-flight entertainment, the PRS had to act on the part of its members to collect revenues from use of music aboard airlines. When British Airways complained to the Copyright Tribunal that they were paying too much for the use of music on their aircraft, PRS investigations revealed the airline to be under-reporting passenger numbers in 1995. After going before the Tribunal, British Airways agreed to pay £300,000 for royalties from 'apparently missed video performances' and the PRS established a formula for calculating revenue due at 6.1 pence per passenger, setting the licence charge for the airline at £700,000 per year (PRS, 1998a).

Globally the world market for recorded music can be divided into key territories representing concentrations of economic activity (Table 6.3). In 1996, with 6.8 per cent of world sales, Britain was ranked fourth behind the USA (30.8 per cent), Japan (17.0 per cent) and Germany (8.0 per cent). Britain has continued to see the value of exports comfortably exceeding imports (Table 6.4). The collecting societies administer royalties for non-British artists when their music is used in the UK, and through reciprocal agreements with affiliated societies overseas, collect royalties for British members whose work is recorded or performed abroad. PRS accounts show that nearly 84 per cent of overseas revenues were received from uses of its members' music by affiliated societies in Western Europe and North America (Table 6.5). Britain is therefore positioned with a concentrated block of the world's wealthiest music markets.

Table 6.3   World music sales by continental territory 1991–96 (US$m)

	Europe	North America	Latin America	Asia	Australasia	Africa	Middle East/Turkey	Total
No. of reporting countries	28 (27 pre-93)	2	17	12	2	10	6	77
1991	10,735.3	8,448.8	1,145.1	5,307.5	610.7	278.6	244.8	26,770.8
1992	10,834.5	9,617.1	1,191.3	6,416.0	601.7	218.5	205.5	29,084.6
1993	10,547.9	10,623.8	1,503.0	7,058.9	612.6	279.9	204.0	30,830.1
1994	11,644.1	12,732.7	2,002.0	8,417.2	684.4	312.7	205.3	35,998.4
1995	13,410.3	13,056.5	1,940.9	9,737.9	790.8	345.9	263.7	39,546.0
1996	13,444.6	13,209.3	2,493.0	9,027.1	936.8	435.9	240.4	39,787.1

Source: compiled and adapted from IFPI, 1997b, p. 107–12.

Table 6.4   Value of UK physical imports and exports of music recordings 1990–96

	Imports £m	Exports £m
1990	109.3	183.8
1991	124.0	196.3
1992	139.9	211.9
1993	158.7	260.0
1994	174.4	283.7
1995	219.5	354.2
1996	278.1	359.2

Source: compiled from *Business and Trade Statistics Ltd* data in BPI, 1997a, pp. 74–5.

Table 6.5   PRS royalties received from overseas affiliated societies 1996

	£
Western Europe	31,551,529
North America	14,423,049
Asia and Australasia	6,593,850
Central and Southern America	1,511,514
Africa and Middle East	1,118,557
Commonwealth of Independent States and Eastern Europe	920,118
Total from affiliates	**63,217,139**
Less expenses	(1,003,738)
Net distributable revenue	**62,213,401**

Source: PRS, 1997b, p. 45.

The size of its own domestic market has meant that the US music industry has a secure foundation from which to exert presence in the global market. The economic and cultural power of the United States continues to provide a cause for concern in the entertainment industries of other nations. While (as we have seen in Chapter 5) Britain's film industry is dominated by American feature films, the music market in Britain has remained dominated by UK talent. US artists do sell well in the UK's singles and album markets. However, despite the powerful presence of American artists in the UK charts, sales figures from the BPI show that British consumers buy considerably more music by artists of UK origin. Indeed, during the 1990s, the gap between sales of UK and US artists in Britain has widened as the proportion of sales for music of US origin gradually decreased (Table 6.6).

Table 6.6   UK music sales by country of artist origin (UK to US comparison) 1990–96

	Singles		Albums	
	UK %	US %	UK %	US %
1990	52.1	31.8	51.5	34.1
1991	59.2	27.3	49.3	35.4
1992	54.4	34.6	48.2	38.7
1993	49.8	31.3	49.3	37.6
1994	51.4	34.0	50.6	37.9
1995	55.9	27.0	55.4	30.5
1996	60.7	25.0	53.1	28.5

Source: compiled from BPI analysis of Gallup/Millward Brown data in BPI, 1997a, pp. 46–7.

While such a trend can be seen as an indicator of consumer loyalty to homegrown talent, there should be caution taken in presuming that such figures represent commitment to any uniquely British pop culture. Music in Britain is a cultural hybrid, the product of influences not only of historically British traditions but of global cultures. Indeed, the diversity of contemporary music in Britain is one of the most immediate indicators of the nation's multicultural identity. The market for recorded music in Britain is therefore not only the product of exchanges in economic trade but also of a plurality of cultural exchanges.

The global shaping of the British music market is also the effect of corporate power in the music industry. Six major companies have continued to dominate the music market in Britain and the world: Bertelsmann Music Group (BMG), EMI Music, MCA Music Entertainment, PolyGram Records, Sony Music Entertainment and Warner Music. Each company has consolidated its presence in the music business by integrating the means for producing, manufacturing and distributing music. The reliability of percentage figures for market shares is open to debate and should only be read as a rough indicator of market presence (Figure 6.2) (*Music Business International*, 1996). However, during the 1990s, the majors appear to have increased their collective share of the UK market from 73 per cent in 1990 to 80 per cent in 1996.

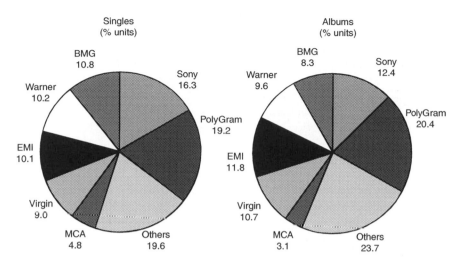

Figure 6.2 Record company market shares 1996 (adapted from BPI, 1997a, p. 46–7)

Where the majors are strongest is in their management of international distribution networks. In Britain, the majors have continued to take upwards of 80 per cent of the distributors' market share for singles and albums during the 1990s (Figure 6.3). As distributors, the majors organize the sale of recordings by artists signed to their own labels or smaller independent labels. The revenue and assets necessary for establishing global distribution networks is beyond the resources of independent companies. Control of distribution therefore prevents smaller companies from competing on the same global scale as the majors.

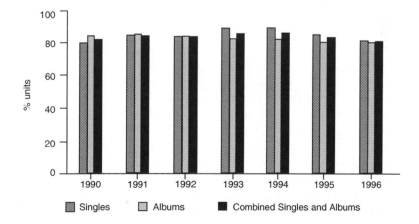

Figure 6.3 Concentration of major record distributors' market share in the UK, 1990–96 (adapted from BPI, 1997a, pp. 40–1, 44–5)

Of the six majors, EMI is regarded as the only British-based company. Like all the majors, EMI is transnational in its reach, organizing production and distribution across all the world's main national markets for music. It is therefore debatable on what terms EMI can be described as 'British'. EMI's British credentials are based on the location of the administrative headquarters in London and the company's association with internationally well-known British artists, including the Beatles and the Spice Girls. Like the entire recorded music industry, EMI origins can be traced back to the manufacturers of sound reproduction hardware who set up business at the end of the nineteenth century. As a result of the depression and the early impact of radio broadcasting, sales of recorded music fell dramatically worldwide, and in April 1931 The Gramophone Company (founded in 1897 by William Barry Owen, the UK agent for Emile Berliner's gramophone manufacturing company) merged with The Columbia Gramophone Company (UK office of the American-based Columbia Phonograph Company) to form Electrical and Musical Industries (renamed EMI in 1971) (Pandit, 1996). During the 1930s, sales of recorded music slumped in the UK, leading to the collapse of many small independent labels, allowing the large recording companies EMI and Decca to achieve a duopolistic control of the British music industry (Frith, 1987).

A significant asset for the majors is their ownership of large back catalogues of recordings. EMI remains the world's largest music publisher with over one million titles in its catalogue. Building the catalogue has become the leading concern for EMI since the 1970s. In 1972, £3.3 million was paid for Affiliated Music Publishers in the UK, followed in 1976 with the £13.7 million acquisition of Columbia Pictures' music publishing division. In 1989, the £187 million acquisition of SBK Entertainment World Inc. bought rights to 250,000 titles, including such well-known numbers as *Singing in the Rain*, *Wizard of Oz* and *Santa Claus is Coming to Town*. Further additions to the catalogue came with the purchase of Filmtrax in 1990, Chrysalis Records in 1991, and the £560 million acquisition of Virgin Music Group in 1992. The catalogue is a stockpile of the record company's intellectual property. New recordings bring in earnings for the record company generally over just a few weeks or months after release. Building a large catalogue makes good business sense, for the catalogue provides the company with more consistent streams of revenue as new and old recordings continually are licensed for public performance or reproduction.

The power of the majors is not only an effect of the presence these companies occupy in the music market. With the exception of EMI, all the majors are part of larger multimedia conglomerates (Table 6.7). Conglomerates are built on the structure of a holding company which owns, often through merger or acquisition, smaller subsidiary companies. It is usual that across the range of companies, the conglomerate is seen to have diversified into a broad range of different business sectors. For the music and media industries, conglomeration and diversification offer key strategic advantages. Recorded music is a leisure good which, unlike food, is not essential to everyday life. Sales of music are affected by relatively unpredictable patterns of consumption dictated by ever-changing trends in public taste. Participation in the music market is therefore a high-risk activity. Through conglomeration, large companies can reap the significant earnings that success in the music business can bring, while also balancing any possible risks or losses from participating in the music market with the company's activity in other relatively less risky business sectors, for example consumer electronics.

Table 6.7   Major record companies

Music company	Bertelsmann Music Group	EMI Records	MCA Records (Universal Music Group)	Polygram Music Group	Sony Music Entertainment Inc.	Warner Music Group
Parent company	Bertelsmann AG	EMI	The Seagram Company Ltd		Sony Corporation	Time Warner Inc.
Other media/ entertainment:						
Filmed entertainment			●		●	●
Radio	●					
Television programming	●		●		●	●
Cable	●		●		●	●
Video	●		●		●	●
Publishing	●					●
Interactive entertainment					●	

Source: Annual reports.

EMI provides an example of the power of conglomerates in the entertainment industry. However, the company also illustrates the business problems that can arise from the creation of large entertainment empires. EMI entered the electronics business through the manufacture of sound and television technology before the Second World War. To extend its involvement in the entertainment and leisure business, in 1970 EMI acquired The Grade Organization, thereby becoming Britain's biggest entertainment conglomerate (Pandit, 1996). However, the acquisition of Grade caused an imbalance between EMI's entertainment and electronics businesses. A downturn in the music market, together with a major loss made by EMI Medical on the research and development of medical scanner technology, weakened the company. Originally attracted by the electronics business of EMI, in 1979 the lighting, consumer electronics and domestic appliances manufacturer Thorn eventually acquired the whole group for £165 million. During the early 1990s, speculation mounted that EMI would be 'unbundled' to form a more valuable stand-alone company (Donovan and Buckingham, 1995). Immediately the demerger of Thorn and EMI was confirmed in August 1996, questions were raised of how long EMI could survive as a separate music company. As the only music major not protected by a larger conglomerate structure, EMI was viewed as ripe for takeover.

Given the size and influence of the majors in the music market, it has become part of the popular imagination to see the music industry as characterized by a David and Goliath struggle of small independent labels against the control of the majors. Often this view is accompanied by the belief that the majors become monolithic purveyors of music for the conservative tastes of a mass market, which is seen to be opposed to the creative innovation of the independents' more niche production. However, this view can be misleading. As Keith Negus (1992) has argued, such beliefs often misjudge the extent to which independents are actually independent. The majors have frequently either bought independent labels or else set up small subsidiary labels in order to sustain an image of independence within the large corporate structure. It is also questionable whether independence necessarily leads to any real alternative to the business practices or creative policies of the majors. While major labels may provide some formulaic music that reproduces existing mass market tastes, equally the majors can only compete by having A&R departments which cultivate the innovative new talent that produce marketable differentiated sounds.

Music Online

Current debates on the capabilities of the World Wide Web (WWW) have recognized new opportunities for the recorded music industry. These possibilities take the forms of online retailing (customers ordering products electronically) and digital delivery (customers purchasing sound files to download onto a computer hard disc). Online retail provides several benefits. Retailers do not have to lease expensive high-street stores. A larger inventory can be offered than is available in most stores. The online store provides extensive choice to consumers in even the most remote locations. Additionally, there is the capacity to offer extensive listings for specialist niche markets which may not be cost-effective given the limited retail space available in many conventional stores.

Forecasts for the impact of electronic commerce on music retailing remain extremely speculative. As yet the most significant gestures towards exploiting online channels for music retail have emerged in the United States. The US example offers some indicators of what can be expected of online retail. Record companies have launched their own online stores, for example

Warners Bros. Records Store (http://store.wbr.com), BMG Music Service (http://www.bmgmusicservice.com) and Sony's The Store (http://thestore. sonymusic.com). While online stores allow record companies to sell directly to customers and circumvent conventional retail chains, it is unlikely that sites dedicated to specific labels will become the future model of online retail. Music consumers are used to the convenience of stores offering titles from many labels under the same roof. It seems unlikely that consumers would choose to replace such convenience with visits to separate stores for PolyGram or BMG titles. Likewise, online customers are unlikely to visit separate sites if choice is provided by one-stop shopping sites. Added to the convenience factor is the general tendency for the majority of music consumers to be led to purchase primarily by knowing an artist, often without any knowledge of, or interest in, the label that the artist records for. The limitations of sites dedicated to a specific label has seen leading US retail chains like WalMart (http://www.wal-mart.com) and Tower Records (http://www.towerrecords. com) enter into online music retail (*Music and Copyright*, 1997a). Music Boulevard (http://www.musicblvd.com) and CDNow (http://www.cdnow. com) have established an early lead in the online retail marketplace.

Based on research conducted in the US, a 1997 report by Jupiter Communications predicted music retailing via the World Wide Web to grow at a rate that would reach $1.6 billion by the year 2002 (*Music and Copyright*, 1997b). In the UK, the opportunities of online retail or digital delivery have to be considered in the context of the general take-up and usage of Internet connectivity. Current evidence would suggest that conditions are not in place to see online transactions make a significant impact on the domestic music market. As part of the BPI's 1998 Music Buyers Survey, a representative sample of 3,235 adults showed that 82 per cent had no access to the Web either at work or home (BPI, 1998a). With an estimated 50,000 music-related sites on the Web, the survey showed that only 5 per cent of the sample visited music sites at any time. The study would suggest that low levels of connectivity and a lack of commitment on the part of users to visit music sites are likely to delay any dramatic growth in online music retailing. It should not be anticipated that the UK will see an increase in online music retailing which is proportionate to the growth forecast by Jupiter in the US.

Price is also an factor to assess when considering the future of online music retail. The Interactive Music and Video Store (IMVS) (http://www.imvs. co.uk), a UK online music retailer established in 1995, formed partnerships with Island and Sony for online retail. In a survey of visitors to their site, IMVS found that over 90 per cent intended to purchase online in the future and use the service to extend their back catalogue (Snell, 1998). Although IMVS had set out to offer titles at discount prices, after postage and packing, the overall cost of an item equalled that of the average high-street store. In comparison, US online stores could offer to UK consumers titles at lower prices even after postal charges. Online retail may therefore result in UK music consumers choosing overseas sites from which to hunt for bargain purchases. A further factor to consider for the music consumer is the cost of phone calls. As long as the charge for local telephone calls remains a significant obstacle to the growth of all Internet use in the UK, it is unlikely that the music market in Britain will witness a boom in online music retailing.

Digital delivery involves the publication of sound files on a server, which are then made available on demand. Fundamental to the exchange of sound files over the Internet is the MPEG sound format, developed at the German research laboratory Fraunhofer IIS Audio and Multimedia in 1987. This audio coding format enables sound data to be compressed without affecting quality (Fraunhofer IIS, 1998). A pioneering example of digital delivery emerged in the UK during 1995 when Cerberus Central Limited (CCL) launched its Digital Jukebox (http://www.cdj.co.uk). The system required users to download the free Cerberus Audio Player and then browse the online catalogue before paying to download single tracks from the Cerberus server. Cerberus quickly established servers in Japan, Brazil and Australia (Cerberus, 1998). The Cerberus example is significant, for not only does it illustrate what a digital delivery system involves, it also indicates the wider questions posed by the impact of digital delivery on the music industry. Central to the power of the major record companies has been their control of the means for the global distribution of music stock. However, by publishing sound files on a server, small companies such as Cerberus can potentially have the same international distribution reach as the majors. One significant difficulty that faced the Digital Jukebox enterprise, however, was that the majors denied Cerberus access to their catalogues. In this way, the majors blocked competition and protected their own plans for online delivery. As a consequence, Cerberus became a niche distributor for many small independent labels, making globally accessible a large number of recordings unavailable in mainstream retail outlets. While the Internet and the World Wide Web may offer small companies the technological potential to compete with the major distributors, from the Cerberus example it is clear that to evaluate the likely impact of digital delivery in the UK, the technological potential of the World Wide Web must be considered in the light of market forces.

An additional factor to take into account when considering the future impact of digital delivery is advertising. While MP3 (digitally compressed) tracks may be published on demand for a potentially huge market, consumers will only demand tracks if they know they are available. Availability must therefore be accompanied by awareness. Conventional music retailing has relied on coordinated marketing campaigns across print and broadcast advertising to make consumers aware enough to step inside a store. The same mix must apply to attracting customers to a virtual store. As long as the majors remain the only companies with revenues large enough to run globally coordinated marketing campaigns, it seems unlikely that companies like Cerberus will be able to effectively promote the artists in their catalogue and so attract customers to purchase online.

Piracy

Like all property, intellectual property can be stolen. At its most basic level, piracy involves the infringement of the mechanical right belonging to a musical work. Although illegal recordings are often given the blanket title of 'pirate', the BPI's Anti-Piracy Unit applies the following classifications to distinguish between different forms of illegal manufacture:

Counterfeit The unauthorised copying of the sound of the original recording, as well as the artwork, label, trade mark and packaging... to mislead consumers and make them think they are buying the genuine article.

Bootleg The recording, duplication and sale of a performance such as a live concert or broadcast without the permission of the artist or record company.

Pirate Unauthorised duplications of music from legitimate recordings for commercial gain without the permission of the rights' owner. [These] may be compilations of tracks which have not been released together before. The packaging and presentation of a pirate copy does not usually resemble a legitimate commercial release. (BPI, 1997b, p. 3)

Illegal recording activity grew as access to the means of cassette tape recording increased. When the CD was first launched in the early 1980s, one of the benefits the industry saw in the digital format was the obstacle it provided to illegal copying. However, rather than prevent illegal recordings, digital reproduction has aided illegal manufacturers, enabling higher quality copies to be produced than was previously possible with vinyl discs or magnetic tape. Home taping now appears to have become accepted by the music industry in Britain as an inevitable and inescapable part of consumer behaviour. While the free exchange of tapes between friends may detract from possible sales, what is of greatest concern to the music industry is commercial piracy, whereby organized groups mass reproduce illegal recordings for sale around the world.

Piracy is now endemic in the world's music market. In figures reported by the International Federation of the Phonographic Industry (IFPI), during 1996 an estimated 1.5 billion cassettes and 350 million CDs were sold around the world, with a combined value of over US$5 billion (IFPI, 1997a). Based on the quantity of seized stock, Britain does not appear to have experienced the same levels of piracy found in other national markets (Table 6.8). In 1995 the piracy level in the UK was believed to stand at 1 per cent, compared to 73 per cent in Russia and some Latin American nations, for example Bolivia (87 per cent), Ecuador (75 per cent), or El Salvador (84 per cent).

Table 6.8   Estimated market for illegal recordings in the UK

	1995	1996	1997	% Change 1996–97
Cassettes				
Bootleg	100,000	80,000	72,000	−10
Counterfeit	1,000,000	500,000	437,500	−12
Pirate	200,000	200,000	180,000	10
TOTAL	1,300,000	780,000	689,500	12
CDs				
Bootleg	1,000,000	800,000	720,000	−10
Counterfeit	400,000	300,000	360,000	20
Pirate	500,000	500,000	500,000	–
TOTAL	1,900,000	1,600,000	1,580,000	−1
Total Units				
Bootleg	1,100,000	880,000	792,000	−10
Counterfeit	1,400,000	800,000	797,500	–
Pirate	700,000	700,000	680,000	−3
TOTAL	3,200,000	2,380,000	2,269,500	−5
Retail Value				
Bootleg	£15,500,000	£12,400,000	£11,160,000	−10
Counterfeit	5,400,000	3,300,000	3,472,500	5
Pirate	3,600,000	3,600,000	3,540,000	−2
TOTAL	£24,500,000	£19,300,000	£18,172,500	−6

Source: British Phonographic Industry, 1998b, p. 1.

Although operating underground, the illegal trade in music recordings appears to uncannily reflect the global economics of the legitimate market. Illegal stock seized in the UK is frequently found to have been imported by using global avenues of distribution. The illegal market delivers stock using global networks to circumvent import controls and obscure the source of orders. Only a fraction of the illegal market in the UK is manufactured in Britain. Asia and Eastern Europe are the leading territories for the production of illegal CDs, with China, Hong Kong, Taiwan, Macau, Malaysia, Russia, Bulgaria and the Czech Republic reported as the main offenders (IFPI, 1998b). Bulgaria in particular has been identified as the source for many illegal recordings found in the UK (Millar, 1997). In 1997, five CD plants were responsible for illegal production in Bulgaria. With two of the plants situated on state-owned land, it was believed that these illegal manufacturers operated with the full knowledge of the Bulgarian government.

To combat the illegal trade, the IFPI has introduced technical initiatives to identify the origin of recordings, together with actively petitioning for international standards in legislation to halt the flow of illegal stock. To monitor the use and reproduction of sound recordings, the IFPI introduced the International Standard Recording Code (ISRC), a twelve-digit alphanumeric code identifying the country, first owner, year of recording, and designation of a recording (IFPI, 1996). This digital fingerprint, encoded at the pre-mastering stage of a recording, is designed to aid rights administration and income distribution, but can also identify the origin of tracks which are illegally reproduced.

Just as the real world music market is divided between legal and illegal trade, so the network economy has become an avenue for the illegal exchange of musical works. As the CD helped rather than hindered the illegal trade, so the nascent potential of digital delivery over the Internet has already raised new issues over protection against further increases in illegal reproduction (Lawrence, 1995; Green, 1997). It is the same benefits of low cost and global reach that make digital delivery attractive for both legal and illegal trade. Sound files can be uploaded and downloaded relatively easily and cheaply. Online delivery creates significant difficulties for rights protection. In 1997 the PRS launched a trial online licence for supplying music in any form, from short clips of less than 30 seconds up to continuous feeds (PRS, 1997a, 1998c).

With users in Britain capable of downloading illegal tracks stored on servers situated in other parts of the world, national legislation alone cannot protect the distribution of works. Moves have been made to internationally harmonize copyright legislation and British law reflects commitments made by various multilateral conventions and treaties on intellectual property law. However, existing copyright law does not effectively cover the publishing of protected works by on-demand services over the World Wide Web. As part of the modernization of international agreements over copyright protection, in December 1996 the World Intellectual Property Organisation (WIPO) drafted the WIPO Performances and Phonograms Treaty (WPPT) at Geneva. Protecting the rights of performers and the producers of phonograms, the treaty included 'the right of making available':

> the exclusive right of authorizing and making available to the public...
> performances fixed in phonograms, by wire or wireless means, in such a
> way that members of the public may access them from a place and at a time
> individually chosen by them. (WIPO, 1996, p. 7)

This new article is broad enough to encompass the publishing of sound files over the World Wide Web and, once the treaty is ratified, the article will be integrated into UK law.

To monitor the illegal online trade, at the end of 1997 the IFPI commissioned a project to scan the Web for MP3 files (IFPI, 1998a). These moves mark the beginning of strategies for the policing of illegal trade in a networked society and represent 'the first real taming of the Web by corporate interests' (Lillington, 1998). However, even with the relative ease of exchanging illegal sound files online, in Britain the most significant impediment to widespread theft could very well be the same factors limiting the growth in electronic commerce faced by the legal retail trade.

Conclusion

Recently the music industry has entered the political agenda in Britain. Following the change of government in May 1997, the music industry became a key feature in Labour's policies for economic growth. Within a few months of the new government taking office, the Department of National Heritage was replaced by the new Department of Culture, Media and Sport (DCMS), tackling a wider cultural remit, including the music business. The DCMS subsequently set up the Creative Industries Task Force, whose membership counted leading names with experience of the music industry, including Richard Branson and Robert Devereux from the Virgin Group, Alan McGee, the founder of Creation Records, and Mick Hucknall, lead singer with Simply Red.

Speaking in New York on 22 October 1997, Chris Smith, the new government's Culture Secretary, addressed representatives of the American music industry and Wall Street financiers to encourage further US investment in British musical talent. Smith argued that, for both the US and the UK, the creative industries had become increasingly important as this sector was now contributing greater value to the national economy than many traditional manufacturing industries (DCMS, 1997a). Indeed, analysis of industrial performance in the UK has shown that for the year 1995–96, in terms of return on capital, recorded music occupied top ranking ahead of pharmaceuticals and electronics (Inter Company Comparisons, 1997). The strength of Britain's music industry is just one indicator of the trend that has seen the service industries rival manufacturing in the shaping of the domestic economy. However, if music is to remain a significant component of the British economy, it will be necessary for the industry to be responsive to new conditions shaping the music market. An immediate concern must be the impact of the network economy on the music market.

While the World Wide Web holds enormous potential for the traffic of entertainment services, the future of online retail and delivery for music sales remain uncertain. In Britain, levels of connectivity will grow and as more homes come online, then electronic commerce will increase. However, it is unlikely that the networked economy will bring about any abrupt change in patterns of music consumption or a radical challenge to the corporate organization of the music business. Online retail simply revises the way in which customers purchase soundcarriers. With mail order clubs already exploiting the convenience of ordering music recordings by telephone, online retail simply adds to the possible range of methods by which customers can places orders for delivery by mail.

Digital delivery however has the potential to bring about a more significant change in how the music market operates. With digital delivery, the costs associated with the manufacture of soundcarriers, the purchase or rental of warehouse storage and the transportation of stock are removed. While this will offer new cost-effective means for the majors to sell their catalogues, it will also provide opportunities for smaller companies to enter into the virtual marketplace. However, the potential impact of such small-scale operators should not be over-estimated. Digital distributors will still need advertising support to attract buyers. Major record companies and large retail chains are likely to retain their dominance in the music business because they have the capital to invest in high-profile advertising campaigns, both through the traditional forms of print, broadcast and outdoor media, and also to buy ad space on other World Wide Web sites. Without such support, small online labels and distributors lack the resources to attract customers or promote their releases. It should be anticipated that, in the network economy, the music market will still remain under the oligarchic control of the majors.

While spreading business internationally has distinct advantages for the major record companies, it also makes EMI and all transnational companies vulnerable to fluctuations in the global market. In 1996, the year EMI was demerged from Thorn, growth in the US market levelled off. EMI's share of US sales fell to 9.7 per cent and the return of unsold stock from US retailers rose to 20 per cent. Commentary on EMI's performance in the US criticized the company's cosy reliance on its back catalogue, together with the costs of commitments to major stars, as factors preventing the company from effectively developing new talent (Buckingham, 1997). Further problems confronted EMI as the collapse of the Southeast Asian economies during 1998 was estimated to have wiped £25 million off annual profits (BBC, 1998a). The Asian crisis and the effect of a strong pound on exports and imports were the main reasons identified for EMI announcing a fall in profits from £380 million in 1996/97 to £307 million in 1997/98 (BBC, 1998b). These problems have raised the very real possibility that EMI will be sold in the not too distant future. Depending on the eventual buyer, the sale of EMI will affect the profile of corporate power in the UK market but is also likely to diminish any claim to a 'British' presence in the global market.

References

BBC Asia Takes Spice Out of EMI Profits, http://news.bbc.co.uk/hi/english/business/newsid_49000/49952.stm (27 May) 1998a.

BBC EMI Faces the Music as Profits Slump, http://news. bbc.co.uk/hi/english/business/newsid_101000/10641.stm (27 May) 1998b.

BPI *BPI Statistical Handbook 1997*. London: British Phonographic Industry, 1997a.

BPI *Protecting the Value of British Music*. London: British Phonographic Industry, 1997b.

BPI 'Internet access', *Market Information*, 101 (1998a).

BPI 'Piracy' *Market Information*, 99 (1998b).

Buckingham, L. 'Out of tune with Uncle Sam' *Guardian* (31 May 1997) p. 26.

Cerberus Company History. http://www.cdj.co.uk/index.html (8 June 1998).

Dane, C., Feist, A. and Laing, D. *The Value of Music*. London: National Music Council, 1996.

DCMS *Chris Smith Urges American Music Industry to Invest in British Talent and Innovation*. http://www.coi.gov.uk/coi/depts/GHE/coi3699d.ok (30 May 1998) (1997a).

Donovan, P. and Buckingham, L. 'Music biz awaits sale of century', *Guardian* (22 July 1995) p. 40.

Fraunhofer IIS 'MPEG Audio Layer-3: History'. http://www. iis.fhg.de/amm/techinf/coding/layer3/index.html (2 June 1998).

Frith, S. 'The Making of the British Record Industry 1920–64', in J. Curran, A. Smith and P. Wingate (eds) *Impacts and Influences: Essays on Media Power in the Twentieth Century*. London: Methuen, 1987, pp. 278–90.

Green, D. 'Music pirates make whoopee on the Net', *Daily Telegraph*, (2nd September 1997), pp. 4–5.

HMSO *Copyright, Design and Patents Act 1988*. London:. Her Majesty's Stationary Office, 1988.

IFPI *ISRC – Essential to Rights Administration in the Digital Age*. London: IFPI, 1996.

IFPI *Pirate Sales '96*. London: IFPI, 1997a.

IFPI *The Recording Industry in Numbers '97*. London: IFPI, 1997b.

IFPI 'IFPI gears up for fight against internet piracy', *Network*, 1 (1998a) p. 3.

IFPI 'IFPI "Going for the Jugular" as music piracy reaches US $5 Billion', *Network*, 1 (1998b) p. 1.

Inter Company Comparisons Ltd. *UK Industrial Performance Analysis 1997/1998*. Hampton: ICC Business Publications, 1997.

Lawrence, A. 'Publish and be robbed?' *New Scientist*, 145 (1995) pp. 32–7.

Lillington, K. 'No! It's not OK, computer', *Guardian: Online*, (16 April 1998) pp. 2–3.

MCPS 'MCPS Consolidated Profit and Loss Account 1996'. http://www.mcps. co.uk/mcps4_2.html (25 March 1998).

Millar, S. 'Alarm as music piracy reaches record level', *Guardian* (1 March 1997) p. 3.

Music and Copyright 'Major record companies follow music retailers into online retailing' (10 September 1997a) p. 3.

Music and Copyright 'Music internet retailing set to reach $1.6bn in, 2002 says Jupiter Report' (27 August 1997b) p. 3.

Music Business International 'Market shares: only part of the story', 6, 2 (1996) p. 13.

Negus, K. *Producing Pop: Culture and Conflict in the Popular Music Industry*. London: Edward Arnold, 1992.

Pandit, S. *From Making to Music: The History of Thorn EMI*. London: Hodder & Stoughton, 1996.

PRS (1997a) 'PRS Launches Trial for Licensing Music on the Net'. http://www. prs.co.uk/7_2.html (25 March 1998).

PRS *PRS: Yearbook and Report and Accounts 97/98*. London: Performing Rights Society, 1997b.

PRS (1998a) 'Copyright Tribunal – Interim Decision British Airways v. PRS'. http://www.prs.co.uk/7_16.html (25 March 1998).

PRS (1998b) 'Facts and figures'. http://www.prs.co.uk/6_1.html (25 March 1998).

PRS (1998c) 'Music licensing and the internet'. http://www.prs. co.uk/3_0.html (25 March 1998).

Snell, T. 'Online market can boost sales', *Music Week*, (2 May 1998) p. 8.

WIPO (1996) WIPO *Performances and Phonograms Treaty*. http://www. wipo.org/eng/diplconf/distrib/95dc.htm (8 June 1998).

CHAPTER 7

New Media

JAMES CORNFORD AND KEVIN ROBINS

In the 1990s, we have seen some dramatic developments in new media technologies. These have given rise to eager speculation and anticipation about a new media order. According to a recent article in the *Financial Times*:

> We are in the midst of a digital maelstrom which is reshaping the traditional computing, telecommunications and consumer electronic industries and promises unprecedented choice for consumers and a new multimedia-rich world of information. (Taylor, 1998)

The excitement is about a technological revolution that promises to fundamentally transform media industries, products and services. A new era of abundance and diversity in entertainment and information is anticipated. However, we are sceptical about this kind of technological enthusiasm. Arguments about technological revolution are by no means new – indeed, they have been used to promote every technological innovation in communications media in the twentieth century (cinema, radio, vinyl records, television, magnetic tapes, video, CDs, CD-ROMs and, now the Internet) (see Robins and Webster, 1987).

Our own approach to new media is more cautious than that of the pundits and forecasters. We want to consider what substance there is to the inflated claims and predictions that are being made. In this chapter we situate technological innovations associated with new media in a wider economic and social setting and draw attention to the significant continuities between new media and old. Many of the new developments, technological and economic, are linked to the opening up of new global media spaces, but our remit here is to investigate the new media in Britain.

New Media – What's New?

What do we mean by 'new media'? It is not just a question of new technologies, but of technological innovation combined with market innovation. More specifically, it is a question of a particular technological development – digital storage, manipulation and distribution of images, text, sounds and video – creating new market opportunities, including:

- Games (in cartridges or CD-ROM format, both for specific 'platforms', such as the Sony PlayStation or the Nintendo N64, and for personal computers [PCs]).
- Edutainment (which merges education with entertainment) and reference products (mainly on CD-ROM).
- Interactive digital television (through terrestrial, cable or satellite signals).
- Electronic publishing and online services, mainly now on the World Wide Web (the Internet-based means of distributing text, pictures and sounds).

For the present we exclude established cable and satellite television, which are an extension of traditional media, and focus on entertainment and information markets. What is it that is distinctively new about new media? We would suggest that digital technologies are associated with three key market innovations:

- *Convergence* – Where traditional (or analogue, that is, using continuous variations in some physical property such as the frequency of the electronic spectrum) media use a variety of non-compatible formats and techniques in their processing of content, new media share a common format – the ones and zeros of digital code. Thus, different modes of presenting information – text, still and moving images, voice and music – can now all be combined in one product or service. This common means of storage and distribution is bringing about a gradual convergence of previously distinct markets and industries. This also engenders new kinds of competitive strategies between corporations.

  Convergence is also becoming apparent at the level of media devices or 'platforms'. The telephone, the television, the personal computer and the video-game machine are rivals in the race to develop a multi-purpose 'information appliance' (Oftel, 1998). The Internet provides voice telephony, video 'webcasting' and audio, as well as text and (still) pictures. Television sets are being adapted to enable them to browse the web. Even telephones can have screens and web browsers built into them.

  There is a gradual convergence of a number of relatively distinct technologies/industries towards the holy grail of the 'information age' – the ubiquitous information appliance that is able to surf the net and interrogate multimedia databases, play music and speech, show films and video, run software, support a telephone conversation and send e-mail.
- *Compression* – Digital technologies enable the compression of signals, allowing for the proliferation of 'channels' as each wire or section of the broadcast spectrum can carry many more times the volume of information than is possible using analogue techniques. This in turn makes possible the development of new markets based on 'narrowcasting' – the transmission of media content to niche or even individualized consumer segments. Market research specialist John Clements envisages 'TV that goes beyond the bounds of entertainment, providing personally relevant information

and opportunities... Post-2000 it will change the face of TV and the ways in which users interact with their TV sets' (quoted in Taylor, 1998). Nicholas Negroponte (1995) refers to this individualization of media as a shift from the 'Daily Us' – where news and entertainment formats are tailored to broad groups – to the 'Daily Me' – where news and entertainment are personalized for the individual reader or viewer. The proliferation of channel capacity also allows for innovations in the scheduling of programmes – for example, 'Near Video-On-Demand' (NVOD), which involves the same programme being broadcast on a number of channels but with staggered start times, thus enabling the viewer to always be within a few minutes of the start of the programme. BSkyB, for example, has plans for its digital satellite television service to dedicate 50 channels to NVOD, offering, several films starting at 15- or 30-minute intervals (Murphy, 1998).

- *Interactivity* – Interactive media are responsive in 'real time' to user input: through clicking on links or selecting menu items with a mouse, through typing input with a keyboard, through a joystick or through voice commands. In some cases, the interaction is with information that is locally stored on a discrete product, for example, a computer game on a cartridge or CD-ROM, or a multimedia encyclopaedia on a CD-ROM. In others, the interaction is with remote databases stored on centralized computers, in the form of a service that is updateable and paid for on the basis of usage time or the number of 'items' used. Increasingly, these two modes are merging, with games and 'edutainment' titles increasingly being 'web aware', coupling the capacity of CD-ROMs to carry large volumes of data, with the Internet's ability to provide updated information from remote databases and to link to other users. The World Wide Web epitomises interactive media. As the European Managing Director of the software company Real Networks puts it:

> The net is interactive, it lets users select the stories that they want to watch in the order they want to watch them. They can also mix and match – getting their socio-political news from the BBC and their world news from CNN. Users can get the TV and radio stations they want from anywhere. (quoted in Shillingford, 1998)

While the new media pundits and prophets seek to persuade us that digital technologies are displacing the old order, we would emphasize that what is actually the case is an accommodation between old and new. Even at the level of the basic technologies, new media rely heavily on established networks and technologies – thus, to use a CD-ROM one requires a personal computer; to use a game console one requires a television set; and to connect to the Internet we require a telephone line. At the level of content, continuity is even clearer – new media are often heavily reliant on repackaged older media content (Microsoft's *Encarta Multimedia Encyclopedia*, for example, is based on Funk and Wagnall's *Encyclopedia*, the *Sunday Times* website is substantially reliant on content from the *Sunday Times* paper, and so on).

And, finally, let us also be clear that, while interactivity is often trumpeted as something wholly new, the idea and aspiration has been around for a long time. We have been able to write to newspapers and phone-in to television and radio programmes for many years. What the new technologies, in fact, permit is a speed-up in the pace at which interaction can take place – almost in 'real time' – and the possibility of actually building interactivity into the heart of new media products.

New Media Order?

Many visions of new media have seen new technologies as inevitably leading to new structures and practices in the media. The most common discourses on the new media share a vision of decentralization, the collapse of media empires, a new level playing field, and a perfect marketplace of ideas. From this perspective the new media technologies are seen as having such radical potential – in terms of their costs, availability, accessibility, and ease of operation – that traditional media systems will be washed away in a flood of decentralized, grassroots activity.

Nicholas Negroponte, a co-founder of the MIT Media Lab (an influential source of new media research and development based at the Massachusetts Institute of Technology), is perhaps the best known exponent of this view. For him, the advent of digital media – what he refers to as moving 'bits' of information instead of 'atoms' of paper – will have dramatic consequences for media structures. He asks:

> If moving these bits around is so effortless, what advantage would the large media companies have over you and me?… Wholly new content will emerge from being digital, as will new players, new economic models and a likely cottage industry of information and entertainment providers. (Negroponte, 1995, pp. 19, 18)

Here the future is presented as one in which the 'mass' media that we have known are replaced by a myriad of small specialist information and entertainment providers: 'the information industry will become more of a boutique business. Its marketplace is the global information highway' (Negroponte, 1995, p. 85).

Wired, the bible of the new technocracy, echoes this theme, albeit with some important caveats. In the series 'Encyclopaedia of the New Economy', John Browning and Spencer Reiss define New Media as follows:

> New Media. Communications for all, by all.

Old Media divides the world into producers and consumers: we're either authors or readers, broadcasters or viewers; entertainers or audiences. One-to-many communications, in the jargon. New media, by contrast, gives everybody the chance to speak as well as listen. Many speak to many and the many speak back.

That doesn't mean tomorrow's prime-time television will consist of home videos and talk shows beamed live from the neighbour's living room. Talent – and marketing muscle – matters, and there will always be hit shows and stars. Television and other old media are not going to vanish, and neither will their proprietors. But they will face new competitors and transformed markets.

New media enables even the smallest, most scattered electronic communities to share – or sell – what they know, like and do. What broadcasting atomized, new media brings back together. (Browning and Reiss, 1998, p. 105)

We might see this as the marketing discourse of the new media interests (Robins, 1997). It is clearly in the interests of this new industry lobby to emphasize the social and political possibilities inherent in the new technologies. But of course, there is a rhetorical trick in their ideal of a media technological revolution. As Nicholas Garnham pointed out a over decade ago, 'this trick is played by concentrating upon the technical potentialities rather than upon the social relations that will determine the form in which those potentialities are realised, and by denying history, by exaggerating the novelty of the process in question' (Garnham, 1983, p. 14).

In reality, the new media are far from being the anarchic, decentralized, democratic infrastructure of a new social and political order. There are clearly new players in the media sector, but the game that they are playing is much the same as it always was. What is most apparent in the new media order is the growing involvement of communications corporations in global strategies of competition for control of lucrative transnational markets. While there are some interesting newcomers to the race – which is what Paul Taylor (1998) calls 'the race for "eyeballs"' – most of the big names in the new media era belong to the familiar and established players in the traditional media, software or telecommunications industries (the Hollywood studios and US TV networks, the BBC and the ITV companies, News International, BT, Microsoft). From an economic perspective, enormous barriers to entry confront any potential competitor. Through a series of assertive tactics – alliances, mergers, takeovers, licensing deals, patents and copyright restrictions – the big players seek to monopolize key, strategic links in the new media value chain.

The new technologies may give consumers more choice (from an expanded set of options), but they also enable the producers of new media products and services to monitor, segment and target audiences in new ways (Gandy, 1993; Lyon, 1998). As Michael Dawson and John Bellamy Foster observe:

The interactive nature of the information superhighway offers the possibility of detailed information on each potential buyer… Nowadays the focus is on 'hyper-targeting' in which the market segment is frequently an individual household or even an individual. (Dawson and Foster, 1996, p. 57)

The new media thus constitute a major leap forward in consumer surveillance, based on the dramatically enhanced capacity of the new technologies to monitor and process the data generated by interactive media usage (a huge extension of the crude sales data and viewing and readership surveys used by traditional media).

A further factor that plays in favour of large and established interests is the cost structure of new media production and distribution. For example, Nick Croydon, joint managing director of multimedia producer Flagtower, describes the complex economic equation of CD-ROM production – one of the most developed or mature parts of the multimedia market:

Each product costs about £500,000 to make, and after distribution, retail and packaging costs we get around £10 to £11 per unit. So you are looking at about 50,000 units to break even on your production costs – and that's pre-marketing. (quoted in Dyer, 1996, p. 116)

These figures are comparable to those that are quoted by Kay Henning (1997) in her *Financial Times* Management Report, which gives a breakeven point of around 40,000 to 50,000 units for most interactive CD-ROM products. Professional multimedia producers in the UK, then, have to confront the familiar media cost structure of high initial costs of production, which need to be spread across a large number of consumers if a particular product is to be profitable. As Henning goes on to point out, with some 10,000 titles on offer in 1995, and some 50 million units sold in that year, the *average* sale is just 5,000 units, implying that the vast majority of CD-ROM titles will make a substantial loss for their producers. It is thus imperative that firms producing CD-ROMs either have very deep pockets, which will allow them to produce several loss-making products in a row before they have a 'hit', or that they produce a large number of products simultaneously, with the expectation that a small number of profitable 'hits' will cancel out the large number of unsuccessful products.

To take another example, that of advertising-funded websites, the issue is slightly different – in so far as it is a question of selling space to advertisers rather than selling products to consumers – but the predicament is very much the same. Forrester Research, a technology consultancy specializing in Internet economics, estimates that maintaining and managing a high-profile World Wide Web site costs an average of $3.1 million per year (*The Economist*, 1998). With such high costs, the site needs to ensure that it attracts a huge number of browsers who will download and view web pages containing advertisements (in the industry jargon 'page impressions'). Such sites therefore need to be marketed – that is to say, they must themselves be advertised in more traditional media – and this simply adds to the cost. 'So what', *The* (usually upbeat) *Economist* asks, 'happened to the Internet's promise?':

> Once upon a time, some hoped and others feared, it seemed to be turning the world upside down by providing a new generation with the means of distributing output at a fraction of the cost of television or print. But distribution costs seem to matter less to the businesses concerned than the marketing and maintaining of a site. (*The Economist*, 1998, p. 101)

While the distribution of content via the Internet may be relatively cheap, the costs of production and marketing for an economically viable web site remain high. The technologies may be new, then, but the underlying economic logics remain the same. For all their established strengths, it is, of course, the case that the new ways of delivering media content are presenting the larger players with new challenges and new uncertainties, bringing them into competition with companies previously operating in different markets. This trend is leading to new patterns of competition and also to new kinds of strategic alliance. For example, among the leading publishers in the reference and 'edutainment' CD-ROM markets (see Figures 7.1 and 7.2) there are examples of:

- software companies (such as Microsoft)
- traditional paper publishers (such as Dorling Kindersley)
- film and television studios (such as Disney)
- newer players (such as Flagtower, Europress or GSP).

In the Internet services market there is a similar range of players, from a slightly different range of industries:

- telecommunications companies (for example BT Internet, Cable and Wireless)
- cable television and telecommunications companies (for example Cable Internet)
- computer software companies (for example the Microsoft Network – MSN)
- entertainment companies (for example Bertlesmann, part owner of AOL)
- newer Internet start-ups (for example Demon – now bought by the telecommunications arm of the Scottish electricity generator, Scottish Power; UUNET – now part of the rapidly expanding US telecommunications operator WorldCom; and Easynet – which has recently become a telecommunications company).

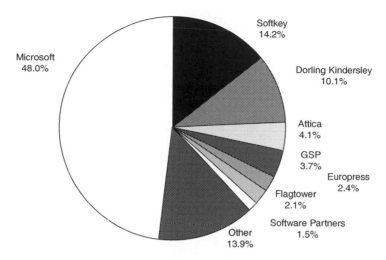

Figure 7.1   UK CD-ROM reference market share 1996 (unit sales)
(*Screen Digest*, 1997)

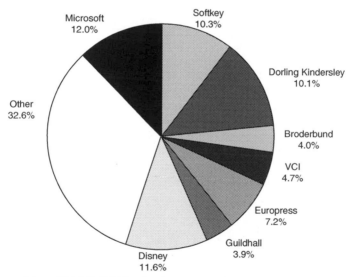

Figure 7.2   UK CD-ROM edutainment market shares 1996 (unit sales)
(*Screen Digest*, 1997)

Finally, in considering the construction of new media industries and markets, we must have regard to questions of regulation (both formal and informal). A common argument from the techno-futurist lobby is that the proliferation of channel capacity – through the more efficient use of wires and radio spectrum that digital compression allows – has undermined the traditional rationale for state regulation of the communications sector. Nicholas Negroponte, for example, argues that the need for regulation will decline in a new 'post scarcity' media environment: 'Guaranteed plurality,' he argues, 'might require less legislation than one would expect because the monolithic empires of mass media are dissolving into an array of cottage industries' (Negroponte, 1995, p. 57). While it is indeed true that the case for regulation on the basis of spectrum scarcity is no longer as robust as it was, it must be pointed out that there are other grounds for government intervention in new media markets.

One concern is that the focus of media control has shifted from control of the spectrum to ownership and control of certain key 'gateways' to services and information. These gateways could take any one of a number of forms – web-browser technology, set-top boxes (which decode and provide access to digital services), even 'portal sites' (electronic programme guides and search engines on the Web). Another focus of concern is the ownership of certain key media properties – above all Hollywood studio back catalogues – which are seen as vital to the economic viability of many new media services, giving their owners a dominant economic position in new media markets. There are also cultural, political and social arguments for sector-specific regulation of new media markets. Here the concern may be with sustaining national cultural identity against the perceived logic of globalization, or it may be a matter of ensuring cultural pluralism and diversity of voices. Finally, there are social arguments for the regulation of media to ensure the universal availability of certain services to all, regardless of means and location.

In thinking about the future of the media, then, it is a question of recognizing the actual economic forces that confound the technological visions, and also of considering the appropriate regulatory mechanisms to ensure that important social values – such as political pluralism, democratic participation and cultural diversity – are taken into account.

New Media in Britain

We will now turn to consider the actual realities of new media in the British context. In spite of the much vaunted digital convergence associated with new media, there are still relatively clear demarcations between different formats, markets, technologies and services. In this section, we want to look at three areas of particular interest in the UK – Internet publishing, digital broadcasting and computer or video games.

The Internet and the World Wide Web: The Logic of Convergence

The Internet, in particular the World Wide Web, is the media domain in which the logic of convergence is most manifest. With the capacity to provide interactive access to text, pictures, speech and music, and – with more band-width or better compression – even video material, the Internet seems to many to be the basis for a new integrated entertainment, communications and information space (for a readable history of the development of the Internet, see Kitchin, 1998).

In Britain, the growth of the Internet has been on a par with most other developed economies (see Figure 7.3), and its household penetration, according to surveys, lags behind only the smaller and richer countries of Scandinavia, together with Luxembourg and the Netherlands (see Figure 7.4). The market research company NOP reports that:

> The number of households in Britain with access to the Internet has more than doubled from just under 400,000 in June 1996 to 960,000 in June 1997, according to NOP Research Group's most recent Internet User Profile Study... This suggests that around one in twenty five of all households in Britain are now linked to the Internet.
>
> ...Overall, NOP's research shows that some six million adults in Great Britain used the Internet in the twelve months to June 1997 and around nine million adults are expected to have used it by June 1998. (NOP, http://www.maires.co.uk/)

BT forecasts that 90 per cent of the country will have an Internet connection by 2010 (Select Committee on Media, Culture and Sport, 1998).

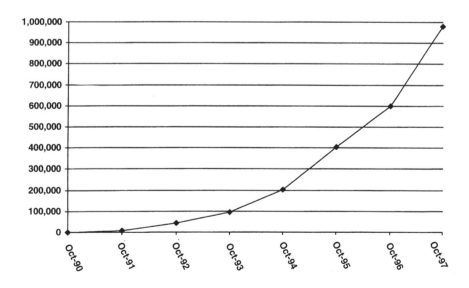

Figure 7.3   Growth in the number of UK Internet hosts (.uk suffix) October 1990 to October 1997 (http:\\www.ripe.net [Résaux IP Européns])

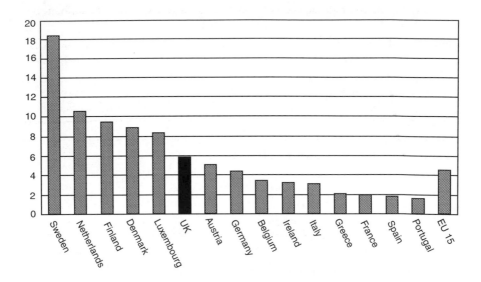

Figure 7.4 Percentage of respondents with home use of the Internet/World Wide Web, Europe, March 1997
(Eurobarometer, http://www.ispo.cec.be/infosoc/promo/pubs/poll97)

The rate of expansion is apparent when one considers that the first commercial provider of dial-up Internet access to households in Britain, Demon Internet, was established in June 1992 and was approaching 200,000 subscribers by May 1998. Demon is now just one of a number of players in a domestic market now dominated by a dozen or so companies (see Table 7.1). Compuserve and AOL (which have now merged) lead the field, with Demon, Microsoft, BT (both in its own right and together with News International in LineOne) and Virgin in the top seven places. Other strong contenders include Cable Internet (owned by a group of cable companies) and the telecommunications and cable company, Cable & Wireless. The number of such major actors entering the Internet market suggests a gathering momentum.

Some of the companies mentioned above (for example Demon) simply provide Internet 'connectivity' and currently have no hand in providing media 'content' and are therefore of limited interest. What is far more significant are those companies and joint ventures that not only provide access to the public areas of the Internet, but also provide 'exclusive content', available to subscribers only. These companies are the mainstream of media and information provision, competing with traditional media for audiences and advertising revenues.

Table 7.1   Internet Magazine's estimates of total 'live' Internet subscribers by ISP, May 1998

Service Provider	Estimated number of 'live' UK subscribers (low estimate)	Estimated number of 'live' UK subscribers (high estimate)
CompuServe	410,000	420,000
AOL	400,000	420,000
Demon	180,000	190,000
Microsoft Network (UK)	130,000	145,000
BT Internet	110,000	130,000
Virgin Net	95,000	105,000
LineOne	70,000	80,000
Global Internet	70,000	75,000
UUNET Pipex Dial	45,000	50,000
EasyNet Group	40,000	45,000
Cable & Wireless	35,000	40,000
Direct Connection	26,000	29,000
Which?Online	23,000	26,000
U-Net	22,000	23,000
Cable Internet	21,000	23,000
Enterprise	12,000	13,000
I-Way	10,000	11,000
Total	1,699,000	1,825,000

Source: Internet Magazine (http//:www.internet-magazine.com/resources/welcome.html).

A good example in the UK is LineOne, a joint venture between BT (which provides the Internet and telecommunications elements) and News International (which uses its newspapers – *Sunday Times, The Times, Sun, News of the World* – and television interests – Sky Television and Fox Television – to provide much of the content). According to the Audit Bureau of Circulation (http://www.abc.org.uk), LineOne provided 5,207,463 web pages in response to requests from users in December 1997 (although the highest audited number of pages downloaded to date has been from the BBC's online offerings with 66,705,338 page impressions downloaded during March 1998 – see Table 7.2). According to a recent report for the Newspaper Society, however, 'only 25–50 sites in Europe generate more than 1 million page impressions per month' (Newspaper Society, 1998, p. 21).

Table 7.2   Top audited UK websites by number of
'page impressions', March 1998

Client	URL	Page impressions	Period
BBC Online	www.bbc.co.uk	66,705,338	1/3/98–31/3/98
BBC Online General	www.bbc.co.uk	41,633,852	1/3/98–31/3/98
Yahoo UK and Ireland	www.yahoo.co.uk	34,579,546	1/3/98–31/3/98
Associated Newspapers	www.soccernet.com	12,617,704	1/3/98–31/3/98
BBC Online beeb @ the BBC	www.beeb.com	12,233,076	1/3/98–31/3/98
BBC Online News	www.bbc.co.uk/news	12,085,272	1/3/98–31/3/98
ITN	www.itn.co.uk	5,964,635	1/3/98–31/3/98
The Times	www.the-times.co.uk	5,208,781	1/3/98–31/3/98
Sunday Times	www.sunday-times.co.uk	5,112,959	1/3/98–31/3/98

Source: http://www.abc.org.uk.

Microsoft Network (MSN), owned by US Software company Microsoft, also has specific British content (for example, material from the satirical magazine *Private Eye*), as well as material originated in the US and elsewhere. AOL, a joint venture founded in 1995 by the US company America On Line (itself only founded in 1985) and the German media giant Bertelsmann AG, is a further example of online services with British-originated material. In 1998, AOL merged with CompuServe's interactive service (although the two companies still trade separately). Thus, only four or five companies – AOL/Compuserve, Microsoft, News International, Virgin and BT – dominate the market for subscription-funded Internet content.

Although barriers to entry in terms of publishing information on the Internet are relatively few – it is fairly inexpensive to have one's own web page – most of the Net's commercially viable content is controlled by, or commissioned by, large companies. The big entertainment, press, telecommunications and software companies are the dominant players.

Web-based media content providers are searching for new ways to maximize their revenues, and to this end they are exploring the possibilities of systems involving the levy of small payments on a 'pay-per-page' basis (this follows the same logic of charging on a 'pay-per' basis which has been emerging in the more established audiovisual sector for over a decade) (Mosco, 1989). However, establishing effective systems of micro-payment has proved technically and organizationally difficult, and the more conventional sources of revenue – subscriptions, sponsorship and advertising – remain, for the time being, the dominant way of financing media activity on the Web.

Digital Television: Compression and Fracture?

Digital television is the new medium in which we can see most clearly the implications of signal compression, which allows for an expansion in the number of channels that can be broadcast by traditional transmitters. In the UK, digital television is widely expected to be the main route by which domestic users will have access to interactive media. Indeed, the BBC, in its evidence to the 1998 parliamentary Select Committee on Media, Culture and Sport, described digital television as 'the natural pathway of choice to digital for "middle England"' (Select Committee on Media, Culture and Sport, 1998, para. 16).

Digital television will be delivered by all three of the current delivery systems for analogue television. Digital *satellite* television, already widely available in Europe, will be led in the UK by BSkyB. Digital *cable* television, already operating in the US, was launched in 1998 in the UK by existing cable operators. In 1998, Britain became the first country to launch a *terrestrial* digital television service. A number of licences for digital terrestrial television have been awarded as 'multiplexes', with each multiplex having the capacity to carry six channels. The BBC has been awarded one multiplex, while the other multiplexes have been awarded, via the Independent Television Commission (ITC), to commercial television companies. British Digital Broadcasting (BDB), a company jointly owned by Carlton Communications and the Granada Group, was awarded a number of Multiplex Service Licences in June 1997 (although it was a condition of the licence that BSkyB, one of the three original shareholders, should withdraw as a shareholder in BDB). A licence has also been awarded to Digital 3 and 4 Ltd, a company jointly owned by the ITV companies and Channel 4. The final terrestrial multiplex licence was awarded in 1998 to SDN – a joint venture between NTL, a telecommunications company; the Welsh fourth channel, S4C; and United News and Media. It is noteworthy that there are no new faces among this list of media corporations.

The introduction of digital television expands the potential for greater segmentation of the audience through specialized niche channels and it allows for augmenting income by means of more precisely targeted advertising and/or direct subscription or pay-per-view revenues. In the longer term the significance of digital television may reside in the potential to integrate it with other digital technologies, in particular the Internet (for example, through web-based interactive channel guides) and much more interactive programming, including 'Near Video-On-Demand', home shopping, banking, and other services. In both the shorter and longer terms, then, digital television is about building on existing strategies.

Digital television must be considered in the context of wider corporate strategies to achieve a competitive position in increasingly contested transnational markets (Bughin and Griekspoor, 1997). The economic logic of market differentiation and consumer targeting is driving the expansion in the number of channels which digital television permits.

Computer Games: Marketing Interactivity

Computer, or video, games are the most developed of the new media, providing the best example of the market appeal of interactive multimedia. With even the latest games consoles – so called 'next generation' consoles – retailing for a fraction of the price of a multimedia PC, there were over 1.3 million such consoles sold in the UK by the middle of 1997 (*Screen Digest*, 1997). Successful games in the console markets – in particular PlayStation and the N64 – can have sales of well over a million units, and an *average* PlayStation game sold 21,000 units in the UK in 1996 (*Screen Digest*, 1997). In terms of the personal computer as a games platform, games have over 70 per cent of the market for PC CD-ROM entertainment software in Britain (*Screen Digest*, 1997). With successful games capable of finding audiences of millions worldwide, computer games are now a well-established consumer industry. The technology used in computer games is at the cutting edge of software and hardware design, incorporating the latest advances in interactive multimedia.

Interestingly, games are – so far – one of the least 'networked' multimedia products. While there are a number of network-based games on the market, and while the development of a viable online games sector has long been a vision of some actors in the games industry, what is significant is that stand-alone games – both for consoles and personal computers – continue to dominate the market. With software (games) locally stored on cartridges or on CD-ROMs, games platforms can access large volumes of data at speeds that are currently impossible using the Internet or other available network technologies (Campbell, 1998).

The market is highly structured and dominated by the decisions of the major console manufacturers – Sony (PlayStation), Nintendo (N64) and Sega (Saturn) – who control and license much of the basic technology. These companies have exploited their control over the consoles to achieve a dominant position in the software market.

In this context Sony's strategy is revealing. Burned by the Betamax/VHS fiasco (in which Sony's technically superior video tape system floundered for lack of any software – films – to play on it), the company held back from the video-console market for many years, only entering seriously with the PlayStation in late 1993. In order to ensure that there were games for the PlayStation, Sony had bought, or partly bought, a number of games producers around the world to ensure a ready supply of PlayStation-compatible games. For example, in 1993 Sony purchased the Liverpool-based company Psygnosis, producers of hits such as *Lemmings* and *Destruction Derby* (although Psygnosis, like many other games developers, also produces games for the PC market and other platforms).

Sony is also able to exploit the synergy between their games and their other media activities. Many films have already spawned computer games – notably the *Star Wars* series and *Blade Runner* for the PC, and *Goldeneye* and the forthcoming *Mission Impossible* for the N64. Meanwhile a number of 'first generation' computer games have been made into movies – *Super Mario Bros.*, *Streetfighter*, *Mortal Kombat* – while more recent games – including *Tomb Raider* and *Resident Evil* – are in development as movies. Sony have already followed this strategy with *Men in Black* – already a movie, video, TV show and magazine, and now a game.

British involvement is predominantly in the field of software (game) development, and in this domain it has a major presence. Clive Shepherd of EMG Entertainment, writing in the *1997 Multimedia and CD-ROM Directory*, explains that:

> Something like 40 per cent of the world's [computer] games are developed in the UK and there are literally hundreds of multimedia developers that have sprung up alongside the growth of CD-ROM... Fees and salaries are generally lower than the USA and continental Europe, [but] the methodologies and technologies are as advanced as anything you will find in the USA and Japan and communications are excellent. (Shepherd, 1997, p. 72)

However, as he goes on to point out:

> Some great software is designed in the UK, although it is more likely to be exploited by an American or Japanese company. There are, of course, exceptions such as Dorling Kindersley and Eidos, although former strong contenders such as Psygnosis, MicroPose, Ocean and Virgin are now at least partially foreign owned. (Shepherd, 1997, p. 72)

Thus, in general, the British games industry already resembles the British film industry, with most of the (relatively) small domestic players dependent on distribution and licensing deals – not to mention financial and technological support – from major Japanese and US companies.

The Novelty of New Media

In this chapter, we have adopted an approach that plays down the glitzy allure of the new technologies. We have looked at new media as industries, and in doing so we have tended to emphasize the elements of continuity. New technologies allow corporate actors to pursue the aims that they have always pursued, but to do so in more complex and sophisticated ways. The new media allow companies to use more sophisticated methods of gathering data on the consumption activities of customers (see Robins and Webster, 1989). Information on audience preferences, tastes and transactions can now be more readily recorded, building up a complex, and even personalized, consumer profile on the basis of longitudinal monitoring. This allows for increasingly sophisticated targeting by advertisers and product developers, and in some cases the data itself can be sold on to other interested parties.

Private media corporations have long sought to commercialize and commodify activities and functions that have traditionally been outside of the market, such as education or information provision through public libraries. New media neologisms, such as 'edutainment' and 'infotainment', suggest the progress that has been made in blurring the boundaries between commercial enterprise and the public realms of education and information.

Companies have long sought to build 'brand loyalty' and to create more direct and immediate relations with consumers. The development of interactive technologies represents a significant development in such strategies. Today, the emphasis is usually on the ways in which such technologies can empower the user. However, it is perhaps more appropriate to see them in terms of how they are strengthening the position of the providers of media services.

Of course, in emphasizing such continuities, we do not want to say that there is nothing new about the new media order. Clearly there are significant innovations going on in the provision of media products and services. But what we want to emphasize is the importance of thinking carefully about what exactly it is that is new about the new media. We do not think that we shall be getting the dramatically transformed media environment that the techno-futurists are forecasting – in fact, the media 'revolution' is more about strategies for deepening and intensifying consumption processes (moving beyond the consumption–time constraints that have limited the revenues and profits that could be garnered from the 'old' media). The newness of 'new' media is of a different order. It is to do with the *enhancement* of existing media products, business models and strategies. What the new technologies permit is the refinement, extension and embellishment of traditional media. We might consider the relationship of new media to old as being like that between an old Hollywood movie and its remake: the characters are the same, the story is the same, but the special effects are more spectacular, and the marketing budget is much larger.

References

Browning, J. and Reiss, S. 'Encyclopaedia of the new economy', *Wired (UK)*, **6**, 5 (May 1998) pp. 105–14.
Bughin, J. and Griekspoor, W. 'A new era for European TV', *McKinsey Quarterly*, **3** (1997) pp. 90–102.
Campbell, C. 'The high price of gaming', *Guardian* (Online), 30 April 1998.
Dawson, M. and Bellamy Foster, J. 'Virtual capitalism: the political economy of the

information highway', *Monthly Review*, **48** (1996) pp. 40–58.

Dyer, A. 'Design council', *Personal Computer World*, November (1996) pp. 116–20.

The Economist 'Internet: brands bite back' (21–27 March 1998) pp. 98–104.

Gandy, O. H. *The Panoptic Sort: The Political Economy of Personal Information*. Boulder, CO: Westview Press, 1993.

Garnham, N. 'Public service versus the market', *Screen*, **24**, 1 (1983) pp. 6–27.

Henning, K. *Multimedia in the UK: Business Opportunities in the Digital Age*. London: Financial Times Telecomms and Media Publishing, 1997.

Kitchin, R. *Cyberspace: The World in the Wires*. Chichester: Wiley, 1998.

Lyon, D. 'The World Wide Web of surveillance: the Internet and off-world power-flows', *Information, Communication and Society*, **1**, 1 (1998) pp. 91–105.

Mosco, V. *The Pay-per Society: Computers and Communication in the Information Age*. Toronto: Garamond Press, 1989.

Murphy, D. 'The film starts whenever you want it to', *Financial Times*, 2 June 1998.

Negroponte, N. *Being Digital*. London: Hodder and Stoughton/Coronet, 1995.

Newspaper Society *New Media Revenue Streams* (Newspaper Society/DTI Sector Challenge Briefing Paper II). Prepared for the Newspaper Society by Electronic Publishing Services, May 1998.

Oftel *Beyond the Telephone, the Television and the PC – Regulation of the Electronic Communications Industry*. 1998. (OFTEL's response to the culture, media and sport select committee inquiry into audio-visual communications and the regulation of broadcasting, http://www.oftel.gov.uk/broadcast/dcms398.htm)

Robins, K. 'The new communications geography and the politics of optimism', *Soundings*, **5** (1997) pp. 191–202.

Robins, K. and Webster, F. 'The communications revolution: new media, old problems', *Communication*, **10** (1987) pp. 71–89.

Robins, K. and Webster, F. 'Plan and control: towards a cultural history of the information society', *Theory and Society*, **18** (1989) pp. 323–51.

Screen Digest 'Interactive entertainment software: rapidly maturing market' (June 1997) pp. 129–36.

Select Committee on Media 'Culture and sport' *The Multi-Media Revolution – Volume 1*, Session 1997–98, HC 520-I, 1998.

Shepherd, C. 'UK market profile, in TFPL Multimedia' (ed.) *The Multimedia and CDROM Directory 1997* (17th Edition). London: TFPL Multimedia, 1997, pp. 71–2.

Shillingford, J. 'Webcasting heralds many new services', *Financial Times* (IT Supplement), 6 May 1998.

Taylor, P. 'Visions of a multimedia-rich millennium', *Financial Times* (IT Supplement), 6 May 1998.

PART II

REGULATION AND MEDIA POLICY

ANNA READING

This second section of *The Media in Britain* is the theoretical and empirical bridge between media institutions – examined in the first part – and media representations discussed in the last part. Here we examine the ways in which the media are regulated through laws and policies in Britain and Europe. The authors consider the different factors that have influenced the development of media policies over the past 20 years, such as the state, governments, the European Union and people's grassroots organizations. In so doing they make an important connection between media companies and industries, the texts they produce and the concerns that people have about the possible effects of media content on people's moralities and identities.

Peter Goodwin begins in Chapter 8 by examining the role of the state in formulating British media policy under Thatcherism and today. He builds on the earlier chapters on broadcasting and looks at the ways in which the state has formulated and developed media policies, especially in relation to broadcasting. Historically, broadcasters maintained that due to spectrum scarcity, broadcasting had to be strictly licensed by the state. However the advent of digital broadcasting has weakened that argument. It brings to light the underlying political motives behind government pressure to maintain control over broadcasting because it was perceived as a more powerful medium than newspapers. Goodwin traces the recent changes in state policy towards the organization of television back to economic, social and cultural developments as well as technological advances. He argues that the New Right's advocacy of a free market, in the 1980s, did not result in a hands-off approach by the government in keeping with this ideology. Rather, Conservative state policy was characterized by a reluctance to give up government influence over broadcasting.

This theme is picked up by Julian Petley in Chapter 9. He begins with a challenge to the dominant view that the content of the British media is relatively unfettered. It is generally argued that the media in Britain are free, but Petley, in contrast, provides an important alternative to this dominant perspective by suggesting the opposite. The view that the media are free was highlighted, suggests Petley, by the reactions to the death of Diana, Princess of Wales, in 1997. At the time, the media were blamed for hounding Diana and calls were made for greater media restrictions, especially the press. Yet if one considers the restrictions that are already in place on the media a picture emerges of tight control: there are already 50 Acts that limit the media's freedom, including laws concerning libel, prior restraint and breach of confidence. Petley considers what these mean in more depth before looking at specific rules in relation to television that control what broadcasters may or may not broadcast. He then considers press regulation which, in Petley's view, is also very restricted in terms of its content. The chapter includes extremely useful direct quotations from primary sources, government papers and documents, as well as key references to other renowned scholars in the area of media law.

Richard Collins' Chapter 10 builds on earlier chapters in Part I in discussing further the themes of state control and media restriction with a broader context. He considers the nexus of political, cultural and technological factors linked to media policy in Europe and addresses some of the developments over the past 15 years within the telecommunications and television industries. It is within these particular industries that the most important policy changes have occurred at the European level. Telecommunications, especially, are increasingly the key medium to consider in relation to policy issues as different media converge through digital telecommunications technologies. Some of the policy controls that both Goodwin and Petley consider come from a concern over the influence of the media on public morality. Yet, these controls are often in tension with commercialization of the media, particularly broadcasting. Collins, too, considers the impetus towards privatization of the media but examines this within a broader European context. Thus, he argues that within Europe there has been a huge growth in commercial television from four private channels in 1982 to 58 channels in 1992. At the same time, however, there have also been concerns over the influence of American media on European identities. These have been articulated in policy terms with calls for a stricter European content quota-system to halt the flow of American TV programmes. This in turn has raised important debates about what actually constitutes European culture and the question of what actually constitutes 'Europe'.

The themes of concern over public morality and the influence of the media, and whose identities are at stake in the making of that culture, are also addressed in Chapter 11 by Anna Reading, but from a very different perspective. Reading considers policy-makers other than the state and governments and instead looks at the grassroots campaigns that have sought to change the media historically and today. These, she argues, fall into three broad categories: those who want to restrict media content that they believe may undermine public morality; those who want to share out the ownership and control of the mass media; and those who campaign to make the media more inclusive of excluded groups such as women and ethnic minorities. Reading argues, as do all the authors in this section, that policy and, in this case, campaigns to change media policy are best understood in relation to broader historical contexts. By looking at emergent patterns over time she suggests that we are able to see the links between, for example, the Co-operative Women's Guild's campaign for literacy in the first part of the twentieth century and present-day struggles by excluded groups to get their voices heard and represented.

What is covered in Part II of this volume concerns policy in relation to the more traditional areas of the press and broadcasting, although Chapter 11 suggests that in campaigns to change the media these often also include other aspects of culture such as theatre and the arts. The final chapter in this section thus provides two important links with Part III of this volume, which considers issues of representation and identity in a range of media, including theatre, museums and music, as well as television and the press.

CHAPTER 8

The Role of the State

PETER GOODWIN

The state intervenes in the activities of all media. It does so in a variety of different ways, and for a variety of different reasons. For example, in virtually every country, even such apparently unregulated media as print periodicals, recorded music or movies are subject to laws – that is state rules – on obscenity, defamation and incitement. All of these media conduct their business on the basis of copyright law. And all can be significantly affected by the state's taxation or competition policy. These are just some examples of the numerous ways in which the state shapes – or tries to shape – every type of media. They also suggest the variety of different reasons why it does so.

Broadcasting as the Extreme Case

So the state shapes *all* media industries. But, in twentieth-century democracies, no other media industry has been as systematically and profoundly shaped by the state as radio and television broadcasting. Two aspects of the history of broadcasting in the UK demonstrate the point. From its birth in the 1920s until 1955, broadcasting in Britain was a state monopoly conducted exclusively by a quasi-state body, the BBC. Even today the BBC – still a public body and still funded out of what is in effect a form of taxation – is the largest single broadcaster of both television and radio in the UK. There is not, and never has been, any equivalent state-sponsored provider of print periodicals, records or films of any way near comparable importance. Even when the UK state did permit broadcasting by commercial companies (television in 1955, radio in 1973), these companies have had to obtain from the state a licence to broadcast – a licence often subject to strict conditions on, for example, content. In peace-time Britain, in the twentieth century, no similar state licences have ever been required to publish a magazine or newspaper, or to make or market a record or film.

Britain is not peculiar in this qualitatively extra degree of state intervention in broadcasting as compared with other media. State monopoly and state ownership in broadcasting have been a feature of virtually every European country and of many other countries in other continents. Even in free-market America, state regulation of radio and television has always been more stringent than state regulation over any other media. Radio and television broad-

130

casting in the USA may have always been overwhelmingly commercial – there was no state ownership of broadcasting and no state funding of it. But to engage in broadcasting in the United States has always required a licence from the state – a licence with often stringent conditions.

Why has there been this especially strong state regulation of broadcasting? In recent years the standard answer has been that traditional analogue terrestrial broadcasting involved 'spectrum scarcity'. To let everyone who wanted to use this scarce resource would result in 'chaos of the airwaves'. So radio and television were a 'natural monopoly' which needed to be either owned or, at the very least, allocated and regulated, by the state. This argument has a powerful corollary. If technological developments eliminated this 'spectrum scarcity' then the rationale for an exceptional degree of state regulation of broadcasting would disappear. Broadcasting would simply become 'electronic publishing' – no different, and no more prone to state intervention, than any other type of publishing (the classic statement of this argument is Pool, 1983).

However, to maintain that 'spectrum scarcity' was the only reason for the especially high degree of state regulation traditionally devoted to broadcasting is a distinctly unhistorical approach to the question. In the real history of broadcasting at least two other factors have been important. First, from its very beginnings, broadcasting has been seen by politicians, rightly or wrongly, to be a peculiarly influential medium, and therefore, particularly necessary to subject to public control. Such control effectively meant regulation by the state. This belief in the peculiar power of broadcasting has remained, and probably grown, as radio was succeeded by television as the major broadcasting medium. Second, whereas modern print media were established and matured under the limited *laissez-faire* 'night watchman' state of the nineteenth century, broadcasting started, developed and came to maturity under the interventionist state of the first two-thirds of the twentieth century. If the public corporation of the BBC seemed a 'natural' way to organize broadcasting in the 1920s, this was, at least in part, nothing to do with the peculiar features of broadcasting. Rather, such a public corporation was also, at the time, seen as a 'natural' way of running a variety of relatively new activities. The institutional arrangements arrived at during the birth of a particular activity tend to become the 'natural' ones for subsequent generations. Broadcasting is a particularly strong case of that rule.

Whatever the historical reasons, television in the 1970s was, throughout virtually the whole of the world, a highly state-regulated activity. In each country it consisted of a handful of generalist channels, largely distributed by means of terrestrial transmission, allocated by, and with a content regulated by, each country's state. There were considerable differences (generally with deep historical roots) between different countries in how that state regulation was applied. In the United States, television broadcasting was permitted and encouraged by the US state to be overwhelmingly commercial and funded by advertising. In most of Europe television was, until at least the late 1970s, a state monopoly funded by a licence fee.

The British Case

On the face of it British television, after the establishment of ITV in 1955, occupied a position somewhere between the US and Continental European models. On the one hand, a substantial section of British television was provided by a public broadcaster, the BBC, financed by the licence fee. On the other hand, BBC television programmes competed for audience share with the commercial, advertising-funded ITV. But beneath this surface reality, two other features of British television in the 1960s and 70s need stressing. First, particularly after the Pilkington report on broadcasting (Pilkington, 1962), ITV was subject to substantial public control by a state-sanctioned regulator, the Independent Broadcasting Authority (IBA), in matters of both programming content and commercial organization. Second, both official UK government policy and the overwhelming majority of elite public opinion in the UK treated the whole of television broadcasting (both BBC and ITV) as a 'public service'.

Forces for Change

From roughly the mid-1970s, a series of developments put into question the traditional organization of television, and therefore the traditionally exceptionally strong role of the state in that organization. These developments were international and can be summarized under four headings.

The first was economic. The traditional models of television organization had developed and reached maturity during the long post-war boom and against the background of welfare and generally state interventionist capitalism – of which they were a part. After the 1973 oil crisis that boom faltered and with it the welfarism and state interventionism that had accompanied it. Broadcasting now functioned in an internationally more competitive environment. The second was both social and cultural. There were widely perceived (if questionable) shifts in popular culture in industrialized societies from the 1970s onwards towards fragmentation of the mass audience and globalization of the national audience. In as much as such developments in popular culture really were taking place, they posed a challenge to traditional forms of television organization, including the UK public service model, which had been built on catering for a national mass audience. The third development was technological. From the mid-1970s onwards two apparently new technologies of television distribution began to become practical. Both broadband cable and direct-to-home satellite broadcasting could greatly increase the number of television channels that could be transmitted, thus mitigating or eliminating the problem of 'spectrum scarcity'. Direct-to-home satellite broadcasting had the additional technological feature of enabling television broadcasting across national frontiers, thus weakening the traditional ability of nation states to regulate television broadcasting within their frontiers.

All of these three developments posed a challenge to the traditional order of television broadcasting. Yet on their own they could do little to rapidly or fundamentally change it. Terrestrial television was peculiarly subject to national state regulation. It could be relatively easily protected against the chill winds of the international economy. National audiences with changing tastes had little or no opportunity to vote with their feet unless the state gave them an opportunity. The new technologies of television distribution were, at the end of the 1970s, still in their early stages. And in their early stages they too were still susceptible to a substantial amount of state intervention.

To work whatever changes they were capable of, the three developments outlined above required a fourth, political, one – the arrival in office of governments who were determined to use state authority to lessen state regulation in television, just as their predecessors had used state authority to maintain it. At the end of the 1970s this was precisely what happened.

The collapse of the post-war boom fostered an international revival of a 'new right' or 'neo-liberal' free-market politics, explicitly critical of state intervention in the economy, which had been out of fashion in the industrialized world since the Second World War. The strength of this revival was first demonstrated by Margaret Thatcher's election victory in Britain in 1979. Just eighteen months later this was followed by Ronald Reagan's victory in the United States presidential election of November 1980.

The Thatcherite 'Project'

In the years since 1979, Margaret Thatcher's administration in Britain has been widely seen as not simply the first 'new right' administration, but also as a particularly determined and (in its own terms) particularly successful one. Critical observers of her government rapidly coined the notion of 'Thatcherism' to explain this determination and success. 'Thatcherism', according to the political theorist Andrew Gamble who has done much to popularize the term, was a political project whose central objectives included 'reviv[ing] market liberalism as the dominant public philosophy and creat[ing] the conditions for a free conomy by limiting the scope of the state while restoring its authority and competence to act' (Gamble, 1994, p. 4).

Such a project applied across all areas of previous state provision – from health care to refuse collection. Television broadcasting was rarely at the centre of its overt concerns, but it could scarcely escape them. One seemingly obvious interpretation of the changes that have taken place in British television since 1979 is that they amount to a progressive, government-fostered erosion of the previously dominant philosophy of television as a public service, and its replacement by the philosophy of television as just another part of the market economy. Such an interpretation embodies a good deal of truth. But it ignores a number of crucial questions.

The first of these concerns the notion of a Thatcherite 'project'. The term 'project' commonly suggests some sort of thought-through and coherent plan of action. Yet, as we shall see, Conservative television policy in the 18 years after 1979 was characterized, not by any coherent plan, but rather by a series of zig-zags.

Second, however determined the Thatcher and Major administrations, or at least their ideological cheer leaders, might have been to create a free-market Utopia, there were various different strategies (each with their own problems) as to how to get there. As we shall see, in the television field at least, the Thatcher and Major administrations never settled on any one of these strategies – rather they lurched from one to another.

Third, however ideologically determined governments may be, in order to implement their policies they have to negotiate with established institutions and confront existing realities, including the unexpected consequences of their own previous policies. Again, as we shall see, this was precisely what happened to the post-1979 Conservative governments in the television field.

Channel 4, Cable and Satellite

Between 1979 and 1983 Thatcher's first administration undertook two major initiatives on television – the establishment of a fourth terrestrial television channel, Channel 4, and the enthusiastic promotion of two new television distribution technologies, broadband cable and direct-to-home satellite. These two initiatives embodied very different approaches to the traditional system of television organization in Britain and the role of state regulation within it. Channel 4 was an extension, albeit a highly original extension, of the public service tradition. It was funded by advertising, but it did not sell this in competition with ITV, and it was bound by a tight government-prescribed remit – to provide alternative programming. In essence the channel was the new Tory government's pragmatic attempt – and, as events were to turn out, it was not an unsuccessful attempt – to extend traditional public service provision to cater for more diverse audiences.

The first Thatcher administration's other major initiative on television was to endeavour to promote cable and satellite broadcasting. This was governed by very different considerations from the creation of Channel 4. Both new technologies were promoted by the Tory government of the early 1980s, not for traditional broadcasting reasons (like audiences and content), but rather, primarily, and quite explicitly, for 'industrial' considerations. Rapid introduction of both satellite and broadband cable were justified as fostering the UK electronics industry. In addition, it was expected that satellite would help the UK aerospace industry, while broadband cable would contribute to UK industrial development in general, by establishing the framework for the widespread growth of interactive services. These industrial benefits would, the government proclaimed, be achieved on the basis of private investment. The government firmly refused to inject any public money into them. In order to encourage this private investment, cable and satellite would be subject to less stringent regulation on content. Terrestrial broadcasting would continue as a tightly regulated public service, but the new technologies of television distribution would be developed by private capital under a looser regulatory framework (see Home Office, 1981; ITAP, 1982).

As events turned out, neither satellite nor cable developed along the lines that the government had mapped out. Government plans for UK-based Direct Broadcasting by satellite foundered because the BBC, either on its own or in alliance with the ITV companies, proved unable to raise the private finance needed to embark on this major and risky project. Cable was also unable to attract the necessary domestic money for extensive building of its networks. The result was that the anticipated benefits for the British aerospace and electronics industries did not happen. When satellite did eventually get going in the UK in the late 1980s, it was as the result of an initiative from a foreign-controlled company (Rupert Murdoch's Sky and then BSkyB), broadcasting from a foreign made and regulated satellite (the Luxembourg-licensed Astra) and broadcasting largely American programming. Similarly, when cable eventually got going in the UK (a little later than satellite) it was on the basis of a massive injection of capital from North American cable and telecoms operators. Like satellite it used little UK-originated technology and little UK-originated programming. It also singularly failed to generate any interactive services alongside its broadcasting and, from the early 1990s onwards, telephone activities. In short, the new technologies of distribution failed to develop either how, or anywhere near as fast as, the Thatcher administration of 1979–83 had planned, and, when they did eventually develop, they failed to deliver the benefits for British industry which the first Thatcher administration had intended.

Lessons from the Early Thatcher Years

The television policy of the early Thatcher years carries with it a number of important, and more general, lessons about the role of the state in endeavouring to shape the media. The first lesson follows from the sharp contrast between the government's essentially public-service driven creation of Channel 4, and the same government's fundamentally industrially driven promotion of cable and satellite. Even apparently ideologically motivated administrations are often inconsistent. State policy towards the media rarely forms an ideologically seamless whole.

The second general lesson is suggested by the fate of the cable and satellite policies of the early 1980s. To put it bluntly, the policy of fostering the two new distribution technologies by means of private finance, so as to benefit British industry, fell flat on its face. State policies towards the media, and that includes free-market policies, can, and often do, fail. But with that lesson goes a third – governments rarely acknowledge failed policies head on, instead they adapt to and often take credit for their unanticipated consequences. This is precisely what the Tory government of the 1990s did on cable and satellite. It embraced Murdoch's BSkyB and the North American control of British cable as examples of the supposed success of attracting inward investment into the new media, by means of a 'liberal' regulatory regime.

However, it would be wrong to conclude from this about-face that government policies of the early 1980s had no effect on the advance of the new broadcasting technologies. In Britain the government allocated a new terrestrial Channel to the 'alternative public service' Channel 4. In France, at much the same time, the government allocated a new terrestrial channel to the commercial, pay-TV Canal-plus. The result of that French move was to limit the scope for 'unofficial' pay-TV to develop in France with the same ease and rapidity with which Rupert Murdoch developed it in the UK.

On the other hand, the creation of Channel 4 in Britain brought with it the birth of a new and influential independent television production sector, with important consequences for the subsequent development of UK television. So the fourth general lesson of the early-1980s television policy in Britain, is that, even when the consequences of state policy on the media are not entirely anticipated, those consequences can still count, and count powerfully.

Lessons from Thatcher's Middle and Late Years

After her second election victory in 1983, Margaret Thatcher's government radically shifted the direction of its television policy towards the public service core of British television. In part, this was because of the marginalization of the Tory 'wets', which gave a freer reign both to the more ideological free-marketeers in and around the Tory party, and to the personal prejudices of the Prime Minister, which were on the whole hostile to the BBC. In part, the shift was because of specific developments in the BBC, in particular its need to push for a heavy hike in the licence fee. Both factors focused attention on one side of the UK public service system – the BBC. The other side of terrestrial television, ITV, at first remained largely immune from government attention.

In 1985 the government set up a committee – under the chairmanship of Alan Peacock – to review the financing of the BBC. Both the background to the committee's establishment and its composition, powerfully suggested that the government had set it up with the specific intention of introducing advertising on the BBC. Such a move would have been a considerable blow against one of the central features of the established framework of British public service broadcasting.

When the Peacock Committee reported in 1986 it did three more or less unanticipated things. First, despite its free-market make-up, it rejected advertising on the BBC in the short term, because it would narrow down viewer choice. Second, it recommended a long-term subscription-based future for the BBC as part of a move towards 'electronic publishing'. Third, it recommended a number of major changes to the advertising-funded sector of British television – including an auction of ITV franchises and Channel 4 selling its own advertising – as part of a move to make these more efficient and market orientated (see Peacock, 1986).

Peacock's recommendation against advertising on the BBC effectively killed off the idea for a decade and more. If even a committee handpicked by the Thatcher government rejected the idea then it was clearly a political non-starter. Peacock's positive recommendations for the long-term future of the BBC were soon quietly forgotten by the government. Thatcher and her colleagues particularly disliked Peacock's idea that as television became simply 'electronic publishing', then it should be freed from 'censorious controls'. So, if it wanted to reform the core of British television, the Tory government of the late 1980s had to pick up and run with the third element in Peacock's recommendations – the ones on ITV and Channel 4.

This it did. In 1988 it published a White Paper (Home Office, 1988) proposing that, in future, ITV licences would be awarded (subject to some conditions) to the highest bidder, that Channel 4 would sell its own advertising (and thus for the first time compete for revenue with ITV) and that the old regulator of commercial television, the IBA, would be replaced by a new far 'lighter touch' regulator, the ITC. These proposals were received with considerable hostility, both from the government's political opponents and from much of the television industry. After intense debate, and with significant modification, these proposals became law in the Broadcasting Act of 1994. There followed the ITV franchise race of 1991, and a new 'more competitive' regime for ITV starting when the newly victorious licensees took their places at the beginning of 1993.

Problems for the Reform

This second period of Tory television policy provides some further general lessons about the role of the state in shaping the media. The first of these is the important role of accident. Had the Thatcher government picked a different set of members for its committee on the financing of the BBC then, in the political climate of the mid-1980s, they could very well have come up with the conclusion that Thatcher, at least, obviously wanted. Had they done so then the government would very likely have taken that course – which would have led to a very different BBC than that which has in fact developed over the subsequent decade.

A second lesson concerns the free-market approach to the media. Both Thatcher and Peacock were free-marketeers, but their shared general political philosophy concealed very different strategies of how to get from existing state dominated television institutions towards their free-market goal. A third lesson can be found in the bitterly contested road from the 1988 White Paper to the new ITV regime. The government faced resistance to its plans from a widespread range of political and industrial opinion, and, as a result, made concessions in its legislation. But the eventual outcome of its measures turned out to be even more modified than might have been expected from the legislative concessions. The new, supposedly 'lighter touch' ITC, set 'public service' requirements on the ITV franchise auction and the new ITV regime, almost as strongly as had its predecessor, the IBA (from which many of the key personnel of the ITC were drawn). Thus, state policy is not just a question of governments implementing their desires. In trying to do what they want, governments encounter powerful entrenched institutions. These institutions can often succeed in adapting to new government measures so as to preserve much of the substance of their previous authority.

Lessons from the Early 1990s

This last lesson from Tory television policy of the mid- and late 1980s is demonstrated again, but in a rather different way, in the next phase of Tory broadcasting policy, the debate on the future of the BBC in the first half of the 1990s. At first sight this provides a striking and puzzling contrast with the previous phase of Tory policy. In the mid-1980s the government had threatened the BBC with a radical change to its funding base which it had only escaped thanks to Peacock. In the late 1980s the Tories had attempted to fundamentally transform commercial television. But in the early 1990s, when the same government for a second time addressed the future of the BBC, its proposals were far more conservative (with a small C), either than they had been for the BBC in the mid-1980s or for commercial television in the late 1980s. Now, according to the Government, the BBC was to continue at the centre of British broadcasting, with its full range of services intact and its licence fee funding preserved, at least to 2002 (see Department of National Heritage, 1994).

Why? One key reason is the phenomenon of 'institutional adaption' which we have already identified with the IBA/ITC. Since a major change in management regime in 1986, when Marmaduke Hussey was appointed chairman of the corporation, the BBC had gone out of its way to demonstrate its adherence to the new government-fostered norms of market rectitude. Most notably it had introduced 'Producer Choice' – an internal market, tested against the outside market, for BBC operations.

But this institutional adaption by the BBC also suggests another lesson about state intervention in the media. The state can shape the media by means other than legislation. Governments have other instruments at their disposal – for example, appointments (like that of Marmaduke Hussey), financial pressure (like the squeeze on the real value of the licence fee exerted from 1985 onwards), and the general climate of opinion they are able to create (very clearly pro-market throughout the Thatcher/Major years). After 1986 the BBC adapted as an institution, and in doing so secured its survival, but it adapted under the powerful direction of the state.

There is one last lesson about the state and the media to be learned from the debate on BBC Charter renewal in the first half of the 1990s. This debate took place against the recent background of Margaret Thatcher's enforced exit from the premiership and of the generally hostile reception given to the Tories' attempts to reform commercial television. With that political back-drop, it is scarcely surprising that in the early 1990s the government displayed considerable caution in its approach to the BBC. To even try to shape the media in a new and radical direction, the state needs political self-confidence. In the debate on BBC Charter renewal in the early 1990s such self-confidence was distinctly lacking.

The State and the Digital Future

In 1993 and 1994 government broadcasting policy on television began to shift emphasis yet again. The new focus of attention was what is a now familiar set of buzzwords – 'multimedia', 'digital revolution' and 'informa-tion superhighway'. There were a number of ways in which the state could have a major effect on how – and how fast – the digital future developed. Three of these caused particular debate during the last few years before the Tories lost office in 1997. They are issues which are unlikely to go away with New Labour.

The first issue revolved around the question of who was to build the 'infor-mation superhighway' of advanced digital networks. One obvious candidate was British Telecom. But British Telecom declared that for it to be worth-while to invest the money required, it was necessary for it to be able to broad-cast cable television over its networks. However, the government had earlier barred BT from carrying television in order to promote the new cable compa-nies and thus encourage competition in the telecommunications market. So here state regulation designed to fulfil one government goal – competition in telecommunications – seemed to many critics to work against another government goal – building the information superhighway (see House of Commons Trade and Industry Committee, 1994). The government, however, chose to stick with its telecommunications competition policy and refused to lift the bar on BT broadcasting television (see Department of Trade and Industry, 1994).

The second issue of controversy in broadcasting policy during the last years of the Conservative administration concerned the ownership of commercial terrestrial broadcasting. In the past, governments and regulators had prevented newspapers having a controlling interest in either ITV licensees or commercial radio. This restriction was firmly enshrined in the 1990 Broadcasting Act. But soon after the new ITV regime come into operation a number of the major newspaper groups started lobbying for it to be lifted. Their argument was framed in terms of the newly developing multimedia environment. This, the newspaper owners maintained, required powerful media companies with controlling interests across different types of media, and so meant allowing newspaper owners to own ITV and commercial radio licences (British Media Industry Group, 1994). This argument was of dubious validity (see Goodwin, 1995). Nevertheless, it appeared in keeping with the new emphasis in Government policy on the multimedia future. The major perceived problem was that to let all newspaper groups own ITV licences would mean letting Rupert Murdoch's News Corporation into UK commercial terrestrial broadcasting. The government eventually met this objection by permitting newspaper groups to own a controlling interest in an ITV licence, so long as they did not control more than 25 per cent of the British national newspaper market (a threshold that excluded not merely News Corporation, but also Mirror Group Newspapers) (Department of National Heritage, 1995a). This exclusion of News Corporation and the Mirror Group was unsuccessfully challenged by the Labour Opposition, now firmly committed to courting the media business in general and News Corporation in particular.

The last strand of the Tory government's focus on the multimedia future was digital terrestrial television. In the mid-1990s the British government was in advance of virtually any other country in its commitment to this new distribution technology. The government presented it as a significant step on the road to a more general interactive and multimedia future (Department of National Heritage, 1995b). Again the argument was dubious – digital terrestrial broadcasting provided no significant interactivity, less channels (perhaps 20) than were already provided to millions of British homes by analogue cable or satellite (perhaps 50) and far less than would be provided at virtually the same time, or even before, by digital satellite (several hundred).

Nevertheless, in the 1996 Broadcasting Act the government provided the framework for the rapid launch of digital terrestrial television. Thanks to that, Britain is likely to be a pioneer, internationally, in digital terrestrial television. Whether this pioneering exercise will prove a successful one, or not, remains to be seen.

This final phase of Tory broadcasting policy suggests one further lesson about the role of the state in shaping the media. It also powerfully reinforces a lesson from the first phase. Even with a government apparently so committed to letting the market take its course, state policy on the media is still seen by particular sections of the media industry as one that can powerfully advance or retard their particular commercial interests. The fact that such industrial interest groups argue their corner in more general terms (like 'we are the ones who will advance the digital revolution') should not be allowed to obscure this increasingly important reality of media politics.

This last phase of Tory broadcasting policy showed, once again, that even governments apparently committed to *laissez-faire* and technological inevitability use the state to promote particular media technologies. As the example of the early Tory government's promotion of cable and satellite had already shown, they may sometimes get this seriously wrong. Digital terrestrial television may well prove to be similarly ill thought through.

All change with New Labour?

The general lessons about the state and the media to be drawn from the broadcasting policies of the 18 years of Margaret Thatcher and John Major are twofold. First, the ways in which the state tries to shape the media are the subject of pressure from interest groups and established institutions, political pragmatism and accident, even in a period of apparently ideologically driven government. Even apparently ideologically driven governments do not simply get their way.

Second, even when policies are apparently driven by a philosophy of 'leave it to the market', the state still counts in media, and counts powerfully. Had the Tory government put advertising on the BBC, really deregulated ITV, established a British Canal-plus rather than a Channel 4, successfully established a national satellite broadcaster in the mid-1980s or allowed BT a free run on cable television, then the British media landscape at the end of the 1990s would have looked very different from the way it in fact turned out.

References

British Media Industry Group, *The Future of the British Media Industry*. London: BMIG, 1994.

Department of National Heritage, *The Future of the BBC: Serving the Nation, Competing World-Wide* (White Paper). London: HMSO, Cm 2621, 1994.

Department of National Heritage, *Media Ownership: The Government's Proposals*. London: DNH, Cm 2872, 1995a.

Department of National Heritage, *Digital Terrestrial Broadcasting*. London: DNH, Cm 2946, 1995b.

Department of Trade and Industry, *Creating the Superhighways of the Future: Developing Broadband Communications in the UK*. London: HMSO, Cm 2734, 1994.

Gamble, A. *The Free Economy and the Strong State: The Politics of Thatcherism*. London: Macmillan, 1994.

Goodwin, P. 'A green light for the Moguls' Charter?', *British Journalism Review*, 6, 1 (1995) pp. 45–50.

House of Commons Trade and Industry Committee, *Optical Fibre Networks*. London: HMSO, 1994.

Home Office, *Direct Broadcasting by Satellite*. London, HMSO, 1981.

Home Office, *Broadcasting in the '90s: Competition, Choice and Quality*. London: HMSO, Cm 517, 1988.

Information Technology Advisory Panel (ITAP) *Cable Systems*. London: Cabinet Office, 1982.

Peacock, A. (Chairman) *Report of the Committee on the Financing of the BBC*. London: HMSO, Cmnd 9824, 1986.

Pilkingon, H. (Chairman) *Report of the Committee on Broadcasting, 1960*. London: HMSO, Cmnd 1753, 1962.

Pool, I. de S. *Technologies of Freedom*. Cambridge, Mass: Harvard University Press, 1983.

CHAPTER 9

The Regulation of Media Content

JULIAN PETLEY

Media regulation is all too often discussed only in terms of the explicit codes governing media content. Important though these are, however, they are by no means the only ways in which limitations are placed on press and broadcasting output. This chapter will therefore begin by taking a critical look at the much-mythologized issue of media freedom in Britain. It will then move on to examine two aspects of the law – libel, and the growth of various forms of prior restraint – which, it has been argued, pose increasingly acute threats to freedom of expression. Finally, we will take a critical look at the actual codes relating to media content, making a clear and forthright distinction between those governing broadcasting, which carry some kind of statutory weight, and those applying to the press, which most emphatically do not.

In the wake of Princess Diana's fatal accident there were widespread demands that the media, which were at first largely blamed for hounding her to death, should be subject to more stringent regulation. Particular animosity was reserved for the tabloid press and their hired paparazzi, and the solution most frequently proposed as a curb on their intrusive behaviour was a privacy law. Two months after Princess Diana's funeral and Earl Spencer's attack on the 'evil' tabloids, a Guardian/ICM opinion poll showed that 81 per cent of those interviewed believed that members of the royal family should be protected by a privacy law, with 55 per cent wanting to see this protection extended to celebrities, and 45 per cent including politicians as well.

What this outcry obscured, however, is that the British media are, by Western standards at least, remarkably tightly regulated. Thus William Waldegrave's 1992 White Paper, *Open Government*, listed 251 statutory instruments limiting the media's ability to report government business, while there are some 50 pieces of legislation that restrict media freedom, such as the Contempt of Court Act, the Obscene Publications Act and the Police and Criminal Evidence Act. Most of these Acts apply to all media, while a few, such as the Broadcasting Act, apply only to radio and television. And the broadcasters, as outlined below, are also subject to various 'internal' regulations, such as *The ITC Programme Code* (Independent Television Commission, 1998), the BBC *Producers' Guidelines* (1993) and the Broadcasting Standards Commission's *Codes of Guidance* (1998).

The sobering fact, then, is that even before the revolutions of 1989, which brought media freedom to Eastern Europe, Britain came only sixteenth in the league of those countries that enjoy freedom to publish. A study by Helsinki Watch, which monitors and promotes compliance with the human rights provisions of the 1975 Helsinki Accords, concluded that 'Britain falls short of protecting freedom of expression guaranteed by conventions and international agreements to which it is a party' (Helsinki Watch, 1991, pp. iii–iv). As Tim Crook has put it:

> In Britain we have a media besieged with guilt over the harassment of Diana, and a defensive, cringing culture where the constitutional role of the press and media is compromised by and ambivalent in its relationship with the establishment. Britain may well have been the 'mother of all liberties' in the history of the English-speaking world, but she is fast becoming somewhat intolerant in her old age and her 'children' have advanced with a much more equitable balance between the rights of a free media and the conduct of government. (Crook, 1998, p. 14)

Britain has no written constitution, and no Freedom of Information Act, and only recently has it incorporated the European Convention on Human Rights into domestic law. Ritual incantations about media freedom notwithstanding, the fact is, as Robertson and Nicol argue, that what freedom the media have had:

> is protected by unwritten convention rather than by a legal constitution [which] means that there is no external brake upon Parliament or the courts moving to restrict it in particular ways, or as the mood of the times takes them. Britain may still be a country where 'everything is permitted, which is not specifically prohibited', but the specific prohibitions have become more numerous, without having to justify themselves against the overriding principle of public interest. (Robertson and Nicol, 1992, p. 36)

In effect, then, there has never been any domestically created, statutory, legally enforceable right to freedom of expression at all, even where matters of genuine public interest are concerned. In law, journalists are not regarded as society's watchdogs and are thus granted no greater rights, freedoms or responsibilities than anybody else. Similarly, newspapers and broadcasters are treated not as Lord Macaulay's 'fourth estate' of liberal democracy, a means whereby those in power can be called publicly to account, but in exactly the same way as any other commercial operation. Indeed, in these days when information is increasingly regarded not simply as property, but as the most valuable of all forms of property, judges, especially in cases in which the media are alleged to have breached commercial confidence, are all too likely to value the property rights of the plaintiff above the media's right to freedom of expression. To quote Robertson and Nicol:

> 'Free speech', in fact, means no more than speech from which illegal utterances are subtracted... In practice, the free press is not a 'free' press: it is what is left of the copy by laws and lawyers. Defamation, blasphemy and sedition have been with us for centuries, but in recent years new rods have been fashioned and old ones polished for editorial backs: breach of confidence, contempt of court, official secrecy, D-notices, incitement to disaffection, prevention of terrorism, copyright – the grounds for censorship are legion. (Robertson and Nicol, 1992, pp. 1–2)

In the space available it is impossible to detail every law touching on media freedom. Instead I shall comment on two areas of the law giving increasing cause for concern: libel, and the growth of various forms of prior restraint.

Libel

To put it simply, libel law protects the right to reputation against defamatory allegations, defamation having been famously defined by Lord Atkin, in 1936, as any publication which tends 'to lower the plaintiff in the estimation of right-thinking members of society generally'.

London has been called 'the libel capital of the world' and 'a town named Sue' because British libel law is much more favourable to libel plaintiffs than that of other countries. First, the burden is on the defendant to prove that the contested material is either fair comment or true; second, there is no 'public interest' defence; and third, British juries, in a clear mark of disapproval of the intrusive antics of the popular press, have shown themselves more than willing to award massive damages to successful libel defendants. Such a combination of factors inevitably produces a 'chilling effect' which may well deter the media from publishing certain stories, even if they know them to be true, particularly when the sheer cost and effort of defending a potential libel action are taken into account. Barendt *et al.* distinguish usefully between what they call the *direct* and the *structural* chilling effect. The former generally

> takes the form of omission of material the author believes to be true but cannot establish to the extent judged sufficient to avoid an unacceptable risk of legal action and an award of damages. This produces the attitude exemplified by most magazine editors and publishers: 'if in doubt, strike it out'. 'Doubt' here, it should be emphasised, relates to their ability to present a legally sustainable defence, not to the editor's view of the validity of the story. (Barendt *et al.*, 1997, p. 191)

The structural effect, meanwhile, is more subtle, but equally restrictive.

[This] is not manifest through alteration or cancellation of a specific article, programme or book. Rather it functions in a preventive manner: preventing the creation of certain material. Particular organisations and individuals are considered taboo because of the libel risks; certain subjects are treated as off-limits, minefields into which it is too dangerous to stray. Nothing is edited to lessen libel risk because nothing is written in the first place. (Barendt *et al.*, 1997, p. 192)

Organizations that spring to mind include such well-known litigants as McDonalds, the Police Federation, Monsanto and the drugs industry, while topics that are clearly highly sensitive are deaths in police custody, genetically modified crops, environmental damage by multinational companies in Third World countries, bribery and corruption in the arms trade, and so on. Perhaps it is hardly surprising, then, that David Hooper, one of Britain's leading libel specialists, has called the law of defamation 'a vast, submerged self-censorship' (cited in Helsinki Watch, 1991, p. 13) and that the environmental campaigner George Monbiot has concluded that: 'the libel laws are as effective a barrier to free speech in Britain as government intervention in Indonesia. And, in the best authoritarian tradition, they rely for their routine observance not upon enforcement, but upon self-censorship' (Monbiot, 1998).

Since fear of prosecution for libel is a powerful incentive not to publish or broadcast, defamation law can be seen as a spur to prior restraint, and it is to this subject that I now want to turn.

Prior Restraint

Prior restraint consists simply of various forms of pre-publication censorship; a newspaper or broadcaster thus constrained cannot 'publish and be damned', since they are damned before they start. That this is unacceptable in a democratic society was laid down by Sir William Blackstone in his *Commentaries* of 1765:

the liberty of the press is indeed essential to the nature of a free state; but this consists in laying no previous restraints on publications, and not in freedom from censure for criminal matter when published. Every free man has an undoubted right to lay what sentiments he pleases before the public; to forbid this is to destroy the freedom of the press; but if he publishes what is improper, mischievous or illegal, he must take the consequences of his own temerity. (cited in Robertson and Nicol, 1992, pp. 19–20)

Recently, however, the notion that prior restraint is an unacceptable shackle on media freedom has been badly eroded, and judges are asked to issue injunctions against the media almost every week. They do not always comply, of course, but all too frequently they do, and sometimes they even ban the media from reporting that an injunction has been granted!

Meanwhile, an increasing number of court cases are held wholly or partly in secret, or the media are barred in other ways from reporting what is going on. In particular, section 39 of the Children and Young Persons Act (which allows for the prevention of the identification of young people involved in court cases) and sections 4 and 11 of the Contempt of Court Act are being applied oppressively and inappropriately by a worryingly large number of judges and magistrates, with the local press bearing the brunt of this culture of judicial secrecy.

A particularly Kafkaesque example of this disturbing tendency was provided by a drugs trial held entirely in camera at the Inner London Crown Court in 1994. The decision to hold the trial in camera was unsuccessfully challenged by two journalists, Tim Crook and Caroline Godwin; as usual, the journalists were not entitled to know why the case was being held in camera, nor were they allowed to mount their challenge at an oral hearing. The defendant was found guilty and subsequently appealed; the entire appeal was then held in camera. Furthermore, as Crook himself puts it, 'because we had to give an undertaking not to reveal the reason for the original trial secrecy, we could not report the Appeal Court ruling. Neither could we say that our appeal was successful, nor could we say that it was unsuccessful' (Crook, 1998, p. 14).

Breach of Confidence

To return to the matter of injunctions, however, it is in matters concerning breach of confidence that these are now most commonly sought. As Tom Crone (1991, p. 83) argues, the law of confidence is becoming a 'boom area' and 'the most significant fetter on a free press'. This area of civil law was first developed to protect trade secrets; gradually, however, the notion of 'confidential information' has expanded to cover any information which has been imparted in confidence. Again, this has to do with the fact that:

> Information has become property, something that can be bought and sold, injuncted and embargoed, almost irrespective of its significance to political debate or current public policy. The laws that permit injunctions and damages for breaches of confidence and copyright are powerful weapons against media use of information supplied by 'moles', 'whistle blowers' and others who leak secrets from within organizations. (Robertson and Nicol, 1992, p. 172)

In breach of confidence cases the crucial stage is the application for an interim injunction suppressing publication of the information in question until the action itself comes to trial. Since this probably will not take place for a long while, by which time the information may have gone stale, neither side is really interested in this distant prospect. If the injunction is granted, the media organization may appeal, or it may simply give up, unwilling to face the spectre of huge legal fees in the defence of an item which may anyway never see the light of day. In the latter case, an interim injunction becomes effectively a permanent one. Here, as indeed elsewhere, Robert Maxwell provides a chilling example: six months before his death he had obtained a High Court injunction banning the media from publishing any suggestion that he or any of his companies had engaged in 'dubious accounting devices' or had 'sought to mislead... as to the value of the assets of the company'. Indeed, this was one of those occasions when the media were banned from even reporting that such an injunction had been obtained.

However, it is not simply the Maxwells of this world who have used breach of confidence legislation to their own advantage; the British government is itself a pastmaster at invoking this law – witness the *Spycatcher* affair. When former MI5 agent Peter Wright published his autobiography in the States, the *Guardian* and *Observer* published its main allegations, and the *Sunday Times* began to serialize it. All were injuncted, not under the already increasingly discredited Official Secrets Act, but under the civil law of confidence. Finally, thanks to the book being widely published abroad, and after interventions by the Lords and the European Court of Human Rights, the media 'won' in that the right to publish was established and the government made to look both foolish and oppressive, but the law was only marginally liberalized.

However, the Lords overturned the injunctions solely on the practical grounds that the material had already been so widely disseminated as to render them pointless. The senior judge in the case, Lord Keith, stated: 'I would stress that I do not base this [ruling] upon any balancing of public interest, nor upon any considerations of freedom of the press, but simply on the view that all possible damage to the interest of the Crown has already been done' (cited in Helsinki Watch, 1991, p. 6). By contrast, the European Court of Human Rights unanimously ruled in 1991 that the injunctions upheld by the English courts after *Spycatcher* had been published abroad were an infringement of Article 10 of the European Convention on Human Rights. Indeed, just how marginally *Spycatcher* changed the confidence law is illustrated by the ease with which, in August 1997, the government used it in order to stop the *Mail on Sunday* publishing the revelations of David Shayler, another disaffected MI5 man.

What this brief review of the laws of defamation and confidence, and of the increasing use of various forms of prior restraint, has attempted to suggest is that freedom of expression is rather more heavily regulated and circumscribed in Britain than might at first appear. Powerful commercial forces with a vested interest in gagging the media, allied with a judicial culture in which freedom of expression seems to count for alarmingly little, not to mention changes in the media themselves, which are beyond the scope of this chapter, have combined to produce a climate in which media content is regulated and restricted less by overt censorship than by more insidious means, the most 'invisible' of which is self-censorship.

Restrictions on Broadcasters

As noted earlier, broadcasters are subject to regulations that apply only to them. These include regulations that permit direct state intervention. Thus Section 8.2 of the BBC Agreement states that:

> The Secretary of State may from time to time by notice in writing require the Corporation to refrain at any specified time or at all times from broadcasting or transmitting any matter or matter of any class specified in such notice; and the Secretary of State may at any time or times vary or revoke any such notice. The Corporation may at its discretion announce or refrain from announcing that such a notice has been given or has been varied or revoked. (HMSO, 1996, p. 10)

Paragraph 10 (3) of the Broadcasting Act 1990 contains similar provisions for the companies regulated by the ITC.

Thus it was, in October 1988, that the Home Secretary, Douglas Hurd, was able, as part of the government's response to the Northern Ireland 'troubles', to act directly to ban:

> Any words spoken, whether in the course of an interview or discussion or otherwise, by a person who appears or is heard on the programme in which the matter is broadcast where:
>
> (a) the person speaking the words represents or purports to represent a specified organization, or
> (b) the words support or solicit or invite support for such an organization. (Curtis and Jempson, 1993, p. 12)

The organizations included the IRA, INLA, Sinn Fein, Republican Sinn Fein and the Ulster Defence Association. The ban was contested by the broadcasting union BECTU, the National Union of Journalists and Article 19 but upheld by the House of Lords in 1991 and by the European Commission on Human Rights in 1994; that year, however, it was dropped by the British government in response to the IRA cease-fire.

For the most part, however, the BBC and independent television (which here is taken to mean ITV, Channel 4, Channel 5 and the cable and satellite channels) are self-regulated by various codes and guidelines, drafted and interpreted by government-appointed bodies such as the Independent Television Commission (ITC) and the Broadcasting Standards Commission (BSC) which lack the force of direct law but which are nonetheless of powerful effect. These codes flesh out the broad principles laid down for the BBC in the Agreement with the Secretary of State for Culture, Media and Sport, and for independent television in the Broadcasting Act. Thus Section 5.1(c) of the Agreement requires the BBC to ensure that all its programmes:

Treat controversial subjects with due accuracy and impartiality, both in the Corporation's news services and in the more general field of programmes dealing with
matters of public policy or of political or industrial controversy, and do not contain
any material expressing the opinion of the Corporation on current affairs or matters
of public policy other than broadcasting. (HMSO, 1996, p. 10)

Meanwhile, Section 5.1(d) lays down the requirement that its programmes
'do not include anything which offends against good taste or decency or is
likely to encourage or incite to crime or to lead to disorder or to be offensive
to public feeling'. Almost identical duties are prescribed by the Broadcasting
Act 1990 for the ITC, except that the latter is also required to draw up and
enforce a Programme Code (Independent Television Commission, 1998)
covering matters such as advertising, impartiality and the portrayal of
violence. That the Act is so much more concerned with impartiality than is
the Agreement is due to amendments by Tory peers who clearly regarded ITV
as a hotbed of left-wing subversion. Thus the Code must not only establish
rules to ensure that 'due impartiality is preserved on the part of the person
providing the service as respects matters of political or industrial controversy
or relating to current public policy' but those rules must indicate:

1. what due impartiality does and does not require, either generally or in relation
   to particular circumstances;
2. the ways in which due impartiality may be achieved in connection with
   programmes of particular descriptions. (ITC, 1998)

The Act also states that, in applying the impartiality requirement, 'a series
of programmes may be considered as a whole' (Broadcasting Act 1990,
pp. 6–7). Here the Tory peers thought they had spotted a loophole, in that if
'balance' were to be allowed to be achieved across a whole series, and not
within each of the programmes constituting that series, how could viewers be
made properly aware of the full, 'balanced' diet ultimately on offer? Thus the
Act lurches into scheduling matters, requiring the ITC to specify the time
limit within which any programme 'balancing' another must be broadcast,
and to ensure that viewers of any 'unbalanced' programme are made aware,
through advance publicity at the time of its transmission, of the forthcoming
'balancing' programme. This, surely, gives a whole new meaning to the term
'political correctness'!
     Unlike its predecessor, the Independent Broadcasting Authority, the ITC
does not have the power to preview or pre-censor programmes. Breaches of
the code, however, can result in a variety of sanctions, ranging from warnings, the imposition of fines and/or on-screen apologies to, ultimately, loss
of the licence to broadcast. The ITC regularly monitors its licensed channels, although investigation of alleged breaches may also be triggered by
viewers' complaints.

The BBC equivalent of the ITC Programme Code is the 276-page *Producers' Guidelines* (BBC, 1993). This is described by the BBC Governors (who are appointed by the Queen on the recommendation of ministers, and who serve as trustees for the public interest by setting BBC strategy and standards, monitoring the observance of its guidelines and assessing overall performance) as setting out 'the editorial and ethical principles that must underpin all BBC programmes'. More specifically:

> They provide detailed guidance for programme makers across a broad range of issues, including accuracy and fairness, taste and decency, privacy, the reporting of crime, political coverage and commercial relationships. They also incorporate a specific code on impartiality and accuracy. The guidelines take account of the legal and statutory requirements on broadcasters – for example, the laws on defamation, national security and copyright and the rules on advertising and sponsorship – as well as the BBC's own internal standards. (BBC, 1997, p. 15)

Under the terms of its Royal Charter and Agreement the BBC is required to publish a Statement of Promises to Viewers and Listeners. This it does annually, and the section of the 1998 edition devoted to 'our programme standards' contains the commitments to be accurate, fair and impartial, represent all groups in society accurately and avoid reinforcing prejudice, and observe the 9.00 pm watershed on television (BBC, 1998, p. 11).

Complaints about programmes are investigated by the BBC's Programme Complaints Unit, whose work is monitored by the Governors. All programme makers are required to cooperate with the Unit's investigations. Where a complaint is upheld, the BBC will apologize, and in some cases an on-air correction may be broadcast. In the most serious cases of breaches of the Guidelines, disciplinary proceedings against the staff involved may be initiated. A summary of all complaints upheld by the Programme Complaints Unit, and an account of the subsequent actions undertaken by the BBC, is published quarterly.

The activities of all broadcasters are also overseen by the Broadcasting Standards Commission. This was set up as the Broadcasting Standards Council in 1988, in response to supposedly widespread public concern about levels of sex, violence and bad language on television. However, this 'concern' was wildly exaggerated by an overwhelmingly Tory press ever eager to echo and reinforce the Thatcher government's bleak and relentless hostility to the broadcasting establishment, and thus it is hard to disagree with Robertson and Nicol's verdict that the BSC is 'another external pressure upon broadcasters to bring their professional judgement (about what the public interest requires to be seen) into line with official judgements about what the public does not need to be shown' (Robertson and Nicol, 1992, p. 606).

The Broadcasting Standards Council was given statutory existence by the Broadcasting Act 1990, and transformed into the Broadcasting Standards Commission by the Broadcasting Act 1996 which merged the Broadcasting

Complaints Commission with it and brought matters of fairness and privacy within its remit. Its chairman, deputy chairman and members are appointed by the Secretary of State, and its duties are clearly laid out in the 1988 White Paper on broadcasting which preceded the Broadcasting Act 1990. Here its role is defined as being to:

- draw up, in consultation with the broadcasting authorities and the other responsible bodies in the broadcasting, cable and video fields, a code on the portrayal of sex and violence and standards of taste and decency
- monitor and report on the portrayal of violence and sex, and standards of taste and decency, in television and radio programmes received in the UK and in video works
- receive, consider and make findings on complaints and comments from individuals and organizations on matters within its competence and ensure that such findings are effectively publicized
- undertake research on matters such as the nature and effects on attitudes and behaviour of the portrayal of violence and sex in television programmes and in video works
- prepare an Annual Report, which the Home Secretary will lay before Parliament and publish (Home Office, 1988, p. 35).

In addition, Section 107 of the Broadcasting Act 1996 required the enlarged BSC to draw up a code:

Giving guidance as to principles to be observed, and practices to be followed, in connection with the avoidance of:

1. unjust or unfair treatment in programmes to which this section applies, or
2. unwarranted infringement of privacy in, or connection with the obtaining of material included in, such programmes. (Broadcasting Act 1996, p. 101)

It is important to note that Section 152(3) of the Broadcasting Act 1990 and Section 107(2) of the Broadcasting Act 1996 require broadcasters, when drawing up or revising their own codes, to 'reflect the general effect' of the relevant parts of the BSC's two codes.

It is frequently asserted that British terrestrial television was 'deregulated' in the Thatcher era. In an economic sense this was indeed the case, up to a point, although as Peter Goodwin argues in Chapter 8, this too is dubious. In fact, deregulation did not extend to relaxing controls over programme content – indeed, quite the opposite. It is all too often forgotten that the Peacock Report argued that, in the future:

What we do expect to disappear or much diminish is the need for negative censorious controls. If the right conditions are established, there will be little need for 'regulation' apart from the general law of the land to cover matters such as public decency, defamation, sedition, blasphemy and most other matters of concern in broadcasting. (Peacock, 1986, p. 133)

Such sentiments were, however, anathema to many Tories. Thus the 1988 White Paper argued that 'because of broadcasting's power, immediacy and influence, there should be continued provisions, through both the law and regulatory oversight, governing programme standards, including the portrayal of violence and sex' (Home Office, 1988, p. 5), while at the same time assuring the reader that 'the Government is also clear that there need be no contradiction between the desire to increase competition and widen choice and concern that programme standards on good taste and decency should be maintained' (Home Office, 1988, p. 1). It was left to irritated Peacock Committee member Samuel Brittan to draw the obvious conclusion:

In putting forward the idea of a free broadcasting market without censorship, Peacock exposed many of the contradictions in the Thatcherite espousal of market forces. In principle, Mrs Thatcher and her supporters are all in favour of deregulation, competition and consumer choice. But they are also even more distrustful than traditionalist Tories of policies that allow people to listen to and watch what they like, subject only to the law of the land. They espouse the market system but dislike the libertarian value-judgements involved in its operation. (Brittan, 1989, p. 40)

It is estimated that the regulation of British broadcasting now costs well over £20 million a year. Much of it is overlapping, and a good deal amounts to nothing more or less than latter-day Bowdlerism. Lord Rees Mogg, the first chairman of the BSC, characteristically once referred to television as a 'guest in the home', and regulators clearly feel that it is one that should be thoroughly vetted before being allowed across the threshold. It is indeed hard not to agree with Geoffrey Robertson's view that:

Speech is not free on British television and radio: it is cribbed and confined not merely by the laws which apply to all media, but by a notion of what is 'seemly' for a general audience to hear and view. Lord Reith, founding father of the BBC, insisted that men dress in dinner jackets to read the radio news, and would not allow divorcees on the airwaves; his spirit lives on in the innumerable codes of conduct designed and enforced by overlapping bodies of Government regulators appointed to minimize any shock or discomfort caused by the electronic guests in British homes. (Robertson, 1993, p. 273)

On the other hand, of course, broadcasting regulation has its positive aspects too; it does not simply regulate out material which some (but not others) may find distasteful but also regulates in features which the majority of listeners and viewers clearly find desirable, such as diversity, 'quality', political neutrality, regionality, educational material and so on. Clearly, a balance has to be struck between, on the one hand, a nannyish over-caution and fear of popular tastes and, on the other, a populist embracing of unfettered market forces. Otherwise one risks turning broadcasting in Britain into the mirror image of its press which, as Colin Sparks points out in Chapter 3, is 'regulated' to a far greater extent by market forces, with consequences which many find unacceptable. There is, of course, the Press Complaints Commission but this not a publicly accountable regulatory body but simply an insurance policy against statutory legislation. As Geoffrey Robertson has damningly put it, the press has:

> established a sophisticated public-relations exercise called the Press Complaints Commission (PCC), with an annual budget of £1 million, to convince Parliament that its ethics are susceptible to what it optimistically describes as 'self-regulation'. But the PCC is a confidence trick which has failed to inspire confidence, and forty years' experience of 'press self-regulation' demonstrates only that the very concept is an oxymoron. (Robertson, 1993, p. 111)

Press Regulation

The PCC came into existence in 1991, replacing the discredited Press Council, as a result of growing public and governmental disquiet at the intrusive behaviour and degraded journalistic standards of the tabloid press. This led to a Committee on Privacy and related matters being established by the Home Office under the chairmanship of David Calcutt QC. The PCC was given two years to try to improve things, but at the end of that time Calcutt reached the entirely reasonable conclusion that:

> The Press Complaints Commission is not, in my view, an effective regulator of the press. The Commission has not been set up in a way, and is not operating a code of practice, which enables it to command not only press but also public confidence. It does not, in my view, hold the balance fairly between the press and the individual. The Commission is not the truly independent body which it should be. The Commission, as constituted, is, in essence, a body set up by the industry, financed by the industry, dominated by the industry, operating a code of practice devised by the industry and which is over-favourable to the industry. (Calcutt, 1993, p. 41)

To replace the PCC, Calcutt proposed a Statutory Press Complaints Tribunal with a fearsome range of powers (Calcutt, 1990). These included not simply drawing up a code of practice and investigating alleged breaches of it, but also stopping publication of offending material, taking evidence on oath and imposing fines. It would be chaired by a judicial figure appointed by the Lord Chancellor, sitting with two assessors drawn from a panel of experts. This was as draconian and authoritarian as the PCC was ineffectual and compromised, and fortunately the government did not accept Calcutt's recommendations; one would hope that this was because they found them incompatible with democratic notions of media freedom, but fear of a press backlash may well have been a crucial factor here. But whatever the case, the fact remains that the manifest shortcomings of the PCC threatened to land the UK with a system of press censorship which would have made the Cromwellian 'licensers of the press' look tame indeed by comparison.

In the intervening years the PCC has tinkered with its code when public criticism of press standards has threatened to get out of hand, appointed a majority of non-press members (none of whom are remotely 'representative' of anything other than the Great and the Good, of course) and shrewdly brought in Lord Wakeham, Mrs Thatcher's chief political fixer, as its chairman, who has proved a formidable political lobbyist on behalf of the press. Nothing can alter the unassailable fact, however, that the powers which it has chosen to give itself are exceedingly limited; thus it cannot (because it will not) stop newspapers from publishing circulation-boosting stories (even if they are untrue or inaccurate), award compensation to victims of the press, oblige papers to display prominently its (exceedingly rare) adjudications against them, or monitor compliance with its code as opposed merely to reacting to complaints. Furthermore, it resolutely refuses to entertain complaints from third parties. It has commissioned no research and, even in the wake of the death of Princess Diana, failed to initiate or engage in any serious debate over press ethics. Nor has it raised even a whimper at the very real restrictions on serious journalism discussed earlier.

To read its code's high-flown rhetoric about 'accuracy', 'opportunity to reply', 'privacy', 'harassment', 'intrusion into grief or shock', 'discrimination' and so on, and then to immerse oneself in the daily, debased reality of much of the British press, which quite clearly cares not a jot for such self-deluding nonsense, is all that is needed to understand why the PCC cannot be seriously regarded as a regulatory body. It is also worth noting that, most conveniently, vast numbers of complaints fall outside its narrowly self-circumscribed remit. For example, in 1997 the PCC received 2944 complaints (the vast majority relating to inaccuracy and not, as might be commonly supposed, privacy); when third party complaints and those falling outside the code are subtracted, the total number of complaints actually investigated was 1510. Of these only 82 were adjudicated, and of these a mere 34 were upheld, a minuscule 1.15 per cent of the total complaints received and a mere 2.25 per cent of those the PCC actually deigned to investigate. This could, of course, be construed as a comment on the standard of the complaints – but it could equally well be taken as a reflection of the true nature, function and loyalties of the PCC. (For a detailed account of a complaint to the PCC see Petley, 1997.)

As John Tulloch has pointed out (1998, p. 77) the PCC is far more like the customer complaints department of a commercial organization than it is a proper regulatory body. That it has absolutely no desire to be the latter was particularly clearly illustrated in the hostility which it manifested towards the European Convention on Human Rights at the end of 1997 and the early months of 1998. In brief, it feared that Article 8 might introduce a privacy law by the 'back door' (as it saw it) and that Article 10, which concerns the right to freedom of expression, would not be strong enough to counteract this. Furthermore, the PCC was alarmed that, under the Convention, it would be classed as a 'public authority'; thus its deliberations could be challenged in the courts and, inevitably, it would be forced to operate in a more judicial fashion. Hence the truly remarkable spectacle of the press campaigning *against* the first measure ever enacted in Britain that attempts to put freedom of expression on a statutory footing, quite apart from having the temerity to suggest that newspapers, alone among institutions with public functions, should actually stand above international human rights law. Quite clearly, for many papers the ability to snoop and poke into private lives (which could indeed be curtailed under Article 8) is infinitely more important than the task of carrying out serious journalism (which may well be helped by Article 10). At the same time, and no less remarkably, Lord Wakeham was lobbying vigorously to the effect that that the last thing that the PCC wanted was any real power or status! Thus, paradoxically, the fact that the PCC is indeed no more than the newspaper industry's creature was ably, if inadvertently, confirmed by its own chairman when he complained that if it was treated as a public body:

> At a stroke the Government would be taking a successful self-regulatory system – the principal aim of which is amicably to resolve disputes under a voluntary Code – and turning it into a legal system. Yet the PCC was never meant to be a legal system... It is only through *voluntary* co-operation of editors that progress has been, and is being, made to raise standards. The Code itself is voluntary: it would cease to exist were it a legal document. (Wakeham, 1998)

We began this chapter by suggesting that the content of Britain's media is rather more heavily regulated than is commonly supposed, and then went on to examine how certain laws, and their interpretation and application by the courts, can act as a significant regulator of media content. However, this legal aspect of media regulation is too often overlooked in favour of an examination of the media's own codes of practice, although these of course have to take into account the laws of the land. Our own discussion of these codes made a particularly firm distinction between those governing broadcasting, which carry a degree of statutory authority, and that applying to the press, which manifestly does not and cannot seriously be regarded as anything other than the newspapers' insurance policy against the threat of statute law.

References

Barendt, E., Lustgarten, L., Norrie, K. and Stephenson, H. *Libel and the Media: the Chilling Effect*. Oxford: Clarendon Press, 1997.
BBC, *Producers' Guidelines*. London, 1993.

BBC, *Governing Today's BBC*. London, 1997.

BBC, *Our Commitment to You*. London, 1998.

Brittan, S. 'The Case for the Consumer Market', in C. Veljanovski (ed.) *Freedom in Broadcasting*, London: Institute of Economic Affairs, 1989, pp. 25–50.

Broadcasting Act 1990. London: HMSO.

Broadcasting Act 1996. London: HMSO.

Broadcasting Standards Commission, *Codes of Guidance*. London: 1998.

Calcutt, D. *Report of the Committee on Privacy and Related Matters*. London: HMSO, 1990.

Calcutt, D. *Review of Press Self-Regulation*. London: HMSO, 1993.

Crone, T. *Law and the Media*. Oxford: Butterworth Heinemann, 1991.

Crook, T. 'An ocean apart on freedom', *UK Press Gazette* (13 February 1998) p. 14.

Curtis, M. and Jempson, M. *Airwaves: Ireland, the Media and the Broadcasting Ban*. London: Campaign for Press and Broadcasting Freedom, 1993.

Helsinki Watch. *Restricted Subjects*. New York: Human Rights Watch, 1991.

HMSO, Copy of Agreement 25 January 1996 between Her Majesty's Secretary of State for National Heritage and the BBC, CM 3152. London: HMSO, 1996, p.10.

Home Office, *Broadcasting in the '90s: Competition, Choice and Quality*. London: HMSO, 1988.

Independent Television Commission. *The ITC Programme Code*. London, 1998.

Monbiot, G. 'Free speech comes dear', *Guardian*, 8 October 1998.

Peacock, A. *Committee on Financing the BBC*. London: HMSO, 1986.

Petley, J. 'No redress from the PCC', *British Journalism Review*, 8, 4, 1997.

Robertson, G. and Nicol, A. *Media Law*. London: Penguin, 1992.

Robertson, G. *Freedom, the Individual and the Law*. London: Penguin, 1993.

Tulloch, J. 'Managing the Press in a Medium-sized European Power', in H. Stephenson and M. Bromley, *Sex, Lies and Democracy*. London: Longman, 1998.

Wakeham, Lord. 'Law would be disaster for PCC', *UK Press Gazette*, 23 January 1998.

CHAPTER 10

European Union Media and Communication Policies

RICHARD COLLINS

Competition is not in fact an end or goal in itself. It is simply the most effective and least risky strategy we have for achieving our real policy goals concerning economic growth and efficient public service. (van Miert, 1996, p. 7)

This chapter reprises a pervasive theme in this volume: that in the last 15 years or so the European media and communications regime has changed dramatically. In the early 1980s it was (almost) universally presumed that efficient delivery of electronic media and communications services to the public required state intervention – characteristically telephony was provided by a state monopoly and broadcasting by a national public service broadcaster. But now private broadcasting is pervasive throughout the European Union and on 1 January 1998 all European Union (EU) states (with the qualified exceptions of Greece, Ireland, Luxembourg, Portugal and Spain) were required to open their telecommunication markets to competition and the private sector. There has been a massive shift in perception – markets rather than states are now widely seen as the instruments through which the European public interest in media and communications can best be secured – as the quote that begins this chapter testifies.

The key agency in this transition has been the European Community – latterly the European Union. The doctrine of 'ever closer union' embodied in the Treaty of Rome has inexorably led to the integration of European media and communication markets on the basis prescribed in the Treaty – notably in Articles 85–90 – of a competitive market. The Delors White Paper (a White Paper sets out policy position whereas a Green Paper advances proposals for discussion and/or consultation) on 'Growth, Competitiveness and Employment' (Commission of the European Communities, 1993a) stressed the economic importance of media and communications. It argued that only energy conservation and management and biotechnology offered comparable possibilities for wealth and job generation to the communication sector. The EU's Information Society initiative, often known as the Bangemann initiative, after Martin Bangemann, the Commissioner who has done so much to advance it, has also reinforced perceptions of the economic

158

importance of the media and communications sector (Bangemann, 1994). As this scene setting suggests, the EU has not initiated any significant measures for radio or the press (but see Commission of the European Communities, 1992 and Harcourt, 1996).

Telecommunications

On New Year's Day 1998 the 'Full Competition' Directive – a community 'law' – (Directive 96/19/EC) came into effect. The ratchet of liberalization has been turning since 1988 when liberalization of terminal attachment (for instance, phones and fax and answering machines) was proposed (and implemented in 1991 with Directive 91/263/EEC amended in Directive 93/68/EEC). Successive Directives have furthered realization of the common market in telecommunications goods and services envisioned in the European Commission's Green Paper (Commission of the European Communities, 1987). The Green Paper began to bring telecoms into line with the Treaty's general economic provisions – notably those on competition (pro), state aids (anti), market integration (pro). It emphasized three principles:

- liberalization of areas under monopoly
- harmonization of the European market
- application of competition rules.

Further Directives followed, notably the Open Network Provision (ONP) Framework Directive (90/387/EEC), the Services Directive (90/338/EEC), the Cable Directive (95/51/EC) and the Voice Telephony Directive (95/62/EEC). The most comprehensive, the Full Competition Directive (Directive 96/19/EC), required Member States to open all telecommunications services to competition (but implementation of its provisions for voice telephony services was delayed until 1 January 1998).

Periodically, the European Commission assesses Member States' progress in liberalizing telecoms. Invariably, the UK is recognized to have advanced furthest and fastest. In 1997, the Commission stated that 'no major problems are expected' in the United Kingdom. In contrast, it said of Belgium:

> The regulatory framework is largely incomplete... On interconnection... no implementing measure is available... transposition of the existing Leased Line Directive [is] incomplete... concern exists regarding Belgium's approach to the regime for new infrastructure... Another outstanding problem concerns the National Regulatory Authority. (Summarized from Annex III of the Communication from the Commission to the Council, the European Parliament, the Economic and Social Committee and the Committee of the Regions on the implementation of the telecommunications regulatory package as extant on 17 November 1997)

Television

Paradoxically, although telecommunications in the European Union are more fully liberalized than broadcasting (or strictly, television), integration and harmonization of the television market have advanced further than telecommunications. Television markets have been converging for nearly a decade and a half following the Commission's controversial 'Television without Frontiers' Green Paper (Commission of the European Communities, 1984). 'Television without Frontiers' contended that a single European television market would improve European competitiveness in the broadcasting and audiovisual sector and that it would also foster pan-European television. European consciousness and culture would be strengthened as European citizens viewed common services and programmes. The Green Paper echoed the European Parliament's Hahn Report of 1982 which stated 'Information is a decisive, perhaps the most decisive factor in European integration' (European Parliament 1982, p. 8). Hahn argued that 'The instruments which serve to shape public opinion today are the media. Of these, television, as an audio-visual means of communication is the most important' (European Parliament, 1982, p. 8). He also argued that political integration of Europe was unlikely to be achieved while 'the mass media is controlled at national level' (European Parliament, 1982, p. 8) and therefore pushed for the integration of markets to make pan-European services possible.

New television services have undoubtedly benefited viewers and listeners by providing new consumption opportunities, extending choice and, in important respects, increasing the range and diversity of broadcasting services. But 'Television without Frontiers' has also been seen as a Pandora's box unleashing a striking increase in the volume of American television programmes on European screens, weakening public service broadcasting and, through wholesale commercialization, polluting the medium best fitted to cultivate political and cultural solidarity among EU citizens. For, rather than fostering pan-European television and promoting European integration, 'Television without Frontiers' created a spectacular growth of commercial television in Europe.

Hodgson (1992) testified to this explosion stating that in 1982 there were four commercial television channels in Europe and by 1992 there were 58. By now there are more than 250 (Commission of the European Communities, 1997a). But growth has taken place in individual national (or linguistic) markets rather than through creation of a pan-European market. Moreover, commercial television spurred a massive increase in European imports of American programming: as between 1984 and 1992 the EU audiovisual trade deficit with the USA had increased ten-fold, amounting to 3500 million ecus per year in 1991 (Vasconcelos, 1994).

'Television without Frontiers' exemplified the Commission's power to initiate new policies without prompting from Member States or the European

Parliament. Initiatives to which the European Parliament and the Member States must (and can only) respond. 'Television without Frontiers' thus perfectly exemplifies what has often been called the European Union's 'democratic deficit' (Commission of the European Communities and European Parliament, 1990).

The Roots of Liberalization

Opening Member States' media and communication markets and creating, so far as circumstances permitted, an integrated single market in media and communications have thus been the main themes of EU's media and communication policy. These initiatives follow the logic of the European Treaty (the Treaty of Rome of 1957, amended at Maastricht in 1992), which constituted the European Economic Community on free market and free trading lines. Accordingly, the 'Television without Frontiers' Green Paper and the Directives that followed it (Directives 89/552/EEC and 97/36/EC) were based on the presumption that broadcasting could be treated as a market like any other. In turn this led to a host of competition cases assaulting the Community's public service broadcasters, and the European Broadcasting Union (EBU) in particular, in which commercial broadcasters (and the Commission's Competition Directorate) argued that public service broadcasters breached fair trading and fair competition principles.

Public Service Broadcasting

The competition provisions of the European Union treaties, and the provisions on state aids – Articles 90 and 92 – in particular, have weighed heavily on public service broadcasters because the licence fee is a hypothecated tax and thus, arguably, a form of state aid incompatible with Article 92 of the EEC Treaty. Doubtless none of this was imagined in the mid-1950s when the Treaty of Rome was drafted. European broadcasting was then dominated by national public service monopolies (apart from Finland and the United Kingdom which, exceptionally, had introduced advertising financed television to Europe in the mid-1950s but did not become members of the European Community until 1973 and 1995 respectively). Broadcasting competition, let alone cross-border broadcasting, was unlikely to have been imagined by the signatories of the Treaty.

'Television without Frontiers' – and the succession of competition cases which followed its publication – has thus reshaped European broadcasting. But the position embodied in them is not unchallenged. Elements in the Commission and the Parliament have testified fulsomely in support of public service broadcasting. See, for example, Carole Tongue MEP's Report (1996) and the European Parliament's Resolution on the role of public service television in a multimedia society and the public service broadcasting protocol added to the European Treaty in 1997 which states, *inter alia*:

> The provisions of this Treaty shall be without prejudice to the competence of the Member States to provide for the funding of public service broadcasting in so far as such funding is granted to broadcasting organizations for the fulfilment of the public service remit as conferred, defined and organized by each Member State.

But, in spite of the Protocol, the internal market is hostile to public service broadcasting. It could not be otherwise for, seen from the vantage point of the neo-classical economic theory underpinning the EEC Treaty, public service broadcasting is aberrant and offensive. The general economic provisions of the Treaty inexorably came to apply to broadcasting once it was defined as a traded service (as it was in the landmark Sacchi and Debauve cases). The Sacchi case established that broadcating was a service, not a product, and that discrimination on the grounds of the national origin of a broadcasting service was unlawful. The Debauve case further confirmed this principle and made it clear that the 'single market' principle established in the Sacchi case applied to advertising as well as to programmes and was not dependent on the tranmission medium (whether cable or terrestrial) used.

The UK is highly exceptional in this context. In contrast to other Member States, its public service broadcasters are very successful. At the time of writing, the BBC and Channel 4 accounted for more than 50 per cent of the share of television viewing – a commanding position enjoyed by public service broadcasters nowhere else in the world. And UK programme schedules are (at least for terrestrial broadcasters – satellite and cable channels tell a different story) dominated by UK programming. The UK's experience is thus quite different to that of its European partners.

European Content on European Screens

Although the UK is no exception to the trend towards a growing presence of imported programmes on European screens, unlike its European partners, the UK maintained a broadly positive 'visible' balance on the audiovisual trade account throughout the 1980s (Central Statistical Office, 1991). In spite of going into 'visible' deficit in the 1990s the UK's deficit in film and television programmes has been more than balanced by net receipts deriving from other film and television services (Office for National Statistics, 1996). Moreover, unlike other EU states, the UK exports significant volumes of films and television programmes to the USA. Thus, the UK has no obvious interest in change to the European status quo which has permitted it both to increase its exports to EU Member States (thanks to the opening of markets via 'Television without Frontiers') and maintain its access to the US market.

In contrast, some other EU countries, and France in particular, are passionately committed to change. For France, liberalization has meant increased import penetration from the USA without the UK's countervailing export successes. For example, between 1986 and 1988 France experienced a striking decline in the proportion of French programming in the key television programme genre of fiction:

> French, or partially French (co-produced), fiction formerly accounted for 49 per cent of broadcast fiction (on three channels) and now accounts for 25 per cent (on five channels). (Personal communication to the author from Mme R Chaniac and M J-P Jézéquel. Responsables de recherche à l'INA 1996)

In consequence, a loose alliance, made up of Member States led by France, Members of the European Parliament and elements in the Commission, notably in DG X, has sought to countervail liberalization and develop an alternative, interventionist and protectionist European audiovisual policy. Jack Lang argued, in the semi-official Community publication *European Affairs,* that 'allowing market forces full play means accepting the disappearance of film production in time. It has long been accepted in France that protective measures are indispensable' (Lang, 1988, p. 16). Indeed Lang argued that the single market served the United States' interests and not Europe's. He wrote:

> The countries of Europe, encumbered as they are with all sorts of historic, linguistic and sociological barriers, were more or less impervious to each other, while the European market – unified – existed only for the Americans. (Lang, 1988, p. 18)

Thus, there are important forces, measures and ideologies that have been mobilized to countervail the effects of the single market, particularly in the broadcasting and audiovisual domain. France and its allies established the MEDIA programme of support for the European audiovisual sector (Council of the European Communities, 1990) and inserted a protectionist European content quota (Article 4) into the 1989 'Television without Frontiers' Directive and have consistently, but thus far unsuccessfully, sought stronger quotas. The Directive of 1989 imposed a 50 per cent European television programme content quota – that is, it limits the maximum possible quantity of US programming to 50 per cent. But the quota was gravely weakened by the rider that quotas are required only 'where practicable'. The UK has interpreted the 'where practicable' provision liberally and has permitted UK-based cable and satellite channels to exceed the authorized 50 per cent of non-European programming. A senior UK official (interviewed 10 February 1992) stated that the UK did not think it 'appropriate' to require satellite film channels to conform to European content quotas and continued: 'we can't expect them to screen Jacques Tati films the whole time'! Tati fans were no better served by the revised Directive of 1997 (97/36/EC).

European Culture and Identity

The European Parliament has stated:

> European media policy... is a touchstone for judging whether the Member States,
> and public broadcasting corporations, are prepared to take European unification
> seriously and adopt a common policy on the media. (European Parliament, 1985,
> p. 35)

Thus far, I have described the European Union's broadcasting and telecommunications policies in economic terms, framing them within a broader, dominant, pattern of market liberalization countervailed, to some extent, by a subordinate and contradictory trend of political intervention in markets. But media and communications in the European Union cannot be understood solely in economic terms for many see their importance as going far beyond economics, as the European Parliament's statement above suggests. And nowhere have conflicts over the identity of the European Union, whether a fully integrated political community or a pragmatic association of nation states in a free trade area, been more intense than in broadcasting and audiovisual policy. This intensity is rooted in the pervasiveness of beliefs in the 'double determinism' discussed above. Beliefs sustained by the celebrated statement of Jean Monnet, the founding father of the European Union, that 'if we were beginning the European Community all over again we should begin with culture' (cited in Commission of the European Communities, 1984, p. 10).

A central thread in EU audiovisual policy has been informed by the assumptions attributed to Monnet – that polity and culture must be congruent if European political institutions are to be robust and legitimate. In 1982, the European Parliament advanced a strong version of this thesis when it looked to television to bind the European Community together. The Parliament pronounced:

> European unification will only be achieved if Europeans want it. Europeans will
> only want it if there is such a thing as a European identity. A European identity
> will only develop if Europeans are adequately informed. At present, information
> vis a vis the mass media is controlled at national level. (European Parliament,
> 1982, p. 9)

In this statement the Parliament clearly articulated the 'double determinism' which has informed so much of European media policy. The first determinism is a technological determinism, a version of the strong media influence thesis, which proposes that attitudes are determined (or at least strongly influenced) by media consumption. The second determinism proposes that political attitudes and identities are determined by cultural identities and that polity and culture must be congruent (Gellner, 1983) if political identities and institutions are to be strong and legitimate.

Certainly, the EU's legitimacy is in question. Positive identification with the European Union by its citizens has declined. It reached a peak in Spring 1991 when 72 per cent of citizens thought 'EC membership is a good thing' and has declined ever since. In May 1994, for example, only 54 per cent thought EU membership was a 'good thing' (*Eurobarometer 41*, 1994) and by 1997 the number of EU citizens favouring the EU had declined to 46 per cent (*Eurobarometer 47*, 1997). The EU thus poses particularly acutely a problem which, the Canadian political philosopher Charles Taylor has argued, is central for modern states – the problem of legitimacy. He states:

> If we define legitimacy in terms of the attitudes and beliefs of members which dispose them to assume or refuse to assume the disciplines and burdens of membership in a given society, we can understand how as legitimacy increases in importance, the more weighty are the disciplines and burdens which must be voluntarily assumed. For the ideal despotism, legitimacy carries a much lesser weight, at least until that point where oppression drives the subjects to revolt. But in contemporary industrial democracies, the everyday operations must call on an ever-present fund of positive identification. (Taylor, 1993, p. 66)

Hence the importance placed on culture (and the audiovisual media as the chief bearers of cultural content and identities in contemporary Europe). Thus, for both political and economic reasons the Europeanization of the audiovisual is seen to be a key priority. Indeed, recent EU policy debates seem to perfectly confirm Lyotard's prophecy that 'nation states will one day fight for control of information, just as they battled in the past for control over territory' (Lyotard, 1984, p. 5).

European Culture

But what is European culture? It is by no means self-evident that a common European culture does exist or that, if it does, it is sufficiently distinctive to differentiate Europe and European politics and values from values, politics and institutions outside Europe. The British novelist Anthony Burgess put this point of view forcefully when he stated:

> I've despaired of finding a culture – other than that of Barbara Cartland, Batman, Indiana Jones and the Coca-Cola can – which should bring Europe and Asia closer together, so I accept, with no sense of despair at all, a Europe united only in its substructure... If we wish to speak of a single European culture, we shall find it only in a tolerant liberalism which accepts those impulses which seem to be disruptive. National culture has nothing to do with political nationalism... We are making an

error of logic if we think that political and economic unity automatically signifies cultural unity. Culture is somewhere else. (Burgess, 1990, p. 21)

Latterly the Commission has identified the 'fight against poverty and unemployment, protection of the environment; Human Rights, freedom and democracy; the wealth and diversity of European culture' as values which 'could form the basis of a European identity' (Commission of the European Communities, 1993b, p. 2). But these values hardly seem to be so distinctively European that they cannot be found elsewhere. Although they may be common to European states, they are not the exclusive property of Europe and so cannot differentiate Europe from non-Europe.

Moreover, hopes that television would prove an effective instrument in fostering European unification have thus far been frustrated. European viewers' behaviour is too different (see, *inter alia*, Assises, 1989; Gunter, 1991) for pan-European services to thrive and no one has yet found a consistently successful programme formula to appeal widely to all European viewers – except, perhaps, American television. A pan-European research team, assembled by the Italian Council for the Social Sciences to analyse 'the contents and narrative structures of television fiction in European countries' (Silj, 1988, p. 1), found that:

> National programmes occupy the top positions in the audience ratings, [but] the public's second choice *never* [original emphasis] falls on programmes produced by other European countries. American is the lingua franca of the European market of television fiction. (Silj, 1988, p. 199)

The Prognosis for European Communications Policy

The globalization of information services through satellite television; expansion of the world's biggest machine – the 'any-to-any' interconnected telecommunication system; the decoupling of cost and distance in telecommunications; and enhanced ability to store and retrieve information in digitized form – whether video, text or sound, all conferred by new communication technologies (see Commission of the European Communities, 1997b), not only accelerate the international circulation of cultural and information products but make the effective exercise of political power to secure cultural sovereignty more and more difficult to achieve.

In consequence, the tensions between the dominant ideology of liberalization and the subordinate ideology of intervention, protection and control, which have suffused the European Union's media and communication policies, are likely to intensify. Within this clash of paradigms, the UK has emphatically been on the liberal side (although, of course, the conflicts that inform the unfolding of EU policy are echoed within Member States); interventionist as well as liberal voices are heard in the UK.

The UK liberalized its telecommunications market earlier than any other EU Member State with consequences that, almost without exception, are seen to have been beneficial. Its audiovisual sector, not least public service broadcasting, is strong and internationally competitive. Unlike any other EU Member State, it has a significant export market in the USA and in consequence broadly favours free trade and opposes stringent European content quotas and other protectionist measures. Moreover, the UK's political history is distinguished by an acceptance and accommodation of difference, for instance, Scotland's different legal and educational systems, the semi-official status of Welsh, and the separate Parliamentary institutions of Northern Ireland. State building in the UK has taken a very different line to the Jacobin nationalist congruence between polity and culture which informed French state building and which animates much EU discourse about cultural sovereignty and 'le défi american'.

However, the UK's experience and strengths are shared by few of its European partners. In consequence, in media and communications, as in other domains, the UK often appears to be the 'awkward partner' (George, 1990). As such it is potentially vulnerable to the adoption of EU policies that respond to the experiences and interests of most of its partners – interests and experiences that, by and large, are different to its own. Thus far, with the exception of modest interventionist and protectionist 'wins' such as the European content quotas in the 'Television without Frontiers' Directive and the establishment of the MEDIA Programme, EU policy in media and communications has run in harmony with the UK's own values and interests. But that may not always be the case. For the doctrine of liberalization recognizes only the economic importance of media and communications – a dimension that, rightly, has been given great salience by both the UK and EU. However, other considerations apply in media and communications and these have, thus far, been subordinated to the dominant doctrine of liberalization in the EU. That may not always be so.

References

Assises de l'audiovisuel *Assises européennes de l'audiovisuel. Projet Eureka audiovisuel.* Paris: Ministère des affaires étrangères, République Française and Commission of the European Communities, 1989.

Bangemann, M. *et al*. *Europe and the Global Information Society: Recommendations to the European Council* (The Bangemann Report). Brussels, (unpublished) 1994.

Burgess, A. 'European culture: does it exist?', *European Broadcasting Union Review, Programmes Administration Law*, **XLI**, 2 (March 1990), pp. 17–21.

Central Statistical Office *Overseas Transactions of the Film and TV Industry*. Newport: Government Statistical Service, 1991.

Commission of the European Communities *Television Without Frontiers*. Green Paper on the establishment of the Common Market for broadcasting especially by satellite and cable. COM (84) 300 final, 1984.

Commission of the European Communities *Towards a Dynamic European Economy*. Green paper on the development of the Common Market for telecommunications services and equipment. COM(87) 290 final, 1987.

Commission of the European Communities and the European Parliament *Europe, Our Future*. The Institutions of the European Community, 1990.

Commission of the European Communities *Pluralism and Media Concentration in the Internal Market*. COM(92) 480 final, 1992.

Commission of the European Communities *Growth, Competitiveness and Employment – The Challenges and Ways Forward into the 21st Century*. COM(93) 700 final, 1993a.

Commission of the European Communities *Reflection on Information and Communication Policy of the European Community*, Report of the group of experts chaired by Mr Willy De Clerq, Member of the European Parliament. RP 1051 93, 1993b.

Commission of the European Communities *Background Report*. The Intergovernmental Conference. B/2/97, January, London: Commission of the European Communities, 1997a.

Commission of the European Communities *Green Paper on the Convergence of the Telecommunications, Media and Information Technology Sectors, and the Implications for Regulation*. COM(97) 623, 1997b.

Council of the European Communities 'Decision concerning the implementation of an action programme to promote the development of the European audiovisual industry (MEDIA) (1991–1995)', 90/685/EEC. OJ L 380, 31.12.90, 1990, pp. 37–44.

Eurobarometer 41, Brussels: Commission of the European Communities July 1994.

Eurobarometer 47, Brussels: Commission of the European Communities, November 1997 (http://europa.eu.int/en/comm/dg10/infcom/epo/eb/eb47/eb47en/higlights.html)

European Parliament 'Resolution on Radio and Television Broadcasting in the European Community' [The Hahn Resolution], OJ C 87, 5.4.82, 1982, pp. 110–12.

European Parliament 'Resolution on a Framework for a European Media Policy based on the establishment of a Common Market for Broadcasting especially by Satellite and Cable', OJ C 288, 11.11.1985, 1985, p. 113.

Gellner, E. *Nations and Nationalism*. Oxford: Blackwell, 1983.

George, S. *An Awkward Partner: Britain in the European Community*. Oxford: Oxford University Press, 1990.

Gunter, B. *The Television Audience in Europe*, ITC Research Paper. London: Independent Television Commission, 1991.

Harcourt, A. 'Regulating for media concentration: The emerging policy of the European Union, *Utilities Law Review*, October (1996) pp. 202–10.

Hodgson, P. 'Introduction', in T. Congdon *et al. Paying for Broadcasting: The Handbook*. London: Routledge, 1992.

Lang, J. 'The future of European film and television', *European Affairs*, **2** (1988) pp. 12–20.

Lyotard, J.-F. *The Postmodern Condition*. Manchester: University of Manchester Press, 1984 [1979].

Office for National Statistics *Overseas Transaction of the Film and Television Industry 1995*. London: Office for National Statistics, 1996.

Silj, A. *East of Dallas: The European Challenge to American Television*. London: British Film Institute, 1988.

Taylor, C. *Reconciling the Solitudes: Essays on Canadian Federalism and Nationalism*. Montreal and Kingston: McGill-Queen's University Press, 1993.

Tongue, C. *The Future of Public Service Television in a Multi-channel Digital Age* (The Tongue Report) Ilford: The Office of Carole Tongue MEP, 1996.

van Miert, K. 'Preparing for 1998 and beyond', *IIC Telecommunications Forum*, 1996 (http://europa.eu.int/en/comm/dg04/speech/six/en/sp96037.htm).

Vasconcelos, A.-P. Report by the Think Tank. Brussels: Commission of the European Communities, DG X, 1994.

CHAPTER 11

Campaigns to Change the Media

ANNA READING

> The reading of novels makes women, and particularly ladies of fashion, very fond of using strong expressions and superlatives in conversation. (Wollstonecraft, 1985, p. 309)

In the 1790s, Mary Wollstonecraft, a campaigner for women's access to 'serious books' and education, argued that a particular aspect of the media – the reading of novels – was having morally deleterious effects on young women's minds (Wollstonecraft, 1985). Two hundred years on, campaigners have expressed concerns over, for example, the effects on people, especially children, of mass media depictions of violence. Other campaigners have expressed disagreement with the way in which the mass media are regulated or have objected to the way in which particular groups in society are (mis) represented. In this chapter I take a bottom up view of the media, empha- sizing people's involvement and activities to change those aspects of the media with which they disagree – rather than giving emphasis to state and corporate power, as in previous chapters. This is because, as Thompson (1997) suggests, it is not only governments and corporations that are inter- ested in cultural regulation and media practice but also a range of other groups within society.

The chapter addresses people's involvement in organized campaigns to change the mass media in Britain, a relatively undocumented area of the media to date. I argue that media campaigns are heterogeneous – varied and different – in three ways. First, they are heterogeneous in terms of their size and scope. Second, they vary in terms of the medium that concerns them. Third, they are different in terms of their mechanisms used to realize change and the degree of praxis they deploy: in other words the link they make between the campaign's theoretical or abstract demands for change and the ways in which the campaign itself contributes to change through media prac- tice. Despite these differences, however, if one examines campaigns to change the media not just today but over time one finds historical continuities that suggest that campaigns fall into three broad categories. There are those that stem from anxieties about the effects of the media on public morality; then, there are those that are based on a desire for greater public input into the mass media; and, finally, there are those that have grown from the realization that particular people – for example women and people from minority groups – are excluded and stereotyped by the mass media. I begin by asking what constitutes a campaign to change the media.

Contemporary meanings of 'campaign' include 'a series of coordinated activities, such as public speaking, designed to achieve a social, political or commercial goal', as well as 'a number of operations aimed at achieving a single objective' (Hanks, 1989, p. 158). The problem with this is that such a definition excludes aspects of human activity in relation to the media that are network or union based, or that have more than one objective. Further, within media and cultural studies the term is, according to Watson and Hill, used to refer to pressure groups that make 'a conscious, structured and coor-dinated attempt' to influence the opinion, or actions of people through the media, such as an election campaign (Watson and Hill, 1993). This raises one of the essential difficulties of pressure groups or campaigns that are specifi-cally seeking to change the media itself: to communicate their message they may well have to use the very medium they may be criticizing. It also suggests that campaigns to change the media work outside of media organizations themselves, which is generally not the case as we shall see.

Further, historically, and today, media campaigns were and are heteroge-neous: they are extremely varied and include a whole range of not only self-identified pressure groups with a single desired outcome but also unions, networks and aspects of the mass media themselves. These 'campaigns' vary in three ways.

First, campaigns vary in terms of their size and scope. Some work inter-nally in particular media companies. An example of one such organization is the BBC's Equality Unit, which seeks to eradicate inequalities based on 'race', gender or disability both within the BBC and the types of programmes that it produces. In contrast, other organizations work across a range of industries. An example of this is the National Union of Journalists. This has 26,514 members in the publishing, magazine, newspaper, public relations and broadcasting industries. The organization seeks to improve the working conditions of cultural production and practice for journalists in their field (National Union of Journalists, 1997). The scope of campaigns also varies in terms of the levels of society and media that they seek to address or change. Thus, some seek change at the national level and work primarily within the British context, such as the Campaign for Press and Broadcasting Freedom or the Campaign for Freedom of Information. These operate at a national level to lobby the government and regulatory bodies to change national policies relating to the media. Other organizations, however, work at a European and international level, trying to influence communica-tion policies and practice both within Britain and abroad, such as the World Association for Christian Communication, Article 19 or the People's Communication Charter, or, they include communication issues as a central part of broader concerns such as the World YWCA (see organizations' websites at end; Reading, 1996, 1997).

Second, these pressure groups, unions and networks are heterogeneous in terms of the mass medium that is their focus of concern. Some organizations work across several different media. Thus the Women's Media Resource Project was established in the 1980s to provide training and resources for women across video, film, radio and print. The National Campaign for the Arts, which deals with public finance, education, media affairs and the fight against censorship, also works across a range of media. Other campaigns however are specifically related to one medium. Examples of these would be the Women's Radio Group or the Independent Theatre Council.

Third, campaigns are heterogeneous in terms of the mechanisms they believe will effect change. Some stress that there must be a degree of praxis – a link between the organization's desired campaign outcomes and how it puts these into practise. Thus at the heart of some campaigns is the belief that an effective mechanism of change is to alter the law. Such campaigns put most of their energies into seeking legal redress and alteration to the laws and regulations governing the media in Britain. Hence, the Campaign for Press and Broadcasting Freedom lobbies governments and parliament to alter media policies to give people a greater say. Others seek change through the mechanism of improved education and special training courses for media workers. This would include union-initiated programmes that seek, for example, to increase the numbers of people from ethnic minorities within the media by providing both special training programmes for those workers as well as training days that address the question of racism (National Union of Journalists, 1997). Other organizations give emphasis to mechanisms that involve increasing public awareness of particular problems within the mass media: thus *Index on Censorship* has sought to make people aware of censorship of the mass media, as well as highlight the continuing imprisonment and torture of writers and journalists under different regimes worldwide.

Another mechanism of realizing change is by producing the kind of media that one wants: this is the samizdat (self-produced) or DIY approach where individuals form networks or organizations to produce their own cultural response and challenge as a supplement or alternative to the mainstream. This may involve samizdat or self-produced and distributed Zines, CDs, tapes, videos, spoken poetry, newsletters or self-managed live events including theatre, music and dance. Hence Undercurrents produces news videos to challenge the bias of mainstream news; women's theatre companies and community theatre companies have given excluded groups a live media voice throughout the 1980s and 90s; the Exploding Cinema in the 1990s used derelict buildings to show radical films by film-makers mixed with performance excluded by the hegemony of the mainstream; and the Home Art Movement circumvented the exclusive practices of art galleries with artists having living room shows (Wilson, 1997). In some cases campaigns directly through praxis are highly sophisticated, as with MedTV, a satellite television

Table 11.1   Different types of media campaigns

	The Moralisers	The Sharers	The Includers
Central Issue	Public Morality	Media Ownership	Media Exclusion/ Inclusion
Concerns	Rising levels of sex and violence	Degree of concentration of media ownership	Institutional exclusion of particular groups. Stereotyping of women, ethnic and sexual minorities and people with disabilities
Desired Campaign Outcomes	* Reduce and censor media sex and violence through legislation and media watchdogs	* Right of Reply * Greater accountability of media * More public access * Freedom of Information Act * Laws to prevent cross media ownership and concentration of power	* Equal opportunities policies in media organizations * Training programmes for excluded groups * Widening of base of representation of excluded groups and reduction in material that degrades or denigrates them
Earlier Campaigns	Campaigns for 'social hygiene', for example National Council for Public Morals	Radical campaigns for a working-class voice in the media, for example Friends of the Oppressed	Campaigns linked to enfranchisement and abolition of slavery, for example Women's Co-operative Guild
Current Campaigns	* Mary Whitehouse's 'Clean up TV' campaign (Founded 1963) leading to the National Viewers and Listeners Association	* Campaign for Press and Broadcasting Freedom (Founded 1979) * National Union of Journalists	* Women in Publishing * Black Media Workers Group * Youth Against Racism in Europe

channel broadcast from London. This uses the voluntary labour of 200 people to provide Kurdish television in a variety of Kurdish dialects for up to 35 million Kurds currently denied political, linguistic and cultural rights in the Middle East (Med Broadcasting Ltd, 1997; Tabac, 1998).

Some campaigns combine several mechanisms of change: the National Union of journalists (NUJ) tackles policy issues as well as providing training. Most campaigns are also involved in some way in some form of media production: the NUJ produces a newspaper for its members – the *Journalist*, the Campaign for Press and Broadcasting Freedom produces the *Free Press*, the National Viewers and Listeners Association has its own newsletter to members and Article 19 has *XIX Bulletin*. Many have their own websites, some of which are cited at the end of this chapter.

Despite, however, the threefold heterogeneity of media campaigns, in terms of their scope, medium and mechanism of change, the organizations fall into three broad categories: there are those concerned with the media's effect on public morality; those concerned with the effects of the concentration of media ownership within capitalist society and there are those concerned with seeking to stop the exclusion and overt and covert censorship of particular groups in society from media organizations and media texts.

The Moralizers

It is not just a contemporary phenomenon that people have worried over the possible effects of the media on public morality. Earlier media campaigns were also concerned, as today, with trying to halt the morally deleterious effects of the media through what was perceived to be a rising tide of violence, blasphemy and 'lewdness' in the media – usually in contrast to an earlier morally 'Golden Age'. These *moralizers* were generally from the middle classes and were especially anxious over the effects of the media on what were considered 'vulnerable' groups in society such as women, children and the working classes. Thus with the growing popularity of the Gothic novel in the late eighteenth and early nineteenth centuries, protests such as that by Mary Wollstoncraft, cited at the beginning of this chapter, were concerned with the impact of sensationalism on women's morals and sensibilities. These concerns continued to be articulated with the development of cheap printed newspapers and magazines in the nineteenth century, known as the 'Penny Dreadfuls', which also elicited protest from the middle classes. With the advent of cinema at the beginning of the twentieth century, it too stimulated disapproval from the authorities and middle classes who argued that it 'glorified crime' and could lead to rising social unrest among the working classes (Robertson, 1985). These campaigns were sometimes effective in getting films withdrawn or censored, however in retrospect the bans sometimes appear ridiculous. Indeed, the first film in Britain ever to be censored was done so after protests from the British cheese industry: the ninety-second film featured magnified bacterial activity in a piece of Stilton and cheese capitalists were anxious that it would put people off eating cheese (Mathews, 1994).

Nevertheless, not all the earlier moralizers were middle class: some of the early movements concerned with social purity included working-class people anxious about the cinema's effects on children (Kuhn, 1988). Neither was it the case that only those on the right of the political spectrum historically sought to limit what they perceived to be those aspects that undermined the moral fabric of society. It should be remembered that it was the Puritans in the seventeenth century who shut down theatres in Cromwell's time and put a stop to fairs and festivals, and later, leftist movements in the early nineteenth century were also against 'licentious' media (Wistrich, 1978). Mary Wollstoncraft (see above) was also one of Britain's early feminists who believed that women should be treated as rational beings and educated in the same way as men.

The right-wing public morality lobby did remain very active, however, throughout the 1930s (Richards, 1984). With the growing popularity of the new mass medium of television in the 1950s and 60s, its ideas were effectively reformulated in the Clean Up TV Campaign founded by Mary Whitehouse in Birmingham in 1964, later called the National Viewers' and Listeners' Association (NVLA).

The NVLA is the key contemporary campaign concerned with the relationship between the possible effects of the media – especially television – and public morality. It has secured nearly 6 million signatures on various petitions between 1964 and 1989 (*The Viewer and Listener*, 1989) and has a current membership of 8,000 plus 170,000 through group affiliations such as Churches and women's organizations (Bayer, 1998b). The Association campaigns against what it perceives to be the erosion of traditional Christian values in British society (National Viewers' and Listeners' Association, 1998). It believes that the values of chastity and the family should underpin society (National Viewers' and Listeners' Association, 1997c) and that the media with their sexually explicit imagery undermine this (National Viewers' and Listeners' Association, 1997d). Thus in 1992 it presented to parliament a petition with 35,000 signatures in a special Campaign to Outlaw Pornography (COP) (*The Viewer and Listener*, 1992). It also campaigns against explicit violence in film, television and theatre (National Viewers' and Listeners' Association, 1997b). Thus in 1996 it produced its third survey of cruelty and violence in films on terrestrial television (National Viewers' and Listeners' Association, 1997a).

The efficacy of the NVLA over the years has been in terms of initiating support for new legislation, with The Protection of Children Act (1979) to outlaw child pornography; the Video Recordings Act (1984) to combat 'video nasties' and the Indecent Displays Act also in the 1980s to combat nude magazine covers on display in newsagents. It also assisted in the establishment in 1988 of the Broadcasting Standards Council (now the Broadcasting Standards Commission) (Bayer, 1998b).

In the 1990s, however, the efficacy of the organization to alter policy or get programmes off-air that it believes go against 'taste and decency' has diminished, according to its General Secretary, John Bayer (1998a, b). This is, in his opinion, because the 1990 Broadcasting Act effectively prevents the Independent Television Commission from previewing programmes and because of the new Broadcasting Standards Commission which has 'no teeth'. Subsequently, the campaign in more recent years has shifted its emphasis away from addressing legal issues towards raising wider public concern over the perceived effects of media violence and sex. This however, according to the NVLA, is difficult because the organization cannot gain access to the print media: 'with increasingly large media conglomerates the press is unlikely to condemn a television company in which it may have shares' (Bayer, 1998a). It may also be that with the end of 18 years of Tory rule in 1997 the organization lost the ear of the government. Nevertheless, the organization is planning to gain support to strengthen the Obscene Publications Act through an amendment to the new Criminal Justice Bill 1998 (Bayer, 1998b).

The Sharers

This is the second category that a variety of campaigns, historically and today, fall into. These are campaigns that seek to roll back laws that gag freedom of speech and information and seek to decrease corporate covert censorship by broadening the basis of media ownership. The sharers have a long genesis – one of the key political campaigns in modern history concerns the struggle to 'free' the media from censorship. This goes back to the campaign against the imposition of censorship by Oliver Cromwell in 1643, most famously articulated in John Milton's classic text *Aeropagitica* in which he argued that people should be able to have access to and read the whole spectrum of views not just those prescribed by the state. This trend to broaden people's access to ideas and increase their share in the media continued in the eighteenth century with people such as John Wilkes, whose struggles are commemorated in a statue on Fetter Lane, London. Wilkes' belief in press freedom led him to launch a weekly paper – the *North Briton* – in 1762, in which he criticized the government and the Crown. His efforts led to other newspapers, despite efforts by parliament to stop them, reporting the procedings of parliament (Griffiths, 1998). The legacy of the effectiveness of this campaign – by Wilkes and others – is one we still have today. Other campaigns for a 'free press' came out of working-class concern for a greater *share* in the press and for a radical voice. Thus, Richard Carlile, for example, who was an active supporter of birth control at the beginning of the nineteenth century, campaigned for a free press to include radical free thought. When he was imprisoned in 1820, his wife Jane continued with the newspaper, the *Republican,* until she too was imprisoned for making written accusatations against the Crown that were deemed malicious (Rendall, 1985). Despite this, the struggle was continued in the nineteenth cenutry by other campaigning organizations: in July 1832 'The Friends of the Oppressed' was established to support those who fought for the rights of the working classes, their aims also included a free and untaxed press (Thomis and Grimmett, 1982). In the twentieth century, the sharers have often been based within working-class campaigns to have their views included. Thus when a film hostile to the revolution in Russia, entitled *Bolshevism,* was to be shown on 16 September 1919, at Majestic Picture Palace in Clapham, 300 Independent Labour Party members protested (Robertson, 1985).

   The key contemporary sharer campaign in Britain is the Campaign for Press and Broadcasting Freedom (CPBF), founded in 1979 as the New Right in Britain took power under Margaret Thatcher. Initially, the campaign argued for a more pluralistic and accountable press and by 1982 it added the call for more accountable broadcasting as well (*Free Press*, 1982). Today, with

1500 individual members, and up to one million affiliate members through its links with a range of other campaigning groups such as PressWise and trades unions such as the NUJ (White, 1998), at the heart of the CPBF's belief is the idea that the essential problem of the media lies in the concentration of ownership in the hands of a small number of media moguls who control vast international conglomerates (Campaign for Press and Broadcasting Freedom, 1998). Thus immediately after Princess Diana's death in August 1997, the Press Complaints Council called for more self-regulation and a privacy law to ban the work of freelance photographers, who were alleged to have caused her death. The CPBF, in contrast, took the view that ultimately it was the owners of the newspapers that had carried sensationalist stories about Princess Diana over the years who were the culpable parties (*Free Press*, 1997). Subsequent work in 1998 centred on increasing parliamentary pressure for a group to discuss the questions of ownership and union rights in relation to the question of privacy (Campaign for Press and Broadcasting Freedom, 1998).

Throughout the 1980s the CPBF began a specific push for a Right of Reply for individuals to address factual inaccuracies and 'for a genuinely accountable system of public service broadcasting and for the break up of concentrated blocks of media power' (*Free Press*, 1997, p. 2). In the late 1980s and 1990s the campaign reacted against attempts by the British Conservative government to commercialize the BBC. It also continued with its work to broaden the base of media representation and the ethnic and gender balance of media organizations through publishing booklets and information on racism and sexism (O'Malley, 1997). Throughout the Thatcher years it pushed for debate on Ireland in the face of censorship of the voices of members of Sinn Fein. It worked with and alongside organizations and unions during the coal dispute of 1984 (O'Malley, 1997). The smashing of the print unions, Murdoch's move to Wapping and the subsequent dispute in 1986–87 led to the campaign's first 'Media Manifesto'. The organization has also worked with other media campaign bodies such as Liberty and, from 1981, with LABFOIC – the Labour Freedom of Information Campaign (then chaired by Robin Cook) to have a Freedom of Information Act on Britain's statute books. The CPBF has campaigned around specific cases such as the *Spycatcher* case, as well as monitoring British elections with, for example, Election Watch in 1992 (O'Malley, 1997).

One of the campaign's most effective mechanisms of change, however, has been its own journal *Free Press* which has, throughout the past 20 years, publicized particular acts of sabotage by the mainstream press against organizations struggling for causes such as peace and the environment. For example, in an early issue of the *Free Press,* a press plot against the Campaign for Nuclear Disarmament was revealed (*Free Press*, 1981). The journal has also been a key way of building links with causes and campaigns for real media freedom in other countries: during the Solidarity strikes in Communist Poland during 1980–81, the *Free Press* journal reported both the strikes in the country and the struggle by workers to change the press in Poland by creating an alternative media structure through Solidarity radio and newspapers (MacShane, 1981).

However, the journal also highlights an important problem with the effectiveness of campaign praxis – with the CPBF there is a contradiction between campaign theory and practice. Although the campaign calls for sexual equality within the press (see *Free Press*, 1991), its own journal was and is structurally gender biased. Mike Jempson's roll call of editors in his retrospective 'Look Back in Angst' (Jempson, 1997) reveals that only one editor of its eight over the past 18 years has been a woman. Nevertheless in 1991 the organization's AGM approved of a Women's Section and published its own 'Code of Conduct on Media Sexism' which states that it seeks to promote (among other things) 'equality of opportunity – employment for women in the media' (*Free Press*, 1991, p. 6). This suggests that despite a campaign's desire for change – such as sexual equality – some areas are not necessarily easily resolved (as indeed the gender imbalance of this book also shows, despite having two women editors who tried to ensure gender parity). In this final section I examine campaigns that have at their heart the desire to include everyone regardless of gender and 'race'.

The Includers

As with the campaigns of the moralizers and the sharers, the includers have an established history of campaigns going back several centuries. Initially, the efforts to make the mass media more inclusive were bound up with broader political campaigns, such as the abolition of slavery in the eighteenth and early nineteenth centuries. As black and Asian people in Britain, at this time, found themselves excluded from the coffee houses where newspapers were read and political information exchanged, they formed their own places where media could be consumed. When black and Asian people found that publishers wouldn't publish their work they also fought to be included. Thus, when a Boston publisher refused to publish poems by Phylis Wheatly, because they would not believe that an Afro-British person was capable of writing poetry with classical illusions, Wheatly mounted a campaign that included the support of the Countess of Huntingdon and the Earl of Dartmouth, along with a petition by a group of Boston dignitaries, resulting in her publication in Britain (Carretta, 1997).

By the mid- to late-nineteenth centuries the includers efforts focused on developing radical publications to give more people a media voice – these went hand in hand with the movement for enfranchisement and state education. Thus, Britain's first feminist publication the *English Woman's Journal* (founded 1858) advocated improved access to education and training for women to write for newspapers (Rendall, 1985). From this came a long tradition by the includers of using praxis as a mechanism of change: alternative media flyers, pamphlets and small circulation newspapers were produced to provide information that was often unreported in the mainstream press such as issues concerned with women's suffrage and the abolition of slavery (Downing, 1995). These were important precursors to political campaigns for racial and ethnic equality in the twentieth century that were combined with the development of a black press in response to exclusion and stereotyping in Britain's mainstream press (Benjamin, 1995).

This form of practical protest and change also continued with The Women's Co-operative Guild (founded 1883). This was an immensely effective precursor to contemporary feminist concerns with women's marginalization in the mass media. By 1930, the Co-operative Guild had 1400 branches throughout Britain holding literacy, typing and reading classes in order to improve women's use of print media. Members produced and contributed to newspapers such as *Co-operative News* and *Labour Woman*, as well as anthologies of their own lives (Davies, 1977). Their concern *to include* – in the form of campaigns for access to the medium of the written word – received renewed impetus in the 1970s with the Adult Literacy Campaign (Lewis, 1978).

A concern with language in a different sense was also articulated by groups in Scotland and Wales from the end of the nineteenth century and throughout the twentieth century. The efficacy of these efforts to include people from lesser-used languages, by providing linguistic rights and minority language mass media, has been enormous over the past twenty years. The Welsh Language Campaign, for example, concerned with the re-establisment of Welsh as a recognized language in Britain, succeeded in 1993 with the Welsh Language Act which requires that any company in Wales dealing with the public and public authorities work bilingually and provide bilingual information. It was also part of the movement behind the establishment and public funding of community newspapers in Wales in Welsh as well as the establishment of public broadcasting in Welsh in the form of Saniel Pedwar Cymru – Wales' equivalent of Channel 4, in which approximately half the channel's output is in Welsh to meet the needs of 500,000 Welsh speakers (Welsh Press Office, 1998).

Feminist campaigns to include more women in media organizations and to change sexist representations have also been successful in many aspects of the mass media in Britain. One of the most vigorous challenges since the 1970s has been in relation to the television industry (Loach, 1987) and feminists over the last three decades have produced a number of reports highlighting the exclusion of women from television (Gallagher, 1979; Baehr, 1981) which have in turn led to effective training campaigns and equality policies. Thus, the Women Broadcasting and Film Lobby, founded in 1979, has pursued a strategy enabling professional women to gain access to senior management. A BBC Equality Network was established in January 1986. At the same time, women are also active in the main broadcasting and print unions in which there is an emphasis on training to enable women's full inclusion. This aspect of the campaign for sexual equality in the media has been important for real change to occur (Loach, 1987, p. 68).

Recent campaigns to challenge racism in the media work in similar ways and also cover the broad range of media forms. The National Union of Journalists with its Black Members Council has fought for better working conditions and training for black journalists (Mathews, 1997) and also works through the International Media Working Group Against Racism and Xenophobia (IMRAX) set up by the International Federation of Journalists to counteract media racism (Iziren, 1998). The Commission for Racial Equality's work has included codes of practice and style guides for broadcasters and journalists and through the Race and Media Awards seeks to reward those who provide informed coverage (Commission for Racial Equality, 1998).

Increasingly, campaigns concerned with racism in the media are cross-European in nature rather than just 'British' based. Thus Youth Against Racism in Europe has worked with a range of organizations including the Gypsy Council, Unison and the Jewish Socialist Group to challenge racism in a key area of the mass media which is often neglected – education. The network, through its anti-racist education pack and speakers, is challenging the basis of much racist education in Europe (Youth against Racism in Europe, 1998). This suggests that as Britain integrates further into the rest of Europe, the efficacy of media campaigns will increasingly depend upon having links and support with groups in other countries.

Concluding Remarks

Overall, Britain has a strong tradition of campaigns to change the media. They vary in their range of activities, but all three categories continue to provide effective challenges – the moralizers in terms of questioning the moral values that the media convey; the sharers in terms of questioning the power that the media wield and the includers by the cultural and political voices that the media still exclude. This is not to suggest, however, that there are no links between the issues tackled by organizations in the three categories. In some ways, for example, the Campaign for Press and Broadcasting Freedom in its attempts to include some policies regarding racial and sexual equality in the media is a sharer but also an includer. Further, it should also be remembered that, although the focus here is primarily in relation to Britain, many organizations now work at a European or global level especially since the globalization of the media itself makes national campaigns less relevant for particular media, such as broadcasting. The degree of their effectiveness in relation to their aims is varied, as the chapter suggests. Some have succeeded in initiating support for getting regulations and laws changed; others have resulted in important cultural shifts enabling more excluded groups to have their voices included; some literally provide alternative views and news within the public sphere by doing it themselves. Certainly, what an examination of campaigns by people to change the media demonstrates is that, even in the face of powerful media conglomerates and governments, there are effective grassroots organizations and campaigns at work and that people do have power if we choose to use it – words and actions do make a difference.

References

Baehr, H. 'Women's employment in British TV: programming the future', *Media Culture and Society*, **3** (1981) pp. 125–34.

Bayer, J. *Interview* (General Secretary of the Viewers and Listeners Association), (1998a) January 25.

Bayer, J. *Interview* (General Secretary of the Viewers and Listeners Association), (1998b) February 25.

Benjamin, I. *The Black Press in Britain*. Stoke on Trent: Trentham Books, 1995.

Campaign For Press and Broadcasting Freedom 'Privacy Seminar', London: The Freedom Forum, 21 February 1998.

Carretta, V. (ed.) *Unchained Voices: An Anthology of Black Authors in the English Speaking World of the 18th Century*, Lexington: University Press of Kentucky, 1997.

Commission for Racial Equality Press Office 'Personal Communication', 16 February 1998.

Davies, M.L. (ed.) *Life as we have known it / by cooperative working women* London: Virago, 1977.

Downing, J. 'Alternative Media and the Boston Tea Party', in J. Downing, A. Mohammadi and A. Sreberny-Mohammadi (eds) *Questioning the media: a critical introduction*, Thousand Oaks, CA: Sage, 1995.

Free Press: The Journal of the Campaign for Press and Broadcasting Freedom 'Press plot against CND', 9 (September/October 1981) p. 1.

Free Press: the Journal of the Campaign for Press and Broadcasting Freedom 'The campaign for press and broadcasting freedom aims to', (November/December 1982) p. 7.

Free Press: The Journal of the Campaign for Press and Broadcasting Freedom 'Code of Conduct on Media Sexism', 4 (June 1991) p. 6.

Free Press: The Journal of the Campaign for Press and Broadcasting Freedom 'After Diana: Four steps to better journalism', 100 (September–October 1997) p. 1.

Gallagher, M. *The Portrayal and Participation of Women in the Media*. Paris: Unesco, 1979.

Griffiths, D. ' Our heroes: a byword for our liberties', *Journalist*, (January/February 1998) p. 26.

Hanks, P. (ed.) *The Collins Concise Dictionary of the English Language*. London: Collins, 1989.

Hoad, T.F. *English Etymology*, Oxford: Oxford University Press, 1993.

Iziren, A. 'What had they got to hide', *Journalist*, January/February (1998) p. 11.

Jempson, M. 'Look Back in Angst', *Free Press: The Journal of the Campaign for Press and Broadcasting Freedom*, 100 (September–October 1997) p. 2.

Kuhn, A. *Cinema, Censorship and Sexuality: 1909–1925*. London: Routledge, 1988.

Lewis, P.M. *Whose Media? The Annan Report and After: A Citizens Guide to Radio and Television*. Consumers Association, London: 1978.

Loach, R. 'Campaigning For Change', in H. Baehr and G. Dyer (eds) *Boxed In: Women and Television*. New York: Pandora, 1987, p. 55–70.

MacShane, D. 'The struggle for Poland's media', *Free Press*, 10 (November/December 1981) p. 6.

Mathews, D. 'Outlook Black', *Journalist* (December 1997) pp. 14–15.

Mathews, T.D. *Censored: What they didn't allow you to see, and why: The Story of Film Censorship in Britain*. London: Chatto & Windus, 1994.

Med Broadcasting Ltd. *The International Impact of MedTV: Kurdish Satellite Television March 1995–1996*. London: Med Broadcasting Ltd, 1997.

National Viewers' and Listeners' Association *More Cruelty and Violence 3: A Survey of Films on Terrestrial Television in 1996*. Birmingham: NVLA Publications, 1997a.

National Viewers' and Listeners' Association *Television and Violence*. Birmingham: NVLA Publications, 1997b.

National Viewers' and Listeners' Association *Television and the Family*. Birmingham: NVLA Publications, 1997c.

National Viewers' and Listeners' Association *Television and Sex*. Birmingham: NVLA Publications, 1997d.

National Viewers' and Listeners' Association 'Many People Believe There is Too Much Violence, Sex and Bad Language on TV: If you Agree then Read On' (publicity material), Birmingham: NVLA, 1998).

National Union of Journalists *Annual Report*. London: National Union of Journalists, 1997.

O'Malley, T. 'Eighteen Years On', *Free Press: Journal of the Campaign for Press and Broadcasting Freedom*, 100 (September–October 1997) p. 2.

Reading, A. 'Me too! Gender and the media in the 1990s', *Common Concern*, (December 1996) pp. 12–13.

Reading, A. 'Women, men and the mass media', *Common Concern* (September 1997) pp. 8–9, 22.

Rendall, J. *The Origins of Modern Feminism: Women in Britain, France and the United States, 1780–1860*. Basingstoke: Macmillan, 1985.

Richards, J. *The Age of the Dream Palace: Cinema and Society in Britain 1930–1939*, London: Routledge and Kegan Paul, 1984.

Robertson, J.C. *The British Board of Film Censors: Film Censorship in Britain 1896–1950*. London: Croom Helm, 1985.

Tabac, H. 'MedTV', paper presented at *GAGGED: The Media and Censorship*, Media and Society B.Sc Student Organised Open Conference, South Bank University, London, 1998.

The Viewer and Listener '25 years on', 1989, p. 1.

The Viewer and Listener 'COP Petition', 1992, p. 1.

Thomis, M.I. and Grimmett, J. *Women in Protest, 1800–1850*. London: Croom Helm, 1982.

Thompson, K. (ed.) *Media and Cultural Regulation*. Open Universiy Press, 1997.

Watson, J. and Hill, A. *Dictionary of Communication and Media Studies*. London: Edward Arnold, 1993.

Welsh Press Office (1998) Interview. 9 June.

White, B. (1998) Personal communication, 'Privacy Seminar', Campaign for Press and Broadcasting Freedom, 21 February 1998.

Wilson, M. 'The gallery at home', *Artists Newsletter*, (December 1997) pp. 10–11.

Wistrich, E. *I don't mind the sex, its the violence: Film censorship Explored*. London: Marion Boyars, 1978.

Wollstonecraft, M. (1985) (First published 1792) *Vindication of the Rights of Woman*. Harmondsworth: Penguin.

Youth Against Racism in Europe 'Anti-Racist Education Pack', London: YRE, 1998.

Websites, as located on 26 February 1998:

    Article 19 – www.gn.apc.org/article19
    World Young Women's Christian Association – www.worldywca.org
    Campaign for Freedom of Information – www.CFOI.org.uk
    Index on Censorship – www.oneworld.org/index_oc/
    Undercurrents – www.undercurrents.org
    Peoples' Communication Charter – pssmaster@waag.or

PART III
MEDIA MATERIAL: CONTENT AND REPRESENTATION

JANE STOKES AND ANNA READING

In Part I of *The Media in Britain* we examined the scope of the media in Britain and the structure of a variety of media industries in turn. We followed this up with a consideration of some of the current debates about the relationship between the state and the media in Part II. Now we turn to the most visible aspect of the media: the texts themselves. In this section we analyse a small sample of the huge variety of media artefacts currently being produced in Britain. There are fourteen chapters in this section, each one addressing a different media text or texts or ideas about the media in Britain.

The debates and developments we have discussed so far all relate to the kinds of media produced in Britain. You will find in the following chapters analyses of artefacts which are traditionally studied on media courses, including newspapers (Cottle, Reading, Russell); magazines (Stokes, Reading); television (Gabb, Owen, Scannell, Sillars); cinema (Russell, Slater, Smith) and websites (Rietveld). The texts discussed are the products of the media industries considered in Part I. But the editors of this volume wish to challenge the idea that these are the only media that can be studied, and therefore we have included some chapters that address media less frequently included in media studies courses, including museums (Crownshaw); novels (Moore-Gilbert) and plays (Sierz). If we want to understand the role of the media in Britain, we need to acknowledge that the category has been too narrowly defined in the past. Media scholars recognize the media as interrelated but are less ready to expand the terrain of texts. We have studied popular media artefacts such as television programmes and films in part because these were neglected by scholars in more traditional fields in the past; now it is time for media studies to embrace 'elite' forms of literature, drama, and public galleries and spaces if it is to develop as a field.

We include in the chapters that follow one on theatre by Aleks Sierz and one by Bart Moore-Gilbert on Hanif Kureishi's novel, *The Buddha of Suburbia*. Both of these contributions show how important drama and literature are to questions of British identity which haunt contemporary media scholars. Questions of what it means to be British emerge in these and other chapters: Jenny Owen's chapter on *The Stephen Lawrence Story*, for example, directly explores questions of black (and white) British identity in the light of the black Londoner's murder at the hands of white youths. British Asian identity is considered as one of 'hybridity' by Bart Moore-Gilbert. In discussing matters of representation of British multicultural society, we cannot ignore the fact of racism. Simon Cottle compels us to confront institutional racism in journalism in his behind-the-scenes examination of employment practices of the industry that may contribute to racism. However, British identity is not necessarily linked with questions of race, and we find ourselves divided on grounds of nationality as devolution breaks up the United Kingdom. The idea of Scottishness as separate from Britishness is considered in two chapters: Murray Smith's piece debates matters of Scottishness raised by the film *Trainspotting*, while Jane Sillars looks at how television drama constructs the idea of Scottish identity. Questions of sex and sexuality are also of interest to media scholars. In my chapter I examine the discourses of sex in girls' magazines while Anna Reading discusses the history of the gay and lesbian press in Britain. Jacquie Gabb considers how fans of *Gardeners' World* create an imaginary garden as they view the show; while Hillegonda Reitveld's essay on dance culture explores how communities of interest have formed around the world for a cultural form which is more typically spatially located. Matters of violence and taste rear their heads in debates about the media and these issues are raised in Ben Slater's piece about *Peeping Tom* and in Jay Russell's chapter discussing the coverage of the film *Crash* and the death of Princess Diana. How to represent the most horrific crime of the twentieth century is the concern of Richard Crownshaw's essay on the Belsen exhibition at the Imperial War Museum.

Evidently, the following chapters are very diverse in terms of themes and subject. They also use a rich vocabulary of media analysis and a wide range of methods. One of the key methods used is *semiotics*, the study of signs. The first chapter in Part III, by Simon Cottle, uses *semiotic analysis* to launch a discussion of racism in the media. Cottle demonstrates the racism at work in the images and headline to a front page story 'Faces of Evil' in the *Bristol Evening Post*. Following this, Cottle looks at the ways in which journalistic norms and practices may foster racist imagery – whether this be intentional or not. Through an analysis of employment and other statistics, Cottle shows that black and Asian people are under-represented in journalism and makes very clear the relationship between representation in media artefacts and representation in terms of employment in the media.

A different method – *textual analysis* – is introduced in the following chapter which also discusses the theme of race. Jenny Owen examines the representation of Britishness in the television documentary, *The Stephen Lawrence Story*, made by Peter Lee-Wright and Yvette Vanson, about the murder of the young South Londoner. Owen subjects the Channel 4 programme to detailed *textual analysis*, examining the sympathetic portrayal of the Lawrence family by the film-makers. This analysis is underpinned by an *historical survey* of the documentary movement in Britain which locates *The Stephen Lawrence Story* within the history of documentary films and reality programming. *The Stephen Lawrence Story* is an example of a political documentary that sets out to challenge and reveal racism. Owen's analysis shows how the programme raises important questions for understanding the media's construction of black and white British identity and citizenship.

The analysis of media content can take many different forms, however, and in Chapter 14 Jane Stokes uses the quantitative method of *content analysis* to examine the importance of sex in magazines for young women and girls. Leading teenage magazines such as *Sugar*, *Mizz*, and *17* are subject to content analysis in order to determine what percentage of copy is taken up with matters of sex. The chapter 'Use it or Lose it' debunks the notion that young people are subjected to bombardment of information about sex in magazines for girls in the 1990s.

The content of the film *Trainspotting* is subject to *textual analysis* by Murray Smith in Chapter 15. Smith discusses the representation of Scottishness in this film and considers the different ways in which the film may be understood as Scottish. The history of the production of *Trainspotting* provides a sound basis for understanding the film and shows how knowledge of a film's history can enhance textual analysis. This chapter demonstrates the efficacy of uniting textual analysis with research into institutions of production and provides a lively and engaging discussion of one of Britain's most successful recent films.

The mechanism of the British film industry is also discussed in the following chapter which provides a reassessment of a classic text of the British cinema: Michael Powell's *Peeping Tom* (1960). In Chapter 16, Ben Slater offers a decoding of this seminal film, deconstructing the complex web of gazes which the film concocts. Slater subjects Powell's disturbing exposition on voyeurism and film-making to careful dissection using Laura Mulvey's theory of the gaze, and provides a rich analysis of the complex pattern of looking within this key text in British cinema history.

Although television and film drama are typically included in media studies text books, the theatre itself is rarely discussed. However, contemporary British theatre is engaged with issues of representation, identity and power – all of relevance to the media scholar; and the theatre is the seedbed of many new ideas and talents. The theatre is neglected to the detriment of media scholarship, and our antidote is provided in the contribution by theatre critic Aleks Sierz (Chapter 17). Sierz examines the classic English drama J.B. Priestley's *An Inspector Calls*, comparing the original, 1940s version of the play with Stephen Daldry's more recent radical production. Sierz shows how ideas concerned with postmodernism may be used to consider issues of representation and class. Sierz's textual analysis focuses on the postmodern aspects of Daldry's production.

Contemporary British drama is also the subject of Chapter 18, although in this particular case Jane Sillars explores Scottishness in television drama. In terms of theme, this chapter clearly shares some concerns with Murray Smith's discussion of *Trainspotting* (in Chapter 15). Sillars considers the role of television drama in 'reflecting and contributing to debates over national identity'. She shows how representations of Scottish people on television have typically been naturalistic representations of working-class folk. More recent images have developed a comedic, whimsical aspect, as in *Hamish Macbeth*, for instance. Despite an interesting consideration of the history of television's representation of Scots, Sillars' discussion focuses more on the institutions of television production than on the texts themselves. The emphasis on the connection between policy and representation also draws on issues raised by Crisell (Chapter 4) and in the contributions to Part II of this book. Sillars discusses the implications of Scottish devolution on British and Scottish identity and broadcasters. This chapter contributes to broadening our understanding of what it means to be Scottish and/or British today.

The role of the fan as analyst has grown in importance in modern media studies. Jacquie Gabb is an avowed fan of gardening programmes and especially of *Gardeners' World* which she subjects to close scrutiny in Chapter 19. Gardening and other 'lifestyle' programmes are ever more prominent in British television schedules and form a popular genre which has so far eluded analysis. Gabb is interested in the pleasures offered to viewers of *Gardener's World* as described in letters from fans. This method of *audience survey research* and *interview* is borrowed from Ien Ang's important study of how viewers watch *Dallas* (1985). Surprisingly, all Gabb's respondents are women, a fact which endorses her hypothesis that the programme offers specifically 'feminine' pleasures. 'Consuming the Garden' shows the significance of gender in the programme, its viewers and the patterns of authority and identity it creates. Drawing on a long tradition of feminist methods, Gabb eschews the notion that the media analyst should be an impartial, dispassionate outsider and integrates her own fandom with her analysis of viewing pleasure.

An interesting feature of the British media, picked up on by Anna Reading, is the fact that we have 'the highest concentration of lesbian and gay press publication in the Western World'. Reading's essay on the gay and lesbian press (Chapter 20) uses *textual analysis* to explore the way in which sexuality is constructed in some of the key British publications for lesbian and gay readers. Reading provides an historical survey of five key publications: *Gay News*; the *Pink Paper*; *Boyz*; *Attitude* and *Diva*. This account is supported by structural analysis in the form of *interviews* with key media producers within the gay and lesbian press. Reading shows how economic pressures of advertisers have impacted on editorial direction and the subsequent construction of sexuality in the gay and lesbian press.

British identity as a kind of 'hybridity' is the theme of Bart Moore-Gilbert's essay on Hanif Kureishi's novels (Chapter 21). Novels are rarely considered in media text books, but they are an important influence on the media world and can find themselves transformed into properties for other media such as television or film. Hanif Kureishi's work has been shown in a range of media, and Bart Moore-Gilbert looks to the source of some of these in his analysis of Kureishi's novel *The Buddha of Suburbia*. Moore-Gilbert examines Kureishi's work as a discussion of hybridity and in this regard his chapter is informed by Homi Bhabha's work on culture and race (Bhabha, 1994). Moore-Gilbert shows how Kureishi is helping to forge a 'Britishness' that does not exclude his characters' 'Indianness'. The *literary analysis* of this novel allows for a discussion of some key facets of the many-sided matter of contemporary British identity and representation.

Cilla Black and the television programme she hosts, *Blind Date*, occupy an important place in British popular culture. Paddy Scannell subjects this programme to a *phenomenological* analysis in Chapter 22. Phenomenology is the study of the structure of the phenomena and is an important aspect of modern media studies which Scannell has addressed elsewhere (for example, Scannell, 1996). The use of setting, participants, studio audience and viewer are all closely examined to show how *Blind Date* constructs a specific phenomenal world.

Novelist Jay Russell investigates the furore surrounding the release of David Cronenberg's film *Crash* and the parallels with the beatification of Princess Diana following her death in a car crash. Russell's piece is a powerfully written essay on the perversity of celebrity in modern Britain (Chapter 23). This chapter follows in the *polemicist* tradition of Dwight McDonald in the US and Richard Hoggart in Britain. It is an example of committed scholarship which characterizes much of the more critical tradition in our field.

Richard Crownshaw (Chapter 24) shows how important museums are for advancing national identities, focusing especially on the questions of British and Jewish identities. Crownshaw argues that museums construct an exhibitionary narration of events which is quite distinct from the actual events chronicled. Through a close analysis of the Belsen exhibit in the Imperial War Museum, Crownshaw's chapter investigates how the museum constructs a history from the perspective of British soldiers rather than from that of holocaust victims and survivors.

The last chapter of this section (Chapter 25) addresses one of the most recent media in our book. The latest medium to be studied in our analytical chapters is the website, which Hillegonda Rietveld explores in relation to contemporary dance culture. Key websites are analysed and their relationship to the broader phenomenon of dance culture is discussed. A detailed historical analysis gives way to a fruitful look at how the subculture of the dance scene uses websites.

All of the chapters in this section present innovative work which the editors hope will give you a taste of the exciting and engaging world of media research and will stimulate the reader to pursue the subject further. Whether you agree with the contributors or not, it is our desire that readers of the following will be encouraged to enter into the debates presented and will want to pursue research and analysis of their own.

References

Ang, I. *Watching Dallas: Soap Operas and the Melodramatic Imagination*. London: Methuen, 1985.
Bhabha, H. *The Location of Culture*. London: Routledge, 1994.
Scannell, P. *Radio, Television and Modern Life*. Oxford: Blackwell, 1996.

CHAPTER 12

Ethnic Minorities and the British News Media: Explaining (Mis)Representation*

SIMON COTTLE

Questions of media representation are not confined to the analysis of media portrayal. When analysing media representations students and researchers sometimes assume that the explanations for these can be recovered from a reading of the representation itself. For example, if a racially demeaning or inflammatory news image is positioned on the front page of a newspaper, surely this can only be accounted for by the racist beliefs of the journalists or proprietors involved? Leaving to one side the possibility that reading an image as 'racist' can sometimes depend as much on the active ascription of meaning by the viewer as the meaning thought to inhere within the image itself, this common-sense view suffers from what has come to be known as 'the problem of inference'. That is, the tendency to 'read off' or infer from an analysis of the media representation possible motivations or explanations for its production – a problem that often surfaces in exclusively text-based approaches to media representations. Simply put, and no matter how methodologically sophisticated some studies may be in terms of their approach to how meanings (and pleasures) are produced within textual features and forms, these cannot substitute for 'behind the scenes' research into the informing contexts and processes of production. The few researchers who have attended to the production side of news representations have thus helped to identify a number of contributing forces and influences that together help explain media representations, and thus overcome the 'problem of inference'. This short discussion focuses on the important concern of ethnic minority representations in news and sets out to outline some of the levels of influence possibly at work in the production of racialized and demeaning news images. If such representations are to be effectively challenged and replaced by more 'representative' images of the communities they purport to portray – including their conditions of existence and in all their cultural complexities – so we must know about the forces that currently produce less than 'representative' portrayals.

* This article is an up-dated and expanded discussion first published as The News Media and 'Race' – A Case of Intended and Unintended Outcomes', *Social Science Teacher*, 1994, **23**, 2, pp. 12–14.

To begin, it is first useful to describe a front-page news report from a recent newspaper that can indeed be challenged as 'racist'. Thereafter we can then briefly consider the different levels of explanations that may be at work in the production of this and, all too often, other representations produced by our news media. I say 'describe a front page' because unfortunately the newspaper in question, the *Bristol Evening Post*, a regional newspaper typical of its type, has refused us permission to reproduce a copy of the front-page article for the purposes of this discussion – notwithstanding that it had already been widely disseminated in the public domain. Curious, isn't it, how newspapers that make much of 'the public's right to know', can themselves run shy of public scrutiny and discussion! The news editor's refusal to grant us copyright permission, on the grounds that 'the interests of the *Evening Post* would not thereby be served', betrays a lack of social responsibility towards its ethnic minority readers and wider community, and simply compounds the original offence caused to them by the production of this particular article.

The front-page article in question produced by the *Bristol Evening Post* comprised the faces of sixteen convicted drugs dealers accompanied with the prominent bold headline 'FACES OF EVIL' (17 April 1996). The sixteen pictures displayed across the front page were police 'mug shots' each with the names of the convicted men captioned beneath. All the faces were black. The *Bristol Evening Post*, a paper not known for its in-depth coverage of Bristol's ethnic minority communities, their different cultures or common difficulties and achievements, evidently felt that such a story was a 'big' story in regional terms and signalled as much with its front-page treatment. While routinely reporting crime related stories in the St Pauls and Easton areas of Bristol – locales associated with the city's African-Caribbean and Asian communities – the paper has also occasionally portrayed in more spectacular ways urban disorders such as the so-called St Pauls 'Riots' of 1980 (Joshua *et al.*, 1983). For the *Post*'s 227,000 or so regular readers, the 'FACES OF EVIL' front page was thus unlikely to do other than confirm prevalent views routinely fed by local news portrayal associating both the locality of St Pauls and its African-Caribbean population with crime and criminality. Of course, the men convicted of drug dealing were legally defined as 'criminal' and all sixteen faces are black. The point here, however, is that without offering a broader context in which to situate the rise of inner city drugs dealing, and without a more differentiated and accurate portrayal of the city's ethnic minority communities and their conditions of existence, such reports serve to sustain racist views of the city's black communities and associated inner city localities as crimogenic – especially when framed with such deliberate sensationalism.

One can question, for example, if the maximum prison sentence of four years meted out to one of the convicted drug dealers, and an average of two years for the rest, warrants the sensationalist label of 'FACES OF EVIL'? Would the *Evening Post* have printed police 'mug shots' of the convicted men across its front page if they had been white? Is it possible that the informing editorial viewpoint would have deemed the story somehow less newsworthy if the men had been white and the newspaper couldn't therefore trade (both literally and semiotically) in a racializing discourse of crime? Do not police 'mug shots' by definition criminalize and, when publicly exposed, help to demonize those caught within the police photographer's frame – an official frame instantly recognizable by the effects of standardized lighting, body posture and facial expression? Should such photos have been given front-page exposure, and anyway how did the paper get hold of these police photographs at such short notice?

The research literature on the British news media and ethnic minorities, both press and TV, indicates that such reporting is not confined to the parochial interests of the *Bristol Evening Post*. Across the years and seemingly as a matter of routine, Britain's black and ethnic minorities have tended to be depicted in terms of a restricted repertoire of representations and within contexts characterized by conflict, controversy and deviance (Cottle, 1992). In the 1960s and 70s, studies observed how immigrants were reported in relation to public health scares, problems of 'numbers' and tensions of 'race relations' – effectively concealing problems of British racism (Butterworth, 1967; Hartmann *et al.*, 1974; Critcher *et al.*, 1977; Troyna, 1981). In the 1970s and across the 1980s, studies identified the ways in which a moral panic orchestrated around 'mugging', the portrayal of black demonstrations, and inner city disorders served to criminalize Britain's black population – ignoring continuing social inequalities and growing anger at policing practices and harassment (Hall *et al.*, 1978; Holland, 1981; Tumber, 1982; Murdock, 1984; Hansen and Murdock, 1985; Cottle, 1993a). In the 1980s and 90s, studies have charted the virulent press attacks on anti-racism campaigns, the vilification of black representatives and the seeming endorsement of statements of 'new racism' by prominent politicians – actively disparaging attempts to further multicultural and anti-racist agendas (Murray, 1986; Gordon and Rosenberg, 1989; Van Dijk, 1991).

Of course, as general findings, exceptions can be found and it is not always exactly clear how news reporting of ethnic minorities has responded to the shifting cultural-politics of 'race' and racism over the years. Commentators have recently begun to recover, for example, the changing cultural representations of ethnic minorities in British television across TV genres from the late 1940s to the present day. These indicate that representations are far from historically static and tend to give expression to the surrounding cultural-politics of 'race' – ideas often associated with positions of 'assimilation', 'integration', 'multiculturalism', 'anti-racism' and/or, most recently, 'new ethnicities' (Hall, 1988, 1995; Daniels and Gerson, 1989; Pines, 1992; Daniels, 1994; Ross, 1996).

If important differences are found across time, there is also evidence to indicate that at least some differences characterize different news forms within and across the news media. The author's study of regional television factual programmes, including news production and output, found that this particular news form has sometimes permitted a more 'positive' and multiculturalist orientation to both its news subject matter and audience (Cottle, 1993b, 1994). Here, a combination of factors contributed to this more 'positive' news portrayal, including a developing newsroom awareness of multiculturalism; the pursuit of minority ethnic audiences as a means of increasing the programme rating; and the programme's populist nature and appeals which inform the selected mix of news stories and features as well as their journalistic treatment. In other words, news representations can exhibit important differences across time, medium and outlet. This discussion now considers some of the forces at work 'behind the scenes' and how these too contribute to a complex of dynamics and levels of influence that can, for the most part, change through time. Though not discounting the explanatory relevance of racist and prejudiced journalists and/or their proprietors for an understanding of the production of racialized and demeaning images of ethnic minorities, research studies tend to indicate, as discussed below, that this individualist explanation often proves less than sufficient. We must also attend to various contexts and dynamics – professional, institutional, commercial, organisational, cultural – and how each impacts on the production of ethnic minority (mis)representations. No doubt each is also implicated in the production of the *Bristol Evening Post*'s 'FACES OF EVIL' front page and others like it. Together they also point to the necessity for a complex and a multi-layered strategy to affect change. For up-to-date research findings and wider discussions of ethnic minority media representations and the shaping influences at work, see Cottle (1999).

Journalist and Proprietor Prejudice

Anecdotal evidence provided by working journalists and observers suggests that many journalists and news proprietors do indeed harbour racist views and sentiments. A casual worker on the *Sun* newspaper, for example, kept a diary in which he recorded how the editors discussed whether to include a picture of one of the 36 winners of the *Sun's* bingo on the front page who happened to be Asian – an interesting counterpoint, perhaps, to the front page discussed above. The *Sun's* acting editor is recorded as saying, 'I'm not having pictures of darkies on the front page', to which the night editor replied, 'That's the last thing our readers want, pictures of blacks raking it in' (cited in Hollingsworth, 1990, p. 132). Proprietorial involvement in setting news policy, hiring and firing senior editors, and even dictating headlines is also well documented. Much might seem to depend, therefore, on the personal views of proprietors, senior editors and ordinary journalists.

However, although it is undoubtedly the case that some, perhaps many, journalists continue to harbour racist sentiments and viewpoints, the routine production of standardized news suggests that if racist views inform the news output, this is informed by professional and organizational goals and not simply by the individual attitudes and prejudices of the news workers themselves. Careful attention to the short exchange above, and its assumption about the racist attitudes of the *Sun's* readership, suggests that more may be involved than simply the editors' personal views. While proprietors undoubtedly wield enormous power and control over news organizations, enabling them on occasion to disseminate personal views, these do not escape the court of readership opinion, nor shareholder interests. News output is generally produced collectively in accordance with a news policy and a shared journalistic understanding of the particular news form produced, its established political orientation, audience appeals and story selections and styles of presentation. The individual prejudices of news workers are thus only likely to be enacted if they conform to the collective news goals and the distinctive market orientation of the news outlet concerned.

It should also be remembered that journalists and some sections of the news media industry have themselves sought to exert pressures for change. The Black Members Council of the National Union of Journalists has produced *Guidelines on Race Reporting* (NUJ, 1995) which seek to curb racist language, sensationalism and defamatory portrayals within the news media industry, and the BBC's *Producers' Guidelines* (BBC, 1996) also provide general rules requiring journalistic fairness, accuracy and impartiality – although clearly these have had varying success.

Social Composition and Journalist Training

A related, perhaps more sophisticated, explanation concerns the social composition of journalists and their forms of professional training and socialization. If journalists are found to come predominantly from white middle-class homes, select educational institutions and share similar middle-ground political values, undoubtedly this will influence the sensibilities and knowledge base informing journalist output. Recent data and discussion of Britain's ethnic minority journalists confirm that a gross imbalance between white and ethnic minority journalists continues to structure training and employment patterns and opportunities within the news media industry (Ainley, 1994). For example, of the estimated 4000 national newspaper journalists only 20 are black or Asian, while a mere 15 out of 8000 work for the provincial press; in the broadcasting industry matters are slightly improved with an estimated 100 black or Asian editorial staff among 3700 – here, the equal opportunities policies, ethnic minority monitoring and training schemes of the BBC are thought to have helped although the researcher reminds us that half of all black staff work on black-only radio and television programmes (Ainley, 1994).

Such figures are an indictment of the British news media and demand concerted action and improvement. However, ethnographic studies of news organizations and professionalism also indicate that processes of journalist socialization may be as important as journalist recruitment. Colleague esteem, successful newsroom acceptance and promotion and, ultimately, career moves depend upon conformity to a news policy and news organization goals, not their disruption. Researchers have often commented on the seeming lack of conflict within newsrooms and the unspoken acceptance of both shared news values and a widespread professional ideology of 'objectivity' – an ideology that may well have the effect of distancing journalists and ethnic minority programme makers from acting as advocates for those minority groups and interests they might otherwise seek to serve (Cottle, 1998).

Competition and Marketplace Pressures

News organizations, for the most part, are in business to make profits and all compete for readers and audiences. This raises a third explanation based in the wider system of commercial constraints and pressures bearing down on the 'cultural industries' and their news output (Murdock, 1982). Surviving in a competitive marketplace means seeking the maximum audience/readers and the maximum receipts from advertisers. In this context, news is produced just like any other commodity for the largest possible group of consumers. Within a predominantly white culture, such an approach will anticipate that the middle ground of white opinion and interests will be catered for while marginalizing minority interests, voices and opinions. Also, high market entry costs and potentially smaller audiences, and hence advertiser reluctance to pay for advertising in such outlets, all inhibit the successful formation and growth of minority ethnic news media – although some have managed against the odds to secure a niche market (Tatla and Singh, 1989; Benjamin, 1995). In the mainstream, market pressures also contribute to press sensationalism and may even lead to the orchestration of 'race' controversy in pursuit of readers, ratings and revenue, as well as the marginalization of ethnic minority programming to the quiet backwaters of the TV schedules.

Bureaucratic Organization

Bureaucratic and organizational pressures within the newsroom, as well as impersonal economic forces outside, also contribute to the production of ethnic minority representations and misrepresentations. Confronted with the daily pressures of news deadlines and the uncertainty of tomorrow's news events, news teams seek, as far as possible, to 'tame the news environment' and 'routinise the unexpected'. One way of doing this is to rely on key institutional sources of news, police or government press releases for example (Hall *et al.*, 1978). The result is that little energy or resources are devoted, as a matter of routine, to the search for non-institutional voices and viewpoints. When coupled with a professional journalistic claim to impartiality and objectivity which, ironically, is achieved in practice via the accessing of authoritative (that is, authority) voices, so the bureaucratic nature of news production is geared to privilege the voices and viewpoints of social power holders, and not those excluded from Britain's powerful institutions. Once again, the voices of white Britain and those institutions with a stake in preserving the status quo are likely to monopolise the opportunities for news access.

Deep-seated 'News Values'

News values also lead to the forefronting of images of ethnic minorities in terms of conflict, drama, controversy, violence and deviance (Hartmann and Husband, 1974; Troyna, 1981). Such deep-seated qualities of 'news' are professionally pursued as a matter of unconscious routine such is their contribution to a journalist's sense of what makes a 'good' story. The question here, then, is not whether these news values are exclusive to 'race' reporting because clearly they inform other news stories as well. Rather, the point is to inquire to what extent they appear to figure in a disproportionate number of stories about ethnic minorities. It is also important to question to what extent such 'news values' can really be assumed to be universal. If found to vary across different cultures, time periods or different news outlets and news media, they most certainly are not beyond criticism nor change.

Culture and Cultural Discourses

Journalists, just like the rest of us, inhabit a social world that is made sense of through language and culture. Culture, in this sense, refers to the taken-for-granted assumptions, values and ways of life that give meaning, sense and identity to individuals and social groups. Journalists inevitably, therefore, give expression to the surrounding cultural terrain which, in the case of Britain, carries the historical traces of imperialism, colonialism and a deeply ingrained sense of white superiority (Hartmann and Husband, 1974; Van Dijk, 1991). From this vantage point it is unsurprising that news language and news texts can become a site for racialised meanings and reproduce the wider cultural field in which ideas of 'race' and ethnic differences are played out – and, to some extent, contested.

Also, as we have seen, journalists are not beyond maximizing a story's news value by actively framing it in relation to current controversies and popular concerns. In other words, journalists can both give expression to the wider play of cultural power, and also play an active role in focusing and orchestrating cultural preoccupations. The active role played by Britain's tabloids in amplifying racist fears and orchestrating racist sentiments should not be forgotten. These, however, are propagated on the basis of varying degrees of professional calculation and conformity to an in-house editorial stance, not simply individual bigotry.

News Genres and News Conventions

If news organizations typically work to an identifiable editorial position and in-house style – the *Bristol Evening Post*, clearly, is not the *Guardian,* and the *Independent* recognizably is not *The Times*, while the *Mirror* is not quite the *Sun* and BBC2's *Newsnight* is not ITV's *ITN* – journalists also reproduce their distinctive news forms according to a number of genre and sub-genre conventions. These also exert a shaping impact upon the selection and framing of news stories although hitherto largely ignored within the research literature. If crime and human interest stories figure prominently in one news outlet, political and financial news may routinely figure within another. If political and economic elites gain routine access in one, ordinary voices may find increased involvement in another. Some TV news programmes involve more live studio discussions and features, while others rely upon edited filmed packages involving interview clips only.

Indirectly, often unintentionally, such differentiated but characteristic forms of news output impact upon the representation of ethnic minorities and associated stories. The popular appeals of regional TV news, for example, have been found to colour minority ethnic representations through a prism of individualism, success and cultural diversity albeit often presented as spectacle and exotica (that is, the 'saris, steelbands and samozas' approach to multiculturalism), leaving issues of structural disadvantage and discrimination largely unexamined (Cottle, 1993b).

Conclusion

Each of the forms of explanation above goes some way in helping to explain the lamentable tale of the British news media and its representations of ethnic minorities. Most, if not all, of them are also likely to have been at work in the production of the *Bristol Evening Post* article discussed at the outset. And each furthermore points to a level of complexity informing detrimental and discriminatory processes that, in the context of news, can result in both *intended* and *unintended* outcomes. The outcomes here, of course, refer to patterns and forms of news representations of ethnic minorities. How exactly such news representations feed into popular and political consciousness and inform wider discriminatory practices takes us beyond the production focus of this short discussion, but the contribution of the mass media to a climate of increasing national and European racisms should not be overlooked.

We have outlined how media representations and misrepresentations of ethnic minorities can be produced by a complex of interrelated professional, cultural, commercial and institutional processes and practices. Confronted with such multiple sources and levels of determination, it follows that improved news representation and access will require a multi-tiered strategy to effect change. In addition to challenging individual racist journalists and their proprietors the following also seem necessary: improved minority ethnic recruitment and access to positions of responsibility and power within British news organizations; enhanced professional training, multicultural awareness and continuing on-the-job monitoring of professional practice; increased resources for improving minority community representation and news media access; a system of financial support and subsidy for at least some ethnic minority and mainstream news media outlets; the development of an expanded range of different news formats and conventions; as well as engagement at the wider level of culture and economy in which patterns of racialized inequality are allowed to persist. Clearly questions of 'representation' cannot be confined to the analysis of media output, but necessarily direct us to the informing contexts and processes of media production.

References

Ainley, B. 'Ubiquitous whites – invisible blacks', *British Journalism Review*, **5**, 4 (1994) pp. 71–84.

British Broadcasting Corporation (BBC) *Producers' Guidelines*. BBC London, 1996.

Benjamin, I. *The Black Press in Britain*. London: Trentham Books, 1995.

Butterworth, E. 'The 1962 smallpox outbreak and the British press', *Race*, **7**, 4 (1967) pp. 347–64.

Cottle, S. '"Race", racialization and the media: a review and update of research', *Sage Race Relations Abstracts*, **17**, 2 (1992) pp. 3–57.

Cottle, S. *TV News, Urban Conflict and the Inner City*. Leicester: Leicester University Press, 1993a.

Cottle, S. '"Race" and regional television news: multi-culturalism and the production of popular TV', *New Community*, **19**, 4 (1993b) pp. 581–92.

Cottle, S. Stigmatizing Handsworth: Notes on Reporting Spoiled Space, *Critical Studies in Mass Communication*, **11**, 3 (1994) pp. 231–56.

Cottle, S. 'Making ethnic minority programmes inside the BBC: professional pragmatics and cultural containment', *Media, Culture and Society*, **20**, 2 (1998) pp. 295–317.

Cottle, S. (ed.) (1999) *Ethnic Minorities and Media Research: Changing Cultural Boundaries*. Buckingham: Open University Press (forthcoming).

Critcher, C., Parker, M. and Sondhi, R. *Race in the Provincial Press*. Paris: UNESCO, 1977.

Daniels, T. Programmes For Black Audiences, in S. Hood (ed.) *Behind The Screens: The Structure of British Television in the Nineties*. London: Lawrence & Wishart, 1994, pp. 65–81.

Daniels, T. and Gerson, J. (eds) *The Colour Black: Black Images in British Television*. London: British Film Institute Publishing, 1989.

Gordon, P. and Rosenberg, D. Daily *Racism – The Press and Black People in Britain*. London: The Runnymede Trust, 1989.

Hall, S. New Ethnicities, in K. Mercer (ed.) *Black Film, British Cinema*, ICA Document 7. London: British Film Institute, 1988.

Hall, S. (1995) Black and White in Television, in J. Givanni (ed.) *Remote Control*. London: British Film Institute, 1995, pp. 13–28.

Hall, S., Critcher, C., Jefferson, T., Clarke, J. and Roberts, B. *Policing the Crisis: Mugging, The State, and Law and Order*. Basingstoke: Macmillan, 1978.

Hansen, A. and Murdock, G. Constructing the Crowd: Populist Discourse and Press Presentation, in V. Mosco and M. Wasco (eds) *Popular Culture and Media Events, The Critical Communication Review* Vol. III. New Jersey: Ablex, 1985, pp. 227–57.

Hartmann, P. and Husband. C. *Racism and the Mass Media*. London: Davis Poynter, 1974.

Hartmann, P., Husband. C. and Clark, J. Race as News: A Study in the Handling of Race in the British Press from 1963 to 1970, in UNESCO (ed.) *Race as News*. Paris: UNESCO, 1974, pp. 91–173.

Holland, P. 'The New Cross fire and the popular press', *Multi-Racial Education*, **9**, 3 (1981) pp. 61–80.

Hollingsworth, M. *The Press and Political Dissent*. London: Pluto Press, 1990.

Joshua, H., Wallace, T., and Booth, H. *To Ride the Storm: The 1980 Bristol 'Riots' and the State*. London: Heinemann, 1983.

Murdock, G. Large Corporations and the Control of the Communications Industries, in M. Gurevitch, T. Bennett, J. Curran and J. Woollacott (eds) *Culture, Society and the Media*. London: Methuen, 1982, pp. 118–50.

Murdock, G. (1984) Reporting the Riots: Images and Impacts, in J. Benyon (ed.) *Scarman and After*. Oxford: Pergamon, 1984, pp. 73–95.

Murray, N. 'Anti-racists and other demons: the press and ideology in Thatcher's Britain', *Race and Class*, Vol. XXVII (1986) pp. 1–20.

National Union of Journalists (NUJ) *Guidelines on Race Reporting*. London: NUJ, 1995.

Pines, J. (ed.) *Black and White in Colour*. London: British Film Institute Publishing, 1992.

Ross, K. *Black and White Media*. Oxford: Polity Press, 1996.

Tatla, D.S. and Singh, G. 'The Punjabi press', *New Community*, **15**, 2 (1989) pp. 171–84.

Troyna, B. *Public Awareness and the Media: A Study of Reporting on Race*. London: Commission for Racial Equality, 1981.

Tumber, H. *Television and the Riots*, Broadcasting Research Unit. London: British Film Institute, 1982.

Van Dijk. T. *Racism and the Press*. London: Routledge, 1991.

CHAPTER 13

Documentary and Citizenship: The Case of Stephen Lawrence

JENNY OWEN

This chapter has two purposes. First, to address the question of methods of analysis – how to analyse television documentaries; and second, to explore the way in which one particular documentary – *The Stephen Lawrence Story* (*SLS*) – addresses notions of contemporary British citizenship and identity.

Students of television documentary are often at a loss as to how they should go about analysing such a diverse product as the television documentary. I would argue that the familiar media studies triptych of 'institution, audience, text' is a good starting point since together they help describe the factors that must be taken into account when studying any television programme.

If we begin by analysing institutional processes we can, for instance, address questions related to the commissioning process and finance. Thus, any analysis of contemporary television documentary would need to take into account an overall decline in the numbers of 'serious' documentaries commissioned by terrestrial television as a result of growing competition in the sector.

For example, while Channel 4's documentary output rose slightly from 279 hours in 1995 to 300 in 1996 (Channel 4 Television Corporation, 1996), the BBC's declined from 1056 hours on BBC1 for 1995/6 to 950 in 1996/7 and on BBC2 from 884 hours in 1995/6 to 821 hours in 1996/7 (BBC, 1996/7). However, the greatest decline in documentary output has been experienced by ITV. A recent report by the Campaign for Quality Television (CQT), *Serious Documentaries on Television*, offers the following evidence: in 1993 ITV companies produced 61 hours of 'single' documentaries, 34.5 hours of documentary series and 22 hours of 'factual entertainment' – in short there was a degree of 'breadth and volume' to its output (Campaign for Quality Television, 1998, p. 4). However, by 1994, argues the report, all the 'serious' documentary strands had been cancelled. Shows with a clear public interest remit, such as *First Tuesday*, *Viewpoint* and *Disappearing World*, were axed to be replaced by a dwindling number of its 'own brand' programme, *Network First*, screened not in prime time but at 10.40pm.

If we then take the second part of our triptych – audience – we find that declining audience numbers for *Network First* meant that from the middle of

1997 ITV ceased to commission any new documentaries for the strand and when its doors 're-opened for business' it 'was not to commission serious documentaries' but to follow the BBC's lead with the production of a long line of 'documentary soaps' (Campaign for Quality Television, 1998, p. 13).

This then was the climate in which the producers of *The Stephen Lawrence Story* were working. While TV documentaries and current affairs programmes of the late 1980s and early part of the 1990s had focused successfully on a number of miscarriage of justice stories (the Guildford Four, the men accused of the murder of Carl Bridgewater), this was now the era of the documentary soap, where programmes like *Neighbours From Hell* were able to draw an audience of 11 million. Producer Peter Lee-Wright, committed to 'partial TV' not 'balanced TV', wanted to explore how the events of Stephen Lawrence's death and the ensuing failure of the judicial system impacted on the family and the world at large; but this kind of subject matter was now relatively 'unattractive' to commissioning editors (Lee-Wright, 1997).

As we have seen, audience figures play a vital part in the commissioning process. While academics and industry insiders of the late 1980s warned of the threat to documentary of increasing competition, they did not foresee the way in which some factual programming might be exploited for its popularity, since it was not the kind of programming they had in mind when they spoke of documentary. For instance, in 1997 the BBC's 'documentary soaps' *Driving School* and *Hotel* routinely attracted audiences of over 8 million and Channel 4's flagship series, *Cutting Edge*, on occasion produced documentaries to compete with the channel's top soap, *Brookside* (Channel 4 Television Corporation, 1996). That said, the success of Channel 4 has been a relative one. On examining the 'top 20' shows across all terrestrial television it is sport and soap which dominate, not documentary (Dyja, 1998).

Finally, if we look at the text we are able to explore the place where meaning is most directly produced for and by the audience; and where we can explore the nature of the 'documentary gaze' and the 'world it brings into sight' (Nichols, 1991, p. 77). In short, an analysis of the text promises insights into the ways in which the use of particular techniques of film-making construct a particular kind of world.

The 'text' that I am most concerned with is *The Stephen Lawrence Story*. This award-winning (CRE prize for documentary 1997), 60-minute documentary was produced by independent film-makers Peter Lee-Wright and Yvette Vanson. First screened on Channel 4 Television in February 1997, it attracted audience figures of 958,000 (or 4 per cent of audience share), while a subsequent transmission in April 1997 commanded a further 424,000 (or 11 per cent of audience share). The subject of the documentary was the death of Stephen Lawrence, a young man who had been 'unlawfully killed in an unprovoked attack by five white youths' (Inquest verdict, February 1997) on April 22 1993. Following the failure of the police and the Crown Prosecution Service to bring the case successfully to court, it had been left to Stephen's parents to try to bring their son's murderers to justice. The five white youths remain at large and the conduct of the police, Crown Prosecution Service and the judicial system is currently the focus of an independent public inquiry.

In 1995 Peter Lee-Wright had secured 'essential and exclusive access' to film the Lawrences. However, as is the way with independent production, Lee-Wright still had to secure backing for his idea from one of the main television channels (Lee-Wright, 1997). This was eventually forthcoming from Channel 4's commissioning editor for independent film and video, Robin Gutch, in March 1996. According to Lee-Wright he pitched the story to Gutch by using the analogy of the Greek myth of Medea. To Lee-Wright the 'Stephen Lawrence story' was the story of a mother whose child has been killed and cannot get justice, a story about an 'absolute and fundamental human response', and it was his aim to produce a 'dialectic between the lawyers' story and the personal story' (Lee-Wright, 1997).

SLS is however, more than dialectic between the lawyers and the family. In particular, the documentary traces the ways in which racism, both institutional and personal, constructs young black British men as criminals, disenfranchises and attempts to exclude ordinary black British citizens, and works to deny what authors Mike and Trevor Phillips, in their book about the impact of the post-war Caribbean presence, have described as the 'irresistible rise of multi-racial Britain' (Phillips and Phillips, 1998).

In fact, *SLS* is important at several levels. First, its presence suggests that in the 1990s, despite the rise of the documentary soap, there remains space (albeit limited) for impassioned and 'political' documentary film-making; and second, it represents a thread of continuity in the tradition of British documentary film-making which has historically engaged with questions of citizenship. This is why we now need to consider *SLS* in relation to the origins of documentary film-making in Britain.

TV Documentary and Citizenship

Documentary film-making in Britain began in the 1920s and 30s; pre-television documentaries were made for either cinematic release (although this became increasingly rare) or for the large numbers of film clubs and workers' associations which were characteristic of the period. This era is usually associated with the name of John Grierson, whose work was influenced both by the imperialistic traditions of early ethnographic film-makers like Robert Flaherty, with his questionable ethical approach to subject and truth, and by the growth of marketing, publicity and public relations in both public and private sectors. For example, it was eventually discovered that Flaherty in *Nanook of the North* (1922), a film which purported to describe the lives of the Inuit, had in fact made 'extensive use of re-enactment' (Kilborn and Izod, 1997, p. 140).

Grierson has come to dominate the period largely because not only did he produce films of enduring interest and quality, he also wrote about his philosophy of documentary film-making in *First Principles of Documentary*, written between 1932 and 1934. It was Grierson of course who famously described documentary as the 'creative treatment of actuality' and who in *First Principles* made the social and aesthetic case for documentary as superior to fictional cinema because it engaged with the real rather than encouraging fantasy and because it worked imaginatively and dramatically rather than confining itself to the aesthetics of the newsreel and the illustrated lecture. Most crucially, however, documentary was not just an 'art form' it also had 'sociological' responsibilities – it had the job of 'making poetry where no poet has gone before'... in 'the streets and cities and slums and markets and exchanges and factories' (cited in Corner, 1996, p. 13).

Documentary of this period was also preoccupied with the problem of how to reconcile democracy with continuing inequality and poverty. However, by the early 1940s, the social democratic didacticism characteristic of Grierson's work had given way to a more overtly propagandist style as befitted the exigencies of war. Films such as *The New Britain* (Ralph Keene, MOI, 1940), *An Airman's Letter to His Mother* (Michael Powell, 1941), *Builders* (Pat Jackson/Ian Dalrymple, MOI, 1942), *India Marches* (1941) and *West Indies Calling* (John Page/Paul Rotha, 1944) asserted a range of arguments to do with the nature of post-war citizenship and the future contract between citizen and state which people might expect once the war was over. *The New Britain*, arguably the most distorted of this collection of films, seemed to suggest that 'happiness' had been at the heart of old Britain and would certainly need to be at the centre of the 'new Britain'; while *An Airman's Letter to His Mother* offered a 'stiff upper lip' paean to 'peace, justice and freedom for all' – all that is who belonged to the 'higher civilisation' – and subscribed to notions of duty, empire, courage and Christianity.

By 1942 *Builders* was offering a more concrete and populist vision for the future – slum clearance, schools and free health care; while *India Marches* referred to the 'struggle for freedom and democracy' that India's people were engaged in as 'Indians' (not as Muslims or Hindus); and *West Indies Calling* cited the 'common citizenship with us', international comradeship and the reconstruction which would need to take place in the West Indies after the war. In this last film there was, interestingly enough, no recognition of the possibility that West Indians might wish to stay in Britain once Germany was defeated. All these films may be viewed at the Film Archive of the Imperial War Museum, London.

After the war documentary film gave way – as did the wireless – to the ascendancy of television. However, many documentaries continued to be preoccupied with defining the relationship which should exist between citizen and state. For instance, seminal television documentaries like Jeremy Sandford's *Cathy Come Home* (1966) addressed the issue of homelessness and the failure of the authorities to deal with the effects of widespread social change; Roger Graef's *Police* (1982) led to changes in the way rape victims were interviewed by the police, while the nature of multiracial Britain was explored in documentaries like *Handsworth Songs* (John Akomfrah, Black Audio Collective, 1986). *Handsworth Songs* focused on questions of race and racism, postwar migration and the poverty of the inner cities, and was 'made in the Griersonian spirit with our own diasporic inflection adding substance to it' (cited in Ross, 1996, p. 40).

Analysing the Text

Historically, documentary analysis has been dominated by a concern with the nature of reality and the extent to which individual documentaries engage with and construct the real. To this end textual analysis has tended to focus on the way different documentary techniques establish truth or verisimilitude.

According to Nichols, there are four main 'modes of documentary' – the expository, the observational, the reflexive, the interactive and combinations thereof. The expository mode is characterized by a 'voice of God' narrator with the viewer directly addressed with titles or voices which advance an argument about the historical world; observational documentaries, currently rather fashionable, stress the non-intervention of the film-maker who appears to cede control; interactive documentaries explore what happens when the illusion of absence (on the part of the film-maker) is taken away and textual authority shifts towards the participants; and the reflexive mode challenges the impression of reality, which the other modes convey 'unproblematically', by focusing on the relationship between the film-maker and the viewer rather than the film-maker and the subject (Nichols, 1991).

SLS is structured using a combination of expository and observational techniques but it is its engagement with what it means to be a citizen in a multiracial society which is the focus of my interest. To this end the documentary offers us a number of story strands – the police story (where various officers strenuously deny the existence of racism: 'it doesn't matter what colour you are, black, blue or pink'... 'the colour of the victim is an utter irrelevance'); the judicial story (which is characterized by the failure to bring the case successfully to court – or what Michael Mansfield QC calls 'prosecutorial reluctance'); the community story (which describes the levels of racial violence in South East London and the failure of local authorities and police to deal with it – 'this society has a lot to answer to. It needs to ask itself why racism? Why?' and 'mostly young people are learning their racism from their parents'); the young people's story (characterized by hopes and fears for the future but emphasizing the importance of engaging with the implications of multiracialism); and last, and most importantly, the Lawrences' story.

The Lawrences' story illustrates the troubling situation in which black people find themselves when asserting their identity as British citizens. How can they be full citizens when they are denied basic rights? For example, when the family's private prosecution fails, Doreen Lawrence observes that she would no longer advise others in the same situation to 'play by the rules' because the rule of law is 'not there for us. The only way we are going to get justice – innocent people – is to do it ourselves'.

The conflict, which the assertion of a black British identity raises, is further explored when the Lawrence's return to Jamaica to visit Stephen's grave. Jamaica or 'home' as Mr Lawrence refers to it, is presented as an island paradise – all waves crashing on the seashore, waterfalls and verdant natural surroundings – and he intimates his longing to stay. For Doreen Lawrence, however, home is Britain and she is vehement on the subject: 'this what the racists want' [for us to go back to the Caribbean]. To leave is impossible: 'black people are here to stay. They fought in the war. They're here to stay.'

These themes of citizenship are continually explored. For example, the documentary skilfully cuts between the failure of the legal process to the thoughts of a group of Stephen's young friends (black and white). The Lawrences' former next door neighbour, a white girl the same age as Stephen, comments: 'It was utopia really. A black family living next door to a white family... we should see that throughout society.'

Another young woman remarks: 'It's up to all of us... the way we think, and our attitudes, and also the way we educate ourselves and our children – we need change in society, not just in the institutions.'

Stephen's black male friends deliver a surprisingly upbeat message about their continued belief in British justice (and one young man says that despite everything he would still like to join the police). This faith is not shared by Neville Lawrence: 'I feel uncomfortable living in a society where I've got no rights. You pay into the system and you expect something back' (Neville Lawrence, *SLS*, 1997).

It is in these ways that the documentary offers a discourse on what it means to be a British citizen – both black and white. This is a discourse most power-fully developed through the testimony of Stephen's mother, Doreen Lawrence. Hers is not simply a legal claim but a moral (and highly emotional) affirmation of her son's human rights. Indeed, her insistence on Stephen's right to justice reminds us that for black people there is no guar-antee that they will be treated as human beings, let alone find justice in the judicial system. Indeed, Doreen Lawrence's struggle to obtain justice for Stephen demonstrates her well-developed qualities of responsible citizenship:

> When I saw those boys in the dock and I think about their parents and I think about how on earth could they sit back and know their son has done wrong and don't say anything. There is no way if one of my children had done anything like that – I couldn't support them in that. (Doreen Lawrence, *SLS*, 1997)

While Doreen Lawrence's maternal devotion is limited by her respect for human life, we can only wonder about the silence of the mothers of the young men who killed Stephen and what such silence says about their sense of civic responsibility, their morality.

Indeed, the absence of any opportunity for the Lawrence family to hear an 'explanation' for their son's death is underlined by the family's barrister, Michael Mansfield QC. He remarks that the most striking element in the case is the extent to which the failure to secure a trial (let alone a prosecution) undermines the position of black people in British society:

> That an ordinary family who are in effect the mainstay of what the great British public would like black families to be... there they are... law-abiding, working hard, sending their children to school, believing in education, believing in a future and there you are, it's all gone. And I think the part played by the judicial system in the demise of their trust and confidence in British society is serious. (*SLS*, 1997)

Finally, the documentary delivers an intensely emotional account of the family's suffering. Lee-Wright makes no apologies for this; for him feelings matter as much as cold facts; indeed, the *SLS* demonstrates that an essential part of justice in a civilized society is the possibility of proper legal redress for pain and suffering. *The Stephen Lawrence Story* may be viewed at the British Film Institute, 21, Stephen Street, London W1P 2LN.

Conclusion

The triptych of 'institution, audience, text' can be a useful model for analysing documentaries. As far as *The Stephen Lawrence Story* is concerned, the fact that Channel 4 (not the BBC) financed the project is noteworthy: although *The Stephen Lawrence Story*'s relative success, in terms of audience figures, demonstrates that there is still an appetite for 'serious' documentaries, these are an increasingly endangered species on ITV and rapidly becoming so on the BBC. It is in the text however that a documentary like *SLS* offers the most fruitful opportunities for analysis, with its emotional and intellectual interrogation of the notion of citizenship.

References

BBC *Annual Reports and Accounts*. 1996/7.
Campaign for Quality Television, *Serious Documentaries on Television*, pamphlet produced by CQT, 1998.
Channel 4 Television Corporation *Report and Financial Statements*, 1996.
Corner, J. *The Art of Record*. Manchester: Manchester University Press, 1996.
Dyja, E. (ed.) *BFI Television and Film Handbook*. London: BFI, 1998.
Kilborn, R. and Izod, J. *An Introduction to Television Documentary: Confronting Reality*, Manchester, Manchester University Press, 1997.
Lee-Wright, P. Interview, 21 March 1997.

Nichols, B. *Representing Reality: Issues and Concepts in Documentary*. Bloomington and Indianapolis: Indiana University Press, 1991.

Phillips, M. and Phillips, T. *Windrush: The Irresistible Rise of Multi-racial Britain*. London: HarperCollins, 1998.

Ross, K. *Black and White Media: Black Images in Popular Film and Television*. London: Polity Press, 1996.

CHAPTER 14

Use it or Lose it: Sex, Sexuality and Sexual Health in Magazines for Girls

JANE STOKES

There have been several claims made recently that young girls might be learning 'too much' about sex from magazines such as *Sugar* and *Bliss*. Magazines aimed at teenage girls and young women are too highly sexualized, according to some critics, and have been blamed for contributing to a perceived increase in promiscuity and a real increase in unplanned pregnancies among British teenagers. Peter Luff, for example, the Conservative Member of Parliament for Mid Worcestershire, has attacked the magazines, accusing them of trading in sexually explicit messages which lead youngsters astray. He even won backing from the then Home Office Minister, Tom Sackville, for a bill to try to force teenage magazines to carry age warnings on sexually explicit material. However, the Labour government believes that these same publications could provide a vehicle for improving young people's sex and health education. Tessa Jowell, the Health Minister, told the Family Planning Association's national conference that young women's magazines 'have an important role to play in communicating with young people in their formative years' (Boseley, 1998, p. 6). Certainly, the magazines justify carrying stories about sex on the basis that this is one of the few means of reaching young people with health awareness messages and information. Magazines can play a role as 'best-friend' to readers at a time in their lives which can be very confusing and muddled: the need for direct, trustworthy information in plain English is clearly very high (Watson, 1997). Research conducted by IPC, publishers of *Mizz* and *19*, showed that 80 per cent of their readers agreed that magazines were their best source of information on 'Sex/Relationships' while 79 per cent agreed that they were their best source of information about 'Issues such as drugs, AIDS, abortion, alcohol' (IPC, 1996, p. 13). Sexually explicit material for teenagers is condemned by many, but magazines may be the best means of ensuring youngsters are informed about sex. But how much do we really know about the content of these magazines? Do they contain sexually explicit features and encourage promiscuity merely to boost sales, as some suggest? Or do they provide clear balanced information on matters of sex, sexuality and sexual health to enable people to make informed decisions about their behaviour? Before we can answer these questions, it is useful to have a more informed idea about the actual content of these magazines, in order to discount the bias of the moralizers on one hand and the publishers on the other. In this chapter I will use content analysis to determine how much discussion of sex magazines for teenagers contain.

A Brief History of Sex in Magazines for Girls and Young Women

Controversy about magazines for young women promoting promiscuous behaviour can be traced back at least to the 1970s with the introduction of the British edition of *Cosmopolitan* in 1972 (Ferguson, 1985; Winship, 1987). This was one of the key launches in women's magazines in the last 30 years and spawned something of a revolution in magazines for women (Viner, 1997). It was the first magazine aimed at single young women that acknowledged that its readership was sexually active; the sexual revolution of the 1960s finally reached the publishing world with this magazine. For some critics *Cosmopolitan* promulgated promiscuity among young people, while others welcomed it as a voice of women's sexual liberation. *Cosmopolitan* was a radical alternative to magazines that had assumed that all sexually active women were married and single women were virgins; it certainly helped put female sexuality at the centre of the debate about women in society. Aimed at older teenagers and women in their twenties, *Cosmopolitan* was controversial because of its liberal attitude toward young women having sex.

In the 1970s also, the first groundbreaking research into magazines for girls was conducted by Angela McRobbie in her study of the teenage publication *Jackie* (McRobbie, 1977). In *Jackie and the Ideology of Femininity*, McRobbie conducted a careful ideological analysis of the content of the 1970s bestselling magazine for teenage girls which was a hybrid of a children's comic and woman's magazine. *Jackie* was aimed at a younger readership than *Cosmopolitan* and did not contain any sexually explicit material. However, McRobbie argued that the magazine promoted a particular attitude towards sex and sexuality through the constraining *ideology of femininity* which she identified. McRobbie's study of *Jackie* initiated a way of thinking about the texts as carriers of a political messages and is an important example of early British cultural studies. Other scholars have built on McRobbie's work and examined the history of the women's magazine in relation to ideas about femininity (Ferguson, 1985; Winship, 1987), while others have focused on women readers and examined the audience for female publications (see, for example, Hermes, 1995).

During the 1980s a number of magazines were published which were aimed at the more brash, streetwise teenage reader. Less concerned with consumption than the 'glossies', and more streetwise than *Jackie* or *19*, maga-

Table 14.1   The launch date, circulation and target audience of selected women's and girls' magazines, in order of first publication

Date	Title	Current Circ.	Publisher	Target	Frequency/Price
1968	*19*	197, 347	IPC	15–24 yr olds	monthly/£1.30
1972	*Cosmopolitan*	460,141	National Magazine Co. Ltd	ABC1 women; 18–35 yrs	monthly/£2.10
1983	*J-17*	162,490	EMAP	Teenage girls and young women	weekly/85p
1985	*Mizz*	150,889	IPC	women 15–24 yrs	fortnightly/70p
1985	*Looks*	222,939	EMAP	women 15–24 yrs	monthly/£1.40
1988	*More!*	430,141	EMAP	women 18–24 yrs	fortnightly/£1.15
1988	*Marie Claire*	455,477	IPC	women	monthly/£2.30
1991	*Pride*		Vee Tee Ay (Voice Communications Group)	African/Caribbean women, 21–35	1991 – bi-monthly 1997 – monthly
1994	*Sugar Magazine*	361,764	Attic Futura	13–19 yr olds	monthly/£1.50
1995	*Bliss*	322,063	EMAP	girls 11–17	monthly/£1.30
1996	*Minx*	no figures	EMAP	women 18–24	monthly/£1.95

Source: Willings Press Guide (1997) Circulation based on Audit Bureau of Circulation (ABC) figures Jan–June 1996.

zines such as *Mizz* and *etcetera* targeted a self-confident teenage audience (Winship, 1985). Old fashioned *Jackie* was ousted by *Just Seventeen* (subsequently renamed *J-17*) as the top selling girls' publication in the early 1990s (McRobbie, 1991, 1994).

With the launch of *Sugar* magazine in 1994, specifically aimed at 13–19-year-olds, an even younger market was being addressed. Publishers Attic Futura had first had a success with the younger teenage reader with *TV Hits* and added *Sugar* to build on their profile as a youth publisher. EMAP launched *It's Bliss* (later *Bliss*) in 1995 and *Minx* in 1996 in an effort to attract this same smart and sassy market. In the 1990s, then, we have seen several new magazines launched which capitalize on the post-laddish spirit of 'girl power' first seen on *The Girlie Show* (Brown, 1996) and much emulated by girl bands The Spice Girls and All Saints. When launched, *Minx* was promoted on slogans such as 'Die of Exhaustion, Not Boredom', and: 'For Girls with Plenty of Balls, clubs and bars to go to.' In its double entendres and playful attitude, especially in its byline 'Use it or Lose it', *Minx* makes plain its attitude towards teenage sex.

Magazines for girls in the 1990s address their audiences in an unpatronising and lively way. *Sugar* is the top selling magazine in its market (see Table 14.1) with a rapidly expanding readership. *Sugar*, *More!* and *Bliss* rank among the 30 top selling magazines in Britain (Peak and Fisher, 1997). The entire sector of magazines for young people is showing remarkable growth in recent years and all of the major publishers now have periodicals aimed at this new niche market (see Chapter 1 of this volume for a discussion of niche marketing in the magazine business). Part of the appeal of contemporary teenage magazines is their direct attitude towards sex and sexuality. But are the readers of *Sugar*, *More!* and *Minx* being presented with too much information about sex, as their detractors claim? Or do the magazines help equip their readers with the information necessary to make their own decisions about sex? These are some of the questions which content analysis can help us to answer.

Content Analysis

There is a vocal minority in Britain who believe that information about sex encourages promiscuity. For these people any amount of sexual content aimed at young teenagers is 'too much'. From a methodological perspective, it is impossible to determine whether there is 'too much' of something in any media product. While *too much* is an extremely subjective value judgement, *how much* is measurable – providing we have a clear definition of what we are looking for. If we have clear knowledge regarding how much of a particular kind of content a medium contains, we will be able to have a more informed discussion of the issues. The technique best suited to *quantifying* the content of any media artefact is *content analysis*. This method is ideal for testing out ideas and hypotheses regarding amounts. Content analysis of media texts requires one to classify and then to count the occurrences of a particular phenomenon (Rosengren, 1981; Berger, 1998).

In this chapter I will subject the seven top circulation magazines for young women to content analysis. I selected titles which were aimed at the younger teenager, that is those which included in their target audiences girls under the age of 18. Of the publications included in this study four are published by EMAP, two by IPC and one by Attic Futura. Table 14.2 lists the magazines and includes the slogan of the magazines to give some flavour of the title's image.

Table 14.2   Magazines selected for this study

Publisher	Frequency*	Title	Slogan
Attic Futura	M	*Sugar*	BRITAIN'S number 1 GIRLS' MAG!
IPC	M	*19*	the bright stuff
	F	*Mizz*	Life, lads and laughs!
EMAP	M	*J-17*	IT'S A GIRL THING!
	F	*More!*	Smart girls get...
	M	*Bliss*	–
	M	*Minx*	For girls with a lust for life

* M = monthly; F = fortnightly
Note: Three consecutive issues of each magazine were studied, beginning with the January 1998 issue for monthlies and the 31 December 1997 – 13 January 1998 issue for the two fortnightly titles (*Mizz* and *More!*). The March issue of *J-17* was not available, so the April issue was substituted instead.

In order to eliminate any bias which might accrue from 'special issues' or unusual editions, content analysis requires studying multiple issues of the text under consideration. In this study, I analysed three consecutive issues of each of the magazines, beginning with January 1998 for the five monthly publications and December 31 for the fortnightlies (*Mizz* and *More!*). The only exception was *J-17*: the March issue was unavailable so the April issue was used instead. This gave me a total of 21 magazines to analyse.

One of the most important stages in any content analysis is the definition of what one is measuring. In this case, we are interested in occurrences of material relating to 'sex, sexuality, and sexual health' in girls' magazines. The first thing we must do, then, is to determine what constitutes 'sex' for our present purposes, and second what is our unit of measurement. The operational definition of 'sex' for the present study is an article that is mostly or exclusively about sex, sexuality or sexual health. The determination of what constitutes such an article is itself somewhat subjective: in an ideal world we would use several different coders and cross-check that they were coding the articles in exactly the same way. This current project does not allow such intensive labour, as I have coded all the material myself. I have had to make a judgement call, based on my knowledge of the medium (and the subject of 'sex') as to what constitutes a relevant article. The unit of analysis in this case is considerably less controversial: it is the page, or the nearest whole page.

I subjected the entire contents of each issue to content analysis, counting every page and classifying the content according to the following mutually exclusive categories:

- Adverts, Fashion and Promotional material
- Features (excluding those about 'sex')
- Features mainly or solely about 'sex'
- Pin-ups
- Letters
- Astrology, Quizzes and Competitions.

Within the first category I counted all promotional material for the magazine including the cover and contents pages plus all features that I judged to be mainly promotional material and the fashion features. These I judged to be largely promotional material because they always list prices and stockists and often constitute sponsored spreads. I took 'Features' to include celebrity interviews, photo stories, vox pop stories as well as 'real life' articles. Articles are coded as 'sex' features separately, in the third category, if they are about sex, sexuality or sexual health. 'Pin-ups' includes all images which are presented for readers to keep: typically these are male pop idols, but in some of the magazines for younger girls these can be of animals or celebrities of any gender (for example, the cast of *Friends*). The category 'Letters' includes all correspondence from readers, whether or not they are mainly about sex/health issues. Finally, 'Astrology, Quizzes and Competitions' is a bit of catch-all including the many features on star signs and destiny and the various quizzes, contests and interactive content.

After counting all of the occurrences of the above in the three issues of each magazine, I calculated the average number of pages in each category, rounding up to the nearest whole page. Table 14.3 presents the average number of pages of each publication devoted to the six different categories, expressed as a percentage of the whole magazine. The second column gives the average number of pages in the magazine, while the subsequent columns are percentage figures. Thus we are able to compare the percentage of pages devoted to each subject by each of the different magazines.

Table 14.3 Content analysis of girls' magazines: percentage of magazine devoted to selected categories

Title	No. Pages+	% Adverts Promos Fashion	% Features	% Sex*	% Pin-ups	% Letters	% Astrology Competitions and Quizzes
Sugar	132	48	20	1	14	6	11
19	127	51	47	2	4	2	4
Mizz	92	26	40	–	13	8	11
J-17	121	46	37	1	1	7	8
More!	100	44	43	7	–	3	3
Bliss	132	48	31	1	8	5	7
Minx	148	51	42	5	–	1	1

* the percentage of feature material devoted to sex
+ the number of pages is the average of the three issues studied

The largest single category is the first one, which includes advertisements, promotional material and fashion spreads. In two magazines (*Minx* and *19*) this accounted for more than half of total. Most magazines had over 40 per cent of their content in this category; the magazine with the least advertising, promotional and fashion copy, with just 26 per cent of the magazine categorized as such, was *Mizz*. In all magazines except *Mizz*, the second largest category was features, the percentage ranging from 20 per cent for *Sugar* to 43 per cent for *More!* The main themes of feature articles tend to be hair and cosmetics, real life stories of various kinds and celebrity interviews: a further content analysis would have been required to break these down, which space did not permit on this occasion. In the area that is of most interest to this present study, features about sex, sexuality or sexual health, there is comparatively little. *Mizz* had no articles about sex in the three issues examined for this study. Of the others, most had on average approximately 1 per cent of their copy devoted to features about sex, with *Minx* and *More!* gaining the most at 5 and 7 per cent respectively.

The relative lack of features on sexual subjects is quite surprising. Also surprising is the wide variation in the amount of space devoted to pin-ups of one kind or another. In general, a large proportion of the magazines in this study is devoted to pin-ups – *Sugar* has the most at 14 per cent of the total magazine. In some cases pin-ups would most certainly constitute sexual material and even border on the erotic. Male subjects are objectified as things to be looked at; expressions such as 'phwooar' and 'eye candy' are frequently used. *Sugar* has a feature on 'top totty' and its February issue announced on the cover 'it's the boy issue', complete with 'totty top 50'. Topping the list of 'totty' is, of course, 'Leonardo DiCaprio All hail the divine one. Sigh...' and an interview with the teen idol of the age is included. While most pin-ups are promotional material, many are of ordinary young men including readers' brothers or boyfriends. However, these images are not necessarily sexual – in *Mizz* they are just as likely to be pop stars and television performers of both genders and cute animals like tigers or koala bears also appear.

The number of pages devoted to letters varies considerably between the magazines. It is here that the titles give their most direct advice and information to readers, much of it about sex. Quizzes make up a large percentage of the last category, and they are often quite informational. They cover a large range of themes, including sexual matters, for example *J-17*'s February issue carried an informative quiz, 'Are you sussed about sex?' The initial coding has not captured all of the material about sex that the magazines contain: sexualized images in pin-ups, quizzes about sexual knowledge and letters and problem pages are also key vehicles for relevant information of various kinds.

Featuring Sex

In general, our preliminary content analysis has found that features on sex, sexuality and sexual health comprise a very small percentage of the content of magazines for teenage girls. The largest percentage of pages devoted to features about sex can be found in *More!*, which includes 7 per cent of such material. The magazine that has caused most controversy, however, is *Sugar*, which contains just 1 per cent content of 'sexual' features. This constitutes just two articles. Both of these articles address homosexuality, but, they do so from the perspective of heterosexual female readers of the magazine. The January issue has one article which I categorized as being a feature about sex with the headline: 'My boyfriend was a girl' and the March issue carried an article about 'My boyfriend left me for my brother'. 'My boyfriend was a girl' is in the 'real life' series and has the subheading:

> Karen thought she had found the best boyfriend in the world. But then she discovered Michael's secret.

To briefly summarize, Karen has fallen for 'Michael' when her friend tells her that he is really a she. When Karen learns she was attracted to another girl she cannot cope and is devastated. The story finishes by telling us that Karen is now going through counselling.

Sugar's story about sexuality in March has a similar theme, but this time it is labelled 'real life trauma'. Shelly was going out with Paul for six months when she walked into her brother's bedroom and found the two boys together:

> '*Oh my God*' I thought to myself. '*This can't be happening!*' Paul and Christian were kissing.

Paul and Christian carried on seeing one another, and Shelly has a new boyfriend:

> Hopefully one day I'll be able to forgive them both and accept what has happened, although that doesn't mean I'll *ever* forget what I saw. I just need time.

The homosexual behaviour of Paul and Christian is seen through Shelly's eyes as a problem she has to deal with. In *Sugar*, themes of sexual identity and sexual orientation are treated as problems for the straight girls who come into contact with gay boys and lesbians. Sympathy is invited for Karen and Shelly, from whose point of view these 'real life' stories are told. 'Michael', Paul and Christian have caused heartache for the girls and are therefore constructed as a problem that readers of *Sugar* might have to deal with. Homosexuality is not presented as a possibility for readers of *Sugar*. Karen and Shelly's experiences are of being hurt by the homosexuality of their peers, and little sympathy is offered for the gay and lesbian youngsters in the stories. The 'real life trauma' involves being confronted with non-heterosexual behaviour, not experiencing it directly.

Other Sexual Content

The magazines contain a lot of information about sex in their letters and problems pages. The magazines also contain a great deal of sexualized imagery which is not very well treated by content analysis – a more semiotic form of analysis is required to garner the nuances from visual material in pin-ups and fashion spreads, for example. Information about how to have safe sex is provided in letters and advice columns and these magazines are very conscientious about providing advice line numbers and helpful contact numbers for people dealing with matters of sexuality and sexual health. If young people are to be fully informed, there should be more direct information in the form of features about sex. Issues of sex, sexuality and sexual health are not widely covered in the magazines we have studied and magazines aimed at teenage girls do not encourage the idea that all youngsters should be having sex. In all instances they encourage youngsters to wait until they are ready and give them the vocabulary and skills necessary to avoid being pressurized into having sex before they are ready.

Matters of homosexuality or bisexuality are sparsely covered: for the lesbian and gay teenagers reading these magazines there is very little they can identify with. Indeed, homosexuality is more often presented as a 'problem' which straight girls might occasionally have to confront in others, but lesbians figure rarely. Young people often feel compelled to conform to heterosexual norms (Holland *et al.*, 1998) and magazines for teenagers should perhaps be doing more to challenge these stereotypes.

Sexual health is not a significant focus in this sample: many magazines are keen to point out the necessity of using a condom, but there was no express information about how to do this. Magazines do need to discuss these issues more if they are to provide the information necessary for their readers to grow up informed about sex, sexuality and sexual health. Teen magazines do not currently serve their gay and lesbian readers well; neither do they provide the information necessary for youngsters to be able to protect themselves from sexually transmitted diseases including HIV/AIDS.

Conclusion

Content analysis has proved to be a very valuable method for gaining reliable statistics to support a hypothesis. We have been able to demonstrate that, contrary to the fears of many commentators, magazines for young women and girls do not contain a large amount of material about sex. By far the majority of the content of these magazines is devoted to promotional and advertising material of various kinds. Perhaps we should be more concerned about the inculcation of teenage girls into a world of conspicuous consumption than the conspicuous display of sexual promiscuity.

References

Berger, A.A. *Media Research Techniques*. London: Sage, 1998.

Boseley, S. 'Teen mags to help fight pregnancies', *Guardian* (27 March 1998) p. 6.

Brown, M. 'The bad girls are back!' *Guardian*, Media section (9 December 1996).

Ferguson, M. *Forever Feminine: Women's Magazines and the Cult of Femininity*. London: Gower, 1985.

Hermes, J. *Reading Women's Magazines: An Analysis of Everyday Media Use*. Cambridge: Polity Press, 1995.

Holland, J., Ramazanoglu, C., Sharpe, S. and Thomson, R. *The Male in the Head. Young People, Heterosexuality and Power*. London: The Tufnell Press, 1998.

IPC *The Ultimate Guide to Girls*. London: IPC South Bank Publishing (Young Women's Group), 1996.

McRobbie, A. *Jackie and the Ideology of Femininity*. Stencilled paper, Centre for Contemporary Cultural Studies. University of Birmingham, 1977.

McRobbie, A. *Feminism and Youth Culture: From 'Jackie' to 'Just Seventeen'*. Basingstoke: Macmillan, 1991.

McRobbie, A. *Postmodernism and Popular Culture*. London: Routledge, 1994.

Peak, S. and Fisher, P. *The Media Guide*. London: *Guardian*/Fourth Estate, 1997.

Rosengren, K.E. (ed.) *Advances in Content Analysis* Beverly Hills CA/London: Sage, 1981.

Viner, K. 'Now we are 25', *Guardian* (6 February 1997).

Watson, S. 'Sweet sex-teen', *Guardian*, Media section (24 April 1997) p. 7.

Winship, J. 'A girl needs to get streetwise: Magazines for the 1980s', *Feminist Review*, No. 21 (Winter 1985).

Winship, J. *Inside Women's Magazines*. London/New York: Pandora, 1987.

CHAPTER 15

Transnational Trainspotting

MURRAY SMITH

Tommy [gesturing at the stark landscape around him]: Doesn't make you proud to be Scottish?

Renton: It's shite being Scottish. We're the lowest of the low; the scum of the fuckin' earth. The most wretched, miserable, servile, pathetic trash that was ever shat in civilization. Some people hate the English – I don't, they're just wankers. We on the other hand are colonized by wankers; can't even find a decent culture to be colonized by. We're ruled by effete arseholes; it's a shite state of affairs to be in Tommy, and all the fresh air in the world won't make any fuckin' difference. (*Trainspotting*)

Trainspotting emerged at a moment when not only British cinema, but *Scottish* cinema, as a distinct entity, was perceived to have an unusual degree of visibility, activity and momentum. Aside from a few notable exceptions (McArthur, 1982; Dick, 1990), Scottish cinema has typically been seen as a 'peripheral sector of what is itself [that is, British cinema] a marginal entity' (Petrie, 1996, p. 93). However, 1995 witnessed the box-office success of two Scottish films, the historical epic *Rob Roy* and the contemporary thriller *Shallow Grave*. Moreover, four new features went into production over the course of the year which could lay claim to being Scottish, including the follow-up to *Shallow Grave* – *Trainspotting* – made by the same trio of producer Andrew MacDonald, screenwriter John Hodge and director Danny Boyle. The funding of the two films, however, immediately draws our attention to some of the layers of the complexity involved in categorizing any such film neatly in national terms: *Shallow Grave* was funded jointly by the Glasgow Film Fund and the London-based television company Channel 4 (total budget at just over £1 million), while *Trainspotting* was, uniquely, financed wholly by Channel 4, the budget of £1.7 million exceeding the company's investment in any other single film. So a non-Scottish company played a major hand in enabling both projects. It is also worth emphasizing that Channel 4 is a television company, and that both films appeared as part of the company's very successful 'Film on Four' series. 'Film on Four' pioneered the practice (in Britain) of a television company producing or co-producing films which would receive a theatrical release prior to broadcast, a formula subsequently emulated by the BBC (who, using this model, co-funded with the Glasgow

Film Fund another one of the four Scottish films in production in 1995, *Small Faces*). So, for all the hoo-ha surrounding the fact that *Trainspotting* was a Scottish film in terms of story material and many production personnel, it is important to see how it fits into a pattern of London-based production, and exemplifies the interdependence of the film and television industries. Such interdependence is a fact of life for film-makers in almost every industry worldwide, but it possesses a special salience in Britain, where the emergence of Channel 4 in 1982 provided, indirectly but effectively, a system of government subsidy for indigenous film-making which had been a feature of many European countries for decades, and long argued for in Britain (see also Hill, 1999, Chapter 5, this volume).

Released in February 1996, *Trainspotting* took £11 million at the UK box office, and went on to become the most successful independent release in the US in 1996, taking $16.5 million in box-office receipts by March 1997. These successes were echoed in many other countries; total worldwide returns thus far are estimated at $60 million. What accounts for the wide success of a film that might appear to have relatively narrow appeal – compared with the contemporary Hollywood blockbuster – in terms of age, region, gender and class? One factor was clearly the aggressive and canny marketing of the film. The film-makers exploited the worldwide interest in British popular culture in the mid-1990s, not only by basing the film on a novel arising out of that culture, but by constructing a soundtrack that mixed contemporary Brit Pop and dance tracks with some of the counter-cultural classics of the 1970s, thus tapping into the musical and fashion enthusiasms of several generations of potential viewers. In this sense, the 'marketing' of the film cannot be clearly distinguished from its 'production'. The film's distributor, PolyGram, launched an expensive publicity campaign (£850,000, or half as much as the film's production costs, for the UK launch) which resembled the heavy publicity associated with the Hollywood 'event' movie more than the modest campaigns associated with 'small' European releases (Wyatt, 1994; Gomery, 1998). Indeed, the publicity for the film showed a wry awareness of this, declaring 'Believe the Hype!' Rather than using the channels and spaces typically used by the large American distributors, however, such as television advertising, PolyGram invested in outlets and sites connected with pop and rock music culture. Similarly, PolyGram collaborated with its competitor EMI (rights' holder of much of the music on the soundtrack) in order to ensure an effective launch of the soundtrack CD tie-in. So, smart marketing was a factor in the success of *Trainspotting*; but exactly *what* was being marketed?

The Lure of America

Trainspotting has been justly celebrated as a breakthrough film for British – and Scottish – film-making. But as the opening scene (and much else in the film) suggests, locating the film in *cultural* terms is as tricky a matter as is categorizing it economically, institutionally and technologically. A gang of skinny heroin addicts rush towards the camera as it tracks back rapidly on a central street in Edinburgh, stolen goods dropping from them as they flee manically, the rhythm of their running picked up and amplified by the pounding, dirty, raw opening of Iggy Pop's 'Lust for Life'. A moment later another layer of sound is added – the voice of Mark Renton (Ewan McGregor) as he intones a kind of heroin addict's manifesto, filled with confident contempt for all the material, conventional comforts he and his pals have forsaken for their true love, H: 'Choose life. Choose a job. Choose a career. Choose a family. Choose a fuckin' big television. Choose washing machines, cars, compact disc players and electrical tin openers... Choose rottin' away at the end of it all...' (*Trainspotting*).

These two sounds – McGregor's Scots' diatribe on the one hand, the unmistakably American drawl of Iggy's voice on the other – provide a path into the complex inter- and intra-national dynamics of contemporary movie culture in general, and the appeal of *Trainspotting* in particular. Iggy's presence and biography is a singularly appropriate one which pervades the narrative in more than the obvious ways (he crops up in the narrative and another of his songs, 'Nightclubbing', appears on the soundtrack). For Iggy is a junkie but also a survivor, the song 'Lust for Life' deriving from a period in the late 1970s when he emerged from a long drug-induced silence to produce two energetic albums. His wasted yet enormously durable frame, subjected to all manner of abuse and exertion – visible in a poster on Tommy's wall several times in the film – matches perfectly the taut, pale skin of the Edinburgh smackheads. Iggy and 'Lust for Life' encapsulate both the characters' and the movie's ambivalent attitude towards heroin – deliverer of both life-wrecking evil *and* delirious pleasure.

And yet Iggy is, of course, American, like so many of the reference points and (trainspotterishly indulged) enthusiasms of the film's central characters. Iggy is joined by fellow junkie-survivor Lou Reed, whose 'Perfect Day' provides semi-ironic accompaniment as Renton, deep in a heroin stupor, is taken to hospital by taxi and dumped outside it. The consumer items enumerated in Renton's litany were, of course, originally driven by the same society that produced Iggy and Lou. Elsewhere in the movie, a naive American tourist in town for Edinburgh's most internationally well-known event – the Edinburgh Festival – is mugged by our friendly local skagheads. For all its 'Scottishness', the impact of America is everywhere in *Trainspotting*. The appeal of American culture to European cultures is a long-established and diverse phenomenon, depending on associations of abundance, glamour, dynamism, social mobility, expressiveness, openness, directness, and modernity (Willett, 1978; Hebdige, 1988; Strinati, 1992; Mulvey, 1996; Hill, 1996). As Andrew Higson has written, Hollywood has become 'an integral and naturalized part of the popular imagination of most countries in which cinema is an established entertainment form' (Higson, 1995, p. 8).

If the rest of the pop-music score is drawn from contemporary British bands, we shouldn't forget that, no matter how brilliantly and distinctively transformed by British traditions and stylings, such transformations – even those of 'Brit Pop' – always carry with them the underlying 'Americanness' of rock as a musical form, invariably being 'refracted' through a 'mythical America' (Hebdige, 1988; see also Webster, 1988). And this is as true of visual as of musical culture. At the most general level, the film exemplifies the incorporation of the music video sequence into narrative cinema – the MTVing of Hollywood, as it were. More specifically, Diane's bedroom wall features a multi-panel, multi-coloured lithograph of herself, mimicking Warhol's portraits of Marilyn and Elvis; in another scene, Renton reads a biography of Montgomery Clift. Sick Boy and Renton impersonate and celebrate Sean Connery-as-James Bond, the perfect symbol of internationalized celebrity culture. Sick Boy may be obsessed by Connery as a Scot, but he is a Scot most famous for an upper-class English character in a highly Americanized series of action pictures – not so very different from the Americanized Australian susperstar, Mel Gibson, playing the role of a militant Scots nationalist in another very successful Scottish film (or at least, a film about Scotland) of recent years, *Braveheart* (1996).

Selling Scotland by the Pound

In playing up the American and international elements of the film, though, we must not lose sight of the local, regional and national cultural traditions which inform the film; it is the dialectic between the regional and 'Hollywood-international' that, I want to argue, is so seductive. The national specificity of the film is apparent in its title – there was much bemused debate over the meaning of 'trainspotting' outside of the UK. The regional and indeed class specificity of the film is immediately apparent from the distinctive accent of the voice-over. The regionalism of voice here is, perhaps, less emphatic than it is in the Irvine Welsh novel on which the film is based, whose phonetic rendering of local dialectic obliges the reader to articulate mentally every syllable ('Yiv goat tae huv fuckin brains tae be a fuckin judge. S no iviry cunt thit kin dae that fuckin joab'; Welsh, 1997, p. 172). The intensity of the novel's 'obscene' language is also somewhat diminished: the word 'cunt', virtually a conjunction in the sociolect of the working-class youths in the novel, is used very sparingly in the film. Nevertheless, McGregor's delivery was strong enough to prompt the re-dubbing of parts of the film for American audiences, exemplifying the commonly expressed fear among distributors that films about Scotland might be 'too Scottish' for wider national and international audiences (see Calderwood, 1996). Indeed, the first club scene in the film jokingly plays up the likely incomprehesibility of the working-class Scots accent to many audiences by setting the dialogue against a wall of disco music and providing subtitles for this scene even in the British release print of the film. (It is worth noting, though, that in France the subtitled version of the film was far more successful than the dubbed version, a fact which suggests how the American market presents rather different challenges to British films from those posed by non-English speaking countries.)

Thus, although ameliorated relative to the novel, *Trainspotting*'s regional, class and subcultural markers are still to the fore. The film's strategy here is a recognizable one, even if it is executed with unusual panache: by playing up the peculiarities of local culture, it addresses not only local but international audiences as well, for the international marketability of an 'art' film like *Trainspotting* depends to a large degree on the 'exoticism' of its regional and local character. (Contrast this with the alternative and overtly transatlantic strategy embodied by *Four Weddings and a Funeral* and Boyle/Hodge/MacDonald's follow up to *Trainspotting*, *A Life Less Ordinary*: although both *Four Weddings and a Funeral* and *A Life Less Ordinary* feature aspects of British national and regional culture, both also pander to the American market through the casting of major American stars such as Andie MacDowell, Cameron Diaz, and Holly Hunter.) Aside from verbal dialect, *Trainspotting* carefully displays national and regional fashions in dress-style and drug-taking (as the story moves into the 1990s, ecstasy becomes more prominent); pub culture and beer drinking; traditional British breakfasts (a big close-up of fried egg, baked beans, bacon and sausage which nauseates the hungover Spud); and shifts in British musical fashion (from 1980s New Wave to 1990s Acid House and Brit Pop). The film also stresses the British national obsession – especially strong in the 1990s, at least in terms of media attention – with football, one which increasingly straddles class lines. This is a passion so strong in the film that even sexual experience is understood by analogy with it. Indeed, the footballing motif is interwoven with both sex and heroin: Renton switches Tommy's tape of himself and his girlfriend having sex with Tommy's '100 Great Goals' tape, and later enjoys a drug-addled viewing of the sex tape; and in the opening montage, a hit of smoked heroin is metonymically rendered by the smack of a football on Renton's forehead, followed by crosscut, graphic mirror-images of Renton collapsing to the left and right of the screen, drug-dazed and football-stunned.

Much of what I've said so far concerns the dialectic between a particular strain of Scots, working-class culture and Hollywood international; but enough has also been said to indicate that there are at least two other cultural fault lines running through and exploited by the film. The first is that between Scottish and English culture, a subject which is particularly acute in the 1990s in light of the movement for devolution (which achieved a breakthrough with the election of the Labour government in 1997, leading to the establishment of a Scottish Parliament in 1999). The second fault line is that between what has rapidly coalesced as 'traditional' heritage culture, and a more sceptical and ironic practice which both appeals to notions of cultural heritage while also mocking them for their anodyne character, their 'cultural racism' (Gilroy, 1987, 1992), or their downright falsity. An early instance of this counter-tradition was *The Ploughman's Lunch* (1981) – in which the eponymous salad is revealed to be nothing more an invention of modern marketing, part of the fabrication of Olde England – and as this example suggests, 'ironic heritage' culture is something shared by England and Scotland, and probably any culture that has developed a heritage industry; an industry, that is, based on selling a prettified, nostalgic image of its host culture as a tourist commodity. We might label this alternative (anti-)tradition 'garbage culture', given its central aim of rubbishing heritage culture, often through an insistent focus on the run-down and the clapped-out, on sites of destitution and impoverishment.

The scene from which the opening quote is taken lies at the point where the two fault lines – Scotland–England, heritage–garbage – cross one another. It manages to have its cake and eat it on both fronts. While dismissing the English as a bunch of wankers, the scene takes a cynical, jaundiced view of Scottish nationalism befitting the egotistical, drop-out anti-heroes that the film centres upon (a point of overlap with the same team's *Shallow Grave*). Similarly, while working in a wee dram of traditional Scottish landscape, Tommy's desire to take a walk in the Pentland hills is dismissed as 'not natural' by Sick Boy, and precipitates Renton's splenetic tirade. And while the film certainly concentrates on the un-heritage Scotland of Leith, with its run-down council estates, dilapidated flats, seedy betting shops, appalling toilets, smoke-filled pubs and loud clubs, we do glimpse some of Edinburgh's grand sights, like Princes Street, as Renton and co. are pursued through the city centre.

But it is not only 'Scottishness' and Scottish heritage imagery that are mocked. When Renton moves to London later in the film, the capital is introduced by a satiric montage sequence featuring many of London's most famous icons, including Big Ben, Trafalgar Square and its pigeons, Carnaby Street, the Lloyds Bank building and the City, a black steel drum player in Notting Hill, Tower Bridge, ice-cream licking tourists, a shot of the Pearly King and Queen smiling and waving from a red London bus. Not only is the image of tourist-friendly London gently sent up by shots of friendly policemen and smiling doormen, but Renton lands a job in the quintessentially 1980s business of estate agency, selling overpriced, misdescribed Victorian conversions to yuppies ('this was boom town, where any fool could make cash from chaos, and plenty did'). Nevertheless, most of the action in this first London interlude occurs in Renton's cramped apartment. Once Begbie and Sick Boy arrive, this space comes to resemble more and more the decrepit hovels they inhabit in Edinburgh. Garbage once again overwhelms and undercuts heritage.

Black Magic Realism

British cinema, including Scottish cinema, is most often associated with a robust social realism, sometimes dour, sometimes mordant – consider the importance, in the canon of British cinema, of the Griersonian documentary tradition, of the Angry Young Man and Free Cinema movements, of Ken Loach, Mike Leigh, Bill Douglas, and Gary Oldman's naturalistic *Nil by Mouth* (1997) (see Higson, 1995, 1998; McLoone, 1996). A straightforward adaptation of Welsh's novel might have fed straight into this tradition, with its stress on working-class culture and vernacular idioms. A large part of the achievement of the film, however, involves a transformation of this realism, accomplished by intensifying the novel's black humour and leavening it with fantasy in the manner of magic realism (drawing perhaps on the non-naturalistic tendencies of Bill Forsyth, Michael Powell and Emeric Pressburger – an acknowledged influence on *A Life Less Ordinary* – and the Scottish novelist Alasdair Gray). The film adopts a stylized *mise-en-scène* in many sequences: consider the exaggerated distances in Spud's interview and Renton's bedroom, the expressionistic colour scheme in the Mother Superior's flat (alternating blood reds and lurid greens), or the flat compositions in which the shapes and colours of characters and buildings are strung out laterally across the screen. These strategies are taken a step further in two sequences: the first involves Renton's hallucinations during his enforced withdrawal from heroin, including a baby which crawls along the ceiling, its head turning through 180 degrees. In the second sequence, point-of-view shots bordered on each side by red carpet render Renton's sensation of sinking into the carpet and withdrawing from the world on a heroin high. The dynamic and graphically playful montage of Renton's collapse in the opening sequence recurs in the short scene in which Spud and Renton drink a milkshake together; rapid-fire montage creates a jagged transition into the scene as the two of them suck the glass empty. On a larger scale, crosscutting works as a structural principal in the film, maintaining an ecstatic momentum from scene to scene, in spite of the film's focus on the more languorous phenomenology of heroin. Throughout, Boyle and his collaborators embrace the possibilities of cinematic form and expression in a way that matches, rather than merely imitates, Welsh's embrace of the possibilities of vernacular language.

Perhaps the most striking instance of this black magic realism, however, occurs in the early scene in which Renton visits the bookies' toilet. As Renton charges into the toilet, the film pauses on the door for a second, framing the sign on the door with a subtitle, so that the whole reads:

The Worst

T O I L E T

in Scotland

Having relieved himself, Renton remembers that he has expelled the two anal heroin suppositories which he had only just inserted, and starts to fish around in the overflowing, disgusting toilet bowl. (Only the scene in which Spud, awakening from a night of incontinent inebriation, splatters his girl-friend's family with his shit-stained sheet as they eat their traditional break-fast, tops the coprophilia of Renton's moment of intimacy with the bookie's toilet.) So much for the harsh realism and black humour. The moment of magic redemptiveness then follows: Renton is forced to delve more and more deeply into the toilet bowl, and eventually disappears head-first into its depths. We see him emerge on the other side in a sun-filled tropical pool, discovering his suppositories like pearls on a shell-covered seabed. The scene operates 'magically' not only in formal terms, by moving seamlessly from the grim detail of ordinary life to a flight of fancy, but thematically too, reiterating the power of heroin to transform – temporarily – the most impoverished real existence into one of sensual richness.

The expansive and confident aesthetic of *Trainspotting* may be taken as emblematic of the way in which British cinema as a whole has diversified in the 1980s and 90s, and this may account in part for the attention it has garnered during this period. Building on its vital role in accruing such prestige – if not financial success – to British cinema, in April 1998 Channel 4 announced the formation of Film Four Ltd, a subsidiary of the parent company which is to act as a 'mini-studio', substantially increasing investment levels and integrating control of production, distribution and television broadcast of its films (see Hill, 1999, Chapter 5, this volume, on 'mini-studios', and more generally on the precarious and qualified nature of the 'success' of British cinema in recent years). Launching the new company, chief executive Paul Webster argued that 'The company sends a message to the international community that we understand that films have to be made and marketed in the same breath. Films are for audiences, and audiences are international' (quoted in Glaister, 1998, p. 23). Such globalization is, as we have seen, a complex 'hyper-cultural' business (Smith, 1997), involving not only the 'Americanization' of Scottish and British culture, but the transformation of American culture as it interacts with these cultures, *and* the selling of these cultures back to American and other international audiences. Even in a film as emphatically specific as *Trainspotting*, the 'local' and 'global' cannot easily be disentangled.

References

Calderwood, A. 'Film and Television Policy in Scotland', in J. Hill and M. McLoone (eds) *Big Picture, Small Screen The Relations between Film and Television*. Luton: University of Luton Press, 1996, pp. 118–95.

Dick, E. (ed.) *From Limelight to Satellite: A Scottish Film Book*. Edinburgh/London: Scottish Film Council/British Film Institute, 1990.

Gilroy, P. *There Ain't No Black in the Union Jack: The Cultural Politics of Race and Nation*. London: Routledge, 1987.

Gilroy, P. 'The End of Antiracism', in J. Donald and A. Rattansi (eds) *'Race', Culture and Difference*. London: Sage/Open University, 1992, pp. 49–61.

Glaister, D. 'Film Four leads British charge', *Guardian* (16 April 1998) p. 23.

Gomery, D. 'Hollywood Corporate Business Practice and Periodising Contemporary Film History', in S. Neale and M. Smith (eds) *Contemporary Hollywood Cinema*. London: Routledge, 1998, pp. 47–57.

Hebdige, D. *Hiding in the Light: On Images and Things*. London: Comedia/Routledge, 1988.

Higson, A. *Waving the Flag: Constructing a National Cinema in Britain*. Oxford: Clarendon Press, 1995.

Higson, A. 'British Cinema', in J. Hill and P. Church Gibson (eds) *The Oxford Guide to Film Studies*. Oxford: Oxford University Press, 1998, pp. 501–9.

Hill, J. 'Enmeshed in British Society but with a Yen for American Movies: Film, Television and Stephen Frears', in J. Hill and M. McLoone (eds) *Big Picture, Small Screen: The Relations between Film and Television*. Luton: University of Luton Press, 1996, pp. 224–31.

Hill, J. 'Cinema', in Anna Reading and Jane Stokes (eds) *The Media in Britain*. London: Macmillan, 1999.

McArthur, C. (ed.) *Scotch Reels: Scotland in Cinema and Television*. London: BFI, 1982.

McLoone, M. 'Boxed In?: The Aesthetics of Film and Television', in J. Hill and M. McLoone (eds) *Big Picture, Small Screen: The Relations between Film and Television*. Luton: University of Luton Press, 1996, pp. 76–106.

Mulvey, L. *Fetishism and Curiosity*. London: BFI, 1996.

Petrie, D. 'Peripheral visions: Film-making in Scotland', in W. Everett (ed.) *European Identity in Cinema*. Exeter: Intellect, 1996, pp. 93–9.

Smith, M. *The Battle of Algiers*: Colonial Struggle and Collective Allegiance, *Iris*, 24 (1997) pp. 105–24.

Strinati, D. 'The taste of America: Americanization and Popular Culture in Britain', in D. Strinati and S. Wagg (eds) *Popular Media Culture in Post-War Britain*. London: Routledge, 1992, pp. 46–81.

Webster, D. *Looka Yonder! The Imaginary America of Populist Culture* London: Comedia/Routledge, 1988.

Welsh, I. *Trainspotting (The Irvine Welsh Omnibus)*. London: Jonathan Cape/Secker and Warburg, 1997.

Willett, J. *The New Sobriety: Art and Politics in the Weimar Period, 1917–33* London: Thames and Hudson, 1978.

Wyatt, J. *High Concept: Movies and Marketing in Hollywood*. Austin: University of Texas Press, 1994.

CHAPTER 16

Offending, Looking, Killing and Film-making: Decoding *Peeping Tom*

BEN SLATER

Opening Sequence

an eye fills the frame – the click of a camera shutter

Leo Marks, who had been an expert code-maker and breaker during the Second World War, considered his screenplay for *Peeping Tom* to be like a code, embedded with a multitude of 'clues' so that the audience 'could discover the clear text' behind the psychopath-protagonist of the film. This is a useful place to begin a study of *Peeping Tom* (directed by Michael Powell, released in 1960) as analysing a text, especially a cinematic text, always involves the unpicking of patterns and motifs within the narrative and visual flow. A film-text can be figured as a cipher – not necessarily with a single, fixed meaning, but a code rich in contradictions, resonances and digressions, which if closely examined might yield a tentative solution to troubling questions. With *Peeping Tom*, there is a mystery that immediately surrounds the film – why was it so vilified upon its release, by the critics who slammed it, and by the audiences who stayed away, thus effectively finishing the career of its prestigious director? It is impossible to provide a definitive solution, but investigation of *Peeping Tom* uncovers a series of meanings and issues that cut right to the core of film-making, in Britain and beyond.

An Assault on Culture

> The only satisfactory way to dispose of *Peeping Tom* would be to shovel it up and flush it swiftly down the nearest sewer... (Derek Hill, *Tribune* cited in Christie, 1978, p. 54)

From its slumbering, mildly salacious beginning to its appallingly masochistic and depraved climax, it is wholly evil. (Nina Hibbin, *Daily Worker* cited in Christie, 1978, p. 56)

I don't propose to name the players in this beastly picture. (C.A. Lejeune, *Observer* cited in Christie, 1978, p. 55)

Reading those reviews 38 years later, livid with moral panic and hatred, it's apparent that there were two variations of opinion – first, that Michael Powell was an accomplished British director who had somehow betrayed his culture by foisting *Peeping Tom* on the world, and the other common theory – that Powell's work had *always* shown troubling signs of a 'vulgarity' and 'morbidity' and, with *Peeping Tom*, these qualities had finally risen to the surface.

Powell was a director whose eminent partnership with Emeric Pressburger under the production name 'The Archers', had brought him international fame and acclaim. *Peeping Tom* was his attempt to establish a new collaboration away from Pressburger with screenwriter Leo Marks. Significantly it was produced for Anglo-Amalgamated, a company cashing in on the market for 'horror' genre films established by Hammer Studios from the mid-1950s onwards. With the script's suggestions of sex, pornography and sadism, *Peeping Tom* must have seemed like an exploitable proposition for its financiers. Thus the film had vulgar 'low-culture' written all over it. So why was Powell dabbling with such salacious material?

Although *The Red Shoes* (1948) had been a massive success, Powell's films with Pressburger had regularly encountered critical resistance and occasionally censorship. The affectionate exploration of Britishness in *The Life And Death Of Colonel Blimp* (1943) inspired the wrath of Churchill, and critics had always been wary of the eccentric plotting, stylistic flamboyance and supernatural mysticism of films like *A Canterbury Tale* (1944) and *A Matter Of Life And Death* (1946).

Along with their trademark visual sumptuousness, Powell and Pressburger's films play fast and loose with film technique and grammar, they conflate and distort time and space, use dream sequences, visual and aural transitions, voice-overs, extended takes, lighting changes, colour stock changes, and actors playing several roles in one film. In short, Powell and Pressburger were interested in manipulating all the possibilities of film, producing works that contain such a surplus of images and ideas that they threatened to destabilize the (realist) narrative flow. Implicit in all of these techniques was a highly developed reflexivity about cinematic language – all their films make the viewer conscious of watching a movie, and that was/is integral to their pleasure.

Peeping Tom was different; it contains remarkably few of the 'tricks' that characterized Powell's best work with Pressburger. Retrospectively it can be seen as a logical end-point in Powell's exploration of the form, because he explicitly set out to look inwards, and a make a film about watching and making films, not a celebration of this process, but rather a dark fantasy about the problems and dangers inherent in images and their reception.

The Plot

At this stage it is worth recounting a simple version of *Peeping Tom*'s narrative. Mark Lewis, the central protagonist, is a serial killer who kills women and films them simultaneously, using a blade attached to one leg of his tripod. He holds down two jobs as a cameraman – he is a focus-puller for a large studio making a comedy and, less legitimately, he is a stills photographer of 'glamour' shots, in a makeshift studio above a newsagent. Through his friendship with a curious young woman, Helen, who lives below him, it is revealed that Mark owns the entire house, and that it belonged to his late father. Dr Lewis was an eminent psychologist who filmed and tormented Mark during his childhood in order to study the development of fear (and sexuality), hence Mark's obsessions in adulthood. He wants to continue his father's research by capturing on film the 'ultimate' look of fear. After killing an actress at the studio, and then his pornographic model, the police begin to close in. Although in love with Helen, Mark decides to finish the experiment by killing himself, and to film it.

Mark Lewis

1960 would be a break-through year for the portrayal of the serial killer in cinema. *Peeping Tom*'s release coincided with an American film by a British director (and one-time colleague of Michael Powell), Alfred Hitchcock. Aside from its ground-breaking audience manipulations, *Psycho* depicted the serial killer as gentle, shy and totally in thrall to his madness. Mark Lewis in *Peeping Tom* is also gentle and shy, but unlike Norman Bates, he is aware of his own psychosis, he knows how his tortured childhood caused his present mental state, and he even exerts some degree of control over it.

Norman Bates, whose pathology has been caused by his abusive mother, is crudely a schizoid, becoming 'mother' every so often in order to enact his monstrous desires, and then return to the normality of Norman. Mark Lewis is, in contrast, a far more complex and ambiguous figure, constantly shifting between positions – seductive, shy, competent, sinister, often in the space of a single sequence, he has no single murderous 'persona'.

Again, unlike Norman, Mark has a project that motivates his killings, the 'documentary of fear'. This involves repeated attempts to record the image of a frightened woman in the last moments prior to her death. It is in this image that he believes he can find some release. He is compelled by what the psychiatrist in the film calls 'scoptophilia, the morbid desire to gaze', which drives him to enact this confluence of sex, filming and death. Partly he wants to 'film what *he* never could', to continue his father's experiments, taking them to their logical but horrific conclusion.

However, Mark's 'documentary' contains an excess of other footage, images that he collects throughout the film. It seems that he is able to discover permutations of his obsession that do not involve killing. For instance he tries to film Helen's reaction to watching the films of his childhood, and he openly documents the police investigation of himself. When he films Lorraine, the model with the deformed lip, he is fascinated with that which he has been instructed *not* to show – her face. Mark is using his camera to break boundaries, to probe into the unshowable. He enthusiastically agrees to help Helen take 'impossible' pictures for her book, and it seems his own documentary will be impossible to complete.

Mark is a subversive and complex figure because he illuminates (with his klieg lights) the connection between voyeurism and cinema – he makes looking a dangerous act for both the giver and receiver of The Look, and he understands, from a childhood of being subjected to the camera's gaze, that these roles are reversible and unstable.

The Look

The role of villain in *Peeping Tom* is not taken by Mark, but rather by his late father and by the technology of film-making itself (and the father is made present in the film through this technology). The projector becomes a monstrous presence in several skewed shots of it glistening and clattering relentlessly as it throws images of death against the screen. Mark's camera is transformed in a different way, it is a physical embodiment of his obsessions, almost another body-part (which he is reluctant to be parted from) – in one scene Mark caresses it neurotically, and when Helen kisses him goodnight he is compelled to kiss the camera too.

In Laura Mulvey's hugely influential commentary on voyeurism and cinema 'Visual Pleasure and Narrative Cinema', she identifies 'pleasure' as being intrinsically bound to the male desire to gaze upon the woman who is castrated or made powerless in the cinematic frame. Mulvey concludes by postulating three types of look in narrative cinema: The look of the camera, the look of the audience, and the looks of the characters within the film:

> The conventions of narrative film deny the first two and subordinate them to the third, the conscious aim being to eliminate intrusive camera presence and prevent a distancing awareness in the audience. (Mulvey, 1988, p. 68)

Peeping Tom anticipates Mulvey's formula – Mark's victims are different kinds of 'exhibitionists' (prostitute, actress, model) designated as Spectacle (all three are involved in a transaction with Mark to reveal themselves to his gaze). Mark is the kind of film-maker Mulvey critiques *in extremis*; for him to film a woman is literally to kill her.

However, while *Peeping Tom* is a narrative film it is also foregrounding the ways in which images are constructed, projected and reacted to, so it actually begins to theorize about the meaning of the gaze within narrative structures. *Peeping Tom* doesn't let us sit comfortably, it breaks the 'fourth wall' (the imaginary rule or barrier that operates in films where the audience are not acknowledged) by explicitly stressing the first two looks and inscribing both our presence and the 'intrusive camera presence' whenever possible. The complexity of this process is frequently bewildering.

The opening sequence contains a long point-of-view shot, as Mark procures a prostitute and goes up into her flat in Newman Passage; she begins to undress; he then makes a strange manoeuvre (explained in the final scene) and starts to close in on the terrified woman. The next sequence shows a projector begin to show a film – and the first frame is immediately familiar, it is the opening sequence all over again. Here the viewer in the cinema is made acutely aware of the process of spectating, and the technology of the film they are watching. The first sequence in full colour is a merging of the film *Peeping Tom*, Mark's documentary, and Mark's point-of-view – all three looks are operating simultaneously. The adjacent scene functions to separate them out, so *Peeping Tom* shows us Mark's projection room. His film is repeating the opening sequence but in black and white, and although the viewer sees what Mark sees, we are distanced because we also see Mark's back as he watches his film. This is also the film's title sequence containing all the credits, and it is energized by Brian Easdale's nagging, insistent piano theme – so the non-diegetic world of going-to-the-cinema is furiously invoked.

This is just one example. The deeper you look into *Peeping Tom* the more complex it becomes in its figuring and refiguring of the Look. During the course of the film every possible specular position is considered and demonstrated, including the position of those who cannot actually see at all (Helen's mother).

Film-making/Serial Killing

As I have stated the numerous films-within-the-film operating in *Peeping Tom* draw attention to the technology of filming, but also emphasize the various frames of reality and unreality that can operate within a narrative film. The studio comedy *The Walls Are Closing In* is patently a parody of the kinds of films Powell hated at Rank Studios (as an in-joke he even casts the near-blind actor Esmond Knight as the director). The authority figures that gather at the studio, the two detectives and the psychiatrist, all appear to have stumbled in from another Rank film, so clichéd and stereotyped are their dialogue and mannerisms (and they fail to solve anything).

There are also the 'virtual' films of the newsagent's pornography, with their sets, costumes and production schedule; and in stark contrast, Helen's children's book about a boy with a magic camera.

Mark's 'documentary' and his father's films exist as authentic 16 millimetre prints projected and re-filmed. The film of his father giving him his first camera is shot with deliberate amateurism, moving in and out of focus when it is held by the step-mother, then adjusted by the unsmiling Dr Lewis (Mark will of course become a focus-puller in adult life, eradicating such flaws). Powell notoriously casts himself as Dr Lewis, and his own son, Columba, as the 8-year-old Mark; another 'in-joke', but one that makes explicit the relationship between the Lewis's activities (both father and son) and the making of cinema – the film director as voyeur, transgressor, and murderer.

Mark is utterly formed and in-formed by film; all his memories bound up with the presence of a camera. When he receives his own camera, it symbolizes his initiation into the father's world. It is a liminal moment, where Mark crosses the threshold between being passively looked-at and becoming the controller of the look.

There is a telling moment where Mark gives Helen a brooch, and as she places it on different parts of her jumper he instinctively imitates her gestures. Mark has spent so long filming/watching that he has become a camera (just as his camera has become part of him). There is a resonance with a statement made by Powell in later years:

> I'm not a director with a personal style, I am simply cinema. I have grown up with and through cinema; everything that I have had in the way of education has been through cinema... its all due to cinema. (Christie, 1978, p. 59)

The Back of the Culture

> Newsagent: Which magazines sell the most copies Mark?
> Mark: Those with girls on the front covers, and no front covers on the girls.
> (Marks, 1997)

The milieu of the newsagent/pornographer where Mark photographs still shots of 'glamour' models was an aspect of pre-1960s Britain not previously seen in a mainstream film. Powell and Marks wanted to show the burgeoning 'underground' culture of pornography, seeking authenticity in casting the real nude model Pamela Green as Millie, and having her then husband/photographer Harrison Marks on set to give technical advice (I believe that he also takes the almost wordless role of Mark's seedy assistant). This shabby world of cheap sets and lurid costumes is the flip-side to the immaculate artifices of *The Walls Are Closing In*. Both are home-grown industries capitalizing on particular desires to look, to fanatasize, and Mark is able to slide between them.

In the scene that introduces the newsagent's setting, an elderly city gent enters the shop on the pretext of buying a newspaper and then inquires after some 'views' (nude photographs). He proceeds to buy the entire book, leaving so quickly he nearly forgets his papers. He hides the photos in what is literally a paper-thin veneer of respectability – an envelope marked 'Educational Books'. In probably the first joke about masturbation in British cinema, the shopkeeper comments, 'Well, he won't be doing the crossword tonight'.

While the gent (Miles Malleson) is inspecting the 'views', a young girl comes into the shop to buy chocolate, which the shopkeeper happily sells to her, but not before she stands unaware in front of a gaudy display of Harrison Mark's photos. Later, the bespectacled newsagent, who is paying for the pornography to be produced, brings them up a pot of tea, but refuses to look at the models. The 'English' cup of tea clashes with the fake 'Paris' of the photography backdrop.

In these sequences *Peeping Tom* accumulates pointed ironies about British society and its double-sided relationship to pornography (and nudity) which anticipate the outraged tone of the film's own critical response. *Peeping Tom* suggests that there is a wider culture of voyeurism (in Britain) which is coupled with a deep hypocrisy about the (illicit) pleasures of watching.

By making this link between everyday practices of watching, pornography and Mark's watching-as-killing, *Peeping Tom* crossed a boundary that critics were not prepared to tolerate. As has often been pointed out, the reviews deploy a language that frequently compares the film to excrement or an animal – it was literally an excessive film with ideas that were out of control, beyond decorum, convention and good taste. The notion of the 'snuff movie', the recording of death, almost unheard of in 1960, is something that (understandably) still causes moral panic and hysteria, but is rarely explored in a 'mainstream' entertainment. The fact that *Peeping Tom* was clearly made skilfully and intelligently only seemed to add to its abhorrence. The critics' views cannot be taken as a true index of public thought (in fact a profession of constant film-goers might have felt particularly threatened by the implications of the film), but they are indicative of a wider reaction, and they certainly helped to ruin the film. Anglo-Amalgamated was frightened by the furore and cancelled distribution and sold the negative, which was heavily cut and retitled in America.

To declare that *Peeping Tom* was completely forgotten until 1978 (when it was reissued and widely re-appraised) may well be an exaggeration, but it does belong to a select group of epochal British films that, in the words of writer/critic Iain Sinclair, 'decay away at the back of the culture' (Sinclair, an unpublished interview with the author, 1997). Like Nicolas Roeg and Donald Cammell's *Performance* (1969) a decade later, it marks the end of an era, raising issues about sexuality and society that could not be comfortably assimilated at the time, prior to the 'liberations' of the coming decade. It is hard to find the British films that *Peeping Tom* influenced. In the 1960s its style surfaces most notably on television, in series like *The Avengers* and *The Prisoner* with their baroque fixations on surveillance, technology and elaborate violence. It is interesting to see its ideas being recycled so many years later in Kathryn Bigelow's *Strange Days* (1996).

Michael Powell did make other films, but not in Britain, and never with the same resources or technical or artistic achievement. *Peeping Tom* finished him, and it provided an excuse for British cinema to back off from self-reflexivity and experimentation, and become ever more absorbed in verisimilitude and realism. The more disturbing territory unearthed by *Peeping Tom* was left aside.

References

Christie, I (ed.). *Powell, Pressburger And Others*, London: BFI, 1978, pp. 53–61.

Croce, B. and Isted, M. 'The naked world of George Harrison Marks', in *Psychotronic Video*, 15 (Spring 1993) pp. 36–40.

Marks, L. *Peeping Tom (The Script)*, London: Faber, 1997.

Mulvey, L. 'Visual pleasure and narrative cinema', in C. Penley (ed.) *Feminism and Film Theory*, London: Routledge, 1988, pp. 57–68.

Sinclair, I. An unpublished interview with the author, 1997.

CHAPTER 17

A Postmodernist Calls: Class, Conscience and the British Theatre

ALEKS SIERZ

I have chosen Stephen Daldry's 1992 production of JB Priestley's classic play, *An Inspector Calls*, as a case study in how class is represented in contemporary British theatre for two reasons. First, because the play itself focuses on the issue of class and, second, because Daldry's version is a good example of how a postmodern style can make an old play look as if it has something new to say about 'now'. The main question is: what does representing class in a post-modern way do to the play's politics?

Although controversial, postmodernism is arguably the best way of describing the condition of today's culture. Since postmodernism is the flavour of the zeitgeist, much of the culture produced in our time bears at least some traces of its influence. Most accounts of postmodernism stress its origins in the failure of the master narratives of the Enlightenment, which used to give us a unified understanding of the world and a clear method for representation in art. As a style, postmodernism is characterized by self-reflexivity, irony, allusiveness. It is cool, stylized, sceptical, parodic, pessimistic. As the cultural expression of a capitalism whose commodities colonize all aspects of life, postmodernism prefers pastiche to authenticity. The political effects of postmodernism are often compared unfavourably with those of modernism – it is seen as an aesthetic that is more concerned with surface than depth, form rather than content, image rather than reality. It prefers a visual playfulness to a deeper engagement with issues. A distinctly postmodern style is usually characterized by a collapse of the distinction between high art and pop culture, a blurring of the boundary between art work and everyday life, and a mixing of different media conventions. Stylistically eclectic, postmodernism often surprises the audience by its daring mix of unusual elements (Lyotard, 1984; Hutcheon, 1988; Connor, 1989; Best and Kellner, 1991; Jameson, 1991).

Its general popularity has meant that postmodern attitudes touch even a traditional art form such as theatre, especially where theatre is a mass medium – in 1993–94 as many people went to the theatre in London as

236

watched live football (Casey *et al.*, undated; Travers, 1998, pp. 8–11). The most popular form of theatre – the mega-musicals of Andrew Lloyd Webber – are the most commodified in the global market. Their mix of high art and pop culture owes more than a little to postmodern sensibility. Because the main characteristic of theatre is that it is a live experience which explores the nature of representation, much straight theatre is also affected by postmodernism. When the curtain goes up, many in today's comparatively sophisticated audience will ask: what is being represented and how?

To answer such questions, I will first look at how the original 1940s version of *An Inspector Calls* used the representational conventions of naturalism to convey Priestley's moral message. Then I will examine Stephen Daldry's 1990s production and ask how far its expressionist style affects the play's political content. In conclusion, I show how the politics of postmodern representation affects the meaning of what happens on stage.

Drawing-room Politics

An Inspector Calls was written during the Second World War by the Bradford-born left-wing writer and dramatist John Boynton Priestley (1894–1984). Often praised for being 'well constructed' and for its theme of 'human responsibility' (Atkins, 1981; Cook, 1997), *An Inspector Calls* was first staged in Moscow in 1945, apparently because there were no London theatres free at the time. A year later, its first London production, at the New Theatre, starred Alec Guinness and Ralph Richardson. Since then, it has been filmed, shown on BBC television and revived on the London stage in 1974 and 1987. It has also become a staple of amateur drama groups and local repertory companies – most productions use the traditional illusions of a naturalistic drawing-room play to convey its political message.

Its plot combines Priestley's moral socialism with his obsessive interest in theories about the circularity of time. When the mysterious Inspector Goole calls on the Birlings, a prosperous middle-class family celebrating their daughter's engagement, it is gradually revealed that Eva Smith, a young working-class woman, who has just committed suicide, was connected in different ways to each member of the family. The Inspector proves that each member of the family was partly responsible for her death. At the end, while the older Birlings (Mr and Mrs) remain complacent, the Inspector's visit provokes a crisis of conscience in their children (Sheila and Eric). In the play's last moments, the Inspector leaves and time suddenly seems to repeat itself.

Although written in 1944–45, *An Inspector Calls* is set in 1912, which is Priestley's way of emphasizing his point that the middle class is on the edge of destruction (the audience knows that this complacent family is just two years away from the First World War). In the play script there's a page of stage directions describing the comfort of the Birlings' home: 'a fairly large suburban house, belonging to a prosperous manufacturer. It has good solid furniture of the period. The general effect is substantial and heavily comfortable... The lighting should be pink and intimate until the INSPECTOR arrives, and then it should be brighter and harder' (Priestley, 1969, p. 161). Despite all this detail, Priestley was not naive about the nature of representation – in the 'Introduction' to his collected plays, he explains that he sets his dramas in 'respectable' sitting rooms as a way of persuading people that they were watching a real story – once they were hooked, he would regale them with his moral message (Priestley, 1948). A naturalistic mode of representing class is thus a means to a political end.

In *An Inspector Calls* this is reflected in the play's language. Although Mr Birling constantly mentions his knighthood and Mrs Birling is always on about class, the family's speech is less a reflection of individual personality than of class character: as when Mr Birling says that the *Titanic* is 'unsinkable, absolutely unsinkable' or when Sheila calls Eric a 'Chump' (Priestley, 1969, pp. 166, 164). The Inspector, significantly, speaks in a different, more rhetorical way. He's an iconic figure, a symbol of justice, a moral reformer who, because he wants to change the world, can afford to ignore class etiquette. Often his language has biblical solemnity: 'Public men, Mr Birling, have responsibilities as well as privileges' (Priestley, 1969, p. 195). The working class, however, is not represented. It is an absence. Eva Smith never appears – she is a hidden victim.

In Priestley's play the Birlings are shown as a solid middle-class, northern family. It is a world where you dress for dinner, have maid servants and where the ladies withdraw from the room after the meal. Yet Priestley's message is that under this veneer of respectability lies an uglier reality. By showing Mr and Mrs Birling as hypocritical, he attacks the double standards of a whole class. They can get away with murder, while the working class (even when industrious) cannot prosper. In the Inspector's last speech, the middle class is warned that if there is no change, the country will be engulfed in 'fire and blood and anguish' (Priestley, 1969, p. 207). The ending is symbolic: while the older generation remains morally irresponsible, Sheila and Eric turn towards change. They have learnt that private behaviour has public consequences. In 1945, this was a call to vote Labour.

However successful, most plays only reach a small, often metropolitan, audience. The way a mass audience got to know about *An Inspector Calls* was through the film version, directed by Guy Hamilton, and released by British Lion in 1954. Its success at cinemas and its frequent rescreenings on television made its way of seeing class seem natural. The bluff, northern accents, the posture of the actors and the sets – especially the dining-room table, that enduring totem of middle-class family life – all create the solid world of the bourgeoisie. Also revealing is the choice of Alastair Sim to play the Inspector; as an actor, he is both benign and creepy. The advantage of naturalism in film is that it shows how the characters react in close-up – we see the Birlings' guilt written on their faces.

But while in the 1950s *An Inspector Calls* was just a successful film, by the 1990s it had become something much more significant – a cultural icon, a symbolic text no longer confined to celluloid but able to crossover from one medium to another. Of course, television's role in this cultural penetration is highly significant. According to the British Film Institute's library records, the film version was screened on terrestrial television six times in the last 20 years alone. With the expansion of satellite and cable television in the 1990s, there have been many more unrecorded screenings. Video versions offer even wider reproduction. Nor is theatre any less popular: not only has *An Inspector Calls* been revived by professional companies, it has also been repeatedly revived by amateur groups. Samuel French's theatre bookshop, which records staging permissions, received more than 120 requests from amateurs from July 1996 to July 1998. And although Stephen Daldry's version hasn't been filmed yet, there is a video record of the stage production at London's Theatre Museum.

Expressions of Style

The origin of Stephen Daldry's revisionist version of *An Inspector Calls*, which was designed by Ian MacNeil (1992), says a lot about the structure of British theatre after a decade of Thatcherite arts policies, when government rate-capping measures forced local councils to cut arts budgets. For although the play got much media attention when it opened at the National Theatre, it began life at a smaller regional venue, the York Theatre Royal. Like many local theatres, York had suffered cuts in its subsidy during the 1980s, with the result that it came to depend more and more on ticket sales for its funding. To achieve good box office, the theatre's programming began to emphasize safe plays rather than riskier fare. By 1989, when Daldry – then a relatively unknown director – came to direct *An Inspector Calls*, the theatre allowed him to put it on because it was thought to be a safe product. Paradoxically, because Daldry and his team were working for very little money, they had a lot of freedom to take risks.

The main innovation made by Daldry and MacNeil was to take what had once been a standard drawing-room thriller and turn it into a strikingly visual piece of theatre. As Daldry told the local newspaper at the time, 'I think there's a need to rediscover Priestley as a radical experimentalist rather than as an old war horse' (cited in Hutchinson, 1989, p. 12). So instead of the usual dining-room set, which represents the home life of the middle classes in much postwar drama, Daldry and MacNeil created a doll's house, 'a box on stilts' (Turner, 1989). Influenced by Expressionism, the production featured not only the six main characters, but also a crowd of outcasts, 'a number of non-speaking extras, the have-nots, gloom-laden with their ragged children' (B.A., 1989, p. 14). By adding this group of extras, which represent the working class (absent from the original play), Daldry and MacNeil turned a domestic drama into a much more socially conscious epic. As Daldry said, 'We are being told by our Prime Minister [Thatcher] that there is no such thing as society. But there is evidence that people are turning against that thinking' (cited in Hutchinson, 1989, p. 12). By representing the have-nots, Daldry was making a political point.

Daldry's *An Inspector Calls* enjoyed a successful run at York from 19 October to 11 November 1989. Later, after he'd directed several successful fringe shows, he was asked to put on a play at the National Theatre. He chose *An Inspector Calls*. When it opened in 1992, it seemed to be the perfect National play – it was well known enough to be popular, but its production was daring enough to look new. The set, with its doll's house on stilts marooned in a symbolic landscape, whose desolate cobbled streets are redolent of factory closures as well as bomb damage, immediately signals a radical departure from tradition. In a final *coup de théâtre*, the house of Birling splits apart and burns to the ground. Daldry's *An Inspector Calls* is certainly spectacular, but how does it relate to postmodernism?

When the curtain rises on *An Inspector Calls*, it is clear that Daldry is opening out the play as if he's making a film. Daldry says his aim is 'to work within a filmic style then re-establish it as theatre' (Royal National Theatre, undated). Many critics think he succeeded. Jack Tinker, for example, says, 'There is an altogether filmic quality' to the play (*Daily Mail*, 12 September 1997). The music played at the start of the performance is from Bernard Herrmann's score for Alfred Hitchcock's 1958 film *Vertigo*, a classic bit of ironic cross-referencing between film and theatre – a mixing of previously separate media which suggests a postmodern sensibility.

The use of an Expressionist style for the overall look of the production is also a postmodern ploy. Daldry and MacNeil mix two historical eras by dressing the Birling family as typical Edwardians and the crowd of silent onlookers in 1940s clothes (a stylistic reference to John Boorman's 1987 film *Hope and Glory* as well as a political reference to the 1945 Labour victory). This kind of playful attitude to the past and the collapse of rigid distinctions between the styles is also typically postmodern.

Scenes of Conflict

The production goes further by blurring the boundary between the art work and the audience. When the Inspector delivers his last speech, in Daldry's version he does it directly to the audience, while the house lights go up so that everyone in the stalls feels they are being addressed. While the Inspector says: 'We don't live alone. We are members of one body. We are responsible for each other' (Priestley, 1969, p. 207), the audience is reminded of the programme note which quotes Mrs Thatcher: 'There is no such thing as society' (Royal National Theatre, 1992). This moment underlines another postmodern characteristic of this production – the way it refers to its own conventions of representation. At the start, a little boy crosses the front of the stage and tries to raise the heavy plush curtains and takes a peek at what's behind. Just as directly addressing the audience draws attention to the play's political relevance, the boy draws attention to theatre as an act of representation.

While the scene when the Inspector addresses the audience works well because its takes the issue of class into the real world, the spectacular ending of the play is more problematic. Although the collapsing house is an entertaining theatrical moment, it is also postmodern in its love of irony, exaggeration, kitsch and parody. It harks back not only to Expressionism, but also to the Hammer horror film; it mixes film images with theatre, seriousness with fun. Some critics doubt whether this works. As Lindsay Duguid (1992) says, 'At times, the production seems to be no more than an ironical commentary on the original text.' And Peter Ansorge equates the play's entertainment values with those of popular musicals: 'The house that visibly crumbled onstage in Daldry's production equals the shock of the chandelier that the Phantom sends hurtling down on the audience just before the interval of Lloyd Webber's musical' (Ansorge, 1997, p. 25).

There are other ways in which Daldry's version subverts the naturalism by which the play usually represents class. The general look of the production suggests the postmodern love of the grotesque. The way the characters are cooped-up inside the doll's house when their meal begins has all the parody, playfulness and pastiche of postmodern style. Their conversation, fractured by the confines of the set, exemplifies the postmodern attraction to fragmented discourse. As the plot develops, the Birlings leave their doll's house (which represents the unreal world of the bourgeoisie) and come down onto the battered landscape (which represents reality). By the end, the younger Birlings are literally stripped of their evening dress – Sheila is down to her petticoat and Eric is in shirtsleeves. The play's moral message about class being a protective cover is thus represented in a visual and playfully punning way.

Central to Daldry's project in reviving *An Inspector Calls* was a desire to return to Priestley's main political message. 'I wanted very much to reclaim the production, to restore Priestley's original politics', says Daldry (Seavill, 1995). 'If we have the moral courage and resources to examine our recent past perhaps we can qualify to "live our lives again" ' (York Theatre Royal, 1989). While Daldry succeeds in making the play an exciting evening in the theatre, not all the results of adopting a postmodern sensibility are equally positive.

The main problem is one of characterization. A naturalistic way of playing Priestley's characters allows the audience to identify with them, to see in their representation of class attitudes its own feelings writ large – the effect is that the audience is implicated and forced to examine its own prejudices. By turning these characters into fanciful figures who inhabit a doll's house, Daldry lets the audience off the hook. For example, Sheila's fiancé Gerald acts as if he's 'oblivious, in a way that is characteristic not only of himself, but of his whole circle and (the play implies) his whole class' (Lesser, 1997, p. 22).

'The Birlings are emblems, not people. In creating high drama, Stephen Daldry has lost the very thing Priestley prided himself on: the common touch' (Duguid, 1992, p. 23). The moral problem of representing class through emblems – a postmodern tactic – arises when this distances the members of an audience from the action, allowing them to see the play as about other people rather than about themselves, thus freeing them from any pangs of guilt.

In any text, class can be represented three basic ways. As a hierarchy (a series of finely graded steps from prince down to pauper); as a tripartite view of society (divided into upper, middle and lower); and as a bipolar view ('them' and 'us'). Each of these descriptions is a rhetorical device which makes a political assumption: the first implies that hierarchy is natural, the second that society is the scene of shifting alliances and the third that the world is split into two antagonistic camps (see Cannadine, 1998, pp.1–23, 163–89). In the 1954 film version of *An Inspector Calls*, the naturalistic style of the representation means that class is represented both as a fixed identity and as a natural hierarchy. The film medium allows us to observe the subtle gradations of power between the older and younger Birlings, and between Sheila and her fiancé. In Daldry's postmodern version, identity is no longer fixed but floating. We can choose to identify with any character or with none. Furthermore, the interpretative model he uses is the polemical one which divides society into two great antagonistic camps: the evil rich and stoic masses. Despite the imaginative postmodernity of Daldry's approach, traditional notions of class remain embedded, are accentuated even, in his production.

Postmodern Populism

So, while Daldry's *An Inspector Calls* is a daring piece of theatre, it is also one that depends on a specific economic framework to find its audience. With subsidy concentrated at the centre of British theatre, people, who want to take their experimentation further than resources at the margins allow, are forced to work at the big national institutions. It's where the money is. When Daldry and MacNeil put on *An Inspector Calls* at the National, they had at their disposal the huge resources of one of the best-equipped theatres in Britain. The theatre's board at first had doubts about reviving such an old-fashioned author as Priestley; then it almost had cold feet about the huge expense of the set (the design concept was the same but had become much more technically sophisticated). In the event, the popularity of the play vindicated Daldry and MacNeil. Whatever was spent on the production was recouped when it was sold to a commercial producer, who put up the money to transfer it to the West End and then Broadway. Its success led to large profits not only for Daldry (who as director gets a share of the box-office receipts), but also for the producer. The National also received a sum from the transfer. In this way, low government subsidies force managements to make arrangements with the private sector to recoup their loses. Policy affects distribution, as well as aesthetics.

Watching a live show can involve unexpected additions to the meaning of the performance. When I saw *An Inspector Calls* at the National in September 1992, just after it opened, heads turned as Neil Kinnock (who had resigned the Labour leadership in July after losing the General Election in April) took his seat in the stalls (Sierz, 1994, p. 36). His presence gave the play an added political charge. For while most of the audience was middle class and middle-aged, their sentiments were liberal. For this reason there was something a bit unsettling about complacent greyhairs hearing a sermon from the stage, then going out into a rainy night, ignoring the homeless begging for money, and getting into their taxis. Thus the issue of class is not just a question of representation, but also a matter of the social circumstances of cultural production.

Conclusion

Although Daldry's *An Inspector Calls* started off with a comparatively privileged audience, it soon found a mass following, becoming the most successful revival of a straight play in the 1990s. While most productions run for a few weeks and are seen by thousands, this blockbuster has been running for six years and has been seen by about 1.5 million people worldwide. Although some musicals score such successes, it is extremely unusual for a straight drama to reach these figures (Agatha Christie's *The Mousetrap* is a rare exception). After being in repertory at the National, *An Inspector Calls* toured Britain, then transferred to the West End, first to the Aldwych, then to the Garrick Theatre. It toured Broadway and the United States. It was also seen in Japan, Australia and Austria. By September 1997, when the production had its seventh cast change, it had garnered '19 major awards' (PW Productions, 1997). These include Olivier awards for best revival, best director and best designer, plus London's *Evening Standard* awards and Critics Circle awards (1993–94), as well as four Tony awards on Broadway (McCabes, 1997). If, as anecdotes suggest, a handful of people walked out because they thought this version of the play was 'socialist propaganda', the great majority of audiences were moved by the experience.

As a cultural icon, Daldry's version of Priestley's text has benefited from the popularity of the Internet. While one Californian website greeted the touring production in April 1996 by saying that 'Bay Area theatregoers should consider themselves lucky' to see it (http://www.dailycal.org/archive), other Internet guides hyped its West End residency (for example, see Albermarles West End Theatre Guide, http://www.albermarle-london.com.inspect). One website offered a free dinner to anyone buying a top-price ticket, another listed revivals of the play in Bradford. An Austrian website discussed the Daldry production while a Canadian site described a local version. Given the role of the Internet – and all other media – in popularizing *An Inspector Calls*, the fact that Daldry's version is a stage play no longer seems as exclusive as it once was. Priestley's play has become a media event, a text that crosses cultural boundaries – a kind of virtual remake.

In conclusion, it is surely ironic that the most successful political play of the 1990s is not an acerbic critique of Tory policy but a revival of a 50-year-old classic. By using daring stylistic devices, Daldry and MacNeil took 'a relatively serious, extremely admonitory play' and gave it 'the thrill and glamour of spectacle' (Lesser, 1997, p. 14). But the way their *An Inspector Calls* represents class has negative as well as positive effects. On the positive side, the shock of the lights going up and the stalls being exposed to the merciless harangue of the Inspector's last speech, emphasizes the play's political message. On the negative side, the huge entertainment value of the costumes and set tends to distract from the humanity of the story. This depoliticizes the play by turning it into a cartoon. On balance, Daldry's *An Inspector Calls* is both more thrilling and less human than other versions. A new aesthetic style often has such contradictory meanings. Just as, in the 1930s, Walter Benjamin saw the art work as both civilizing and barbaric, so in the 1990s the best theatre is often both experimental and entertaining at the same time (Benjamin, 1970). Even if Daldry's *An Inspector Calls* is not a completely postmodern work, it still contains the tensions of the postmodern condition – where a belief in change coexists with sceptical irony.

References

Ansorge, P. *From Liverpool to Los Angeles: On Writing for Theatre, Film and Television*. London: Faber, 1997.

Atkins, J. *J.B. Priestley: The Last of the Sages*. London: John Calder, 1981.

B.A. 'An Inspector Calls' review, *Yorkshire Post* (21 October 1989) p. 14.

Benjamin, W. *Illuminations*. London: Jonathan Cape, 1970.

Best, S. and Kellner, D. *Postmodern Theory: Critical Interrogations*. London: Macmillan, 1991.

Cannadine, D., *Class in Britain*. New Haven: Yale University Press, 1998.

Casey, B., Dunlop, R. and Selwood, S. *Culture as Commodity? The Economics of the Arts and Built Heritage in the UK*. London: Policy Studies Institute, undated [1996].

Connor, S. *Postmodernist Culture: An Introduction to Theories of the Contemporary*. Oxford: Blackwell, 1989.

Cook, J. *Priestley*. London: Bloomsbury, 1997.

Duguid, L. 'An Inspector Calls' review, *Times Literary Supplement* (25 September 1992) p. 23.

Hutcheon, L. *A Poetics of Postmodernsim: History, Theory, Fiction*. London: Routledge, 1988.

Hutchinson, C. 'Under closer inspection', *Yorkshire Evening Press* (18 October 1989) p. 12.

Jameson, F. *Postmodernism, or, the Cultural Logic of Late Capitalism*. London: Verso, 1991.

Lesser, W. *A Director Calls: Stephen Daldry and the Theatre*. London: Faber, 1997.

Lyotard, J.-F. *The Postmodern Condition: A Report on Knowledge*. Manchester: Manchester University Press, 1984.

McCabes, M. 'Awards for *An Inspector Calls*', publicity list of main awards, London: Michael McCabes Associates, 1997.

MacNeil, I. *An Inspector Calls, Model of the Set for the National Theatre Production* Theatre Musuem, London, 1992.

Priestley, J.B. 'Introduction', in *The Plays of J.B. Priestley*, Vol. 1. London: Heinemann, 1948, pp. i–xiii.

Priestley, J.B. '*An Inspector Calls*', in *'Time and the Conways' and Other Plays*, Harmondsworth: Penguin, 1969, pp. 157–220.

PW Productions *An Inspector Calls*, publicity leaflet for the Garrick Theatre, London, 1997.

Royal National Theatre *An Inspector Calls*, programme for the production, London, 1992.

Royal National Theatre 'Platform Papers no. 3: Directors' pamphlet. London: Royal National Theatre, undated [1993].

Seavill, R. 'J.B. Priestley's utopian vision', interview with Stephen Daldry in the programme of *An Inspector Calls*, Garrick Theatre, London, 1995.

Sierz, A., ' Polishing the kitchen sink' *New Statesman and Society* (11 March, 1994) pp. 34, 36.

Travers, T. *The Wyndham Report: The Economic Impact of London's West End Theatre*, London: Society of London Theatre, 1998.

Turner, F. 'An Inspector Calls' review, *Guardian* (6 November 1989).

York Theatre Royal *An Inspector Calls*, programme for the production, York, 1989.

CHAPTER 18

Drama, Devolution and Dominant Representations

JANE SILLARS

This chapter looks at questions of the representation of nationality in a period of political and cultural transformation. Constitutional changes within the United Kingdom, emerging alongside technological and economic shifts in the ecology of broadcasting, are currently reconfiguring the structures and the meaning of 'the national'.

The chief concern here is with the representation of Scotland, at the level of institutional structures and within the specific genre of television drama. As a form that is increasingly produced and sold within an international market, television drama provides a means to examine what visions of the nation circulate internally and externally, and how dominant discourses can be reproduced or reworked.

TV Institutions, Political Culture and National Identity

Television in the United Kingdom has always reflected the nation in both its institutional organization and its modes of representation. As with other European nations the development of terrestrial television evolved within the regulatory structures of the bounded nation state. Within the complexity of the British experience, as a state made up of several nations, broadcasting has presented a powerful unifying voice for a coherent national identity.

The role of the BBC, in radio and television broadcasting, has been crucial in the production and maintenance of a shared British national identity in the twentieth century. This unity is reinforced through the form and the content of the media and through their relations with their audience. Through most of its history the BBC has operated largely centralized processes of funding, production and transmission. Its relation to the life of the nation has been cemented through its imbrication with the institutions and daily rituals of British life: both the official structures of monarchy, religious festivals, sporting events and state occasions; and the individual patterns of everyday life (Scannell, 1990).

The introduction of commercial television in 1954 changed the landscape of independent and public service broadcasting alike. ITV's regional structure prompted greater emphasis on representing the geographical variety of British life. However, the uneven distribution of audiences, economic forces, and production and commissioning infrastructures across the UK has meant that even the arrival of two further channels (4 and 5), supplied by independent producers, has done little to shift the concentration of broadcasting power and production from the South East of England.

However, the structures of British broadcasting do recognize the diversity of regional identity to some extent. This is accommodated through the mixture of network programming – serving the whole of the UK – and opt-out provision – which allows regional and national broadcasters to offer distinctive local programmes to their audiences.

Television production in Scotland has expanded with the development of this opt-out provision. However it remains bound within over-arching British institutional structures of commissioning and broadcasting. This mix of dependence and control, which is manifested throughout Scotland's media provision, has led to its description as 'semi-autonomous' (Meech and Kilborn, 1993). This inbetween status of Scotland's broadcasting institutions – caught between the regional and the national – has historically mirrored Scotland's broader constitutional position as a stateless nation within the multination state of the United Kingdom.

Now, however, the constitutional relations of the nation are undergoing reform. The successful 1997 referenda on devolution for Scotland and Wales and the establishment of the new Northern Ireland Assembly all promise to radically reshape the political contours of British national identity. In Scotland the political arguments around devolution, intensifying since the 1970s, have been accompanied by debate on the changing cultural identity of the nation. New representations of Scottishness – perhaps most strikingly in literature, but also across theatre, classical and popular music and film – have contributed to a wider renegotiation of questions of nationality. (Murray Smith's Chapter 15 on *Trainspotting* is further evidence of this trend.)

Within broadcasting there has been some recognition of this shifting terrain. The establishment of a national station, Radio Scotland, by the BBC in 1978, was seen as anticipating 1979's first unsuccessful referendum on Scottish parliamentary devolution. However, for the most part, institutional responses have followed in the wake of political and cultural changes, although the content of much Scottish-produced opt-out programming has often engaged directly with these discussions.

This relative stasis of Scotland's broadcasting structures is currently embodied in the government's legislative regulations for devolution. The Scotland Bill marks out broadcasting as a 'reserved power' to remain in the control of Westminster. This has proved one of the more controversial aspects of the legislation; the Scottish National Party has raised several parliamentary questions on this topic, and several lobby groups, including the Voice of the

Listener and Viewer, have expressed broader public concern over the implications of this omission.

In the absence of governmental guidance, existing terrestrial channels are reacting in different ways to this constitutional change. Channel 4's response to the changing shape of Britain has been the most evident. Its establishment of a new Nations and Regions office in Glasgow in 1998, under Stuart Cosgrove, marks a move to address these potential new configurations (as well, perhaps, as an acknowledgement of its historical under-representation of programme-makers outside the South East). The two major Scottish broadcasters, BBC Scotland and the Scottish Media Group, which owns independent companies Grampian and Scottish Television, seem content with maintaining the status quo. Both have shaped their response to devolution as primarily a question of the reporting of news and current affairs in the new parliament (see Schlesinger, 1998, for a fuller discussion of these questions).

Even this limited model has generated massive problems for the BBC. The relatively modest proposal to provide an opt-out extended Scottish news at six o'clock, in place of the current mix of network and opt-out, provoked expressions of cabinet concern. Despite intense lobbying by Scottish BBC executives, the Board of Governors announced, late in 1998, their intention to block this change, owing to their determination that the corporation should not 'run ahead' of constitutional change (quoted in Wells, 1998, p. 1). This interpretation was met by vigorous protests from the BBC's own Broadcasting Council for Scotland, and the angry resignation of one of its members.

The ongoing furore over this single issue indicates how much is at stake in these questions of cultural and political representation. It demonstrates how the relations between institutional and constitutional structures can be uneven and uneasy. It shows how bitter the arguments can be over both the pace and the actual meaning of change.

Television and Globalization

The interplay between dominant and minority nationalities is obviously complex. It is made more so by unfolding in a wider and shifting international context. As Andrew Crisell makes clear in Chapter 4, television increasingly operates not only in a national, politically bounded space, but within the economic structures of a global marketplace (Hoskins *et al.*, 1997).

Recent changes to the technologies of television, and in particular the emergence of satellite and cable modes of transmission, have already begun to fragment television audiences and transform the relationship between television and the nation. The capacity of cable and satellite signals to cross national boundaries has redrawn the lines of television and the ways it imagines and addresses its audience. The growth of a global television market (currently dominated by US production) has further altered relations between producers, audiences and the nature of the national identities they inform and represent. Many critics have begun to address this rearticulation of the global, the national and the local which is reconstructing economic, political and cultural structures.

In terms of cultural representation this process poses crucial questions to a small peripheral nation such as Scotland. Film-makers and institutional bodies, such as Scottish Screen and the Scottish Arts Council, are beginning to address the problems of how an economically underdeveloped infrastructure of audiovisual production participates in the realm of cinema production (McIntyre, 1994). In the light of growing convergence between the technologies of film and television, the issue of how forms of representation circulate and how they may be altered by these processes is becoming pressing for both media (Caughie, 1996).

Television Drama and Identity

Within the ecology of British broadcasting, drama has always held a privileged position. Perhaps because of the cultural prestige borrowed from the established art forms of theatre and literature, television has invested heavily in drama – whether in the form of single plays or classic, literary serials. One of the most expensive forms of television production, drama has continued to maintain a strong position in the schedules and with audiences.

Television drama also plays a central role in reflecting and contributing to debates over national identity. It explores historical, political and cultural questions of nationality; and works to frame notions of Britishness. Explicitly and implicitly it raises debates over the nature of class and society, the individual and the collective, agency and identity.

As with other forms of programming, television drama has been predominantly commissioned and produced from London. This centralization of power and money has been intensified within the costly realm of drama, where high budgets and production values for the most part prohibited the provision of opt-out drama and ensured that regional producers were dependent on network commissioning and funding.

Within Scotland the growing production infrastructure over the 1970s and 80s made inroads into BBC and ITV networks. BBC Scotland's drama department became best known for the series of plays scripted by Peter McDougall, depicting the trials of West of Scotland, working-class masculinity – such as *Just Another Saturday* and *Just A Boy's Game*.

The strong tradition of working-class naturalism is one that has been explored across a range of Scottish cultural production from theatre (*Men Should Weep, The Gorbals Story*); to film (*Floodtide, The Big Man*); to literature (*Dear Green Place, No Mean City, Laidlaw*). Identified by critics as Clydesideism (see McArthur, 1982), this mode renders Glasgow as a tough, uncompromising, urban sprawl; deformed by the experiences of industrialization, yet united by a sense of working-class community which is nonetheless rigorously controlled by codes of masculinity and femininity (Scullion 1995).

The recognizability of these depictions means that they can be readily mobilized. Their economic worth can be seen in the character of TV detective Jim Taggart, the embodiment of the values of Clydesideism, who has given Scottish Television its most successful presence in the lucrative ITV network schedule, and generated overseas sales. *Taggart* remains an effective brand, despite the death of its eponymous hard-man hero. In fact, over its extended life the series has examined changing images of Glasgow, and the tensions between its industrial past and an increasingly service-driven economy. Not only have *Taggart*'s protagonists changed to a woman and a middle-class man, but many storylines have exposed divisions between those living in the affluent 'new' Glasgow and those whose material lives remain untouched by the city's vaunted transformation.

Television drama clearly not only replays dominant representations but can begin to challenge and deconstruct them. John Byrne's two major drama series, *Tutti Frutti* and *Your Cheatin' Heart,* produced by BBC Scotland for the network in the 1980s, offered a new comic vision of Scottishness which successfully addressed Scottish and British audiences alike. In *Tutti Frutti*, the tale of a group of old-style rockers reuniting for a chaotic anniversary tour offered the means for a sustained interrogation of the changing relations between men and women. With the character of Vincent, the tough guy whose implacable masculinity literally goes up in flames at the end of the series, Byrne provided a powerful metaphorical destruction of the dominant figure of the Glasgow hard man, imploding within his own machismo.

Byrne, who designed as well as wrote the dramas, abandoned modes of naturalism in favour of an excessive and stylised *mise-en-scène*, offering new visions of Scotland. Along with other Scottish film and television creators like Bill Forsyth and David Kane, he has tapped into the alternative tradition of whimsy and surrealism – where the imperatives of class and place are side-stepped through comic reverse. If naturalism proposes that people are shaped by environment, then whimsy presents means by which they negotiate their placing. In their stories of capable women and inept men and their parodic deployment of traditional notions of class and identity, these producers have demonstrated how dominant models are open to reworking and re-creation.

An alternative example of the strategic use of whimsy can be found in one of the most successful television exports from Scotland in recent years, *Hamish Macbeth*. Apparently another formulaic genre drama, featuring the adventures of MC Beaton's fictional Highland policeman, Hamish, and his Westie terrier Wee Jock; its announcement filled the hearts of Scottish cultural analysts with dread. With the scenic West Highland village of Plockton starring as Loch Dubh and a credit sequence of picture-postcard images of Highland cattle and bagpipes, the series appeared to hark back to the most clichéd and reductionist shortbread-tin picture of Scotland. It was not a vision that immediately impressed: 'The opening moments of... *Hamish Macbeth* were enough to make your heart sink' (Dunkley, 1995, p. 17); 'I spent the first 10 minute of *Hamish Macbeth* fearing the worst' (Close, 1995, p. 28).

However, its exploitation of other familiar references was acknowledged to be subtle and skilful: 'a bit like *Twin Peaks* meets *Northern Exposure*' (MacLeod, 1995, p. 11); 'it does owe a debt of gratitude to both *Whisky Galore* and, just perhaps, *Local Hero*' (Laing, 1995, p. 16). With its close-knit rural community, quirky narratives, eccentric characters and easy-on-the-eye scenery, *Hamish Macbeth* clearly fits cosily in the gentle sub-genre of Sunday evening viewing, which stretches from *All Creatures Great and Small* to *Ballykissangel*. However, the most obvious point of comparison, with ITV's period rural cop show *Heartbeat*, is not one that met the approval of *Hamish Macbeth*'s spiky star, Robert Carlyle. 'I thought, this is nice, it's different. It's commercial television, but it is not – it is fucking not – *Heartbeat*' (quoted in McKay, 1995, p. 8).

In fact the casting of Carlyle was crucial in distinguishing the series and speaking to a broader, younger audience. It drew on a reputation built through a challenging repertoire of roles as drunks and psychotics like *Safe*'s Nosty and *Cracker*'s Albie, anticipating his scary portrayal of Begbie in *Trainspotting* (discussed by Smith, Chapter 15, this volume). Carlyle's role transferred some of the edge of Clydesideism's charged representation of working-class masculinity to the cosy environment of the Highland lawman. It is a clear demonstration of *Hamish Macbeth*'s success in utilizing a range of references to speak to the largest possible audience.

Produced by independent company Zenith for BBC Scotland, the programme's producer, Deirdre Kerr, was always aware of the need to address several audiences. In pre-broadcast interviews she privileged the local audience, but made clear the economic need to communicate beyond it. 'It's incredibly important that Scotland likes this series. We made this for Scotland, we made it for the rest of the country and we made it for overseas sales – in that order' (quoted in Docherty, 1995, p. 3). The use of heavily stereotypical depictions of Scotland works to market an exportable product; while the ironic framing of these stereotypes – from the postcard frame of the opening credits, clearly marking them out as generic representations, to the knowing play of the narratives – addresses a local audience as in on the joke. Just as the 'locals' of Loch Dubh perform their eccentricities for visitors, so we as their local audience are invited to share in the process of playing up to stereotypes in pursuit of gain.

The delight in teasing the uninformed outsider works at a narrative level to reverse traditional inequalities of power between centre and periphery as the community frequently outwits outside authorities impinging on their independence. However, I think the problem of wider questions of power and representation remains. While *Hamish Macbeth* wittily demonstrates how Scottish-produced drama can play with dominant imagery in often creative and challenging ways it does not address the questions of whether indigenous production can begin to move beyond these discourses; how it might engage with the politics of a changing cultural identity; and how these changes might be represented to a wider audience.

In this light, an instructive contrast can be drawn between the economic success of *Hamish Macbeth* and the two series produced for BBC Scotland by writer Donna Franceschild. *Takin' Over the Asylum*, a series set in a Glasgow mental hospital, was one of the most moving dramas of recent years. It went on to win a Bafta award for best series, but tucked away on BBC2 failed to attract more than 1.5 million viewers (Calderwood, 1996). Her second series, *A Mug's Game*, told the story of a working-class woman in the decidedly anti-romantic location of a fish-packing factory in the Western Highlands. Its factory and council estate locations dramatize precisely those symptoms of modernity and the mundane that most representations of the Scottish Highlands determinedly suppress. As with her earlier series, these were not images that appealed strongly to the viewers. The respective fate of these programmes is partly attributable to generic differences, and shows a public service system that is still willing to accommodate both challenging and mainstream work. However, it also makes clear the economic attractions of the familiar; attractions strengthening in a climate of transnational trade.

Conclusion

Devolution for Scotland is emerging following a period of intense political and cultural debate. Over the past two decades a cohesive, but necessarily contingent, Scottish identity has been deployed as a politically useful tool. As part of this process there has been a trend to explore differences *from* Englishness; while differences *within* Scottishness have been put to one side. Questions of gender and sexuality, of ethnicity and religion have been routinely ignored, although there are welcome exceptions emerging in critical writing recently (Whyte, 1995; Boyle and Lynch, 1998). These questions are fighting their way onto a new political agenda. They will be vital for the Scottish parliament, along with the need to address the broader requirements of a geographically and linguistically diverse nation, many parts of which have suffered severe economic underdevelopment and depression. These issues of identity and development in a postmodern, post-industrial world do not necessarily sit comfortably with the traditional images of Scotland.

Questions of identity are complex and contested. Television mobilizes different signifiers of place and identity across and within genres; speaking to audiences imagined as local, national and international. Within Scotland this is a period of political transformation that exposes some of the limitations of institutional structures shaped in a different historical moment. The new political settlement within Britain creates opportunities and challenges. Broadcasters and producers working in this evolving environment need to discover the resources and the representational strategies to respond creatively to change.

I would like to acknowledge gratefully the assistance of my colleague, Raymond Boyle, in shaping the arguments expressed here, and for his generosity with his ideas and his time.

References

Boyle, R. and Lynch, P. (eds) *Out of the Ghetto? The Catholic Community in Modern Scotland*. Edinburgh: John Donald, 1998.

Calderwood, A. 'Film and Television Policy in Scotland', in J. Hill and M. McLoone (eds) *Big Picture, Small Screen: The Relations Between Film and Television*. Luton: University of Luton Press, 1996, pp. 188–95.

Caughie, J. 'Scottish Television: What Would It Look Like?', in C. McArthur (ed.) *Scotch Reels: Scotland in Cinema and Television*. London: BFI, 1982.

Caughie, J. 'Questions of represention', in E. Dick (ed.) *From Limelight to Satellite: A Scottish Film Book*. Edinburgh/London: Scottish Film Council/British Film Institute, 1990.

Caughie, J. 'Logic of Convergence', in J. Hill and M. McLoone (eds) *Big Picture, Small Screen: The Relations Between Film and Television*. Luton: University of Luton Press, 1996, pp. 215–23.

Close, A. Review, *Scotland on Sunday* (2 April 1995) p. 28.

Craig, C. *Out of History: Narrative Paradigms in Scottish and British Culture*. Edinburgh: Polygon, 1996.

Docherty, G. 'Laid-back lawman', *Daily Express* (8 March 1995) p. 3.

Dunkley, C. 'Review', *Financial Times* (29 March 1995) p. 17.

Hebert, H. '*Tutti Frutti*', in G. Brandt (ed.) *British Television Drama in the 1980s*. Cambridge: Cambridge University Press, 1993, pp. 178–95.

Hoskins, C., McFadyen, S. and Finn, A. *Global Television and Film: An Introduction to the Economics of the Business*. Oxford: Clarendon Press, 1997.

Laing, A. 'Hail Carlyle, man of many parts', *Herald* (8 March 1995) p. 16.

McArthur, C. (ed.) *Scotch Reels: Scotland in Cinema and Television*. London: British Film Institute, 1982.

McArthur, C. 'The Cultural Necessity of a Poor Scottish Cinema', in *Border Crossing: Film in Ireland, Britain and Europe*. Belfast and London: Institute of Irish Studies and British Film Institute, pp. 112–25.

McCrone, D. *Scotland: The Sociology of a Stateless Nation*. London: Routledge, 1992.

McCrone, D., Morris, A. and Kielty, R. *Scotland the Brand: the Making of Scottish Heritage*. Edinburgh: Edinburgh University Press, 1995.

McDowell, W.H., *A History of the BBC in Scotland*. Edinburgh: Edinburgh University Press, 1992.

McIntyre, S. 'Vanishing Point: Feature Film Production in a Small Country', in J. Hill, M. McLoone and P. Hainsworth (eds), *Border Crossing: Film in Ireland, Britain and Europe*. Belfast and London: Institute of Irish Studies and British Film Institute, 1994, pp. 88–111.

McKay, A. 'Nuts and dolts', *Scotland on Sunday* (18 March 1995) p. 8.

MacLeod, P. 'Macbeth of the loch', *Sunday Mirror* (4 March 1995) pp. 11–12.

Meech, P. and Kilborn, R. *Media and Identity in a Stateless Nation: the Case of Scotland*, in *Media, Culture and Society*, 1993, pp. 245–59.

Nairn, T. *The Break-Up of Britain*. London: Verso, 1977.

Nelson, R. *TV Drama in Transition: Forms, Values and Cultural Change*. London: Macmillan, 1997.

Scannell, P. 'Public Service Broadcasting: The History of a Concept', in A. Goodwin and G. Whannell (eds) *Understanding Television*. London: Routledge, 1990.

Schlesinger, P. 'Scottish Devolution and the Media', in J. Seaton (ed.) *Politics and the Media: Harlots and Prerogatives at the Turn of the Millennium*. Oxford: Blackwell, 1998. pp. 55–74.

Scullion, A. 'Feminine Pleasures and Masculine Indignities: Gender and Community in Scottish Drama', in C. Whyte (ed.) *Gendering the Nation: Studies in Modern Scottish Literature*. Edinburgh: Edinburgh University Press, 1995. pp. 169–204.

Wells, M. 'Uproar as BBC kills 6pm Scots bulletin', *Scotsman* (21 November 1998) p. 1.

Whyte, C. (ed.) *Gendering the Nation: Studies, in Modern Scottish Literature*. Edinburgh: Edinburgh University Press, 1995, pp. 169–204.

CHAPTER 19

Consuming the Garden: Locating a Feminine Narrative Within Popular Cultural Texts and Gendered Genres

JACQUI GABB

In this chapter I seek to explore the implications of my own, and other (female) fans', pleasure in *Gardeners' World*, looking into how it captures and secures such a large and loyal following. Ien Ang's earlier study into the viewing pleasures of *Dallas* grounds its analysis within the subjective stand-point of her own fandom. Rather than qualify and apologize for her partiality, Ang uses it as the starting point for her study (Ang 1985). Within my analysis of *Gardeners' World* I have adopted a similar stance. I have used my own interest and viewing pleasures as a way into my analysis, and as a useful means of constructing a dialogue between myself and my informants.

Within traditional media analysis subjectivity has been sanitized from the text. However feminist analysis has confronted the masculinist objectivity that claims (scientific) objectivity, instead positing a reflexive account, where 'self-criticism and self-doubt [are] set in progress' (Westkott, 1990, p. 59), as a progressive model that accommodates the inherent subjectivity of any research process. Hence my identification as a fan, the professed partiality within my analysis, does not negate any critical insights but merely grounds them within my own subjectivities.

Much existing feminist research into the media has tended to concentrate its analysis upon daytime television (Modleski, 1990) and traditionally defined women's genres such as soap opera (Brunsdon, 1981; Hobson, 1982). Some research has considered the definitions of what constitutes a women's genre (Kuhn, 1984), looking into how the female (social) subject may be arguably constructed by the feminine narrative. But while programmes may be typically compartmentalized into gendered genres (Fiske, 1989), such rigidity not only reifies the social subject/spectator, it also delimits what may be included. To actually catalogue programmes into distinctive (gendered) categories actually excludes more programmes than it includes. To argue that only women's genres have open narratives and multiple storylines ignores the hybridity of many contemporary programme types, such as the police series. In addition, it also delineates which programmes are worthy of consideration. Those omitted from 'the lists' have been cast out into the academic hinterland: too 'ordinary' to be of interest. Yet they are significant, and do attract a relatively large, and most certainly loyal, audience. Gardening programmes have fallen within this void.

While *Gardeners' World* may reach an average audience of approximately 5 million viewers (calculated from *Radio Times*, issues from 1 July to 1 August 1996), a figure greater than any other 'minority programme', it has not received any critical attention. And although this viewing figure is only a fraction of the popularity afforded to traditional feminine genres, such as soap opera, this should not leave it outside the academic gaze. During peak – spring/summer – season gardening programmes average about 12 hours airtime per week on British television. And gardening itself is also becoming big business. Fifteen million of us garden each weekend, spending £2 billion per annum on our gardens (Levene, 1996). Gardening programmes are the primary means of 'advertising' gardening as a recreation and a pleasure, arguably serving to perpetuate and increase this mass popularity. By neglecting such minority programmes within feminist and/or television analysis we are not only denying the importance that they play within millions of women's lives, but also their interrelationship with other media texts and their more complex ideological functions. As women engage with the gardening narrative they are not only consuming the garden but also the privileged position of the private, self-contained family within society. Minority programmes *are* significant, both within their own terms of reference and also within the larger, social, picture.

While there is commonality between all gardening programmes, here I concentrate on one specific text, *Gardeners' World*, as it is by far the most popular of the genre, and through its structure and presentation arguably hails an (ideal) female audience. Drawing upon Ien Ang's methods (Ang, 1985), I placed an advertisement in the local newspaper, the *Hull Daily Mail*, asking for 'fans' of *Gardeners' World* to write and tell me why they watched the programme. In response I received over thirty letters. All of these respondents were female, and all declared an evident passion for gardening and this gardening programme in particular. From these letters I selected a typical sample, of eight women, to be interviewed in more depth. In concentrating my analysis upon only female fans it is not my intention to suggest that *Gardeners' World* offers an exclusively feminine pleasure, in fact part of my academic interest arises from the programme's broad-based popularity. As Geoff Hamilton points out:

> The only thing viewers have in common is an interest in gardening. Age, income, size of garden, level of understanding can be totally different. (Levene, 1996, p. 2)

Gardeners' World unarguably has both male and female 'fans', however, I intend to show that it hails a predominantly female audience. In response to my open letter to 'fans' of *Gardeners' World*, *all* of the thirty or so respondents were female. Attendance at the annual *Gardeners' World Live* show, held in 1998 at the NEC in Birmingham, was also predominantly female. And while no gender breakdown of the *Gardeners' World* audience is readily available, I wish to suggest that gardening, gardening programmes, and specifically *Gardeners' World*, *are* hugely popular with women, a disproportionate affiliation which is neither a matter of chance nor coincidence. On a regular basis Geoff Hamilton would purposefully privilege his address to the female audience: 'If your old man thinks this is too expensive...', 'Get your old man to knock up some 2x2 frames...' (*Gardeners' World*, 1996). All television programmes carefully, and strategically, identify their *ideal* audience, and *Gardeners' World* is no exception.

The Perennial Soap Opera

Although my research into *Gardeners' World* starts with the television text, I have endeavoured to steer clear of a purely text-based analysis. Such a methodology can too easily become fundamentally reductive, being over-reliant upon specific textual examples for the sake of academic expediency. Instead I have utilized a more expansive approach that incorporates the social (female) subject and 'her' negotiated pleasures from the text. There is also a tendency that is evident within some feminist analysis, whereby texts are subjected to a process of resignification, as a means of locating a feminist agenda that is all too absent from the mainstream media. The result of such a framework is that the gendered (social) subject often becomes essentialized; the female viewer becomes conflated with femininity, and the feminine is then displaced on to the female body (Tasker, 1991). To avoid such simplifications, I aim to locate the viewing pleasures within a broader context.

The viewer is not seen as a product of the (feminine) text, but is posited as a social subject, whose gendered identities are composite and contingent. *Gardeners' World* ably addresses this fluidity. It explicitly employs the conventions that are associated with the most popular women's genres, incorporating the broader (domestic) context of most women's lives within its feminine narrative. With its open structure, multiplicity of 'storylines', and lack of narrative closure, *Gardeners' World* appropriates soap opera conventions and reproduces them within its own unique 'herbaceous' narrative. The centrality of nature's cyclic process, the ongoing saga of the 'television garden' project, and the familiarity and ordinariness of the presenters' faces, are all characteristics of traditional soap opera. It serves up a familiar blend of education and entertainment: a formula that 'educates (with a very small "e")' (Kenyan, 1990, p. 4). Enabling an identification with the storylines and characters alongside an escapist narrative, it takes the spectator outside the mundanity of 'her' domesticity. It both facilitates fantasy while analogously reproducing the concerns of many women's lives.

Members of the female audience of *Gardeners' World* feel passionately that the programme is their own; it is specifically, and individually, tailor-made for them. 'Just sitting down in the evening, feeling that the programme was mine... it was my programme. I could just sit there and it used to absorb me completely' (Rosie M). Using the feminine language associated with 'mother' nature, it slips almost seamlessly into the television genres traditionally associated with the female audience. Characteristics traditionally denoted as feminine, such as fertility, nurturing and beauty, are all celebrated within the television garden, in a rare and spectacular representation of maternal plenitude. The audience is implored to look after their tender (dependent) seedlings. Many female names and garden flora are interchangeable, for example Rose, Poppy and Lily. And gendered adjectives are the descriptors of feminine and horticultural beauty alike. Indeed the language of the garden, in all its representations, is so heavily gendered that gardening and plants become 'marked' as female, signifying a femininity which sutures the programme (with its male presenters) and the female subject. Masculinity is largely absent from this arena, being pushed to the margins of manual labour and/or hard landscaping, or discreetly contained within the garden shed alongside all the (technical) garden machinery.

The garden and its flowers represent and symbolize femininity. The female viewer thereby feels comfortable within the narrative of the garden as it offers her an expression of her own (constructed) maternalism. 'It's like being a mother again. Watching your little plants, nurturing them and feeling sad if they die. All these maternal instincts come into it really' (Rosie M). Irrespective of their own maternal and/or familial status – not all fans of gardening programmes are mothers! – the audience is implored to 'give' their love, affection and time to the garden and its plants, on the promise of reciprocity. 'Gardening is like no other leisure activity because we gardeners actually create hundreds, perhaps thousands, of new lives each season' (Hamilton, 1993, p. 95). Unlike the emotional investments tied up within the family, these attentions are supposedly 'guaranteed' to give you something back in return. 'Give them a bit of encouragement to show them that you love them, giving them a feed... then they'll reward you with their very best display of colour' (Hamilton, 1996b). Thus, under the aegis of Geoff Hamilton, *Gardeners' World* evoked the *myth* of the garden, the role of 'Mother Nature', the precariousness of life, and the ever-present need for the virtues of nurturing and growth to secure its loyal female following.

The television garden represents the female viewer's (domestic) subjectivities and thus privileges her viewing pleasure. The inanimate routine of gardening 'chores' become conflated with the 'living' needs more usually aligned to her family members. It is not only her children and/or partner who need to be cared for, the garden also needs to be nurtured and looked after or it too might fall into disrepair, and she be deemed negligent, inadequately equipped to deal with her familial responsibilities. Tania Modleski's 'ideal mother' is figuratively identifiable within this *living* scenario (Modleski, 1990). The domestic (familial) routine that constructed Modelski's maternal subject is embedded within the daily needs of the garden. The female spectator not only provides the central support mechanism upon which her family depends, she is also the 'mother' to all her plants. It is only through her skills, dexterity and loving attention, coupled with those of her ally 'mother nature', that her family and garden will flourish. The fictional 'ideal mother' becomes identifiable and realized within this *living* context.

Authority and the Anchor-man

Once the female audience inhabits this domain of the 'ideal mother', then Geoff Hamilton may appear to appropriate the role of the (symbolic) 'father': 'Geoff was the Governor and always will be' (Tony C). 'I cannot imagine doing anything in the garden without first thinking what Geoff would advise' (Maggie F) (*Radio Times*, 24 August 1996, p. 139). Hamilton presented *Gardeners' World* from 1979 until his death in 1996, being known both inside and outside the gardening industry as 'the grand old man of the garden' (Levene, 1996, p. 2). His popularity had risen in line with the ratings of the programme itself. With his amiable manner, and informal dress code, he was instantly recognizable, and was duly adored by millions of gardening fans. But while his direct address to the female viewer may appear to characterize him as the absolute patriarch of the gardening world, such interpretation would exclude many of the feminine pleasures that are present within the text. I wish to posit that Geoff Hamilton was so popular with the female audience precisely because he signified something greater than (masculine) expertise. As I will show, Hamilton represented a complex blend of patriarchal authority and feminine (maternal) power, singularly embodied within a male physique.

Traditionally the presenter signifies the ultimate authority: articulating the producers' voice, 'he' controls the gaze. Yet while most other 'famous' television gardeners apparently relish the mantle of (patriarchal) expert, Geoff Hamilton endeavoured to rebuff this title. He subverted the direct address of the anchor-man, successfully overturning the authoritarian relationship between the television expert and 'his' audience. By describing his own expertise as the result of experience he placed it within the audience's grasp. He constantly addressed the audience – 'we gardeners' – bringing himself down from the echelons of stardom to within our reach; he was one of us. 'I think he just came over as such a simple person. That was his appeal really, he was so simple and down to earth... [He] made you feel "we can do that"' (Rosie M). Hamilton encouraged his armchair gardeners rather than give them instruction. He addressed 'his' viewing public as knowledgeable friends, an identification that was further enhanced by his body language. The (subservient) gesture, kneeling before us, represented *his* identification with *us*: he was our equal, open and vulnerable like any 'ordinary' gardener.

Geoff Hamilton established a contract between the viewer and himself, drawn up by mutual agreement. Like other presenters of his kind, he cajoled the viewer into an illusory dialogue, an intimacy that made us feel special, uniquely identified. The (female) audience of *Gardeners' World* believed his credible performance and invested heavily in his character. The responses to his death illustrated the extent of such affections and how deeply embedded he was within their 'real' lives. 'We are richer than we could have possibly imagined thanks to this gentle, lovely man. We shall miss him – very, very much' (Daphne W). 'The death of Geoff Hamilton will leave a huge gap in the lives of gardeners everywhere. Geoff sowed seeds not only in the soil but in the heart' (Dorothy B) (*Radio Times*, 24 August 1996, p. 139).

Transformations of Gender

Although it is relatively easy to see why the female audience invested so much of their emotional energy in Geoff Hamilton and the narrative of the garden, their *identification* with his character is more problematic. The explanation for this lies outside traditional textual analysis, demanding a far more progressive interpretation of gendered representation and feminine spectatorship. Geoff Hamilton arguably embodied the archetypal patriarch – the director of the gaze, the mediator of knowledge – but such authority was forever unstable as it was antithetical to the feminine form and content of *Gardeners' World*. Thus an enigma was created, a paradox that can only be resolved by dissipating the masculinity of his character and elevating the authority of the female spectator. This transformation of the female (amateur) gardener into the (masculine) gardening expert is achieved through an identification of herself within the (maternal) gardening narrative: a process of empowerment that facilitates both a fantastical identification with the garden and a figural identification with its textual representatives. Facilitated by the feminine language of flowers and the maternality of the gardening narrative, the female viewer *becomes* 'the garden' and thereby the 'natural' embodiment of expertise. 'She' usurps the traditional role of the authorial presenter.

'Woman' is not easily incorporated into the mainstream narrative, her social status as *object*, rather than *subject*, ensures that she continually slips from (active) spectator to (passive) spectacle. Therefore it might appear that the male presenter within the gardening narrative is hard to displace, for 'he' easily adopts the role of the protagonist, directing the narrative action within the passive spectacle of the garden. However, although the garden as a cultural artefact may be equated with masculinity, its mediated representation signifies the feminine process of gardening, the constant reassertion of essential maternalism. I wish to suggest that when Geoff Hamilton and other (male) presenters *invade* the garden – representing masculine culture over

nature, penetrating the (feminine) garden text – the female spectator strategically (mis)reads this image. Rather than 'man' transforming nature into
culture, she emasculates the symbolic (male) presenter, making 'him' part of
the 'natural' gardening narrative: a process that Geoff Hamilton ably facilitated. 'My garden at Barnsdale has really wheedled its way into my heart and
soul, and I'm now firmly transplanted and growing away' (*Radio Times*, 24
August 1996, p. 139). Within this environment the male presenter becomes
absorbed into the feminine subject, his role as the gardening presenter
becomes conflated with the garden narrative; *he* becomes feminine, *he*
becomes *her*.

However, although the female spectator may recognize the *representation* of
Geoff Hamilton as feminine, his 'real' character, as a man, remains intact. In
this way, Hamilton's *representation* becomes unstable, while his *gendered identity* as a male individual remains secure. It is not Hamilton who is emascu-
lated – his 'fans' are far too devoted to commit such a sacrilege – instead it is
the representations of gender that he personifies which are disrupted, and
with them the privilege afforded to the male (social) subject. The activity of
consuming the gardening text thereby reverses Laura Mulvey's assertions of
the female viewer's inherent masochistic pleasure at her mis-identification
(Mulvey, 1989). Rather than the female spectator undergoing a process of
identificatory 'transvestism', it is Geoff Hamilton who necessarily masquer-
ades; it is he who must continually perform his (male) identity.

When Hamilton's masculine identity becomes too fragile it is shored up by
a strategic use of the (gendered) garden. The feminine narrative of the flower
garden is cast aside for the masculine productivity of the vegetable plot, his
television address is (re)directed at the male viewer, and there is an assertion
of his character's 'real life' masculinity. 'What you saw was what you got with
Geoff Hamilton. The affable bloke-next-door image was the real man' (Titch-
marsh, cited by Pasco, 1996, p. 12). However, the evocation of the 'real man'
contradicts his beautification of 'the (garden) set', and the maternal narrative
of growth and nurturing, making such items a source of great complexity.
'Masculine' features become insecure as Geoff Hamilton constantly expresses
his belief that the garden must look attractive as well as be productive.
'Growing vegetables, fruit, herbs and flowers all mixed together in glorious
profusion... The feathery foliage of these carrots adds a delicate effect to this
border' (Hamilton, 1996a, p. 39). He does not adhere to the functional
imperative that forms the basis of other proponents of the recycling movement. While peers such as Bob Flowerdew, a regular guest presenter on
Gardeners' World, advocate the use of recycled fridges, tyres and carpet,
Hamilton's organic gardening always retained its (feminine) aesthetic.

Spectacular Identifications

The potential for subversive and successful female viewing pleasures is not solely reliant upon the character of Geoff Hamilton and/or his interrelationship with feminine narrative of the garden; it may also be attributable to the representation of the television garden itself. Within the television garden the female spectator is offered the possibility of multiple identifications, a process that substantially disrupts the female gaze. Rejecting the requisite masochism of the traditional female subject position (Mulvey, 1989) and the vagaries of mis-identification proffered by textual (feminine) 'others', 'she' is able to achieve a more satisfactory viewing pleasure. Within *Gardeners' World*, the dialogue between the feminine text and the female subject is not a passive discourse, but requires that 'she' actively construct the narrative. While the television garden may represent her femininities and maternalism, she also expects to insert her own life within this story. Such intervention within the narrative is not solely figural, it is not prescribed by the bodily boundaries that restrict the traditional mainstream narrative; her identification may operate outside the material world, within the symbolic, imaginary realms of abstraction and fantasy. Her *fantastical identification* can be a physical transformation. 'I just get lost in the programme. I end up dreaming of all the flowers and the colours, sometimes I reckon I can even smell the flowers' (Mary S). 'All the flowers are so beautiful... and the colours. It's like a weekly trip to paradise' (Audrey V).

Hence the gardening narrative not only encourages women to appropriate the (active) male gaze, it also facilitates a non-figural identification that explodes the restrictive categories that exist within the conventional binary of the sexes. It facilitates a truly spectacular identification. Within this scenario, colour, shape and form are everything. Using the techniques that are traditionally afforded to representations of women, the garden is fragmented into close-ups. It is carved up into a fetishistic representation for the spectator to consume; a display of (floral) femininity. Yet the paradox is that this fetishistic representation of femininity is arguably made for, and consumed by, predominantly women. Thus the totality of this (homoerotic) process enables the female viewer not only to gain pleasure from the televisual spectacle of visible femininity, but also encourages her to place herself within this frame.

Imagining the Feminine Narrative

The female subject thus gains satisfaction from her fantastical identification with the garden because it fulfils the conscious (or unconscious) desire for pleasure. She is encouraged to inhabit subject positions and scenarios that she would not assume in real life, experience an emotional intensity that she is usually denied. 'Through fantasy she can move beyond the structural

constraints of everyday life and explore other, more desirable situations, identities, lives' (Ang, 1996, p. 93). The television garden allows the female
viewer to *be* someone else, indulging her fantasies of owning a perfect house
and garden, of *being* an expert (gardener). It encourages her to invest herself
within the garden. She embodies the spectacular visual pleasures: she *becomes*
the garden. *Gardeners' World* and its like, are partly successful precisely
because they transport the viewer outside of her real existence, into imaginary
worlds. The female viewer does not confuse reality (her own garden) with
fiction (the television garden); she is all too aware of its 'essential artificiality'
(Seiter *et al.*, 1996, p. 146). Instead she subsumes herself, her life, and her
experience deeply within the larger narrative of 'the garden'.

Perhaps *Gardeners' World* has firmly secured the top slot in the television
gardening market because it has recognized a community's desire for a deeper
(maternal) investment within the narrative of the garden. However, the
progressive readings of the female audiences' viewing pleasures and their
multiple (spectacular) identifications suggest that there are hidden depths to
the television garden that are not apparent to the passing glance of the disin-
terested critic. Through my analysis I have shown that gardening programmes
represent a significantly progressive (feminine) narrative that sets it apart from
other 'ordinary' programmes. However, I believe it is also timely for academic
criticism to stop endlessly looking at traditionally defined gendered genres
such as soaps, and look into those marginalized, previously ignored,
programme slots. Otherwise the variety of our viewing pleasures become
fixed within an essentialized (feminine) form that stands at odds with the
contingency of the (female) social subject. The female audience is not a
passive recipient of feminine texts, nor does 'she' restrict her viewing to a
narrowly defined genre. Women watch all programme types and find a diversity of pleasure therein. It is the *variety* of these programmes and pleasures
which reflect the complexity and individuality of the female spectator. My
analysis of *Gardeners' World* provides just another piece in the jigsaw.

References

Ang, I. *Watching Dallas: Soap Opera and the Melodramatic Imagination*. London:
    Methuen, 1985.
Ang, I. *Living Room Wars: Rethinking Audiences for a Postmodern World*. London: Rout-
    ledge, 1996.
Brunsdon, C. 'Crossroads: notes on soap opera', *Screen*, **22**, 4 (1981) pp. 32–7.
Fiske, J. *Television Culture*. London: Routledge 1989.
Gardeners' World, BBC2, 1 April 1996 to 1 August 1996.
Hamilton, G. *Gardeners' World Practical Gardening Course. The Complete Book of
    Gardening Techniques*. London: BBC Books, 1993.
Hamilton, G. 'Inspired Creations', *Gardeners' World*, March (1996a) pp. 37–42.
Hamilton, G. *Geoff Hamilton's Barnsdale Collection* (video). BBC Television, 1996b.
Hobson, D. *Crossroads. The Drama of a Soap Opera*. London: Methuen, 1982.

Kenyan, J. 'Making a *Gardeners' World* programme', in J. Kenyan and P. Franklin (eds) *The New Gardeners' World Handbook*. London: BBC Books, 1990, pp. 1–7.

Kuhn, A. 'Women's Genres', *Screen*, **25**, 1 (1984) pp. 18–28.

Levene, L. 'The star turns of rockery 'n' roll', *Independent* (17 May 1996) Section 2, p. 2.

Modleski, T. *Loving with a Vengeance: Mass-produced fantasies for women*. New York: Routledge, 1990.

Mulvey, L. *Visual and Other Pleasures*. Basingstoke: Macmillan Press, 1989.

Pasco, A. 'A man for all seasons', *Gardeners' World*, November (1996) pp. 10–13.

Radio Times, 1 July to 1 August 1996.

Radio Times, 24 August 1996, p. 139.

Seiter, E., Borchers, H., Kreutzner, G. and Wrath, E.-M. '"Don't Treat Us Like We're So Stupid and Naive" – towards an ethnography of soap operas', in H. Baehr and A. Gray (eds) *Turning it On. A Reader in Women and Media*, London: Arnold, 1996, pp. 138–56.

Tasker, Y. 'Having It All: Feminism and the Pleasures of the Popular', in S. Franklin, C. Lury and J. Stacey (eds) *Off-Centre. Feminism and Cultural Studies*. London: HarperCollins Academic, 1991, pp. 85–96.

Westkott, M. 'Feminist Criticism of the Social Sciences', in J. McCarl Nielson (ed.) *Feminist Research Methods. Exemplary Readings in the Social Sciences*. Colorado: Westview Press, 1990, pp. 58–64.

CHAPTER 20

Selling Sexuality in the Lesbian and Gay Press

ANNA READING

Gay men have got more in common with a clubbing *Loaded* reader than with a dull old Nelly. (Collard, 1997)

In the 1990s there was an increasing interest in sexuality in media studies, as well as an increasing acceptance of gay and lesbian sexuality in some areas of popular culture – as signalled by the inclusion of out gay characters in popular British soaps. These changes may be understood as part of a broader development in the mass media involving the increasing commoditization of minority cultures: this has involved the proliferation of niche rather than mass markets and the exploitation of aspects of people's identities, including our sexualities. From one or two gay newsletters in the 1970s distributed through alternative networks, lesbian and gay glossies such as *Attitude* and *Diva* have become readily available in high-street stores. At the end of the 1990s, Britain has the highest concentration of lesbian and gay press publications in the western world, with approximately ten free publications going out to clubs and venues in London alone (Collard, 1997). Now, even the mainstream tabloid newspapers, according to the editor, accept the importance of the gay press in British culture: 'Even the *Daily Mail* sends a bike to collect the *Pink* if it hasn't got a copy' (Clements, 1997).

This chapter takes these developments as its starting point to look at the relationship between the market, sexuality and the magazine industry by exploring the effect on editorial direction of increasing market profiles and advertisement revenues of lesbian and gay publications in Britain. As with Simon Cottle's earlier chapter on ethnic minorities, this chapter suggests that questions of representation may involve an analysis of media content but also 'behind the scenes' research into production processes. The methods used here involved contextualizing an analysis of the content of five key lesbian and gay magazines with historical background and interviews with magazine editors and production staff conducted in 1997. I begin by discussing the concepts and relationships between sexuality and gender.

Sexuality and Gender

Sexuality may be understood in a variety of ways. First, for some, sexuality is the result of our nature – we are born with a predisposition to be heterosexual, bisexual or homosexual. For others, such as Sigmund Freud, sexuality is the result of our psychopathology: we are born bisexual but through the psychological relationships of early childhood develop desires for those of the opposite or same sex (Freud, 1974). These perspectives are essentialist: they assume that sexuality, either from birth or once laid down in early childhood, is fixed and unchanging. Yet other writers on sexuality, such as Michel Foucault, have offered another way of understanding sexuality. Foucault has suggested that sexuality may be understood in a non-essentialist way as 'the name that can be given to an historical construct' (Foucault, 1979, p. 105). In other words, sexuality may be something constructed over our lifetimes and within the context of our own particular historical epoch. Building on Foucault's assumption, sexuality in this chapter is understood to be a mixture of our innate being as people, as well as being constructed and reconstructed by the world in which we are immersed. This social constructivist view of sexuality is developed by Jeffrey Weeks (1985, 1996) who suggests that our innate sexuality is unfixed and may take a variety of forms. This polymorphous sexuality then becomes inscribed in the ways of our given society at a particular point in time. Thus in twentieth- and early twenty-first-century Britain, sexuality is understood in terms of a binary division between heterosexuality and homosexuality, 'between the norm and the perverse, or in practice between hegemonic heterosexuality and dissident homosexuality' (Weeks, 1996, p. 75).

Further, sexuality from this social constructivist perspective is constructed in a way that is gendered. Gender, rather than being something fixed from birth, may also be understood as socially constructed in particular ways. In our epoch, gender is the way in which biological sex differences are exaggerated, built upon and given different meanings and values through the social scaffolding of femininity and masculinity. In the 1990s to say that sexuality is gendered doesn't mean that homosexuality and heterosexuality for men and women are essentially different but that they are forged in ways that ascribe different meanings and values for masculine sexuality and feminine sexuality. The social construction of women's sexuality, for example, is still more highly controlled than that of men through both social pressure and the threat of violence. Masculine and feminine versions of the same aspect of sexual behaviour consequently often have very different connotations, with the masculine version seen as positive and the feminine as pejorative. A man may be virile but a woman is a nymphomaniac. A man may suffer from impotence (and be 'cured' with Viagra) but a woman is frigid. Masculine sexualities have also had a vocabulary and visibility that femininine sexualities have not. Thus, historically, female homosexuality was not outlawed in the same way as male homosexuality because those in authority could not believe female homosexuality was possible (Spencer, 1996). Mark Simpson has argued that this is also due to the ways in which male sexuality is inscribed through masculinity: male homosexuality places a powerful threat to patriarchal capitalism's imperative for men to 'always be a fucker and never a fucked' (Simpson, 1996, p. 246). In the 1990s this gendered divide is articulated in a way that has valorized female homosexuality through the phenomena of lesbian chic in popular culture (Hamer and Budge, 1994).

Indeed, the cultural industries and the mass media generally are key players in the construction, meaning and value of gendered sexualities. Terry Sanderson's *MediaWatch* has shown, for example, how the mainstream mass media, especially the tabloid press in Britain, have silenced and linguistically queer-bashed gay men and lesbians (Sanderson, 1995). In this way we see how Week's assertion that homosexuality is constructed as the perverse or dissident in our society is in part constructed through the mass media. However, in the past 30 years, Britain has also seen the development of a strong lesbian and gay press. As this has developed, in what ways have increasing market profiles and advertisement revenues affected the construction of sexuality in lesbian and gay publications? (For an analysis of gay and lesbian broadcasting see Keith Howes, 1993.)

Selling Homosexuality: From Newsletter to High Street

Lesbian and gay communities or groups have existed in Britain for a long time (Weeks, 1977; Bray, 1982; Faderman, 1985) with, historically, a variety of media, especially literature, expressing same sex love. In Britain this extends as far back as the first presses. Before the advent of restrictive Victorian morality, people wrote quite openly about loving relationships between people of the same sex. In the eighteenth century people talked of 'romantic friendship', for example, between women (see Faderman, 1985) and Wordsworth wrote of 'sisters in love' on 'Deva's banks'. A number of journals appeared in the 1870s publishing homosexual poetry as part of the Oxford fashion for 'boy worship' (Kaplan, 1997).

However, a specifically gay and lesbian press did not arise in Britain until the late 1960s. This can be understood as part of wider social movements such as the women's movement and those concerned with 'the politics of sexuality' in response to the legal, social and cultural oppression of homosexuals (Weeks, 1996). Editorials were directed by the fact that these were newsletters, sold not for profit, but published for campaigning organizations, such as the Gay Liberation Front's *Come Together*, *GGASlight* in Scotland, the *Gazette* and *SMG News* (Mason, 1996). Then, in 1973, *Gay News* was founded, which was more than simply a newsletter. As an activist fortnightly paper, its editorial extended the constituency of the gay press and it became, as Michael Mason argues, one of the most influential lesbian and gay publications produced by the modern gay movement. It was a vital focus for information and spawned the help line Gay Switchboard, as well as Gay Sweatshop, the influential theatre company. Sexuality in *Gay News* was constructed in a way that broke the silence surrounding homosexuality at the time and combined it with an 'activist' struggle against oppression of gay and lesbian men and women. The very use of the word gay in defiance of pejoratives for homosexuality at the time served to validate homosexuality in a way never done so before.

Then, Millivres, a small retail and mail order bookshop stocking US 'picture mags', which had moved into publishing with *Zipper* magazine and *Him Exclusive* (North, 1995), began to realize the potential market for a monthly gay magazine. In 1983 the company bought in the staff from *Gay News* and relaunched it in the form of *Gay Times*. With this change the editorial direction moved towards that of the classic style magazine with serious news alongside arts, trends and erotica. This was a way of reaching a wider market and it also, according to production staff, extended the boundaries of lesbian and gay sexuality: David Smith, editor of *Gay Times*, stated that by looking at everything from Russian laws on homosexuality to ecstasy raves from a gay perspective the publication reinforced a positive sense of gay identity. The magazine, rather than being just for gay activists, was and is an umbrella publication appealing to readers 'from as young as 16 to 86' (Smith, 1997).

The next extension into the market came in November 1987 with the *Pink Paper* (circulation 55,000), fondly abbreviated to the *Pink*, launched not as a monthly magazine but as a weekly tabloid. Originally a campaigning paper, then bought up by the Chronos Group, its unusual distribution method (free through gay bars and clubs), as well as its relaunch in 1995, gave it both a cultural twist and mass appeal, making it a key part of national gay life. Its editor, Paul Clements, divides the publication historically into the old *Pink*, in which editorial direction was in terms of constructing sexuality around the discussion of the oppression of gay people in the 1980s, and the new *Pink* in the 1990s, which seeks to counteract 'drab news' and the 'victim mentality' 'by leading the way in outness' (Clements, 1997).

The launch of *Boyz* in 1991 took the emphasis in editorial on an upbeat out gay sexuality – and the market for a gay publication – even further. Also distributed free through pubs and clubs its circulation soared to 100,000. The editorial direction of *Boyz*, according to its editor, is based on 'the politics of defiance'. Thus, said one article, 'who cares what straight people think anyway' (*BOYZ*, 1997b, p. 18). It also offered a construction of gayness as working class and male. Thus one article railing against 'snobs' and the 'educated' suggested a name change for its readers from the 'classic gay', 'Nigel/Tarquin' to something 'modern-ish working class' like 'Kevin/Darren' (*BOYZ*, 1997b, p. 18). Another article satirized the middle-class view of working-class masculinity:

Acting nancy maybe all very politically correct and desirable in a multi-cultural tolerant yadda yadda yadda but everyone knows that butch boys get more shags. Here's how to clump that dolliness, the *Boyz* way. (*BOYZ*, 1997a, p. 8)

The article then advised gay men to jam sump oil under their bitten finger-nails; give up on perfumes in favour of their own 'pong or swafega' and moon and get 'your cock out. Especially on the bus' (*BOYZ*, 1997a, p. 8).

The tone of defiance and satire marked the start of a new editorial direction and diversification in the print representation of sexuality to include a construc-tion of gay men as up-beat, cool, working class and irreverent (Gage, 1997).

Attitude (circulation 60,000), launched by Northern and Shell in 1994, added to this diversification in a different way. As a glossy monthly magazine distributed through high-street companies like WH Smith and Menzies, its market is the urban or metro, media-literate, style-conscious, consumerist and middle-class gay man. Unlike any of the other publications, the editorial direction of *Attitude*, according to its editor, is 'post-gay'. In this respect it 'takes a pot shot at certain aspects of gay identity with its sense of self-irony' (Collard, 1997). It also does not flinch at including stories about 'breeders' (heterosexuals) or by them or for them. In this sense the construction of sexu-ality in the publication disrupts the usual dichotomy between hetero and homo sexuality.

This growing diversity of representations in the gay press was added to in 1994 with the launch by Millivres of a bi-monthly publication, *Diva*, aimed at the lesbian market and which quickly achieved a circulation of 30,000 (Millivres Ltd, 1997). The editorial direction and look of the magazine was in some ways based on what women generally liked in the broader women's magazine market: the editor said, for example, that they wanted a magazine that should be 'lovely to hold like *Marie Clare*' (Rodgerson, 1997). At the same time, the editor was keen to construct a positive picture of lesbianism, that reflects 'real women's lives, rather than the lesbian chic found in the mainstream press' (Rodgerson, 1997).

Diva is unusual in the lesbian and gay market in Britain in that it is aimed specifically at women. It uses the term 'lesbians' rather than 'lesbian and gay' – unlike other publications. The editorial emphasis in *Diva*, according to its editor, was to construct a sense of lesbian sexuality that was not marginal or an adjunct to gay men's sexuality and which includes a range of different kinds of women. Indeed, while some gay publications do indeed aim and claim to include lesbians – such as *Gay Times* – my own content analysis of gay publications in June 1997 suggests that they were still overwhelmingly male in editorial direction and market orientation: for example, in *Gay Times* 87 per cent of photographs were of men, while 13 per cent were of women. (*Gay Times*, 1997). The pattern is similar with the other gay publications with the proportion of photographs of women highest in the *Pink* at 35 per cent.

Furthermore, the differences in markets and magazine competition, also, interestingly, have influenced representations of sexuality and editorial direction of lesbian and gay publications in other ways that are gendered. Lesbian sexuality in *Diva* is constructed in a way that is global rather than UK-centric and primarily urban, as in the gay men's magazines. In *Diva*, content may include articles on 'Being a Lesbian in Argentina' to 'Hockey Night in Haringay' to the lesbian delights of Vancouver (*Diva*, 1997). The letters page includes writers from Australia, Ireland and South Africa, as well as from Cardiff and London. The magazine always includes an international news section. This, however, is not because lesbians are necessarily more international in outlook, but is the result of market forces: approximately 10 per cent of its 30,000 circulation is through overseas distributors, with copies going to other European countries as well as the US, Australia and New Zealand. While there is a global market for a UK lesbian magazine, for the UK gay men's magazine market there are too many strong, English language competitors – at least two leading publications in the US and in Australia four to five. This, according to *Diva* and *Gay Times* marketing director, Kim Watson, accounts for the different editorial directions and consequent constructions of sexuality in *Diva* and in gay men's magazines (Watson, 1997a).

In addition, the relationship between advertising and editorial direction in gay men's magazines and *Diva* is also gendered. Lured by the potential of pink pound profits (Watson, 1997b), mainstream advertising companies began placing ads in gay press titles in the early 1990s (Baker, 1997). Gay men's publications, like *Genre* in the US, then began to emulate heterosexual men's magazines such as *Esquire* to get more adverts (Gluckman and Read, 1997).

This was also the case in the UK. *Attitude*, according to its editor, was created to meet the demands of advertisers who wanted a magazine which was not about, 'banging on a drum and waving a rainbow flag... yet not sleazy' (Collard, 1997). The magazine, in its editorial emphasis on lifestyle, in some ways emulates heterosexual men's magazines such as *GQ* and *Loaded*. Its coverlines and picture are designed not to outrage people at points-of-sale in supermarkets and not to 'put people off reading it on the train' (Collard, 1997). Its emphasis on style and media celebrities melds well with mainstream ads for consumables. So popular (that is, profitable) was the publication in 1998 that its editor, James Collard, was appointed editor of the US's leading gay magazine, *Out*, to revamp it along the same lines (O'Rourke, 1998).

The launch of *Attitude* on the basis of the perceived potential profits to be reaped from the pink pound subsequently impacted on *Gay Times*, which shifted its editorial and brought forward its lifestyle content and pushed news and politics further back. This, according to David Smith, is because mainstream companies do not like their adverts alongside stories of murders of gay men. The result is a tension between retaining 'honest, true journalism' and taking mainstream high-paying advertisements (Smith, 1997).

In contrast, the pressure on *Diva* to capitulate to advertisers, and to change editorial direction and representations of lesbian sexuality accordingly, is far less because it has a virtual monopoly. Its editor said that so far there had been no conflicts of interest. 'We're clear that they are only buying ad space, not us' (Rodgerson, 1997).

Thus, since the 1970s, with the market expansion of the gay and lesbian press, the representation of sexuality in these publications has diversified to include gay activists, middle-class professionals, lesbian mothers, working-class muscle-marys, as well as queer breeders. This diversity, however, is still largely premised on the traditional dichotomy of homo/heterosexuality. It is also gendered. Further, as publications try to extend their market reach and increase profits, editorial direction has changed in the more glossy publications to please advertisers, resulting in a commoditized sexuality more akin to a style we can buy like music or clothes. Nevertheless, it is the lesbian and gay press that has continued to provide a positive alternative to the hegemonic view in the mainstream press of homosexuality as perverse.

References

Baker, D. 'A History in Ads: The Growth of the Gay and Lesbian Market', in A. Gluckman and B. Reed (eds) *Homoeconomics: Capitalism, Community and Lesbian and Gay Life*, London: Routledge, 1997.

BOYZ 'Backchat', (19 July 1997a) p. 8.

BOYZ 'Free yourself from poofery', (19 July 1997b) p. 18.

Bray, A. *Homosexuality in Renaissance England*. London: Gay Men's Press, 1982.

Clements, P., Interview, 21 July 1997.

Collard, J., Interview, 24 July 1997.

Diva, June/July 1997.

Faderman, L. *Surpassing the Love of Men*. London: Virago, 1985.

Foucault, M. *The History of Sexuality*, Volume 1. (translation Robert Hurley) London: Allen Lane, 1979.

Freud, S. 'Three Essays on the Theory of Sexuality', in James Strachey (ed.) *The Standard Edition of the Complete Psychological Works of Sigmund Freud*, Volume 7. London: Hogarth Press and the Institute of Psychoanalysis, 1974.

Gage, S., Interview, 21 July 1997.

Gay Times (June 1997).

Gluckman, A. and Reed, B. 'The Gay Marketing Moment' in A. Gluckman and B. Reed (eds) *Homoeconomics: Capitalism, Community and Lesbian and Gay Life*. London: Routledge, 1997, pp. 3–10.

Hamer, D. and Budge, B. (eds) *The Good, the Bad and the Gorgeous: Popular Culture's Romance with Lesbianism*. London: Pandora, 1994.

Howes, K. *Broadcasting It*. London: Cassell, 1993.

Kaplan, M.B. *Sexual Justice: Democratic Citizenship and the Politics of Desire*. London: Routledge, 1997.

Mason, M. 'Out of the Closets, on to the Sheets: Gay Men's History', in *Stonewall 25: The Making of Lesbian and Gay Comment in Britain*. London: Virago, 1996, pp. 98–110.

Millivres Ltd. *Diva – Media Pack*. London: Millivres Ltd, 1997.

North, L. 'Cottage industries' *Gay Times* Issue 200 (1995) p. 62.

O'Rourke, I. 'Pecs out for the lads', *Guardian* (17 January 1998) pp. 4–5.

Rodgerson, G., Interview, 3 June 1997.

Sanderson, T. *MediaWatch: The Treatment of Male and Female Homosexuality in the British Media*. London: Cassell, 1995.

Simpson, M. *It's a Queer World*. London: Vintage, 1996.

Smith, D., Interview, 3 June 1997.

Spencer, C. *Homosexuality: A History*. London: Fourth Estate, 1996.

Watson, K. Interview, 3 June 1997a.

Watson, K. 'The Pink Economy', unpublished paper, Millivres Ltd, 1997b.

Weeks, J. *Coming Out: Homosexual Politics in Britain from the 19th Century to the Present*. London: Quartet, 1977.

Weeks, J. *Sexuality and its Discontents: Meanings, Myths and Modern Sexualities*. London: Routledge and Kegan Paul, 1985.

Weeks, J. 'The idea of sexual community', *Soundings: A Journal of Politics and Culture* 2 (1996) pp. 71–84.

Electronic Source:

http:/www.gaytimes.co.uk/

CHAPTER 21

Hanif Kureishi and the Politics of Cultural Hybridity

BART MOORE-GILBERT

In recent years, 'hybridity', 'hybridization' and cognate terms have become key concepts in the investigation of issues of identity and belonging, especially in so far as these have been inflected by the complex histories of (post)colonialism and globalization (see, for example, Hall, 1991, 1993; Chambers, 1993; Gilroy, 1993; Young, 1995; Werbner and Madood, 1997). In the formulation of these concepts and in their application to the analysis of such issues, the work of Homi Bhabha has been perhaps the most influential, spreading out from literary criticism to contemporary art history, sociology and film theory. Indeed, it could be argued that current New Labour thinking about the 'Third Way' owes something to Bhabha's criticism which, from the late 1980s, was using such terms as 'the third space' in an attempt to envision a new kind of 'postmodern politics' in the wake of the decline of traditional Left assumptions, analyses and strategies (Rutherford, 1990; Bhabha, 1994).

The influence exerted by Bhabha's various formulations of the categories under discussion rests to a considerable degree on their highly theorized and abstract nature, which has enabled them to be transplanted in modular fashion across a variety of terrains of social practice and fields of knowledge. However, little has been done in the way of testing Bhabha's models of hybridity and hybridization in concrete studies which might illuminate in a practical way both their strengths and possible weaknesses. To this end, this chapter will attempt a dialectical process of reading Bhabha against Hanif Kureishi and vice versa. Kureishi represents a suitable test for Bhabha's theories for several reasons. First, he is one of the most dynamic and high-profile cultural producers within the first generation of British-born citizens with an 'ethnic' or postcolonial background. Second, Kureishi works in a variety of media, including literature, drama, film and television and in doing so, crisscrosses the traditional divide between 'high' and 'popular' cultural forms. Third, and most importantly, in most of his work Kureishi raises in an immediate and empirical form precisely the sorts of issue that so preoccupy Bhabha at a theoretical level.

I will be arguing that a central element of the work of both these figures is the conviction that postcolonialism and globalization involve a challenge to the traditional identity of the 'host' nation as much as of those cultural communities whose migration to the West reflects the demand for a mobile, flexible workforce in a world economy that has become increasingly integrated since the fall of the communist European empires (and the Soviet Union). However, I will suggest that whereas Bhabha is overwhelmingly, even uncritically, positive about the opportunities offered by the processes of cultural hybridization which accompany postcolonialism and globalization, for both the individual and the sociocultural fomation(s) from which that individual comes, Kureishi's response to these developments is far more ambivalent.

Because space is limited, I will focus on only one of Kureishi's texts, *The Buddha of Suburbia*, which has claims to be considered exemplary of his work. Since the television series of *The Buddha* (co-scripted by Kureishi) is so faithful to the novel, especially in terms of the issues under discussion here, my usage of the term 'text' refers to both the novelistic and television versions of the narrative. With the possible exception of *My Beautiful Laundrette* (1985), *The Buddha* is certainly the best known of his pieces, and is probably the one that has enjoyed the greatest critical and commercial success. It won the prestigious Whitbread award for Best First Novel published in 1990 and has since sold almost 400,000 copies. It has been translated into more than twenty languages, including Japanese and Hebrew. (To this extent, the text can be considered as a cultural commodity of precisely the kind that characterizes the workings of the new global economy.) In its incarnation as a four-part BBC television programme (first shown in 1993), it reached an audience of 5 million. Finally, it comes roughly in the middle of his career to date, and both takes up themes elaborated in his earlier plays and films and anticipates his later work as a novelist and short-story-writer.

It is in Bhabha's work that perhaps the greatest claims for the politically and culturally enabling possibilities of hybridity and hybridization have been made in contemporary sociocultural criticism. Throughout his career, Bhabha has consistently elaborated these concepts in terms of their potential for subordinate or oppressed social and cultural constituencies to effect a 'strategic reversal of the process of domination' (1994, p. 112). Such arguments were first announced in the context of Bhabha's early essays in the field of 'colonial discourse analysis', a disciplinary intervention primarily identified with the work of Edward Said and, more specifically, with his *Orientalism* (1991). Bhabha's early essays represent both a refinement of, and reaction against, his mentor's work. For Bhabha, *Orientalism* is flawed by its static and binary conception of colonial relations, in which power rests overwhelmingly with the colonizer and is mediated only in a willed and intentional way. Because *Orientalism* fails to pay sufficient attention to the psychic domain in colonial relations, according to Bhabha, he fails to register the conflictual and contradictory nature of colonial discourse which, if read 'correctly', in fact registers as much anxiety about – and desire for – the colonized as it does the colonizer's confident and conscious sense of superiority over – and difference from – the colonized.

In the unstable economy of affective and psychic (self-)identifictions and counter-identifications which Bhabha sees as more truly characteristic of colonial relations and the regimes of representation produced by the dominant order, he discerns the grounds of a different process of contestation of that dominant power than is conceived in earlier postcolonial thinkers. In Bhabha's account, *Orientalism* in practice pretty well writes out the possibility of effective resistance to colonial rule; by contrast, Fanon (1986) sees violent confrontation as the only effective challenge. By contrast, Bhabha has argued that, as an 'in-between' figure who is 'not quite/not white' (1994, p. 92), the western-educated and often highly Anglicized native of nineteenth-century India (who exemplifies cultural hybridity in many of Bhabha's early essays) troubled and subverted the gaze of colonial authority by virtue of inhabiting a subject position which shuttled in an unstable continuum between 'Englishness' and 'Indianness'. For Bhabha, such fluidity presented insoluble problems of epistemological and psychic (self-)identification for a system of power which was characteristically based on the colonizers' ultimate assumption of absolute, ontologically grounded differences between themselves and the colonized.

In more recent essays, Bhabha has extended such arguments to analysis of some of the challenges posed by postcolonialism and globalization, which are entwining hitherto comparatively distant and distinct cultural formations in ever-closer conjunctions. One manifestation of this new cultural/political dispensation is the migration of significant numbers of formerly colonized peoples to the western metropolis, a development that poses urgent questions about identity, belonging and cultural tradition to such migrants, to their 'host society' and to their 'society of origin' alike. For Bhabha, the conflict which has sometimes accompanied this process of 'translation' is characteristically generated by essentialist conceptions of cultural identity and the confrontational politics which these often generate. On the one hand, the host culture has proved all too liable to require the migrant to 'assimilate' to what it assumes unquestioningly to be superior, even 'universal', norms and values – sanctified by reference to their long and 'organic' evolutionary development. This has at times encouraged a defensive reaction among migrants in the form of 'cultural nationalism', which can issue in an intransigent or 'fundamentalist' defence, also in the name of authenticity and tradition, of the integrity of social practices and beliefs brought from their culture of origin. For Bhabha, it is essential to find means of mitigating such polarizations so that productive negotiations between the historically dominant and subordinate, or majority and minority, formations are made possible. The usefulness of concepts like 'hybridity' in this context is that their differential and relational conception of identity makes fixed oppositions between Self and Other untenable; consequently, any politics erected on 'the traditional grounds of racial [and cultural] identity are dispersed, whenever they are found to rest in narcissistic myths of Negritude [for example] or White cultural supremacy' (Bhabha, 1986, p. ix).

Bhabha's conception of hybridity offers a significant challenge to dominant metropolitan discourses of inter-cultural relations, whether those associated with 'multi-culturalism' or 'cultural diversity'. The former exists in two principal versions. The first offers a vision of cultural mixing on the melting-pot model, in which differences between cultures become 'progressively' effaced through a dialectical teleology of sublation and synthesis. The second version tends towards a greater acceptance of cultural difference; this is, however, accompanied by the value coding of the 'host' culture as 'tolerant', 'liberal' and so on, and thus accords it privileged status. The doctrine of 'cultural diversity' also exists in two characteristic versions. The first, a modernized version of primitivism, valorizes the 'exotic' and authentic differences of migrant culture, often as a means to provide an 'internal' critique of the shortcomings of the host society (its lack of community, sexual repression and so on). The second version, commonly associated with far-Right politics, suggests that the differences between cultures (habitually defined in racialized terms) are so absolute as to make their coexistence in the same geographical space, in conditions of even relative peace and equality, a practical impossibility. By contrast with all these models of inter-cultural relations, Bhabha invokes Derrida's figure of the hymen in *Dissemination* (1981) to illustrate how hybridity can work to provide a 'third space' between any two given (sub)cultures. This ambivalent 'border-area' enables historically subordinate formations to 'negotiate' with (rather than simply confront or submit to) dominant ones and allows the construction of alliances between marginalised (sub)cultures without, in either instance, necessarily leading to synthesis into a new composite: 'It is an operation that *both* sows confusion *between* opposites *and* stands *between* opposites at "once".' (Bhabha, 1994, p. 127. For more detailed analysis of Bhabha's theories of hybridity, see Moore-Gilbert, 1997.)

The Buddha of Suburbia is paradigmatic of a lot of recent work emerging from postcolonial and migrant 'minority' formations in the contemporary West to the extent that it corroborates Bhabha's argument that an insistence on fixed conceptions of identity and an over-valorization of the authenticity of cultural tradition lie at the heart of much contemporary inter-cultural conflict. *The Buddha* also seconds Bhabha in identifying metropolitan racism as the most pernicious of the variety of essentialisms that it analyses. To a figure such as Helen's father, hybridity poses a major threat to the purity of metropolitan civilization, particularly through the 'degeneration' which inter-racial relationships are assumed to unleash. Such ethnic absolutism is expressed most damagingly in physical violence. In one attack Changez has the initials of the National Front carved into his stomach; Jamila, meanwhile, has ample raw material for her research into racial attacks on migrant women. On a less dramatic scale is the everyday prejudice (characteristically mediated in banter) of the kind suffered by Haroon in his work for the Civil Service, to which he attributes his continuing failure to be promoted. Such 'humour' embodies the widespread fear of difference which is apparent even in 'respectable' metropolitan culture. One example of this is the complaint of the seemingly thoroughly 'decent' Ted to Haroon: 'Buddhism isn't the kind of thing [Margaret] is used to. It's got to stop!' (p. 48). Underlying such comments is the assumption that it is the migrants' duty to efface all traces of their 'original' cultural identity, as suggested by Jean's demand that Haroon become 'Harry': 'It was bad enough his being an Indian in the first place, without having an awkward name' (p. 33).

One of the most interesting insights of *The Buddha* is its ironic perception that an equally flawed logic of 'assimilationism' organizes some kinds of 'radical' metropolitan anti-racism. The politics espoused by Pyke's troupe, for example, tends to homogenize the margins by subordinating their various and particular experiences to a crudely deterministic, singular (and Eurocentric) model of class conflict. (Moreover such a politics promotes confrontation with the dominant order, rather than subversion of it, which Kureishi and Bhabha alike see as the ultimately more effective political strategy.) Thus, kinds of difference, which are clearly evident and important to Karim, for example between black British and British Asian experience, or between different religious or gender fractions within British Asian society, tend to be discounted within a master-narrative that privileges class above all other forms of identity and belonging. (Compare Spivak's (1993) reminder of the necessity of a persistent recognition of the heterogeneity and 'otherness' of 'the subaltern'.)

Kureishi's text is equally subtle and effective in its critique of quite different kinds of metropolitan anti-racism that seem, by comparison (on the surface, at least), to respect the differences of 'minority' cultures. However, Kureishi implies that beneath Helen's spontaneously open-hearted endorsement of Haroon's 'right' to be in England, for example, lies a patronizing exoticism which implicitly forbids him to become culturally 'contaminated' by the centre. Such neo-primitivism, *The Buddha* suggests, is a trap into which well-meaning 'liberals' are all too prone to fall. Thus Eva dislikes Margaret in part because the latter is 'just' English and, conversely, prizes Karim because he is 'so exotic, so original!' (p. 9). Whether at Carl and Marianne's home in Chiselhurst, or Dr Bob's apartment in New York, the ethnicity of the cultural 'Other' is consistently represented in *The Buddha* as an object of consumption by the liberal centre, whether it is embodied in alternative modes of thinking (Haroon's 'spirituality'), in the promise of novel kinds of sexual experience (Karim is an object of desire for many of the white characters in the text, male and female) or in the more mundane material form of artefacts such as the 'lacquered boxes on the dresser, the silk cushion from Thailand' (p. 186), which decorate so many bouurgeois domestic interiors in the text.

Such attitudes are taken to extremes by the seemingly more politically sophisticated radicals represented by Shadwell's theatre group. With ironic echoes of colonialism's admiration for the 'unspoiled' native (which, so paradoxically, characteristically accompanied its 'civilizing' mission), Shadwell sneers at Karim's inability to speak an Indian language and the fact that he has never visited the sub-continent. The pernicious lengths to which Shadwell is prepared to go in his insistence on authenticity are indicated in his requirement that Karim both change his accent and employ 'a jar of shit-brown cream' (p. 146) in order to be able to play the role of Mowgli 'properly'. (This 'browning' of Karim in fact brilliantly symbolizes Kureishi's point that ethnicity – and cultural identity more generally – are, to some degree, constructed rather than innate or given.) Shadwell's demands are thus justifiably represented in *The Buddha* as little more than a different means of regulation, even subordination, of the 'Other' in the contemporary metropolis. Moreover, Shadwell's consistent manipulation of Karim through the director/ actor hierarchy (like Pyke's) effectively symbolizes the way in which western radicalism's desire to help give voice to, or liberate, the oppressed can involve a reinscription of the very (neo-)colonial assumptions to which it is ostensibly opposed (for more on this topic, see Spivak, 1987, 1993).

However, *The Buddha* is equally sensitive to the potential dangers of a recourse to notions of authenticity in certain kinds of minoritarian cultural nationalism. Kureishi is vigorously sceptical about the essentialist conception of identity on which the quest for, or return to, 'roots' in such movements often embodies. Thus Anwar's reaffirmation of cultural tradition in its 'pure' form is invariably shown as having destructive effects. His antipathy towards Hindus resonates ironically with the text's references to the terrible intercommunal violence that accompanied the partition of the sub-continent in 1947 and Karim identifies Islam as particularly susceptible to the extremism that Anwar embodies: 'Like many Muslim men – beginning with the Prophet Mohammed himself, whose absolute statements, served up piping hot from God, inevitably gave rise to absolutism, Anwar thought he was right about everything. No doubt on any subject ever entered his head' (p. 172). Jamila is, of course, the chief victim of Anwar's 'regression' to an originary conception of cultural identity. In detailing the blackmail that leads to Jamila's forced marriage, as well as Anwar's oppression of his wife, Kureishi emphasizes the subordinate role to which women are habitually placed (or returned) in the discourses of cultural nationalism, especially when these are inflected by religious zeal.

Yet Kureishi's treatment of cultural nationalism is not wholly unsympathetic, as Jamila's investment in a secular version of it implies. (Jamila, it might be argued, embodies to a considerable degree the 'conscience' of *The Buddha*.) Her rejection of the western canon in favour of the black radical intellectual tradition and her refusal to recognize the beneficial influence of Miss Cutmore's education are certainly satirized. But Kureishi represents Jamila's reactions as a stage through which it is perhaps necessary and inevitable that she should go, especially in so far as it is an immediately effective means to organize against the pressures exerted by the dominant culture. Indeed Jamila never renounces her determined anti-racism, a commitment that is used recurrently to show up in a negative light Karim's wavering loyalties to the community to which he, at least partly, belongs. (And, of course, Jamila's radicalism also reflects Kureishi's desire to challenge the widespread perception among metropolitan radicals that all British Asians are simply victims within metropolitan society.) To this extent, then, *The Buddha* seems to endorse the legitimacy of what Spivak has defined as 'a *strategic* use of... essentialism in a scrupulously visible political interest' (1987, p. 202).

However, the narrative voice much more obviously and consistently endorses the kind of hybridity initially represented by Haroon, which does not discount either the legitimacy of 'filiations' to one's 'original' cultural traditions or of 'affiliations' to one's host society (for detailed discussions of these terms, see Said 1983). Even at the outset of the text, when Haroon is at his most Anglicized, there are strong suggestions that his 'Englishness' is to some degree tactical, a form of mimicry which, like Amar's preference to be identified as Allie, is a means of deflecting the racist gaze of the dominant culture. As Haroon's self-confidence grows, so he increasingly reaffirms his non-western roots. Karim notes: 'He'd spent years trying to be more of an Englishman, to be less risibly conspicuous, and now he was putting it ['Indianness'] back on in spadeloads' (p. 21). But it is precisely Haroon's understanding that his roots are located in an 'imagined India' (p. 74), with all the provisionality that such a construct implies, which distinguishes him from Anwar. At the latter's funeral, Karim has a moment of epiphany that strongly affirms his father's pragmatic model of cultural self-identification: '[My father] wasn't proud of his past, but he wasn't unproud of it either; it just existed, and there wasn't any point in fetishizing it, as some liberals and Asian radicals liked to do. So if I wanted the additional personality bonus of an Indian past, I would have to create it' (pp. 212–13).

In its unrelenting and highly effective assault on a variety of essentialist notions of cultural authenticity and the confrontational politics of belonging to which they often give rise, *The Buddha* certainly lends considerable support to Bhabha's arguments about the potential of hybridity to help effect a new cultural/political dispensation in a contemporary metropolis that has been culturally and demographically transformed by post-war patterns of migration. Karim's nickname is, of course, 'Creamy' ('not quite/not white') and it is possible to see in his 'ambivalence' and shifts of subject position a successful and deliberate process of subversion of foundational conceptions of western and non-western identity alike. Karim's decision to settle in West Kensington, which he describes as 'an area in between' the inner-city and the suburbs (p. 127), in a city which is itself a space mediating the wider worlds of East and West respectively represented by Bombay and New York, might be taken to symbolize Karim's achievement of the kind of 'border-line' cultural location that Bhabha finds so productive. And the concluding scene could be interpreted as suggesting that Karim has finally carved out a 'third space' in which his 'double consciousness' (see Gilroy, 1993) can flourish. Neither fully assimilated as a 'brown-skinned Englishman', nor 'rejectionist' in the manner of a cultural nationalist like the older Anwar, Karim might seem to have evolved into a triumphant example of the 'new breed' of Englishman that he anticipates at the outset of his narrative, a hybrid being who will 'translate' or negotiate between all of the (sub)cultures to which he is both filiated and affiliated, without privileging any of them.

Yet *The Buddha* can also be interpreted in much less optimistic terms than this account might suggest, for three principal reasons. First, Kureishi lays great stress on the pain and loss that hybridity can involve. From this perspective, Karim's triumph at the end of the text could be seen as merely temporary, one more breathing space of the kind he enjoys after Anwar's funeral. It could even be argued that because so few of the dilemmas over his cultural identity have really been resolved, at the end Karim is in fact stranded between identities, in a predicament that is always as likely to prove painfully conflictual as pleasurably empowering. Second, while *The Buddha* celebrates Karim's assumption of new identities as a potentially liberating strategy, it also recognizes that, however much they may be mediated and conventional in themselves, forms of social classification based on ethnic, class, sexual and gender identities are objectively real to the extent that they are capable of exerting strong material pressures on the individual subject, as is illustrated by the effects of almost every instance of prejudice that occurs in *The Buddha*. Indeed, one inference to be drawn from the text in this respect is that those who are less privileged in terms of their class positioning and education than Karim may find it proportionally harder to escape 'into the border-lands'. Finally, the text warns that alliances between different kinds of marginalized cultures may be much more difficult to construct in practice than Bhabha recognizes. Anwar's hostility to Hindus, Changez's dislike of Pakistanis, and the antagonism between Karim and Tracey, who is black British, are reminders of the dangers of assuming any necessary common interest among ethnic minorities. Meanwhile Haroon's homophobia and Karim's sexism and occasional snobbery indicate the obstacles to building bridges between such groups and those whose marginalization arises from other histories of oppression. To this extent, *The Buddha* implies that Bhabha's conception of the liberating effects of hybridity – whether in the social, political or cultural domains – may be, if not utopian, at least prematurely optimistic.

References

Bhabha, H. 'Remembering Fanon; Foreword to F. Fanon', *Black Skin, White Masks*, trans. C.L. Markmann. London: Pluto, 1986 (first published 1952).

Bhabha, H. *The Location of Culture*. London: Routledge, 1994.

Chambers, I. *Migrancy, Culture, Identity*. London: Routledge, 1993.

Derrida, J. *Dissemination*. Chicago: Chicago University Press, 1981.

Fanon, F. *Black Skin, White Masks*. London: Pluto, 1986.

Gilroy, P. *The Black Atlantic: Modernity and Double Consciousness*. London: Verso, 1993.

Hall, S. 'Old and New Identities, Old and New Ethnicities', in A. King (ed.) *Culture, Globalization and the World-System*. Basingstoke: Macmillan, 1991, pp. 19–40.

Hall, S. 'Cultural Identity and Diaspora', in P. Williams and L. Chrisman (eds) *Colonial Discourse and Post-Colonial Theory*. Hemel Hempstead: Harvester Wheatsheaf, 1993 (first published 1990) pp. 392–403.

Kureishi, H. *The Buddha of Suburbia*. London: Faber, 1990.

Moore-Gilbert, B. *Postcolonial Theory: Contexts, Practices, Politics*. London: Verso, 1997.

Rutherford, J. 'Interview with Homi Bhabha: the Third Space', in J. Rutherford (ed.) *Identity: Community, Culture, Difference*. London: Lawrence & Wishart, 1990, pp. 207–21.

Said, E. *The World, the Text, and the Critic*. London: Faber, 1983.

Said, E. *Orientalism*. London: Penguin, 1991.

Spivak, G. 'French Feminism in an International Frame', in G. Spivak, *In Other Worlds: Essays in Cultural Criticism*. London: Routledge, 1987 (first published 1981) pp. 134–53.

Spivak, G. 'Can the Subaltern Speak?', in P. Williams and L. Chrisman (eds) *Colonial Discourse and Post-Colonial Theory*. Hemel Hempstead: Harvester Wheatsheaf, 1993 (first published 1988) pp. 66–111.

Werbner, P. and T. Madood (eds) *Debating Cultural Hybridity: Multi-Cultural Identities and the Politics of Anti-Racism*. London: Zed, 1997.

Young, R. *Colonial Desire: Hybridity in Theory, Culture and Race*. London: Routledge, 1995.

CHAPTER 22

Blind Date and the Phenomenology of Fun

Paddy Scannell

Everyone knows that the British television programme, *Blind Date*, is fun. This does not necessarily mean that everyone will like it or will find it entertaining. But whether something is fun or not is not, in the first place, a matter of opinion. It is an achieved and accomplished phenomenon. This means that for fun to happen it must be made to happen. Fun, like everything else, is an organized and managed affair. 'Phenomenology' is a *logos*, or discourse, about *phainomena*, things that show themselves (Heidegger, 1962). Fun is a human, social phenomenon. It shows up, is manifest, as one aspect of ordinary life. To study it is to examine what it is and how it is achieved.

Fun is an occasional, now-and-then thing. *As* an occasional thing, fun must create its own occasion. And the irreducible components of any occasion are time, place and person(s). An occasion can be defined as a particular 'totality of involvements', a specific set of concerns, a 'care-structure' (Heidegger, 1962; Dreyfus, 1991), that work together to produce the occasion (whatever it may be) as that which it is meant and intended to be. Thus, whether it be a child's birthday party or a royal coronation, each occasion has a specific care-structure that produces it *as* a coronation or a birthday party. The care-structure of an occasion is the totality of commitments and concerns that are necessary for its realization as the particular thing that it is.

The Care-structure of *Blind Date*

The object of *Blind Date* is fun. Its care-structure is the management of the occasion in such ways as to secure this objective. How, then, is it managed? Let us begin by thinking about its temporal 'when', its spacial 'where' and social 'who' – the *deictic* components that combine to make it the occasion that it is (*deixis* studies the use of words that indicate time, place and person in any actual utterance) (Levinson, 1983). The temporality of the programme can be thought about in two ways. There is the time of its transmission and the time of the programme itself. The programme's time-slot in the schedules is linked to the pleasures of the weekend. As a hugely popular programme,

Blind Date is strategically positioned on Saturday nights so as to win viewers to ITV at the start of the evening and, hopefully, keep them through the next few hours. But what is the temporality of the programme? We know of course that the show is pre-recorded week on week. But it is recorded in such a way as to preserve the effect of liveness and immediacy so that viewers experience it as if it were happening for the first time *now*. The 'now' of the programme is its now of concern, the now in which the programme's care-structure unfolds and is realized. For each and every viewer it is the now of their concern with the programme, of being engaged and caught up in it *now* in the moment of viewing.

What is the significance of this? A key expectation that we have of fun is that it should be spontaneous. Laughter cannot be forced. It comes spontaneously or not at all. We can all tell the difference between 'polite' laughter, 'hollow' laughter, 'bitter' laughter and the real thing which has an explosive, immediate and spontaneous character. The now of the programme must appear to be live and immediate – as if it were happening for the first time, now – for it is this that guarantees the effect of spontaneous enjoyment which is the hallmark of fun. There is of course a paradox here. The seeming spontaneity of the programme is a most carefully planned and managed effect that is crucially dependent on a temporality so organized as to produce the effect of the live, immediate, unfolding *now*.

Let me now turn to the programme's where. We can obviously say that the programme takes place in a studio which I have defined elsewhere as 'the institutional discursive space of radio and television' (Scannell, 1991, p. 2).What happens in the television studio, whether it is a political interview, a talk or game show, is a particular, organized social interaction. The nature of any interaction is always shaped by the 'social architecture' of the space in which it takes place. The design of the lecture theatre 'gives' the possibility of the lecture. The design of the church fore-structures the activities that can take place within it. The social arrangements of space are always formally indicative of the particular involvement-wholes that they are designed to elicit. The studio arrangements of *Blind Date* indicate the nature of its occasion.

To open this up, we need to bring in the question of the programme's 'who'. There are two issues here: 'Who are the participants?' and 'Who is the programme for?' Are they the same? Evidently the participants in the show include Cilla Black, of course, and all those who volunteer to play the game of 'Blind Date'. But what of the studio audience? Are they part of the show, or is it that the show is produced and performed for them? And what of viewers? I want to suggest that the studio audience is part of the show which is, first and last and in every particular, *for* the television audience. If this is so, it must be possible to show that it is so by a careful analysis of how the programme works as a set of social interactions.

Given the programme is for viewers, we need to think again about its 'where', for it exists simultaneously in two quite distinct spaces. The show is in the studio. Viewers are 'at home', watching in various domestic set-ups.

How are these two quite separate spaces linked together by the programme? One way to answer this is to consider who goes where: does it appear that the show enters our space (it comes to us) or is it that we, the viewers, enter its space (we go to it). Certain kinds of programme 'talk' to us in the places where we live and in which, among many other things, we watch television and listen to the radio. DJ talk on radio overwhelmingly talks to people in the contexts of their daily lives and concerns (Montgomery, 1986). Television and radio 'bring' us news. From their studios they speak to us of the great public world, bringing us information from all over the world and presenting it to us in our homes. News enters into the 'life-worlds' of countless millions via the television set in households and the contexts of everyday existence (on the life-world see Honderich, 1995).

The social organization of *Blind Date* is not like this. It is rather, an invitation to enter the social space of the television studio. It is not much fun watching other people having a good time if we ourselves feel excluded from what's going on. How are viewers included in the programme? Consider the role of the studio audience. Clearly the programme is performed before 'live' audiences, but this does not necessarily mean that it is performed *for* them. In fact the studio audience is there for us, the viewers. How so? Well, consider the well-known fact that studio audiences, in shows like this, are always rehearsed. They are advised when to applaud and cheer, and join in. Their behaviour is treated by the producers as part of the overall effect of the show, as something to be managed and controlled with viewers in mind. But does a show like *Blind Date* need a studio audience? If the show is for an absent audience of viewers, why not perform directly to them and do without a studio audience? Would anything be lost? The answer is, surely, obvious. The studio audience is vital to creating the atmosphere of the show, its 'mood'. Mood is a fundamental concern of any phenomenological analysis (Heidegger, 1962). The studio audience in *Blind Date* is essential to the creation of a specific public mood – a collective willingness to have a good time, a shared disposition to laughter and fun.

Fun is a spontaneous thing. But the conditions in which fun can spontaneously be had have themselves to be created. Mood is something you have actually to get into, and there are ways of doing this and aids to getting there. In television shows the studio audience is always 'warmed up' to get it in the right mood for the show. This warm-up helps to prevent the show from starting 'cold' and so having to work to get into its desired and appropriate mood. For viewers the effect of a live and present studio audience, when unobtrusively managed and controlled, is to produce the essential sense of the show as a public, sociable occasion, of which they themselves are a part.

The Social Relations of *Blind Date*

How are viewers made part of the show? It all depends on the programme host or presenter, whose key role in the management of the occasion we must now consider. The interactive organization of *Blind Date* – its template or fore-structure – is reducible to a format that goes back to the beginnings of broadcast entertainment (Scannell, 1996). In essence the show is a set of interactions between:

- host and participants (who play the game)
- host and studio audience
- host and viewers or listeners.

These three different circuits of interaction are 'in play' throughout the show and what holds them together, at all times, is the performative skill of its presenter, Cilla Black. The people who play the game and the studio audience all contribute to the performance, but it is the host – and she alone – who has overall responsibility for the management, control and direction of the show from the moment it starts to the moment it finishes. Cilla Black is a highly paid, professional entertainer. No one else is. All the other participants in the studio are 'ordinary people' for whom being in the television studio is a rare and unusual experience. How do you get an appropriate performance, in the very public space of a television studio, from people who are not paid and professional performers in public? Remember, this is 'live' television. Those who play the game are out there in front of a real 'live' studio audience. What if they get stage fright and dry up? The demonic problem of live broadcasting is the ever-present possibility of the whole thing suddenly going wrong. Part of the programme's care-structure is a concern to avoid technical failure and ensure performative success. This responsibility is vested in the whole invisible production apparatus of television. But what is highly visible from start to finish is the programme presenter. The production team delivers the show technically. Cilla Black delivers the show as 'the real thing', the thing that makes millions watch, week in week out. How does she do it?

It is worth recording an episode of *Blind Date* and going back and watching the beginning. If you can do this, pay careful attention to how Cilla Black makes her entrance. Note especially her 'body language', how she uses her hands and arms for instance. Characteristically, as she comes in she raises both arms, a gesture that acknowledges the cheers from the studio audience and the start of a complex interweaving of the three sets of interactions that she must keep going throughout the show. Cilla comes downstage to a pre-arranged position in front of the studio audience and a studio camera. She has begun to speak to the studio audience as she walks to her camera spot. Now she addresses her talk direct to camera, to absent viewers 'out there somewhere' watching.

The direct address to camera produces a look and discourse which is peculiar to television and essential to the interactive regime that it routinely establishes between institutions and audiences. In narrative cinema, and in fictional television, the actors in the story never look directly to camera. The regime of oblique looks and glances in film and television drama creates a self-sustaining world whose fictional 'reality' would be destroyed if ever the actors went 'out of character' and looked or spoke directly to the audience. To sustain their imagined worlds' fictional narratives rigorously exclude any acknowledgment of the real world in which viewers (or readers) are situated. It is an essential aspect of the ordinary, everyday worldliness of radio and television that they are in continuous dialogue with their audiences, thereby acknowledging that both – institutions and audiences – are part of the same 'world' with the same basic assumptions about and attitudes towards this world-in-common that broadcasting creates. (The significance of 'being in the world' is the central concern of phenomenology, see Heidegger, 1962; Arendt, 1989; Dreyfus, 1991.)

Cilla Black ensures that viewers are part of what's going on by talking to them directly and thereby bringing them into the picture and into the show. We effortlessly understand her talk and body language as a complex weave of interactions between herself as host, the studio audience, those who play the game each week and ourselves as viewers. The play of these interactions folds us into the show as it unfolds. We, the viewers, are not detached observers of *Blind Date*. We are active participants, part of the action. We are made so by the performative skills of Cilla Black.

Game for a Laugh

Fun is a manifold thing. Can we pinpoint what its basis is in *Blind Date*? What is the game here, how does it play and who plays it? To answer such questions we need to consider the programme's 'horizon'. The horizon is a phenomenological term for the always prior taken-for-granted attitudes, assumptions, knowledges and competences that make up the given and presumed background of any particular social world (Gadamer, 1993). The horizon indicates the limits of possibility, the boundaries of that world (whatever it may be). *Blind Date* presumes that there might be something entertaining in the idea of inviting ordinary members of the public (male and female) to take part in a game in which someone will select, from a choice of three, a partner from the opposite sex for a 'blind date'. They will go off together on this 'date' and a television crew will compile a record of the date itself and then interview, separately, each of them to get their candid opinion of the other and how the date went. Both will return to the studio in a subsequent show for a playback of their date and a discussion with Cilla of how it went and how they now feel about each other. What is the horizon of the assumptions that all this could be the source of public entertainment on television?

The world that is mobilized by the programme is the ordinary everyday life-world of all the show's participants and especially the audience watching at home. The concerns of the programme and the concerns of its audiences in the studio and at home have the same common ground. The core of the programme – its focused thematic concern – is a particular kind of social encounter that arises in the contexts of everyday life in the kind of world that we (as members of a modern, western society) inhabit. The possibility of the kind of social encounter that *Blind Date* presumes is not a given in every human society. The regulation of opposite-sex encounters in many parts of the world would frown at the very idea of 'blind' dating. But in our world – our historically and culturally specific world – blind-date encounters are, in themselves, indicative of the horizon of social structures that we all inhabit. In particular they indicate the everyday unavoidable and necessary business of negotiating encounters with strangers, for the essence of *Blind Date* is the idea of a social encounter with someone you've never met before in your life – a total stranger.

How to deal with 'the stranger that comes among us' has been a rich theme in literature and movies, in anthropology and sociology, for it indicates the boundaries, the limits, of the social and the sociable. 'The Stranger' appears as a threat to the shared world of a society's members. 'He' is the outsider, the unknown, a possible threat with a potential for disruption, disorder and danger. Modern societies have an unprecedented social complexity. The routines of daily life with which we are all familiar, require us to deal with strangers every day and in many different contexts. Being at ease in the company of strangers on a crowded street or tube, or dealing with strangers in a bank or shop requires specific social skills and ways of dealing with the situation (Goffman, 1963). In our kind of society we have learnt to become familiar with strangers and to minimize their potential threat by a complex range of 'politeness' strategies (Brown and Levinson, 1987) that are displayed in our talk and body language. It is within this horizon that *Blind Date* operates, mobilizing assumptions about how social encounters between strangers might be 'engineered' as a source of fun.

Part of the complex character of fun is that it can include 'making fun' of other people. Fun can be risky; it can have an edged and edgy quality; it can slide into mockery and teasing; and if it does you have to prove that you are 'game', you can take it, you won't get flustered or lose your rag. You cannot do this for to do so destroys the required, obligatory mood. When fun is being had, no one is allowed to spoil it. Participants in *any* interaction have a moral obligation to maintain the nature of the situation even if it should turn out, in the case of fun, that the fun is being had at their expense. In *Blind Date*, the risk lies mainly in the second part of the game. The first part – the pairing off game – is played for laughs. It is a light-hearted affair with a nicely balanced tension. Who will she pick? Will it be the one we like, or the prat who fancies himself? And do we, the viewers think it will work? Will they hit it off or not, on the date itself? The programme's sting lies in the subsequent feedback as the couple sit beside each other and talk it through with Cilla, for it often turns out that the date was a rocky experience, one way or another, for both concerned. It is here, in the feedback about the date, that participants are vulnerable to self-exposure, to wittingly or otherwise revealing aspects of their personality that may expose them to teasing, mockery and perhaps public dislike.

Conclusion

I have offered no more than a sketch-map of *Blind Date's* care-structure, the totality of involvements that it seeks to elicit, all of which are gathered together under the rubric of 'fun'. What does this kind of analysis tell us, not just about a television show, but more generally? It is fundamentally concerned to show that human activities and practices are meant and intended, and that this is the basis of the meaningfulness of human, social life. Care-structures are, to put it another way, meaning-structures. Phenomenology's core assumption is that the human world is a world of concern (Heidegger, 1962; Dreyfus, 1991). We *are* our concerns, and this shows up in every aspect of human life. Those concerns are always historically and culturally specific (Gadamer, 1993). It would be hard to imagine a human society that had no sense of fun. But, on the other hand, what is gathered as fun in the care-structure of *Blind Date* is particular to our times and our world – the contemporary world of modern, western societies, of which television is itself an integral, constitutive part.

References

Arendt, H. *The Human Condition*. Chicago: Chicago University Press, 1989.
Brown, P. and Levinson, S. *Politeness*. Cambridge: Cambridge University Press, 1987.
Dreyfus, H. *Being-In-The-World*. Cambridge, Mass: MIT Press, 1991.
Gadamer, H-G. *Truth and Method*. London: Sheed and Ward, 1993.
Goffman, E. *Behavior in Public Places*. New York: Free Press of Glencoe, 1963.
Heidegger, M. *Being and Time*. Oxford: Blackwell, 1962.
Honderich, T. *The Oxford Companion to Philosophy*. Oxford: Oxford University Press, 1995.
Levinson, S. *Pragmatics*. Cambridge: Cambridge University Press. 1983.
Montgomery, M. 'DJ talk', *Media ,Culture & Society*, 8, 4 (1986).
Scannell, P. *Broadcast Talk*. London: Sage. 1991.
Scannell, P. *Radio, Television and Modern Life*. Oxford: Blackwell, 1996.

CHAPTER 23

Di/Crash

JAY RUSSELL

If Diana Spencer's spectacular, mechanized death hadn't existed, it most surely would have had to be invented by JG Ballard.

In the tabloid/television orgy-cum-beatification that followed the demise of the princess, the extreme, if uncomfortable, truths of Ballard and Cronenberg's *Crash* suddenly seemed far less obscure. The *Daily Star's* day-after *Playboy*-like centerfold of Di and Dodi's mangled Mercedes, with its massive 'Tunnel of Death' headline, could only make the ostensibly outré eroticism and cheekily self-conscious techno-fetishism of *Crash* (the movie) seem far less alien and infinitely more comprehensible. Ballard, whose ancient, perhaps not entirely serious, remark characterizing *Crash* (the novel) as a 'cautionary tale' – a line unearthed and much repeated in press reports during the interminable brouhaha that surrounded the release of the film – eerily comes off as less of a pervert and more of a prophet. We don't even need to see those hideous photos of dying Di in the metallic ruins (although sooner or later, offered up on a website somewhere along with video clips of Pammy and Tommy Lee screwing like gophers, we probably will); the important thing is just knowing that those pictures are out there in the mediasphere.

1997 was quite the year for manufactured and wildly inflated media events in the United Kingdom; for spectacles and *situations*: 'saint' Diana, 'depraved' *Crash*, 'innocent' Louise Woodward. (And where would we be, in these zany fin-de-millennial days, without all those 'post-ironic' quotation marks?) Not to mention the rise and free fall of the Spice Girls *and* the thirtieth anniversary of Dead Elvis. It's almost (but not quite) a shame that goofy old Guy Debord blew his brains out a few years too soon, because he surely would have gotten a blast out of it all.

Diana's death was, of course, the holy of media holies; the biggest, bestest thing to happen to tabloid life since the hideousness of the Royal Wedding itself. On the one hand, there's no denying the significance and power of the story of the death crash in 'objective' news terms – deservedly or not, Diana was/is one of the most famous people in the world – but on the newsprint blackened other hand, the very terms of what is 'news' have been first fabricated and then set in stone as a pure consequence of the entrenchment of vapid tabloid values throughout what currently passes for journalism in Britain and, thanks in no small part to the pernicious likes of Murdoch and pals, throughout the world. Naturally, while eschewing 'Tunnel of Death' headlines *per se* on Crash Day, the BBC chose to pre-empt all non-Diana programming from *all* its broadcast channels for virtually the entire day; its so-called *Category One* death plan. (Very Michael Crichton.) Now the BBC is every bit as detestable a media organization as is News Corporation – perhaps more detestable given its pretence of seriousness and authority, not to mention John Birt – but what rationale could possibly exist for duplicating broadcasting on both terrestrial channels for hour after blather-filled hour?

JG Ballard might know.

Diana, Our Lady of Perpetual Paparazzi, was already a near-perfect Ballardian figure. For all intents and purposes, she was plucked – tragically, as it happens – from schoolgirl adolescence to be rewoven from whole cloth for the media by the royals for their own invariably self-serving ends. With each passing year and new trauma, Diana seemed to exist and act to greater degrees strictly for the benefit of the media: the virginal, perfect bride; the troubled, bulimic young woman; the vindictive, spurned lover; the loving, perfect mother; the committed, caring activist; the tragic, dead princess. Image after image after photo-shopped image, tailored and moulded to suit the moods and modes of the day; designed first for and then, rolling snowball that it became, *by* the tabloid editors and proprietors for whom every new click on the icon meant another happy visit to the bank.

To be fair to the various McKenzies and Morgans of Fleet Street-cum-Wapping, Diana's relationship with the nation's irredeemably loathsome, but ever-so-popular, tabloids (and their increasingly indistinguishable broadsheet – and corporate – big brothers) was entirely symbiotic, like those African birds that peck the ticks off the backs of rhinos (although which of the two was the bird and which the animal's arse remains entirely a matter of perspective). Diana's endlessly empty exploits – from the picturesque ski-trips to the photo-op hospital visits, from the exquisite *mise-en-scène* of the *Panorama* interview to her warmed-over Jackie O. romance with the son of the equally Ballardian owner of Harrods – were supposedly irresistible, but frankly inexplicable to the majority of people who lead normal, mundanely complicated lives. Diana's every action seemed perversely calculated to titillate and tease the tabloid editors, even as she and her minions declared her annoyance and dismay over the horror they ostensibly inflicted on her existence. But what existence did she have other than the one she made for the sake of the press and which the press tried, in equal measure, to make for her? If ever a Lady did protest too much... (Charles: 'That was no Lady, that was my ex-wife.')

Of course, an insistent and genuinely perverse eroticization always lay at the heart of Diana's media portrayals. From the start, as a gangly kid, both establishment and tabloid culture insisted on the magnificence of her beauty, but this over-determined, nigh-universal exaggeration of Diana's manifestly modest, wouldn't-kick-her-out-of-bed-for-eating-crackers *physical* appeal has always been unfathomable, except as an extension of the continuing, unspeakably dull English self-delusion that Britain is somehow still top of the world.

In the years since Diana's unveiling, there has been a fevered mania for photographs of the princess that could in any way be viewed as physically revealing or sexually provocative, but that might have been out of some sad, 1950s soft-core porn rag: the crotch shot elevated to the status of royal portraiture. This pathetic game of photographic peeping-tom was made that much more perverse by the glaring immediacy of Diana's self-image problems and obvious eating disorder(s). The less sexy she actually became, the more desirous, it seemed, the tabloids had to make her appear for the slavering hordes of readers who could always flip to Page Three for the cheapest of all possible thrills.

As Diana grew older, and visibly more comfortable within and about herself (especially post-Charles), this eroticization of her took a different tack. The mania for cheesecake shots naturally continued apace, but Diana's increasingly dubious (at least from the establishment's perspective) romantic liaisons provided a new and more titillating focus of attention for the press. The story of the soldier who risked beheading (yeah, right) to bed the princess may have been a gift from the gods, but Dodi Al Fayed – *Dodi!* Could you make it up? – was every salacious editor's sweatiest wet dream come true. Diana and Dodi's 'true love at last' angle was good for some play, sure – although it played even better in the context of fleshing out the depth of her 'tragedy' post-mortem – but the vulgar Hollywood exoticism, the raw middle-eastern *otherness* of the once-upon-a-time virgin's new lover was the really juicy bit. The mother of the future king was doing it with a dirty Arab! (Come home Edward Said, all is forgiven.) What better to set to racing the tiny hearts of the legion of Little Englanders who write and read the tabloids? Even in death, it is hinted, Diana and Dodi were in each other's arms. Why else, conspiracy theories notwithstanding, weren't they wearing their seat belts? Death, in media terms, offers the rarest, if still relatively taboo, taste of the erotic, with sad Tory MP Stephen Milligan and his orange slice and bondage gear at one end of the spectrum, Princess Di in her crushed Mercedes at the other.

The death of the famous is the most potent distillation possible of that erotic forbidden fruit. JG Ballard exposed and explored this region of taboo in *Crash*, as well as in a series of short stories and quasi-surreal literary doodles, notably *The Atrocity Exhibition*. Ballard's preoccupation has been, against all odds, immaculately realized in celluloid by David Cronenberg. Ballard and Cronenberg's triumph – and their sin, at least in the eyes of the ever hypocritical tabloids – was to feel no guilt, demonstrate no shame in overtly portraying, in a *non-condemning* manner, this supposedly forbidden avenue of the erotic. The price of this honesty was a wholly manufactured tabloid fury and (yet another) demand for greater censorship; the price of the tabloid's *dis*honesty may yet be censorship of a whole other kind in the form of privacy and libel laws and restrictive industry codes.

Ballard told an interviewer in 1970:

> A car crash harnesses elements of eroticism, aggression, desire, speed, drama, kinaesthetic factors, the stylizing of motion, consumer goods, status – all these in one event. I myself see the car crash as a tremendous sexual event really… That's why the death in a crash of a famous person is a unique event… it takes place within this most potent of all consumer durables. (cited in Re/Search, 1984, p. 156)

If at the time Ballard was speaking the automobile was indeed the most potent of consumer goods – and certainly the environmental movement has run a sharp key along the gloss of that finish – the information age has transmuted some of that sheen of desire from the strictly material to the media-processed physical; from items to own, to icons to be. This has been true to some degree throughout this century – it is, of course, the quicksand foundation that Hollywood is built on – but never to the omnipresent extent of the present day. What is Michael Jordan, for example, but the Cadillac of the 1990s? ('If I could be like Mike…' is the song Nike wrote to sell their sneakers.) And Jordan doesn't pollute! Well…

Diana's death achieves the Ballardian sublime not just because she was a famous person killed in a crash, but because her death, following logically from the ridiculous, media-led spectacle of her life, represents the triumph of the personality as consumable. And her star-studded funeral and posthumous media existence represent nothing less than the apotheosis of this most rabid, nigh-cannibalistic form of consumption. As this is written, seven months after her death, Diana continues to sell newspapers and magazines and television time (not to mention tribute albums and lottery scratch cards and teddy bears and countless other tacky doo-dads and tchotchkes) and will no doubt go on doing so for a long time to come. Tabs of ecstasy are even being stamped with Diana and Dodi's name on one side, and 'RIP' on the other (Nicoll, 1998). Damn, if that ain't nineties apotheosis, what is?

In the same 1974 introduction to the French edition of *Crash* in which Ballard referred to the novel as a cautionary tale, he wrote:

> I feel that the balance between fiction and reality has changed significantly in the past decade. Increasingly their roles are reversed. We live in a world ruled by fictions of every kind – mass merchandising, advertising, politics conducted as a branch of advertising… the increasing blurring and intermingling of identities within the realm of consumer goods, the preempting of any free or original imaginative response to experience by the television screen. We live inside an enormous novel. For the writer in particular it is less and less necessary for him to invent the fictional content of his novel. The fiction is already there. The writer's task is to invent the reality. (reprinted in Re/Search, 1984, pp. 97–8)

Beyond his anticipation and rather more elegant and parsimonious articulation of a subsequent decade's worth of postmodern theoretical claptrap,

Ballard is eerily prescient about the state of human affairs at the end of the 1990s. Although Ballard's fetish for mutilated celebrities is not front-and-centre in Cronenberg's movie, it is now impossible to consider the film without recourse to Diana's demise, for the seemingly outlandish fiction of *Crash* stands revealed as nothing less than one of the 'enormous novels' of our time. In the name of 'road safety' – but not entertainment, oh, my, no – the airways are filled with the likes of ITV's *Police, Camera, Action*, featuring nothing *but* images of car crashes and drivers doing 'crazy' things. But of course this is *reality-based* programming. So that's okay then. Not at all depraved and corrupting like, say, a Cronenberg film.

The most striking thing about Cronenberg's *Crash*, beyond the breath-taking, Canadian cold, precision of its direction and construction, is the sense that one is observing another species. The characters in *Crash* don't seem to live in a recognizable, workaday world with the kinds of petty, bill-paying, Tesco-shopping concerns that consume most of our lives. In that sense, it's almost like some anthropological documentary or – harking back to Ballard's literary roots – a science fiction film. The figures in *Crash* could well be an alien species, so dislocated are they from the common place of human emotion and interaction. And it is from an analogous distance and with an almost equivalent alien-ness with which many of us observed the behaviour of the grieving 'masses' in the days surrounding Diana's death.

During the week of Diana's funeral, with every media source dominated by the (lack of) story, as the mountains of flowers watered by streams of strangers' tears grew ever higher, Britain briefly became another country. Not because, as media pundits trilled, the clichéd English reserve was shattered or transformed – clearly, nothing has *really* changed – but because people we know simply did not behave like people we know. The spectacle of the funeral and the week of wake was a kind of macabre carnival in which ordinary Brits suspended their normal critical faculties in order to indulge in a veritable orgy of self-pity. Just as the staged – and 'real' – car crashes in the world of Ballard and Cronenberg provide for the characters a portal into some normally inac-cessible realm of experience and sensation, so did Diana's death provide a path into a place where her mourners do not normally or willingly tread. It was as if, for a week or two, a kind of boon had been granted, wherein, as in real carnival, masks could be put on – or taken off – to reach expression and passion otherwise stifled. To this day, it is simply not credible that those tears and howls of anguish which echoed from the Paris underpass to Kensington Palace, were really shed for the stranger who was Diana; surely the pain had more to do with – as in Ballard's 'fertilizing' instant of the car crash – a reve-lation about those things in all of us, and which may be different for each of us, that normally cannot be faced, which must be left unexposed.

In any case, Diana is still dead, at least physically. And that is undeniably a tragedy for her children and for those who genuinely knew and loved her. But in a sense – at least, a Ballardian sense – Diana died a long time ago, when that unlucky teenage girl was plucked from obscurity and garlanded with a crown of tabloid thorns for her invented sins. The Diana that survived after that day, the media Diana, will undoubtedly exist for as long as the Wapping presses roll and the satellites look down. ('Her darkest hour is somebody's bright tomorrow', as Elvis Costello sings.) Just as the industries for Elvis – Presley, that is – and Marilyn Monroe and Kurt Cobain and James Dean bustle happily along, bigger now than ever they were when the mere mortal beings walked the earth, so too is Diana destined for eternal media life. There'll no doubt be a report, one day soon, that she's been spotted in a burger bar or a Butlins camp, and of course she'll be commemorated on limited edition plates and coins offered up beside the fake jewel crosses and bust-enlargement devices in the back pages of the tabloids, certificates of authenticity and all.

Diana has left the building.

References

Nicoll, R. 'Diana, the movie, or a tale of taste and hypocrisy' *Guardian* (15 January 1998) p. 4.
Re/Search *J.G. Ballard*. San Francisco: Re/Search Publications, 1984.

CHAPTER 24

Ethnic Identity and Cultural Heritage: Belsen in the Museum

RICHARD CROWNSHAW

Introduction: 'The Texture of Memory'

James Young argues that when reading museum exhibitions of the Holocaust we must not mistake artefacts from the past, the remains of historical events, for the events themselves. More precisely, the arrangement of artefacts in a museum exhibition must not be mistaken for the order and way in which past events happened. We must instead attend to the museum's placement of artefacts in a narrative and to the meanings thereby generated. '[E]xhibitions at Holocaust museums can be approached as aesthetic, artistic creations... even... where the artefact is treated as holy object' (Young, 1990: p. xxii). Writing on museums in general, Douglas Crimp concurs. The exhibition of artefactual evidence that the Holocaust (or any other historical event) happened should not be confused with evidence of the museum's interpretation of history (Crimp, 1997). Otherwise, the meanings generated by museums in their ordering of display – meanings dictated by, as Young puts it, 'the taste of their curators, the political needs and interests of their community, the temper of their time' – appear natural rather than contrived (Young, 1990, p. xxii).

By examining the Holocaust exhibition at London's Imperial War Museum (IWM), this chapter will show how the Holocaust is exhibited from the point of view of British experiences and memories of the Second World War rather than from the perspective of the Jewish majority who suffered the Holocaust. In particular, by focusing on critiques of the IWM, namely by Tony Kushner, the museum's version of the Holocaust will be explained in relation to the post-war British identity built from such a selective version of the past. The IWM's performance of this national identity will be scrutinized for the memories and experiences excluded by the museum and the idea of Britishness in which it participates. Extending Kushner's critique, the museum visitor's negotiation of British memory and identity will be considered. The meaning of exhibitions is dependent not only on the positioning of their artefacts but the visitor's interpretation and negotiation of them. Kushner does not account for this economy of seeing between exhibition and visitor (or spectator). A theory of museum spectatorship will be developed from previous studies of museums to analyse this economy. Only by recognizing the possibility of negotiation can artefacts be revealed not as direct extensions of the past but as part of an exhibitionary narration (contrivance) of it. As Young might put it, Kushner does not 'address the physical and metaphysical qualities of these memorial texts, their tactile and temporal dimensions:… "the texture of memory"' (Young, 1993, p. xxii). This chapter, then, will render the idea of Britishness (underpinned by the display of artefacts) less monolithic, and theorize the possibility of the museum visitor's intervention in British collective memory to remember what it forgets.

Holocaust Memory and the Idea of Britishness

For cultural historian Tony Kushner, the politics of display in the IWM are the culmination of a process of Anglicization of Holocaust Memory in Britain. Kushner indicts the museum for presenting the Holocaust, and in particular Belsen concentration camp, from the point of view of the British liberators rather than the Jewish majority of victims and survivors (Kushner, 1997). This display is symptomatic of the way in which British collective memory has forgotten memories other than those of the liberators in order to appropriate the Holocaust as a moral reason for allied involvement in the war (Kushner, 1997). (On this note, historian David Cesarani [1997] raises the question of how much a priority the liberation of Belsen actually was, and whether it could have been liberated earlier.) This exhibition is not just symptomatic of the state of British memory but central to it. Belsen has, until recently, been a symbol for the Holocaust in the British historical imagination since 1945. Generally, at the time of their liberation, western camps such as Belsen received more media coverage than their eastern counterparts because western forces liberated them. Auschwitz, although liberated before Belsen (in January 1945), had, in the immediate post-war period, little or no representation. As awareness of the eastern camps grew, images of western concentration camps were used by the media to explain the functions and death-tolls of eastern death camps (Kushner, 1996). Even during the 1995 VE Day commemorations images of Belsen were still circulated in the media to epitomize the Holocaust.

Kushner's analysis is an extension of his wide-ranging and seminal attempt, in *The Holocaust and the Liberal Imagination*, to map out the contours of mainly British memory inscribed in a range of responses to the Holocaust (from the popular to the political to the artistic) from the first awareness of its occurrence to the present day. Kushner's thesis shows how these private and public acts of remembrance produce a collective (collected) memory that is structured by a liberal-humanist ideology. In the immediate post-war years liberal humanism allowed a rethinking of national identity in terms very different to those of the Nazis. Whilst the expanding Nazi state was based on the exclusion of the cultural, religious and ethnic differences primarily embodied by its Jewish inhabitants, Britain sought to redeem nationalism by not recognizing such differences.

To officially draw attention to the particularity of the indigenous and immigrant Jews in Britain might, it was feared, invoke the same kind of deadly resentment of them induced by Nazism (Kushner, 1997). Consequently, liberal humanism marginalized Anglo-Jewish memories of the Holocaust from the public record. Despite the limitation on the number of Jewish immigrants – only a few thousand were admitted in the immediate post-war period (Kushner, 1994) – the marginalization of Holocaust experiences of those who arrived in Britain before, during and after the war created a very exclusive version of the past. Immigrant and indigenous Jewish relations to the war, and British experiences of it, were profoundly incongruous.

The projection of post-war national identity, the idea of Britishness, was as homogeneous as the 'past' from which it was built. Post-Holocaust Anglo-Jewish identity had to negotiate the difficulties of the inscription of its particular history into this idea of nationhood. Or put another way: Jewish identity had to contend with its inscription by a nationalism that ignored the particularities of Jewish histories. For Kushner, the legacies and ramifications of liberal humanism – the policies and structures of remembrance it informed and the identities it constructed – can still be felt today in the IWM. It remains to be seen whether the IWM's plans to extend itself and house a larger, permanent and more comprehensive Holocaust exhibition (opening in 2000) will attend to the deficiencies of its predecessor (Imperial War Museum, undated). While it is hard to critique his suggestion of a nationalized British Holocaust memory, Kushner's reading of the IWM inadequately theorizes the museum practices involved in nationalization. Before his critique can be demonstrated by reference to the IWM, and supplemented by a theorization allowing the possibility that the visitor might see meanings there other than those intended by the museum, a detailed description of the IWM's Holocaust exhibition is needed.

Reading the Imperial War Museum's Holocaust Exhibition

The Holocaust exhibition is divided into two parts, conceived separately. The first is much smaller and, in effect, serves as an introduction to the second, primary exhibition of the liberation of Belsen concentration camp, 'Belsen 1945'. The two exhibitions will be described as continuous with each other and later counted as one in their analysis. The first exhibition positions the museum visitor as a 'witness'. As the visitor walks into this alcove, she or he is forced to confront two blown-up life size photographs of camp scenes presumably witnessed by the liberators. (We are not told what or what types of camps have been photographed.) The first photograph shows a row of camp buildings, out of which are spilling dozens and dozens of dead, undifferentiated and un-named 'life-size' bodies. On the left is a similar sized photograph showing row upon row of unidentifiable bodies that have been laid outside a camp's internal compound. These visual displays are 'witnessed' first, and then one has to turn round to see the explanatory text. From the visitor's point of view, this explanatory text is not in the same visual field as the photographs. The effect of this spatial arrangement is presumably to put the visitor in the position of liberator/witness stumbling across the shocking scenes – scenes so shocking that they apparently defy explanation and meaning. The small text panel briefly defines the Holocaust, its victims and the camp system.

Adjacent to these photographic displays are nine encased artefacts including Nazi and Jewish correspondence. These artefacts are not arranged in any kind of chronological order. It is not the unfolding of history that is witnessed here – although each artefact is contextualized by an explanatory panel below – but the artefactual burden of proof. For example, there is Josef Kramer's correspondence as Commandant of Natzweiler Camp in which he cites the Keitel Decree (7 December 1941). The decree essentially responded to 'threats' to national security by legislating the 'disappearance' of those 'threats' (people). A letter from Bureau D11 Oranienburg (an administration centre for the camp system) cites Himmler's orders that the concentration camps be cleared of Jews, who were to be sent to Auschwitz death camp. A used canister of Zyklon B registers the effects of these orders. The victims and survivors, as opposed to the perpetrators, are represented via a pair of striped trousers, a yellow star, and messages written on cigarette papers by Josek Zajac to the Polish resistance detailing camp life. A letter from British Army photographer Sergeant AN Midgley details scenes of Belsen when liberated.

The visitor's perspective of the Holocaust is more specifically focused from the point of view of the British liberators in 'Belsen 1945'. 'Belsen 1945' primarily consists of the exhibition of artefacts, such as film footage, photographs, and other historical objects. These are accompanied by captions containing the personal remarks of liberators and factual text panels providing a historical narrative and framework. (Rarely are the remarks of camp internees represented.) The exhibition begins with explanations of the complex functions of the camp, the military truce that allowed the liberation, and opposite, a photograph of what must have been witnessed on entering it: inmates carrying out day-to-day activities such as washing and eating among the filth, the dead and the dying. A text panel details a chronology of the relief of Belsen, another, the units involved in the relief operation. Photographs of the clearing of bodies follow.

Film footage taken by the British Army between 17 April and 21 May 1945 is shown on video. (Although on video, the film narrative is still as the military edited it.) The footage can be roughly divided into three sections.

The first gives the impression of entering the camp for the first time. What are found upon entry are scenes of daily activity (cooking, washing) in a debris-strewn area. The emaciated and half-dead inmates walk around in a 'zombie' like state, passing the bodies of the fully dead. This section concludes with the arrival of the British troops *en masse*, and the feeding and gratitude of the inmates. In the second section bodies are removed to mass graves by bulldozers or former camp guards. The local citizenry are forced to watch. A religious service is conducted over the pits of the mass graves, and distraught military personnel leave the site. Mass graves are filled in with bulldozers. The final section attempts to picture the restoration of normalcy. Inmates are hospitalized, typhoid zones are demarcated and mobile bacteriological units work against the epidemic. Finally, the camp buildings are bulldozed and the last of them is ceremoniously incinerated along with the cloth portrait of Hitler that drapes it.

Three oral testimonies can be listened to while watching the footage. One is the testimony of broadcaster Richard Dimbleby, another is of medical officer Dr MM Raymond. The last testimony is that of Zdenka Erlich, the only one by an inmate, who tells the story of how she crawled from hiding to be found by a soldier and saved by his arrangement of her medical treatment. Another panel of photographs follows, this time of inmates feeding in squalid huts, being evacuated and hospitalized. A panel of statistics of death and survival rates before and after liberation precedes photographs of those responsible. The trial and execution of the perpetrators (camp guards and commandant) is explained by accompanying text.

The exhibition also covers the rehabilitation of the camp's survivors, not just their hospitalization, but also in educational terms – preparation to return to a normal life. Contrary to Kushner's argument about the IWM's lack of representation of Jews, the Jewishness of Belsen as a Displaced Person's camp is noted, as is the Jewish cultural renaissance that took place there, albeit in brief terms (Lavsky, 1997). A case of eighteen artefacts includes administrative plans for the relief operation, medical equipment, photographs of the medical personnel who used it and their personal letters, diaries and notebooks, and the belongings of former inmates. There are photographs of children, children's scrapbooks, letters to relatives in Palestine, clothing, witness' passes to the trials, and a record of Jewish survivors published by the Central Jewish Committee of Belsen (September, 1945).

Kushner's main complaint about the IWM is that it mainly portrays victims and survivors, via the point of view of the liberators, as dehumanized and without individuality. Such images outweigh those of Jews returning to normalcy (Kushner, 1997). The IWM, then, adds to the familiar, ubiquitous and iconic deathly image of victims and survivors. This imaging of the Jew extends to other artefacts that, for the most part, refer to the Jewish body as victimized. The display of Jewish testimony is minimal. The lack of Jewish voices adds to the process of de-individualization and dehumanization. It not only the humanity and individuality, but the Jewish specificity of these internees that disappears behind their iconic representation. To extend Kushner's logic, if Jewishness is at all represented it is predominantly in death. British collective memory remembers Jewish particularity as a thing of the past, either dead or dying rather than admitting the Jewish perspective of living memory to its idea of Britishness (Crylser and Kusno, 1997). Reading the IWM's Holocaust narrative as the effacement, decay and dehumanization of Jewishness, via the point of view of the liberators, however, does not take into consideration the visual economy between spectator and artefact. A method of reading the museum is needed to account for the museum's spectatorship.

Accounting for Spectatorship in the Museum

This method can be drawn from previous theorizations of museum spectatorship as they relate to the evolution of the institution of the museum. Tony Bennett, in a modification of Michel Foucault's *Discipline and Punish*, identifies an economy of seeing between spectator and exhibition in the museums and expositions of the nineteenth century. He argues that, thanks to a shift in display techniques to the chronological arrangement of artefacts (informed by advances in biological and geological sciences), as opposed to their classification according to type, together with museums allowing the working classes through their doors, a wider section of society could now see the evolution of civilization from the dawn of mankind to modernity. What is more, museum spectators could see their own position exhibited in this evolutionary scheme and themselves as the beneficiaries of the progress of civilization (Bennett, 1996). Perhaps more importantly, it was not just the progress of mankind that was witnessed, but the formation of a national identity that could be traced back to its evolutionary origins. The visitor was not only party to a nation that was the product of the evolution of civilization, but living proof of this ascendancy. In effect the visitor became an extension of the museum's exhibition – an artefact. If the exhibition was extended to the visitor, he or she saw in other visitors him or herself as the product of civilization. Seeing oneself as ideal reinforced the desire to participate in the national identity exhibited in the museum. In this way museums attempted to regulate (civilize) the beliefs and desires of those who passed through their doors. In order to do this they had to make visible the principles of power by which national memory and identity were constructed and visitors regulated, and make transparent the manipulation of artefacts for these ideological ends (Bennett, 1996). Applied to the IWM, Bennett's model might explain the desire to participate in national memory and identity, given the benefits participation brings. The museum visitor can share a sense of moral wellbeing with a nation that liberated concentration camps and thereby redeemed the war effort. What is more, the visitor feels in a privileged position, able to see the ideological operations of the museum (mapped onto others) and thus enjoy the illusion of not being ideologically manipulated by them. However, it is the desire to participate in a beneficial memory and identity that lays the foundations for future desires to reinterpret the museum.

Such benefits can only be felt if artefacts are seen to have the historical power to anchor the exhibition's meaning. Theodore Adorno points to a modernist crisis of seeing in the museum, at the end of the nineteenth century and the beginning of the twentieth. The movement of modernism in the arts and sciences, that sought new ways to explain and rationalize the world, and to break from previous traditional and superstitious explanations, found itself in opposition to the work of the museum. While museums mummify cultural traditions, preserving artefacts as extensions of past cultures (Adorno, 1995), artistic modernism sought to negotiate a new and rapidly changing world rather than conserve an old one. As Adorno argued, museums in their attempt to save past cultures, through the preservation of their artefacts, speeded up the decay of cultural traditions. Wrenched from their original surroundings, cut off from the living culture of which once they were an organic part, artefacts, when placed in the museum, 'are in the process of dying' (Adorno, 1995). For Adorno, the failure of artefacts to recall the past is inevitable, but it is possible for the visitor to breathe a 'second life' into them (Adorno, 1995). The artefact is always already mediated by those who view it and the memories it invokes in them (Adorno, 1995). Artefactual meaning, then, is subject not only to the spectator's gaze but also to his or her memories. Applying this modernist perception to the IWM, the artefact can be reinvested (resurrected) with historical resonance, but this time of a more personal nature – allowing an intervention in the collective cultural memory that the museum narrates.

Andreas Huyssen accounts for museum spectatorship in a postmodern age. If modernism sought a break with past traditions, today's postmodernism, in its various cultural practices, and in its suspicion of the way in which our sense of history has been manipulated in the past for ideological ends, has been accused of breaking with the idea of history altogether. Yet, as Andreas Huyssen suggests, the continuing popularity of museums might have some-thing to do with a desire to reinvest artefacts with a historical presence, to prop up the historical narratives that our postmodern age has supposedly forgotten, and to form identities in relation to the past that have been unmoored by what he believes is a recent historical amnesia (Huyssen, 1995). Huyssen argues that the desire for links with the past does not lead to a naive museum spectatorship. Instead, the museum gaze is focused by the nature of the artefact. On the one hand the artefact is obviously divorced from its orig-inal surroundings and use, so that it seems opaque to meaning. On the other hand, its transcendence of time and space and physical presence in the museum is evidence of its historical weight, pull and resonance (Huyssen, 1995). Thus, the overall effect of displaying artefacts is to invoke and inevitably frustrate the visitor's historical imagination. The artefact seems to refer to the history whence it came but the reference is incomplete. Artefacts

invoke memory work in the spectator that can never fully realize the
museum's intentions, leaving space for the spectator's more personal interpretation of artefacts, memories of events they did not necessarily experience,
and intervention in a collective memory. In Huyssen's theory, museums such
as the IWM are used as the only available cultural apparatus by which one's
historically constituted identity can be restored. This does not reinforce the
museum's intended meanings but is a reappropriation of the power of its artefacts to remember contemporary ethnic (Jewish) identities, the past roots of
which have been forgotten by the museum.

Conclusion: Witnessing Ethnic Difference in the Museum

By developing an appropriate model for reading the IWM's Holocaust exhibition, the critique of British memory and post-war identity can be extended
and sustained. A theorization of artefacts and the visual economy that determines their meanings accounts for the potential appropriation of museum
narratives as historical evidence by which to remember what the IWM and its
idea of Britishness forget. In other words, in the museum collective memory
can be widened to include different ethnic experiences, and in particular
Jewish ones. This does not mean that artefacts can be appropriated to
generate another exclusive version of history. Artefacts, as Huyssen has
argued, have proved themselves far too ambiguous to sustain anything but a
glimpse of different identities, perspectives and memories (Huyssen, 1995).

References

Adorno, T.W. Valery Proust Museum, *Prisms*. Cambridge, Mass: MIT Press, 1995.
Bennett, T. 'The Exhibitionary Complex', in R. Greenberg, B. Ferguson and S.
    Nairne (eds) *Thinking About Exhibitions*. London: Routledge, 1996, pp. 81–112.
Cesarani, D. 'Introduction', in T. Kushner, D. Cesarani, C. Richmond, and J. Reilly
    (eds) *Belsen in History and Memory*. Ilford: Frank Cass, 1997, pp. 16–20.
Crimp, D. *On the Museum's Ruins*. Cambridge, Mass: MIT Press, 1997.
Crysler, G. and Kusno, A. 'Angels in the temple: the aesthetic construction of citizen-
    ship in the United States Holocaust Memorial Museum', *Art Journal (Aesthetics and
    the Body Politic)*, **56**, 1 (1997) pp. 52–64.
Huyssen, A. *Twilight Memories: Marking Time in a Culture of Amnesia*. London: Rout-
    ledge, 1995.
Imperial War Museum, *The Holocaust: A Major Permanent Exhibition for the New
    Millennium* (A Report). London: Imperial War Museum, undated.
Kushner, T. *The Holocaust and the Liberal Imagination: A Social and Cultural History*.
    Oxford: Blackwell, 1994.

Kushner, T. 'The memory of Belsen', *New Formations*, No. 30, Winter (1996) pp. 18–32.

Kushner, T. 'Introduction', in T. Kushner, D. Cesarani, C. Richmond, and J. Reilly (eds) *Belsen in History and Memory*. Ilford: Frank Cass, 1997, pp. 1–16.

Lavsky, H. 'A Community of Survivors: Bergen Belsen as a Jewish Centre after 1945', in T. Kushner, D. Cesarani, C. Richmond, and J. Reilly (eds) *Belsen in History and Memory*, Ilford: Frank Cass, 1997, pp. 162–77.

Young, J.E. *Writing and Rewriting the Holocaust: Narrative and the Consequences of Interpretation*. Bloomington: Indiana University Press, 1990.

Young, J.E. *The Texture of Meaning: Holocaust Memorials and Meaning*. New Haven and London: Yale University Press, 1993.

CHAPTER 25

Spinnin': Dance Culture on the World Wide Web

HILLEGONDA C. RIETVELD

This chapter will address the World Wide Web (or the Web), using the specific context of post-rave dance culture as a case study, since it is a contemporary subject in which websites are proliferating. After a discussion of what is meant here by dance culture, the formats and some of the social functions of a range of available communication media (that is mediascape) in this context will be addressed. That way, it can be shown that formats found on the World Wide Web do not appear out of thin air, but have historical links with a pre-exisiting mediascape. Following this, a choice of dance-related websites will be discussed in order to show a diversity of the potential uses of this communication medium, as well as some of its limitations. Finally, this chapter will 'zoom out' of the specific discussion with regards to dance-related websites and produce a more general conclusion on the basis of its case studies. This chapter constitutes a case study in the use of new media raised in Chapter 7 of this volume.

The World Wide Web is based on a protocol (that is, a set of computer rules and language) called hypertext, which was introduced in 1993–94 (Segal, 1995) and which allows the user to point and click on links that will connect to other websites. I will therefore argue that the consumer of the World Wide Web produces specific individual pathways of hypertext links and that the producer of a website is not entirely in control of these routes. So, although it is of importance to research the context of production of a website, its ultimate identity depends on the affective field of the user, who puts a site in particular context. Since British websites are linked to non-British sites, a national identity of a hypertext web communication is sometimes difficult to maintain; this important point will be clarified at several points in this chapter. Words from critical theorist Roland Barthes, written in the pre-Internet 1970s, are appropriate in relation to both the way in which the World Wide Web follows formats of exisiting media and in which web pages can be linked by the user through a unique pathway: 'there is one place where this multiplicity is focused and that place is the reader, not, as was hitherto said, the author' (Barthes, 1977, p. 148).

The World Wide Web is part of the Internet, which also features communication devices such as e-mail, mailing lists, Telnet, Fetch. Unlike other Internet tools, the World Wide Web is not exclusively text based; instead it also features sound and images (still and moving). This is possible because the Internet is a digital form of communication, which requires a particular way of understanding various, previously analogue, media which are not only text based, but also audiovisual in character. Historically, communication technologies have predominantly been analogue, which means that the carriers of sound or images in some ways resembled what they represented; sound waves were recorded and stored in a different way from visual information. This is not the case with digital information, where a message is reduced to a series of binary numbers, one and zero, indicating 'on' or 'off'. As Negroponte points out: 'in the digital world, these differences blur or, in some case, vanish: they are all bits... subject to the same commingling and multi-use that define multimedia' (Negroponte, 1995, p. 54).

Bits, which are digital units, are usually programmed into what is historically and culturally familiar to the producer and the user of such a medium, so that a CD resembles a vinyl record and a digital camera resembles a photographic film camera. It is therefore not surprising that when hypertext (the protocol for websites) was introduced, the design and use of such a digital communication tool depended on the media histories of its producers and users, the participants of the World Wide Web. So, websites are produced in the image of a pre-exisiting mediascape. For example, in the context of popular-music-related websites, Hayward noted in 1995 that:

> With few exceptions, these have primarily operated as promotional and/or informational services and have not, as yet, comprised anything more than an adaptation of existing music industry and 'fan' practices into a new medium. (Hayward, 1995: 29)

Retail mail order sites were early music industrial successes in the development of the World Wide Web (Hayward, 1995). In addition to mail order catalogues, websites are linked to a mixture of DJ mailing lists (for record requests) and e-mail-based discussion groups; the latter can be archived as, for example, on British-based *Breaks* site (1998). As the technology develops, websites are starting to include features comparable to video, television, dance radio, jukeboxes, dancezines and flyers. (See Chapter 6 for a discussion of the music industry in Britain.)

During the twentieth century, the activity of dancing to records has become a sophisticated leisure industry, including jukebox dances in the USA (Joe, 1980; Chanan, 1995); jazz dances in Europe around the Second World War (Joe, 1980); the 1950s twist craze which eventually developed into the even more popular disco era of the 1970s (Joe, 1980; Dawson, 1995; Mutsaers, 1998); the developments in Jamaican styled reggae sound systems (Hebdidge, 1990) and American hip hop, electro and rap (Toop, 1991; Rose, 1994); and the house music phase of the 1980s and 90s (Rietveld, 1998).

During the post-rave mid-1990s, the umbrella term 'dance culture' has gained currency in the UK to indicate a variety of dance clubs and parties. Dance music genres used at these occasions have been specifically produced by and for DJs first and foremost and usually feature emphasized rhythm sections and prominent bass lines.

'Dance culture' also points to specific uses of material spaces and 'club' technologies, which enable the sharing of these musics by dance crowds; for example, sound systems provide inescapable tactile-acoustic experiences due to the levels of sound amplification combined with the use of a bass-heavy rhythm section in the music, while the use of visual effects (such as flashing lights, smoke and visual projections) defuse a focused gaze (Rietveld, 1998). Economic attitudes towards the production and consumption of dance musics can range from unscrupulous entrepreneurial capitalism to anarchist free parties.

Insight into the economic importance of dance culture was gained in 1993, when the Henley Centre for Forecasting estimated that the consumption of raves in the UK alone was worth between £1 and £2 billion in one year (Veares and Woods, 1993). Examples of 'super clubs' are the Ministry of Sound in London and Cream in Liverpool, which have a reputation well beyond their local reach and which organize occasional club nights abroad (for example, on the Spanish holiday island Ibiza, during the summer months). The Ministry of Sound owns a merchandise shop in London and, in addition to a website, launched its own magazine, *Ministry*, at the end of 1997. Dance spaces outside of the legislated environment have a more temporary quality, such as empty warehouse spaces, agricultural fields and even city streets, as has been demonstrated by London protest group Reclaim The Streets (RTS) (McKay, 1998). These ephemeral events range between the extremities of political awareness actions, such as RTS, and purely money-grabbing events.

From the above it becomes clear that the concept of post-rave 'dance culture' belies the variety of dance music genres and types of participant as well as the range of levels of their engagement. Although dance culture can mean an occasional night out for most, to some an overwhelming passion for dance music and its cultural meanings can blur the divisions between work and leisure. This diversity is illustrated in, for example, detailed investigative journalism of the acid house and rave scene (Collin, 1997); the memoirs of a succesful acid house party organizer (Anthony, 1998); popular fictions by participants (Geraghty, 1996; Champion, 1997); collections of interviews with musical professionals, DJs and record producers (Flemming, 1995; Kempster, 1996); and research into dance drugs, especially ecstasy (Saunders, 1995).

British academic book publications in the field of dance culture are just an example of a breadth of approaches, such as popular cultural studies (Redhead, 1993; Redhead with Wynne and O'Connor, 1997; Rietveld, 1998); media studies and subcultural theory (Thornton, 1995); (post)colonial theory (Sharma *et al.*, 1996); or gender and drugs studies (Henderson,

1997). O'Hagan has identified a 1998 UK profile of genres, which includes drum 'n' bass, house, garage, techno, trance, hardcore and gabba, whereby the Beats Per Minute (BPM) range from 100 BPM to over 190 BPM, which indicate a splintering of post-rave dance music styles and their modes of consumption (O'Hagan, 1998). So, as post-rave dance culture and its modes of critical comment continue to evolve, mutate and fragment, updates of academic studies are required.

Crowds do not always simply go out to the nearest dance club. They are willing to travel long distances to experience their favourite DJs, to meet up with a familiar dancing crew or to explore new territory. As can be witnessed in magazines such *DJ, Mixmag, Wax, Jockey Slut, The Face, i-D* or *Muzik* within the UK, people travel to other neighbourhoods, towns, cities and country settings, south to north and vice versa. Going out dancing can even turn into an extended holiday; each summer Brits can be found dancing to garage and 'Balearic mixes' in the mostly British-run clubs of the Spanish holiday resort island Ibiza (such as Cream or Manumission), while each winter groups of (mostly white) 'Bohemian' Brits go to the province of Goa in India to dance with other 'western' tourists and some young locals to trance and techno.

The spread of information of what's on, and where, works across a variety of communication media. An analysis of these has been provided by Thornton, who argues that 'media and other culture industries are there and effective right from the start. They are central to the process of subcultural formation' (Thornton, 1995, p. 117). In other words, cultural meanings of dance (club) cultures are produced within communication media. This may explain some of the motivations of punters to travel to places they have never been to, in order to experience what is represented as 'the real thing', an authentic experience of a certain event, a DJ, a type of dance music, a crowd, or a location.

Thornton divides the dance-related mediascape in micro-media (directed at the 'crowd' itself), niche media (such as the popular music press) and national mass media (newspapers and broadcasting). Micro-media are the media that are closely identified with a sense of authentic cultural formation and are characterized by low circulation, narrow targeting and the use of exclusive jargon. They include word-of-mouth and word-on-the-street (fly posters and spray paint), flyers, listings, fanzines, pirate radio, e-mailing lists and Internet archive sites. According to Thornton, micro-media are not the 'authentic' media they seem to be. For example, with a lack of tight deadlines, amateur print media, such as dancezines, often lag behind events. Dancezines, fan-produced small press, are therefore more nostalgic than the up-to-date news provided by the mass media, despite the great difference of agendas between the latter and micro-media (that is, the mass media address a larger and more general public and often present a 'dominant' morality). Thornton contends that the mass media have been instrumental in shaping a notion of underground resistance around dance culture; especially the tabloids (such as the

Sun and the *Mirror*), which produced a moral panic about British rave culture in the late 1980s (Rietveld, 1993; Thornton, 1995).

In addition, the niche media, such as the music and style magazines (for example *Mixmag*, *The Face*, *i-D*) 'pull together and reify the disparate materials which become subcultural homologies' (Thornton, 1995, p. 151). For example, they provide photo illustrations of the 'look' of a particular scene, in addition to record reviews and interviews with participants, so that the dress and speech styles, music genres and other cultural aspects of a 'subculture' (that is subcultural capital, as Thornton [1995] suggests), as well as certain social traits in people are seen as homologous, that is, directly related with each other. So, the wide spectrum of media associated with dance culture are presented by Thornton (1995) as marketing devices which combined have produced subcultural capital for its cultural industry. The influence of the niche media in the creation of 'subcultural' can be well demonstrated when the notion of a musical scene is exported. For example, British music and style press (such as *DJ*, *Muzik*, *NME*), including a selection of prominent British dancezines (like *Jockey Slut*), are eagerly consumed in Western Europe and in the larger cities of the USA, Canada, Japan, Australia, New Zealand and South Africa. This produces a demand for recordings and styles of consumption which are given prominence in these publications. A recent example is a response by Sydney-based DJ and academic Chan to an e-mail request on how Australians have made drum 'n' bass (originated in London) their own:

> A lot of people got into d&b [drum 'n' bass] as the 'next big thing' over here and have subsequently dropped it in line with those 'great guiders of subcultural standards' – the UK music press. (Chan, 1998, e-mail)

To return to the point made in the introduction regarding that we must acknowledge a pre-existing mediascape to the World Wide Web, a similar spread of media (micro, niche and mass media) can be found interlinked on the World Wide Web. Although the Web, and with it the Internet, has potential for the equal exchange of cultural knowledge, it operates within the context of hegemonic international relations which can be found in its related media conventions.

In addition to a shared understanding of 'subcultural capital', a shared experience of dance music at (similar) dance events provides the cultural cement of networks of communication between the participants of contemporary dance culture. Although Thornton contends to the contrary, word-of-mouth information as occurs between friends and professionals (DJs or organizers) can be based on personal experience in addition to mediated meanings from tabloids, niche magazines or legal radio stations; for example, anyone who has been present at a (post-)rave dance event will know how sensationalist the mass or niche media can be in their reports.

Critical dance-related small press (such as *The Herb Garden*, *Dream Creation inc*, *Squall*, *SchNEWS*) provide a view on dance culture that is different from the exotic representations often found in mass-produced print media. Pirate radio stations such Soul Nation in Manchester or Freak Radio in London are more than advertising spaces for clubs and one-off parties; they supply communities with alternative musical spaces which the legal stations, due to commitments to a variety of funding bodies, cannot always provide (Brown, 1997). Within the context of dance culture, the use of the World Wide Web must therefore be understood as a range of voices, from an alternative media space which addresses a presumed known audience (such as the political direct-action *Network 23* site) to a commercial site which advertises its wares (like the *Ministry of Sound* website).

Gibson (1997) has inquired into a possible use of the World Wide Web as an autonomous site of resistance. Gibson suggests that 'the Web... forms a sort of support system for a subculture' (Gibson, 1997). Although Gibson undertook his research in the context of an Australian rave scene, a British example of the World Wide Web as a site of resistance is Mike Slocombe's *Urban 75*, which has been in operation since 1996. Its content has a history in the micro-media of punk and football fanzines of the 1980s (Haynes, 1995). It features critical articles on the specific aspects of the dance culture as well as a direct-action page on actions such as road protests and protest dance parties. A football fanzine page and a detailed description of Mike and the *Urban 75* team roots the site in a material lived context; the cultural context of this site explains its ideas, which were shaped in the now defunct community squat the Cool Tan Centre and an extended social family around the pubs and dance spaces around Brixton's Coldharbour Lane area in London, UK.

However, it is difficult to know who gains access to the site and what will be done with the information. For example, when in 1995 the Criminal Justice Act, 1994 (or CJA 94), was tested for its section with regard to raves, *Urban 75* provided updates on the whereabouts of a test-case party, The Mother, to see if and how the relevant part in the CJA 94 would be implemented to stop this dance event. Although the police task force may have used the related telephone information line or informants for finding the law-breakers, the updates on the World Wide Web may have made this even easier. The Mother dance event did not happen; the main access roads to the secret site (somewhere in the West Country) were blocked and the sound rig confiscated. In addition to this particular website of resistance, Mike has created web designs for several companies and institutions, providing them with street credibility or subcultural capital. Website *Urban 75*, then, has a double function: it is an advertisement for the skills of the creators of this site and a tool for a critical political practice, ironically partially financed by 'the other side'. Rather than being autonomous, *Urban 75* negotiates a space of resistance in the contradictory realm of popular culture.

An example of a populist commercial website is *0171 Internet Radio*, which is sponsored by server Demon and the publishing corporation EMAP and has been modelled on a combination of niche magazines and local dance radio. It features listings and role-model photographs of punters and DJs, local listings of London-based club nights and pirate radio stations, chat and discussion rooms, plus a connection to the radio-modelled audio stream facility (in this case a type of net-radio). There is also a party database, which ambitiously aims to cover all the continents of the globe (only a few dates for Australian events, but a much larger list of US events), which may distract the Net surfer to embark on a 'transglobal' net travelling adventure away from London.

How this list is used depends very much on the user. the Net-radio feature may be more fun for the geographically removed Anglophiles than for Londoners themselves, who are surrounded by pirate radio on the airwaves at no extra cost to one's phone bill. On the other hand, if the audio stream technology becomes more accessible and less unwieldy, it may show a way to avoid the British licensing regulations for radio, providing an alternative to the legal hazards of producing pirate radio (Green, 1997). In this sense, *0171* is a site of resistance, albeit in the form of enterprise capitalism versus the state, a situation which seems typical to the history of British dance culture during the last ten years (Rietveld, 1993, 1998; Thornton, 1995).

The distribution of soundfiles potentially offers more than a modelling on radio. It has been argued that the World Wide Web could, in principle, cut out the music industry and enhance or supplement what Hayward describes as a type of 'infra-net' (Hayward, 1995), connecting like-minded musicians and fans. Currently, this takes place in symbiosis with 'traditional' media technologies (such as postal mail and audio cassettes). For example an Australian musician commented in an e-mail that:

> I heard a RA file of some nice d'n'b [drum 'n' bass] produced in the states, I e-mailed the guy and asked for a tape copy (as my link wasn't fast enough to d/l [download] the full hour – and I only have an 8bit/22khz sound card), and he posted it. It was the first d'n'b album I received – and it was a demo produced by an American. My style has been more influenced by him than any single Sydney artist because of that simple fact. (Willis, 1998, e-mail)

A potential of 'cultural exchange' (Wallis and Malm, 1990) is shown here. However, web technology, as at the time of writing, is not yet the ideal communication technology for the streaming of sound files. This is due to an unequal distribution of access to compatible hardware in the context of rapid software developments; a new computer is currently out of date within about four months. The distribution of cultural artefacts and exchange of ideas is not entirely free-flowing, but is produced within the matrix of material power relations of production and consumption which existed as the World Wide Web came into being.

Straw has suggested that musical practices are not stable entities in a localized vacuum; instead, there is a cross-fertilization within music scenes (Straw, 1991). As Chanan points out, this is a characteristic of recorded music:

the record industry... was immediately international in character. A recording could be made anywhere and then be easily transported across the ocean to be mass-produced in a different location. (Chanan, 1995, p. 5)

Dance records are sometimes produced with a local audience in mind, especially when the local competition between DJs is strong. Once a dance music genre has been established on the international market, overseas audiences are catered for as well, producing a transcultural music scene with local musical dialects (Savage, 1996; Rietveld, 1998). A difference between the previous media and the World Wide Web is the sense of immediacy when travelling from one site domain to another. For example, links are provided to sites that are outside the editorial control of a home site, such as discographies of relevant artists and of record labels which are run by clearly identifiable companies and artists on the one hand and by enthusiasts on the other hand. The complex networks of relations between cultural identity and market interests is hereby demonstrated.

On the Web this network of cultural relations seems to have a close proximity to the participant; to 'surf the Net' gives a sensation of floating through an instant network of spatial relations which are not restricted to geographical boundaries. In a similar way, the time of transfer of information has been reduced considerably in comparison to the worldwide distribution of analogue forms of communication. Depending on the media format that is produced by a website, this speed could, in principle, increase the level of interactivity between the participants of dance music scenes. To use one of McLuhan's concepts (1994), the world as represented on the World Wide Web seems to have 'imploded' to the here and now of my computer screen.

Although dance-related websites may serve a clearly identified geographical area or cultural scene, due to the easily linked networks it becomes at times problematic to find a located sense of 'Britishness' in the thousands of dance culture related websites which are either initiated in Britain, related to a once British-identified dance music genre or which are frequented by a British audience. In addition, once information becomes available on the World Wide Web, it becomes accessible to an audience that is much wider than the producers can predict and even control. Information about events and products, which was once the exclusive knowledge of identifiable cultural groups of people, becomes available to a large group of users with various agendas which range from participation to surveillance. The production circumstances of websites are important for our understanding of them as researchers and as reflective practitioners, but to the general clicking and surfing participant, context of use is an overriding principle. Therefore, although British produced websites may be identifiable as such, their national cultural boundaries blur in the process of consumption.

Availability of technology and of know-how (from how to operate the hardware and software to understanding the cultural context of a website) limits the potential of the World Wide Web. For example, to date it is still difficult to assess the material impact of the World Wide Web on dance culture since, so far, access to the Internet has been exclusive to certain social groups, such as academic students, which do not include all participants of dance culture. For the researcher, therefore, questions of locality and access must be raised in terms of, on the one hand, power-relations in, and on the other hand cultural and material contexts of the modes of production and consumption of, the World Wide Web.

References

0171 internet radio (1998) http://www.0171.com/the radio/menu.html

Anthony, W. *Class of 88: The True Acid House Experience*. London: Virgin Books, 1998.

Barthes, R. 'The Death of the Author', in S. Heath (ed. and trans.) *Image–Music–Text*. London: Fontana Press, 1977, pp. 142–8.

Breaks (1998) http://www.breaks.com

Brown, C. 'Kiss off to another galaxy', *DJ*, **2**, 4 (1997) pp. 48–9.

Champion, S. *Disco Biscuits: New Fiction from the Chemical Generation*. London: Hodder and Stoughton, 1997.

Chan, S. *youthspace@unsw.edu.au* (e-mail discussion list), 1 March 1998.

Chanan, M. *Repeated Takes: A Short History of Recording and its Effects on Music*. London and New York: Verso, 1995.

Collin, M. (with J. Godfrey) *Altered State: The Story of Ecstasy Culture and Acid House*. London: Serpent's Tail, 1997.

Dawson, J. *The Twist: The Story of the Song and Dance that Changed the World*. Winchester, MA: Faber and Faber, 1995.

Flemming, J. *What Kind Of House Party Is This?* Slough: MIY Publishing, 1995.

Geraghty, G. *Raise Your Hands*. London: Boxtree Ltd, 1996.

Gibson, C. 'Subversive Sites: Rave Culture, Empowerment and the Internet', *IASPM Conference: Site and Sounds: Popular Music in the Age of the Internet*, UTS, pp. 21–3 July 1997.

Haynes, R. *The Football Imagination: The Rise of Football Fanzine Culture*, Popular Cultural Studies No. 8. Aldershot: Arena, 1995.

Hayward, P. 'Enterprise on the new frontier: music, industry and the Internet', *Convergence*, **1**, 1 (1995) pp. 29–44.

(also http://www2.rz.hu-berlin.de/inside/fpm/hayward.htm)

Hebdige, D. *Cut 'n' mix: Culture, Identity and Caribbean Music*. London: Routledge, 1990.

Henderson, S. *Ecstasy: Case Unsolved*. London: Pandora, 1997.

Joe, R.A. *This Business of Disco*. Lakewood, NJ: Billboard Books/Watson-Gutpill Publications, 1980.

Kempster, C. *History of House*. London: Sanctuary Publishing, 1996.

McKay, G. (ed.) *DiY Culture: Party and Protest in Nineties' Britain*. London: Verso, 1998.

McLuhan, M. *Understanding Media: Extensions Of Man*. London: Routledge, 1994.

Ministry of Sound (1998) http://www.ministryofsound.co.uk/home.html.

Mutsaers, L. *Beat crazy: A pophistorical study of the impact of the transnational dance crazes twist, disco and house in the Netherlands*, PhD script, successfully submitted to University of Utrecht, Utrecht, 1998. (available from author on request)

Network 23 (1997) http://www.network23.org.

Negroponte, N. *Being Digital*. London: Hodder and Stoughton, 1995.

O'Hagan, C. *British Dance Culture: Diversity of Sub Genres and Associated Drug Use*, unpublished research paper presented at *Discussing Dance Culture*, South Bank University, 8 April 1998.

Redhead, S. (ed.) *Rave Off, Politics and Deviance in Contemporary Youth Culture*, Aldershot: Avebury, 1993.

Redhead, S. with D. Wynne and J. O'Connor (eds) *The Clubcultures Reader*. Oxford: Blackwell, 1997.

Rietveld, H.C. 'Living the Dream', in S. Redhead (ed.) *Rave Off, Politics and Deviance in Contemporary Youth Culture*. Aldershot: Avebury, 1993, pp. 41–78.

Rietveld, H.C. *This Is Our House; House Music, Cultural Spaces and Technologies*. Aldershot: Ashgate, 1998.

Rose, T. *Black Noise: Rap Music and Black Culture in Contemporary America*. Hanover, NH: Wesleyan University Press/University Press of New England, 1994.

Saunders, N. *Ecstasy and the Dance Culture*. London: Nicholas Saunders, 1995.

Savage, J. 'Machine Soul: a History of Techno', in J. Savage (ed.) *Time Travel. From The Sex Pistols To Nirvana: Pop, Media And Sexuality, 1977–96*. London: Chatto & Windus, 1996, pp. 310–23.

Sharma, S., Hutnyk, J. and Sharma, A. (eds) *Dis-Orienting Rhythms: The Politics of The New Asian Dance Music*, London: Zed Books, 1996.

Segal, B. (1995) A short history of Internet protocols at CERN, *CERN* – http://wwwcn.cern.ch/pdp/ns/ben/TCPHIST.html

Straw, W. 'Systems of articulation, logics of change: communities and scenes in popular music', *Cultural Studies*, October 1991, pp. 368–88.

Thornton, S. *Club Cultures: Music, Media and Subcultural Capital*. Cambridge: Polity Press, 1995.

Toop, D. *Rap Attack 2: African Rap to Global Hip Hop*. London: Serpent's Tail, 1991.

Urban 75 (1998) http://www.urban75.com.

Veares, L. and Woods, R. 'Entertainment', in *Leisure Futures*, Vol. 3, London: The Henley Centre for Forecasting Ltd, 1993, pp. 86–9.

Wallis, R. and Malm, K. 'Patterns of Change', in S. Frith and A. Goodwin (eds) *On Record: Rock, Pop and the Written Word*. London: Routledge, 1990, pp. 160–80.

Willis, S.M. *youthspace@unsw.edu.au* (e-mail discussion list), 11 March 1998.

Index